BARLEY TO BAYONETS

Barley to Bayonets

A Biography of
Nineteenth-Century Bulford,
Before the Soldiers Arrived

❧ ❧ ❧

PETER BALL

HOBNOB PRESS
2015

First published in 2015 by
The Hobnob Press,
30c Deverill Road Trading Estate, Sutton Veny, Warminster BA12 7BZ
www.hobnobpress.co.uk

© the estate of the late Peter Francis Ball, 2015
The Author hereby asserts his moral rights to be identified as the Author of the Work.

All rights reserved. No part of this publication may be reproduced, stored in a retrieval system, or transmitted in any form or by any means, electronic, mechanical, photocopying, recording or otherwise, without the prior permission of the publisher and copyright holder.

British Library Cataloguing in Publication Data
A catalogue record for this book is available from the British Library

ISBN   978-1-906978-20-4 hardback edition
       978-1-906978-21-1 paperback edition

Typeset in Minion Pro 11/14 pt. Typesetting and origination by John Chandler
Printed by Lightning Source

Front cover illustrations (clockwise from top left):
Crosskills Reaper (see page 165); Rev Dr J.J.S, Mountain (see page 199); 1872 Review (see page 266); John Sawyer (see page 223).

Contents

Peter Ball, an Appreciation, by Peter and Christine Goodhugh   vii
Foreword   ix
List of Figures and Illustrations   xii

1   SETTING THE SCENE *First impressions ~ Villagers ~ Village mores ~ Physical environment ~ Environmental impact on villagers ~ Shops ~ Entertainment*   1

2   LIVING CONDITIONS *Housing ~ Diet ~ Prices and income ~ Poverty ~ Drinking ~ Health and insurance ~ Rural unrest ~ Emigration*   15

3   HORIZONS AND COMMUNICATIONS *Road communications ~ Turnpikes ~ Draw of Salisbury and Amesbury ~ Village insularity ~ Horizons of gentlemen and yeoman farmers ~ Economic horizons ~ Cultural horizons ~ National and international horizons ~ Anthony Gapper / Southby ~ The village on the eve of the army 'invasion'*   53

4   FULL CIRCLE OF OWNERSHIP: BULFORD MANOR AND THE VILLAGE *Inheritance of Bulford ~ The Southby / Gapper family links ~ Anthony Southby's heirs ~ James Ledger Hill ~ The farms of Bulford Manor ~ Consolidation of farms ~ Ownership by the Secretary of State for War ~ Cottage tenants*   82

5   THE SEYMOUR ESTATE AND THE LEASEHOLDERS OF WATERGATE FARM *Inheritance of the Seymour Estate ~ Leaseholders of Watergate Farm ~ Gentrification*   113

6   'NAG'S HEAD' AND THE THIRD ESTATE *The 'Nag's Head' ~*   137
Orchard End ~ Exchange of lands and the wider picture

7   THE AGRICULTURAL HEARTBEAT OF VILLAGE LIFE   149
Climatic influences ~ Cycles of the farming year ~ Livestock ~ Arable ~ Changes in farming ~ Farm infrastructure ~ Economics of farming ~ Trees ~ Farm management

8   CHURCH AND CHAPEL *Clerical provision ~ Resident Parish*   175
Priest ~ Neglect of the Parish Church ~ Growth of Dissent ~ Founding of Bulford Chapel ~ Chapel influence on the village ~ Response of the Established Church ~ Bulford's first Parish Priest ~ Status and lifestyle of incumbents ~ Parish governance ~ Church and Chapel relationships ~ Parish Clerk

9   BULFORD PAPER MILL AND ITS PAPERMAKERS *Early*   212
paper making at Bulford ~ Lawrence Greatrake ~ Papermaking at its zenith ~ Characteristics of the papermakers and links with the cloth industry ~ The ownership of Bulford Mill ~ Papermaking processes and its demise at Bulford

10 EDUCATION AND SOCIAL MOBILITY *Bulford's first schools*   227
~ Impact of schooling ~ Sunday Schools ~ The Education Act of 1870 and the new Village School ~ The curriculum and compulsory education ~ Social mobility

11 'RIGHT ABOUT TURN': THE COMING OF THE ARMY   259
Changes to the village in the latter half of the century ~ 1872 Autumn Manoeuvres ~ Bulford Camp beginnings ~ The permanent camp and the railway ~ Impact on the village

APPENDICES *Family Trees ~ Prudence Sawyer ~ Churchwardens ~*   285
Incumbents ~ Bulford Papermakers

Notes   303
Bibliography   338
Index   345

Peter Ball, an Appreciation

PETER AND CHRISTINE GOODHUGH

We first knew Peter in 1977, when he came to live in Amesbury on taking up the deputy headship at Bulford School. At that time the school was run in a more traditional manner, thus anything considered 'avant garde' would have been viewed conservatively.

Into this atmosphere Peter arrived for the appointment interview, resplendent in his very trendy, shaggy Afghan overcoat. The buzz in the staffroom ran along the lines of, 'He'll never get the job dressed like that!' Needless to say, and to the surprise of his future colleagues, he won over the interviewing board and got the job. He loved sharing his ideas with others and bringing history to life; letting children discover it for themselves. His enthusiasm is evident in this book.

This was also the time when Amesbury was working towards celebrating its millennium. As part of the programme of events we undertook an archaeological excavation, overseen by Salisbury Museum, off the north-west corner of Amesbury Abbey Church nave. Clearly, if Peter had ever considered an alternative career, it could have been archaeology. His enthusiasm, attention to detail and meticulous recording were marvellous. We did not find what we had originally expected, but instead a wealth of alternative artefacts and evidence. Peter also collaborated on the book about Amesbury's history produced for the millennium. The particular topic he chose was to research the fragments of the Saxon crosshead found in the Abbey church in the 19th century, reflecting his interest in religious history. The resulting account was a clear example of his ability for orderly and wide-ranging research and recording.

In 1981, Peter and his family moved to Roffey in Horsham, West Sussex, where he was appointed Head of Nuthurst C of E Primary School.

After a few years, there was another move to Highweek Village on the edge of Newton Abbot, Devon. Here, Peter took up the headship of Wolborough C of E Primary School, where he remained for 22 years until his retirement.

Over the ensuing years we kept in touch, receiving postcards from unusual, distant and sometimes rather exotic locations; indications of his great love of travelling and experiencing widely differing cultures. As we are conveniently located for friends using the A303, we would receive unexpected, but very welcome, visits from time to time, updating us on all that was going on in his family's life and, latterly, about progress on this book. For Peter, visiting Wiltshire to research this book was never a chore and was something he really enjoyed.

Peter had a long-standing interest in Bulford, its history, people and environs. Evidence of this emerged some years ago when he investigated, at some depth, Bulford's watermill and paper-making industry. His interest widened, resulting eventually in this book.

In writing *Barley to Bayonets* Peter has brought to life a small and largely overlooked Wiltshire village. His account has a warmth, interest and sensitivity that purely academic works may not embrace. It exemplifies his ability to explore a subject in detail and in depth, whilst retaining an intimate association with the subject matter. The project was conducted over several years. However, even Peter's enthusiasm and drive could not hold back a sudden and terminal illness. Peter managed to write the book, but was unable to see it through to the final published article. Fortunately, completion of the book has been made possible by the help of a number of friends to whom the Ball family is sincerely grateful, and particularly to John Chandler who has brought it to publication.

We feel that our association with Peter, professionally and socially, has been a privilege that we will treasure. *Barley to Bayonets* will be a constant reminder of a good friend.

Peter and Christine Goodhugh
January 2014

Foreword

MY ASSOCIATION WITH Bulford started in the 1960s when my father was posted to the Camp and we lived at 1 Milston Road. These were happy childhood years when we spent hours cycling and walking around Bulford Fields, Beacon Hill and the local lanes. Later, 1977 to 1981, I returned to work at the new Village School and it was at this time that I started studying the history of the village as a project with my class. Now, over thirty years later, this has finally resulted in this book. I was always intrigued by what the village was like before the influence of the army and this book attempts to shed light on Bulford Village in the nineteenth century, chronicling the changes that occurred with its arrival at the century's end. It is not so much a history of the village as a physical environment, but more an attempt to penetrate the lives of the village community. Any historian, let alone an amateur historian, who thinks that they can achieve this is sadly deluded, but nevertheless I have tried to scratch the surface, using quotations from contemporary sources wherever possible. I have also endeavoured to set Bulford Village in a wider context by drawing on other contemporary, or near contemporary material relevant to the region or to the lives of those who called the village their home at some point during the century. I have strayed into the early twentieth century as what has been called the 'long nineteenth century', the period between the Napoleonic Wars and the outbreak of World War I, seems to create a logical timeframe for this book, but these are excursions. I have not taken this timeframe up to 1914 as the building of the permanent Camp in the early years of the twentieth century hardly qualifies as being on 'the eve of the coming of the army' as stated in this book's title.

With this study focusing as much as possible on the people of the village, hence the word 'biography' in the book's title, what soon becomes clear is that their community horizon is much wider than the boundaries of the Parish of Bulford. The village community extended into Durrington with the 'Nag's Head' straddling both parishes, but more part of Bulford than Durrington, and of course family connexions did likewise. The community of Bulford Chapel extended into all the surrounding parishes and drew in very closely Ratfyn in Amesbury, due to family links which were at the foundation of the Chapel's creation. The world inhabited by the upper echelons of village society extended way beyond the Parish and in some cases actively embraced the wider British Empire. An individual's outlook is formed by their family context, and in an effort to explore this I have delved into the family histories beyond the village of key members of its society: the Lord of the Manor, the first Parish Priest and the first Mistress of the Village School. Whilst exploring these bye-roads, I was struck by the immediacy of the Empire on various people's lives, warning me against the temptation to see village society as an isolated backwater. I have also indulgently explored connexions with the USA of one of the village papermakers.

This brings me to the point that to do justice to my themes can only be achieved by reference to individual family histories, and in this regard this book is sadly lacking. What little I have achieved has been the result of the generous sharing of information, and checking the accuracy of my conclusions, by the descendants of villagers who are historians of their own families. I am very grateful in this regard to Eve Magee, Margaret Fay, Janine Hyatt, Jack Sturgess, Ann Sawyer and her late mother Prudence, Tim Perrot and the late 'Old' Farmer Hann. I owe them a huge debt. My researches have taken me a great deal to Canada, unfortunately not literally, and so I have been reliant on information from Ann Boa, Don and Judy Fleming, Adam Birrell and Eve Magee, who herself has travelled there researching her family history. I have been greatly assisted by the staff in Salisbury Library and the various archives that I have visited and would like to mention in particular Georgiana Uhlyarik (at the Art Gallery of Ontario where I did not visit) who researched a document for me. While on the subject of libraries, I would like to thank John Chandler for his encouragement for me to begin my research when he was the Librarian at Amesbury. Other villagers and those associated with the village (past and present) have helped me: Rev. Peter Beale, Tony Hadley, Dr Goodson-Wicks, Sally Hickman, Peter Wicks and CSjt Povey on behalf of General Sir Nick Parker. I would like to apologise to any villagers whom I may have upset by misrepresenting their forebears. I am very happy to put such instances to rights at the first opportunity as well

Foreword

as adding anything that might be communicated to me to further elucidate this account of the village in the nineteenth century. This book is very much a work in progress.

I have benefited enormously from the help, support and guidance in this book, as in two previous forays into print, by Peter Goodhugh and John Chandler. Despite their expertise, all the conclusions, misunderstandings and mistakes in the book are mine. Last of all, I must record a big 'thank you' to my wife Pamela who has lived with this book, especially over the last three years, and encouraged me to see it through and has read the manuscript. I now know why authors are so indebted to their spouses who have to live with a book, like another person in the relationship.

Peter Ball
Newton Abbot
April 2012

Notes on text

THROUGHOUT THIS BOOK, I have used the old money and units of area. To have done otherwise would have given quotes from sources less authenticity, and if I had put present day equivalents in brackets afterwards, it would have destroyed what little flow that there is in the text. I have used square brackets when making any insertions into a quote. I have reproduced the spellings found in the documents, and any contractions used. The ubiquitous family name of 'Sturgess' is also found as 'Sturges' or 'Sturgis', and there is little consistency in the documents. I have more often than not used the 'Sturgess' form, but the other variations can also be found.

List of Figures and Illustrations

The author and publisher acknowledge with gratitude the permission granted by the copyright holders to reproduce these figures and illustrations, as credited below.

Figures
1. Mid century age profile of the village
2. 1851 'Census Map' *based on map in Wiltshire and Swindon Archives*
3. Bulford Bazaar poster, 1903 *Wiltshire Heritage Museum*
4. Swing Riots
5. 1881 Advertisement for a new tenant for Lower Farm *Wiltshire and Swindon Archives*
6. The development of Watergate Farm
    1773 Andrews & Dury Map *Wiltshire and Swindon Archives*
    1817 OS Map First Series, 1817, sheet XIV *courtesy of Ordnance Survey*
    c1820 Henry Seymour's Map *Wiltshire and Swindon Archives*
    1838 Tithe Commutation Map *Wiltshire and Swindon Archives*
    1869 Lucius O'Brien Sketch (detail) *permission from the Art Gallery of Ontario*
    1887 OS Map sheet LIV *courtesy of Ordnance Survey*
7. Elementary Standards
8. Bulford watermark *courtesy of Ann Sawyer*

Illustrations
1. 1773 Andrews and Dury Map *Wiltshire and Swindon Archives*
2. 1887 OS Map Wilts sheet 14 *courtesy of Ordnance Survey*

List of Figures and Illustrations

3 Watergate Lane *in Lucius O'Brien's sketchbook donated to the Art Gallery of Ontario by the late Isabel S. Grant, Shanty Bay, Ontario, 1992. Copyright 2012 Art Gallery of Ontario*
4 Road over Beacon Hill *Wiltshire and Swindon Archives*
5 Nine Mile River *photographed by author in 2011*
6 Engravings by Anthony Gapper (Southby) *images courtesy of Biodiversity Heritage Library*
7 Bulford Manor House from the East *photographed by author in 2011*
8 1897 OS Map of Bulford Manor *courtesy of Ordnance Survey*
9 Bulford Manor House Accounts *Berkshire Record Office*
10 Upper and Lower Farms in 1880 *Wiltshire and Swindon Archives*
11 Lower Farm *photographed by author in 2011*
12 Lower Farm tenancies *map accompanying 1881 lease of Lower Farm. Wiltshire and Swindon Archives*
13 1897 map of Upper and Lower Farms *Wiltshire and Swindon Archives*
14 The Seymour Estate at its maximum extent of 1628 acres *Wiltshire and Swindon Archives*
15 North barn of Watergate Farm *photographed by author in 2011*
16 Site of waterwheel *photographed by author in 2011*
17 Water meadows *c.1820 Henry Seymour's Map. Wiltshire and Swindon Archives*
18 Watergate Farm granary *photographed by author in 2011*
19 The 'Third Estate' *The National Archives*
20 Orchard End *photograph by permission of Jonathan Stone*
21 Crosskills Reaper
22 Parish Church 1869 *in Lucius O'Brien's sketchbook donated to the Art Gallery of Ontario by the late Isabel S. Grant, Shanty Bay, Ontario, 1992. Copyright 2012 Art Gallery of Ontario*
23 Parish Church 1895 *photograph by Canon Ruddle of Durrington. Wiltshire and Swindon Archives*
24 Bulford Chapel *photographed by author in 2011*
25 First Chapel Manse *photographed by author in 2011*
26 Rev Dr Jacob Jehoshaphat Salter Mountain *photograph given to author by Ann Boa*
27 Mary Anne Knight *photograph courtesy of Margaret Fay*
28 Bulford Mill *Wiltshire and Swindon Archives*
29 John Sawyer *courtesy of Ann Sawyer*

30 Richard Duke's School *photographed by author in 2011*
31 Politeness *Wiltshire and Swindon Archives*
32 School Copybook *courtesy of Ann Sawyer*
33 Farmhouse and new Manse *photographed by author in 2011*
34 School plans *Wiltshire and Swindon Archives*
35 1872 Review at Beacon Hill *Wiltshire Heritage Museum*
36 Church Parade with Tented Camp beyond *permission of National Army Museum*

Publisher's Note

PETER'S UNTIMELY DEATH, on 2 September 2013, occurred tragically before he was able to see his book in its finished form, although he was correcting page proofs until a few days before he died. During the ensuing months some publishing decisions, relating to the book's title, its illustrations and the index in particular, have had to be made without his guidance, and some errors and inconsistencies must remain, despite the best endeavours of his family and myself. I should be grateful to hear of any serious shortcomings that readers may come across, and will try to make amends in future printings.

John Chandler
Hobnob Press

1
Setting the Scene

First impressions

It was an eight mile drive to Bulford, [from Porton Station] so that we had plenty of time to admire the airy distances of the plain. The evening sun bathed in gold light, the great expanses of rolling downland, wide fields of young wheat and oats, scattered farm-houses, villages of thatched cottages and distant, half-hidden spires. So great was the peace that we sat for most of the way in our misty cab without speaking. In the dusk we drove down-hill into Bulford ... It was a quaint little village.

THESE WERE THE first impressions of Mary Hamilton who, in May 1900, travelled to Bulford in a four wheeled cab to meet her husband serving with the Royal Irish Fusiliers encamped on Bulford Fields. A villager Prudence Sawyer, twenty-one at this time, described her home as a 'pretty little village nestling in the heart of Salisbury Plain, with about 350 inhabitants. Most of these were agricultural workers.' The village was built around the confluence of the Avon and Nine Mile River, so called, it is said, because when travellers crossed it they were nine miles from Salisbury. All wheeled traffic had come through the water of Nine Mile River and a byepath was made for pedestrians alongside, called Water Street. This is the picturesque heart of the village where one can still gain an impression of what it must have been like during the whole of the nineteenth century.[1]

To try and get a sense of the village, all the twenty and twenty-first century development of the village, the army camp, the high hedges and fences along Water Street demanded by present day privacy and security, the tree plantations around the junction of Bulford Droveway and Milston

Road and those on Bulford Fields need to be swept away, along with the railway embankment skirting the south and east. Bulford Village can then be seen to be as a small community at the heart of Salisbury Plain. The village would have felt more open and rural then with three farms at least in the village itself, with their farmyards, orchards and meadows right at its heart. The road from Milston to Bulford, present day Milston Road, was a track called 'Broadway' on account of its width, with nothing to see but miles of plain. Bulford was a compact little village. Notes for the census officer in the middle of the century say that,

> The Parish of Bulford consists of the village of Bulford (excluding the Nag's Head Inn which is in Durrington Parish) and two outposts which are –
>
> 1st The Hamlet called Longs Pennings situated a mile distant on the cross roads from Bulford to Andover over Beacon Hill and consists of four cottages and Farm buildings
>
> 2nd The Hamlet called Tidworth Pennings [known as Robbins' Pennings in 1877] situated 1½ miles distant at the end of a broad wagon track road that turns sharp off to the right a little beyond John Robbins' farm house [Upper Farm]. It is just opposite the first turning down to Milston (on the left). It consists of two cottages and extensive farm buildings.[2]

Villagers

THE SIZE OF the village was limited by the number of mouths that could be supported through the success of its farming. At the time of the 1851 census, the village population stood at 408 in eighty-three households including the two Pennings and two outlying farms. This was its highpoint. In 1801 the population stood at 228, rising steadily each year to the 1851 peak. Ten years later it decreased to 383 with the 'Decrease attributed partly to the temporary absence of several families, partly to the high rate of mortality among old people since 1851, and partly to migration.' Thereafter it levelled out to the 340s until the army camp was created. The cause of the migration could well have been that the village had outgrown its ability to feed its population adequately and, being no longer economically viable, had to reduce in size. The population in 1901 then jumped to 1,386 but 435 of these were construction workers employed in building the new camp, and 608 were soldiers, leaving the village population unchanged at 343. The 1851 and 1861 census returns show the age profile of the village (*Figure 1*).

Age bands	1851	1861
0–10	28 %	26½ %
11–20	21 %	19 %
21–30	11½ %	16 %
31–40	13½ %	12 %
41–50	9 %	11 %
51–60	8 %	9 %
61–70	3 %	4½ %
71–80	2 %	2 %
81–90	½ %	½ %

Figure 1 Mid century age profile of the village

Two things jump out from these figures, the first of which is the consistent picture in the two sets of census returns. The second is the number of juveniles, with over a quarter of the population under the age of ten. The 28 per cent of 0 to 10 year olds in 1851 has been reduced by a quarter to 19 per cent (11 to 20 year olds) a decade later pointing to a high infant mortality rate. This is echoed in the burial registers from 1861 to 1871. Of the 68 burials recorded, 24 were aged 60 and over as one would expect, but 23 (a third) were under the age of 16. The human story behind the deaths of these children can be glimpsed from the absence register of the chapel which tells of John and Betsy Thorn, living at Bulford Pennings in 1861. Betsy's 'heart [was] nearly broken thro' the death of her two children.' Emma and Samuel Sawyer went through the same anguish at the same time, with Emma turning to religion for comfort. The absence register records, 'The death of two of her children has been as life from death to her. Thus was she first led to Jesus.'[3]

The church registers from 1841 to 1851 show men married between the ages of 19 and 34, with 26½ years old being the average. The women were aged between 19 and 26, with 23 being the average age. Two men and three women were described as being under age when they married, the women were 19 and the men were aged 19 and 21. The largest family groupings in the village were the Sturgess/Sturges/Sturgis households. The earliest recorded presence of this name in the village was in 1608. In 1852 there were 56 Sturgesses out of a total population of 408. During the nineteenth century they were divided into five 'clans', two of which intermarried but two remained totally distinct throughout the century. Two of the 'clans' were builders with the rest being agricultural workers and a butcher. This all points to a close knit village. The marriage registers cited above show that nineteen of the twenty-seven weddings at the parish church were purely village affairs, seven had the grooms coming from out of the village, overwhelmingly from the Avon valley – only one bride was an 'outsider', and she only came from neighbouring Durrington.[4]

Village mores

IT IS HARD to comment on the general level of morality in the village. Bastardy records exist for the village at this time and when a man and a woman were expelled from the chapel at the same time for immorality, it is natural to draw conclusions. With the isolation of the village, compared with nowadays, it would be natural for a group mores to evolve. One person to fall foul of this was the village shoemaker and shop owner called James Chalk, who in 1810,

> having excited the indignation of his neighbours, by gross and scandalous misconduct towards an apprentice boy, his effigy was paraded through the village, with proper marks of ignominy, and at length consigned to the gallows ... when he asked a farmer friend, "What had I best do?" and was frankly answered, "Go hang yourself!" the wretched man followed his advice, and was some time after found suspended a corpse.

He was ostracised despite being a man of standing. He was, for example, one of the signatories to registering houses for Dissenting worship in 1805, showing that even for the most respected there were boundaries which could not be crossed. There was a follow up to this sad tale as we shall see in Chapter 9.[5]

One group of 'outsiders' excluded for most of the century from statistics and for whom we have a record was the gypsies. An Elisa Woods

Setting the Scene

lived on Bulford Fields, as also did a gypsy named White. The latter struck the woman with whom he was cohabiting with a stick and kicked her, leaving her by the roadside. He was apparently jealous of her relationship with 'another member of the tribe'. The woman was picked up in a cart in which she died. The attitude of villagers to the gypsies was no doubt antagonistic to 'outsiders'. In a court case in 1835 gypsies on the downs were picked on as scapegoats and accused, falsely as it turned out, of helping with the theft of a saddle and bridle for a horse stolen from Watergate Farm. The 1891 census in April of that year recorded three gypsies living in tents, a Lucy Smith and her two daughters Sarah and Frances.[6]

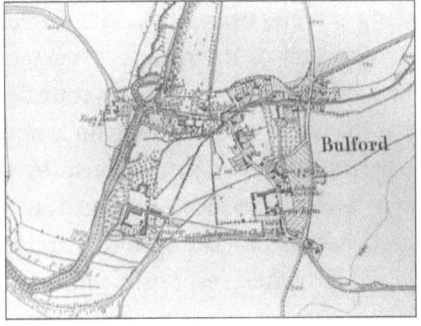

1 *1773 Andrews and Dury Map*
   (Wiltshire & Swindon Archives)

2 *1887 OS Map Wilts sheet 14*
   (courtesy of Ordnance Survey)

Physical environment

THE VILLAGE CHANGED little physically during the course of the nineteenth century as the two maps in *Plate 1* clearly show. The main thoroughfare from west to south was the road across Bulford Bridge which doglegged to the south after crossing the Nine Mile River. There was little change shown here, other than the building of the chapel at the top of Watergate Lane, the demolition of Bulford Mill spanning the mill leat, the development of Lower Farm and the 'Rose and Crown', and the building of the new school on the other side of the High Street from the farm. A second arm of the village is the development along Water Street, from the dogleg in the High Street to the corner of Milston Road and Bulford Droveway leading up to Sheep Bridge, and on to Tidworth (or Tedworth as it was known at the time). The main change shown here by these maps is the disappearance of a group of cottages clustered around this junction. This basic shape still forms the historic centre of the present village and would be recognised by nineteenth-century villagers were they to return. Something to strike returning villagers would be the lack of water. Frank Sawyer who was water keeper for six miles of the Avon upstream from the village, tells how in the nineteenth century, water covered three times as much ground as at present (he was writing in 1953) and the river made a greater impact. This was due to a variety of reasons. One was the areas of water meadows which were submerged to encourage the growth of grass, and the associated ditches and drains which made them possible. These he described as now being 'a scene of neglect. The carriers, which in bygone years brought life-giving water to the meadow vegetation, are now dried-up ditches – drains have been trodden flat with countless hooves of cattle.' Another reason is that the water level of the Avon is now lower than it was. This is due to water extraction by humans, but also by the trees. The trees of the river valley were a resource to be managed as a crop. The tree growth was regularly harvested by pollarding and 'shrouding'. Frank Sawyer describes how Seth, an old 'drowner' responsible for managing the water meadows in the valley in the last quarter of the century, drew attention to the trees, now sixty years later.

> Jest thee look et thay withy bids en thay thir wold pollards vallin en sprawlin all awver tah placin. Al on em be drinking ep tha water is vast is a thirsty 'oss ... None of em wir lowed ta git like thay be now. All thay withy bids wir planted zince I kin mind, en us used to keep em cut [*Just look at those withy beds and those old pollards falling and sprawling all over the place. All of them are drinking up the water as fast as a thirsty horse ... None of them were allowed to get like they are now. All those withy beds were planted since I remember, and we used to keep them cut.*]

Frank Sawyer calculated that there were about a million withy and alder trees along his six mile reach of the river which would extract a million gallons of water from the river in the growing season. Floods were inevitable, like the one in November 1823 which damaged Bulford Bridge, and were more frequent than today. The low lying meadows, in addition to the water meadows, would have been frequently inundated.[7]

Setting the Scene

3 *Watergate Lane. This view, sketched on 7th April 1869 by Lucius O'Brien, nephew of Anthony Southby, shows the farm buildings of Watergate Farm once the new farmyard had been created north of Watergate House. The point from where this sketch was drawn, is marked on the 1861 Census Map in Figure 2. (Sketchbook donated by the late Isabel S. Grant, 1992; copyright 2012 Art Gallery of Ontario)*

The natural world would have been more immediate. The roads, which were tracks, provided a haven for wildflowers as did the fields before chemicals were used to control weeds. A sketch drawn 7 April 1869 shows a bend in Watergate Lane, and looks across meadows to the buildings of Watergate Farm (see *Plate 3*). It is a tree-lined dirt road with thick verges and a stile next to wattle fencing which gives a precious authentic contemporary picture of the village outskirts. Prudence Sawyer, who was born only ten years after this sketch was drawn, recalls that the roads where grass and weeds grew between the wheel ruts, and wild-roses formed hedges on either side. Mary Hamilton had similar memories of roses and an abundance of wild flowers. She wrote that,

> The wild flowers would suddenly surprise me – masses of them growing along the sides of the roads; delicate hare-bells, like flat blue rosettes, campanulas, as large as Canterbury bells; Queen Anne's lace; and low growing camomile with its daisy like flowers and comforting aromatic scent. In the cornfields there were scarlet poppies and cornflowers and great dog daisies, and, on

the edge of the fields, tansy with its pungent smell and frond-like leaves of rich green.[8]

The downs, too, beyond the fields had a different aspect than today. The rough pasture used by the army for training was covered in turf with,

> a smooth elastic character which makes it better to walk on than the most perfect lawn. The sheep fed closely, and everything that grew on the down were close cropped by the sheep and – grasses, clovers, and numerous small creeping herbs – had acquired the habit of growing and flowering close to the ground ... .

All has now changed with the disappearance of the many flocks of sheep. The insect and mammal and bird life must have been richer as well. We have a record in the church accounts of six pence being paid for a dead polecat in 1789, as well as £1 2s 2½d for a hundred and twenty-two dozen sparrow heads. The churchwardens, at this time, were responsible for the eradication of vermin and offered rewards. We also have a record of curlew, snipe, quail and woodcocks from hunting records. Bustards were almost certainly not seen in Bulford during the century as they were on the verge of extinction. Raven were also a rarity at the beginning of the century, soon to disappear, having been decimated by the huntsman, but one of the three remaining breeding colonies remaining in Wiltshire in 1887 was nearby at South Tidworth. The downs abounded with hares and a good day's hunting could bag up to forty-seven. This was in addition to partridges and pheasants. The average kill over twenty-one hunts between 1837 and 1893 was thirty partridges and seventeen hares; these hunts took place in September after the partridge season opened on the first, and before the pheasant season opened a month later. One hunt, however, was in October when a pheasant was bagged. There were good and bad years, for example on 5 September 1849 it was recorded that 'Partridge very scarce in the bottoms this year'. When Bulford Manor was put up for sale in 1886, the advert publicised 'capital trout fishing' and stated that, 'There is invariably a good head of game, and the [hare] coursing is some of the best in the South of England.' National papers regularly reported on the Bulford Stakes for hare coursing, and announced fox hunting meets. It is not surprising therefore that when a Bulford Gentleman giving up hunting put up for sale, 'Twelve couple of

Setting the Scene

HOUNDS, running Hare or Fox, entire Fox Hound blood, and in perfect hunting condition', that the advertisement appeared across the whole of South England. When in September 1842, 'A bevy of quail was sprung ... in a small piece of gorse on Bulford lees', several sporting parties who had already arrived in the vicinity from London were in good spirits. Field sports drew people from afar, and an amusing hunting anecdote appeared in the press in 1849 which reported that, 'a tooth of an extinct species of Rhinoceros ... has lately been found by Dr Southby [Lord of the Manor], at Bulford ... in a deposit of superficial gravel. What would our Sportsmen say, now-a-days, at finding such game as this in the little Wiltshire Meadows?' Fish were aplenty and in spring and early summer, the water meadow drains and drawings were a mass of crawling caddis, snails, shrimps and fly larvae and consequently the trout population of the river was more abundant than nowadays as these waterways were the trout nurseries. To sum up, not only were the fauna and flora richer, but the outdoor life of the villagers, who would think nothing of walking to Salisbury and back, put them in closer contact with their natural environment.[9]

The down side of this was that the inhabitants of Bulford were also at the mercy of the elements. On a fine, sunny May evening, all could look enchanting as Mary Hamilton recorded, but it was a different picture during the winter months. Thomas Davis, the estate manager at Longleat, writing about farming in South Wiltshire in 1811, summed up the climate as follows:

> The cold sharp air of the Wiltshire Downs is so well known, as to be almost proverbial. The height of the hills, and their exposure to the south-west wind from Bristol and the British Channels, the want of enclosures in the vallies, and the draught of air that necessarily follows the rivers, undoubtedly contribute to make this district healthy for both men and beast; but the length of the winter consequent to such a situation, is certainly unfavourable to many purposes of agriculture. [10]

Environmental impact on villagers

THOMAS DAVIS SHOULD have added that the same 'unfavourable' conditions for agriculture on the Wiltshire Downs equally applied to the people living there. Winters were to be endured in houses with neither adequate heating by today's standard nor protection from rising damp. For the soldiers in tents on the downs it was worse where, one November, there were deaths from pneumonia. It is hardly surprising to find that rheumatism was a frequent complaint amongst the population. Alice Ventum, for example was 'confined to her house ten or twelve years through rheumatism'. Another member of the chapel congregation, Mary Ann Ranger from Durrington, 'had a long illness during the past winter'. The pastor, John Protheroe, had to leave the village for health reasons and he wrote from London on 8 October 1847 that 'the loss of my health and a fear that did I return to Bulford I should lose even the little strength that remains,' was the excuse for his absence. An analysis of the illnesses recorded in the *Chapel Church Book* between 1835 and 1840 show that these peaked from January to March, and started rising again from September. What is surprising, though, is the dramatic rise in July at the height of summer. Bad weather had to be endured. Snow, rain and bad weather were frequently cited for non attendance of chapel in the winter months and there was the usual incidence of winter illness. One particularly bad outbreak of influenza, which if the figures for chapel attendance are extrapolated across the whole village brought down a quarter of its inhabitants, occurred in February/March 1837.[11]

Keeping warm and dry was always a problem. A fictitious shepherd on the Plain told a visitor in the early years of the century that 'we have seldom smoke in the evening for we have little to cook, and firing is very dear in these parts.' Agricultural labourers survived on faggots and furze from the downs and peat, if they could afford it. In the 1840s a wagonload of peat cost about four shillings and six pence with five or six shillings transport costs on top of that to bring it from the New Forest. William Hudson wondered, 'How labourers at that time, when they were paid seven or eight shillings a week, could afford to buy fuel at such prices to bake their rye bread and keep the frost out of their bones is a marvel to us.' Perhaps many could not as the shepherd mentioned above later added that rheumatism, 'is but a bad job, especially to people who have little or no fire.' Coal was becoming part of the economy. Thomas Davis noted that ' ... the general introduction of pit coal, which farmers are enabled to bring back on their return wagons from market, has very much lessened the consumption of wood for fuel.' It was, however, a commodity restricted to the yeomen of the village and the blacksmith, and even then, the rise in prices for coal from Newcastle and Somerset, 'Radstock coal', was causing landlords to grow more wood for fuel. In February 1812, a quarter (of a hundredweight) of coal for the Manor House cost twelve shillings, and fourteen quarters were bought altogether that month from Thomas Croome at a cost of eight pound and eight shillings. Bulford had little woodland and in common with 'the centre of the county finds a serious want of wood ... '. Villagers struggled against the bad weather to keep both warm and well.[12]

There were also bouts of exceptional weather and good and bad years. Judging by the harvest 1806, for example, was a good year. A letter from Matthew Devenish, J.P. of Dorchester written in March 1875 about the founding of the chapel by his father in 1806, recorded remarks by the latter's servants that, "the chapel cost Master nothing for the harvest that year was so abundant they were sure it more than paid for the chapel". On the other hand, 1810 was not so good and there was a drought in May when 'there has been so little water in the meadows, that it was difficult to produce a fine specimen of long grass.' The year 1826 was also a year of drought and was followed in the thirties by a series of bad harvests which were a factor in people leaving the valley to emigrate to Canada. In 1898 a very dry summer presented problems for the cavalry camp in Bulford. The river was low and a report added that there was 'no doubt a bacillus scare' in the water supply. Perhaps this is the explanation for the peak in illness in July from 1835 to 1840 already noted above.[13]

Shops

LIFE GOES ON through all the environmental ups and downs and in a more agrarian society, villagers were more self sufficient than nowadays, using their gardens to grow vegetables and to keep a pig. Nonetheless there was a need for shops. The unfortunate shoemaker James Chalk, whom we have already met, had a shop in 1810, presumably a shoe shop, but we have to wait till 1829 for further evidence. Charles Adlam ran a shop, which had a garden and orchard and was valued for parish rates purposes at eight pounds. This could possibly have been James Chalk's shop because he was a man of means, described as a yeoman. Directories from 1851 onwards reveal that there were three shops for most of the time. Some shopkeepers had other trades as well, like George Kill who was also a carrier in 1851. The widow Mary Love ran a shop from at least 1851 which was then in the hands of her daughter Elizabeth in 1861, and then her widowed son William in about 1880. In 1889 a William Swatton took over a shop, probably

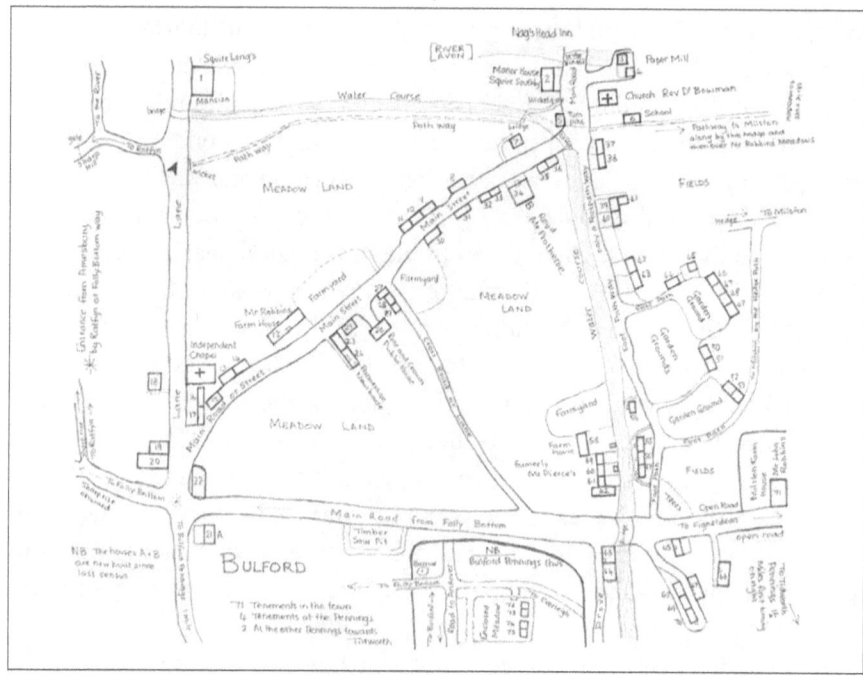

Figure 2 1851 'Census Map'. This map has been redrawn, with nothing added except the arrow which marks the spot where Lucius O'Brien did his sketch in April 1867. The map duplicates the hedge path to Milston, and includes Upper Farm (no.71), and the Pennings on the Seymour Estate (houses 72 to 75). I have indicated the River Avon. There are some very faint names against some of the houses on the map, no doubt belonging to the original version. These are: 30 and 33, William Sturgess; 31 and 32, Samuel Sturgess; 35, George Weeks and 36, Sturgess. (basd on WSA 2916/24)

The Army Deeds dated 31st March 1898 have the following names against properties: 1, George Melsome; 2, James Ledger Hill; 3 & 4, J Sawyer, W. Birmingham, E. Kimber; 6, H. Andrews; 7, H. Candy; 19, S. Andrews; 22, Vallis (now garden and marked site of Chapel); 31, C. Swatton; 33, Post Office, Mrs J. Rowden; 34, Avondale School; 35, W. Sturgess; 36, J. Weeks; 39, J. Sturgess; 40, J. Sturgess, R. Dymer; 42, Ann Adlam; 43, C. Hickman; 44 and 45, J. Kell; 58, Mrs Latimer, (Messrs Bartlett tenants); 59, J. Bailey; 60, E. Keel; 61, W. Hedges; and 63, A. Swatton. In addition there is a new house on the corner opposite the Church occupied by J. Sturgess; and a new house beside the Chapel occupied by S. Andrews.

William's. In 1875 Mrs Jane Rowden had a grocer's shop which she ran for at least twenty-four years, situated on the main road until it was demolished with road widening in the twentieth century (*Figure 2, no.33*). The post box which used to be on the toll keeper's house (*Figure 2, no.5*) was subsumed into her shop when it became the village's first Post Office in about 1895, and Jane was the sub post-mistress. (The Post Office moved to the corner of Orchard Way in 1927, which was then a byeway called Cross Road or Cross Lane.) A second shop on Main Street (*Figure 2, no.7*) was run by Hannah Candy for the last five years of the century, and she had taken over from her father Edward Weeks who traded for the twenty years previous to that. Both Hannah and her husband Charley Candy had been in service in the village, but she was widowed before taking over the shop. Before him, Edward Pain kept the shop from at least 1841. An interesting example of shop keeping as a sideline was the village blacksmith Robert Lake, who in 1885 was a shopkeeper as well. Ten years later he reverted to being solely the blacksmith but the 1901 census describes him as a baker's shop keeper with no further mention of being a blacksmith. The bakery flourished and that year there were three baker journeymen in the village who probably worked with the Lakes (although they could have been employed in the Camp). The smithy was located behind both Lower Farm and the chapel. Robert's shop (*Figure 2, no. 47*) was situated off the Old Coach Road. Later it was run by Mrs Lake and it was the last shop, other than the Post Office, to continue trading in the village up until the early 1960s. Prudence Sawyer recollected 'only two small shops in the village – no baker, grocer or butcher.' There was a bacon curer who processed the villagers' pigs. The best picture of the shops comes from Mary Hamilton's short stay in the village although she has a more generous assessment of the shop situation. Perhaps Prudence Sawyer's recollections were focused on the early twentieth century when the position deteriorated. Mary Hamilton, however, wrote:

> A tinkling stream ran through it [the 'quaint little village'], and to get from shop to shop you crossed this on wooden planks. Not that there were many shops. A tiny butcher sold legs of lamb. From the baker I could buy cottage loaves, and light sandwich-cakes. The grocer only supplied a few necessities. Anything else could be sent for from Salisbury. A carrier's cart, covered with a canvas, used to call for orders. There was nothing he would not bring, from needles and thread to bunches of bananas.

Her last remarks no doubt explain why, as has already been noted, George Kill combined being a shopkeeper with being a carrier – a mobile shop perhaps? [14]

Entertainment

THE PURPOSE OF this opening chapter has been to endeavour to set the scene to illuminate the context for subsequent more focused chapters, and many of its themes will be revisited and expanded. The picture that has been drawn so far is of a resilient community which had to look to itself for survival and amusement. And this they did. Prudence Sawyer talks of the villagers holding 'their little fairs, stalls etc with fairings of all sorts' where the 'Rose and Crown Hotel', then the village pub, now stands; and there was the 'travelling musician' John Montanero who died in the village in 1869 who, and the likes of him, would have brightened up such occasions. There were all the activities centred on the church and chapel, including the choir at the former, and there was a choral society and the Bulford brass band. The village had a Reading Room on land donated by the Lord of the Manor where, in 1889, an entertainment of vocal and instrumental music was held. On big occasions, the whole village came together, as during the celebrations for Queen Victoria's Diamond Jubilee which was marked by a cricket match and a bonfire on Beacon Hill. On these national celebrations, and for village fetes, the Manor House lawns were opened to the village, and there is still a gateway in the garden wall which allowed access. Bulford's band played on both evenings for dancing at the Bulford Bazaar held on the Recreational Ground in aid of the Church Restoration Fund in June 1903 (*see Figure 3*).[15]

Figure 3 Bulford Bazaar poster, 1903 (Wiltshire Heritage Museum)

There are many areas that this opening chapter does not address, for example the pubs and churches, farming and industry, and education, but these will be covered in succeeding chapters.

2
Living Conditions

'It seems impossible to find a more beautiful and pleasant country than this, or to imagine any life more easy and happy.'

Housing

WANDERING THROUGH THE picturesque parts of Bulford Village where thatched cottages come down to the river, it is easy to agree with the above quote of William Cobbett's, writing about the Avon Valley and riding through Bulford on Monday 28 August 1826 before staying the night at Amesbury. Images are conjured up of contented people, working on the land and living in a close community. This picture is very misleading; life for most was hard and, for some, desperate. William Cobbett, who had been brought up as a farm labourer in Farnham, and later was a farmer himself, felt passionately for the condition of agricultural workers, whose livelihoods, as he saw it, were being sacrificed at the expense of farming 'improvements'. Their hours of work were long, diet was meagre and housing left a lot to be desired. He had written in a letter five years earlier that,

> Improvement is a mark of good taste, and its pursuit attended with more pleasure, perhaps, than any other. But, if the thing cannot be accomplished without producing the fall, the degradation and misery of *millions*, it is not an improvement. The gay farmhouses with pianos within were not *improvements*. The pulling down of 200,000 small houses and making the inhabitants paupers were not an *improvement*. The gutting of cottages of their clocks and brass-kettles and brewing tackle was no *improvement*.

Although writing with a political agenda, he knew his facts. A Parliamentary Commission reporting in 1867 on the *Employment of Children and Young Persons and Women in Agriculture*, found that housing conditions in the chalkland regions of Dorset and Wiltshire were deplorable. Is there any evidence to suggest that Bulford was an exception in this respect?[1]

It is impossible to know precisely about housing conditions of the agricultural workers in the village and its outlying pennings, but we can gain a general insight into the issues from detailed minutes of a discussion about 'The Dwelling houses of the poor' held in November 1863. It was between the clergy and leading laymen ('Consultees') who represented the parishes in the Northern Division of the Amesbury Rural Deanery, which included Bulford, and their collective view is worth quoting in full. Francis Stephen Long of Watergate Farm was present and we can rest assured that if the drift of the discussion was way off beam for Bulford, he would have said so.

> It was assumed at once that the present cottages of the poor, or labourers generally were not what they might or should be ... But what did constitute a good house? It was thought that 3 rooms on the ground and first floor ought to be the general rule, but at the same time it was obvious that to fix such a rule if probable or possible to be done, lead to some of the very evils now complained of unless an agreement in writing were made to prevent it having more rooms than wanted would lead to taking lodgers. On the other hand as rent must bear some proportion to the accommodation provided, it must not be fair to make anyone rent a home larger than he might need. It would therefore be needful to build cottages of different sizes, and the tenants should be made to understand when they entered that they would be tenants at will. One shilling per week was thought to be enough rent for any labourer to pay, indeed it was the difficulty in providing the rent which led many persons to seek lodgers. Still whatever might be the sum fixed it was thought that any labourer would be willing to pay a little more for a comfortable house near his work than pay less and have some distance to go daily to his labour.
>
> The Law of Parochial Settlement was thought answerable in a great degree for the present scarcity of housing for the labouring population, but the Laity were of opinion that the Land owner was in duty bound to provide sufficient accommodation for workers of the soil and it was not quite certain that the keeping down the number of residences, did not in

Living Conditions

other ways, indirectly burden the ratepayers more than the opposite course. There were also some difficulties in the matter. In some places there were many small freeholders, where all was invested in a few small houses, for which they extracted a comparatively exorbitant rent, and on which they spent a minimum in repairs or improvements. The laudable example of some land owners in erecting fit houses for labourers of their Tenant Farmers would, it was thought, if followed by a majority in a short time uproot this evil for was it likely that a labourer would occupy such a house if he could get a better, at the same rent? But then it had been urged that land owners could not afford to build houses, since they are no sufficient investment for capital. Assuming (which scarcely anyone present admitted) that this was a question of capital and interest, How much return ought to be expected? Three per cent was thought enough and obtainable and one Lay Consultee stated that he had built a detached house of 3 rooms above and below (the chief materials being on the spot) for £75.0.0 which would certainly bear that interest rate.

However the Lay Consultees present did not accept the principle, that this was a question of percentage, but as affecting the welfare of the people at large, and the duty of landowners (several present being such).

Discussion followed about who should pay for any necessary repairs. 'This was not quite settled, but it was not thought impossible at all, that it might be made the subject of an agreement between the owner and the Tenant of the soil.' The clergy at the meeting then raised the question of the 'The aged poor', those who had no means of paying the shilling a week's rent.

As regards the state of the poor we were disgraced, it had been said that dogs and horses were better housed than men in England, that the English labourer had no forethought no ideal of a future, that even the worn out slave of a Southern State [of America] was better off than a worn out labourer here, the one had a home on the Estate, the other had rarely anything to look to in old age but the Union [workhouse]. No doubt there had been a great deal of exaggeration in these statements.

The discussion went on to discuss the relative conditions of 'workers of the soil' on the continent. It was felt that things were better here than in Spain and Italy, but not so compared with France and Belgium as 'here the soil is in the hands of a few, there much divided.' [2]

The focus of the discussion then turned to the condition of cottages in the locality, the villages north of Amesbury. 'The present position of many cottages on low-land and near water was thought by some to produce consumption and decline, and it might be in some cases', whereas others thought new cottages were not so well built as they were a generation ago. Then the sizes of cottages were again discussed.

> The sizes of rooms and houses must of course be varied. In the case of families it ought to be the rule to have no less than 3 bedrooms in others not less than 2 bedrooms for cases of emergency by sickness or death. A case was named where 13 persons were sleeping in one room and others not so bad but still grievous were cited.

Returning to the construction of cottages, the minutes continue,

> In S Wilts, one great difficulty was the cost of good building materials, Inferior bricks, no stone, and chalk a bad material for receiving mortar, these were great drawbacks. Still there was one material which, if only properly protected from wet from above makes a sound and durable and cheap and warm wall viz a mud wall of this it was thought houses might be built in couples for something like £75 or £80 ... For covering the general feeling was in favour of slate or tiles. A statement had been made by the Reg[istrar] General adverse to thatch, as being a harbourer of disease but it was thought scarcely worth considering. The real objections to thatch are 1 harbouring vermin 2 constant need of repair 3 danger from fire.

After a brief discussion in favour of almshouses, the meeting wound up when, 'It was proposed by Mr F S Long [of Bulford] ... "That the Rural Dean be requested to communicate with the bishop, suggesting that the subject of Labourers' dwelling houses may be submitted for the consideration of the Clergy and Lay Consultees of this Diocese, for consultation on the said subject".'

Those taking part in the discussion evidently felt pleased with the way it went, but what little evidence can be shed on the state of housing in Bulford? Census statistics show that the village housing stock stood at fifty-three in 1801 and rose steadily, peaking at eighty-one in 1871. (This increase could have been partly accounted for by the division of existing houses.) Of

Living Conditions

these houses, two contained two households in 1801, four in 1831. Mid century saw the housing stock failing to cope with population expansion so that in 1851 there were nine houses containing two households and in 1861, eight. Thereafter, pressure on housing decreased so that by 1891 there was a surplus of housing with no house having two families living in it, and there were three uninhabited houses. The Deanery discussions, therefore, were happening at the time when the pressure on village housing was at its most intense. During the twenty years after 1871, the number of houses went down by eleven. Presumably the least satisfactory houses were the ones to disappear first, leaving the better ones and this has to be borne in mind when looking at those remaining today. Cottages disappeared from the Tidworth Pennings (near Sheep Bridge) and at Corner End (*Figure 2, no.65, 67-70*), for example, and these could well have been more basic cob constructed dwellings.

Bulford was lucky in having well established builders, the Sturgesses, and what they built was to a high standard. The three labourers' cottages attached to Lower Farm in 1881 (*see Figure 4*) were 'brick, flint, and concrete built, and slated, each containing Five Rooms, with Woodhouses, Gardens, and a Well.' Not all houses were of this standard for, according to Prudence Sawyer, they were, 'made of mortar stones and brick, with wheat straw and cowhair to bind all together, and the roofs were thatched to keep out the weather'. 'The bigger houses were tiled with stone, slates were then but little known.' The cost of building a new 'cottage and fuel house' in the village was put at £133 in 1874 – about twice the sum mentioned in the meeting for a basic cob house. This was for a well built cottage by the Sturgesses and the proof is in the pudding for when a gas explosion in one of their cottages next to the chapel happened in the 1970s, it withstood the blast when "most of the front of the house seemed to be on fire" and part of the roof landed in the road. It was one of the four cottages in the village owned by the chapel, three of which in 1874 were thatched, the fourth having a slate roof. The chapel accounts noted that 'nothing is said of repairs to which old thatched cottages are frequently liable'. The chapel was a good landlord which upgraded its cottages. That occupied by a Mrs Highal in 1874 had the old thatched (?) roof removed, the brick and flint walls raised with new wall plates to support the rafters in order to 'Slate the Roof with Countess Slates – Ridge tiles pointed in sement', and the chimney heads raised to a proper height. A new partition was put in and the old brick floor down stairs was

Figure 4 1881 Advertisement for a new tenant for Lower Farm (Wiltshire and Swindon Archives)

replaced by a new floor with 'one inch Red floor Boards' on oak joists resting on sleeper walls. Lath and plaster ceilings were put up in all the new work, with two coats, and all the windows were made good, including glazing when required. The estimate for these improvements was £55 10s 0d.[3]

It would appear that the Manor and Watergate Farms were also good landlords who kept 'their cottages in good tenantable repair' as the 1883 lease of Upper and Lower Farms puts it. This was a two year lease stipulating that the Lord of the Manor had to make any repairs first, and provide all materials for any subsequent repairs and maintenance: sawn timber, bricks, tiles and lime (but no thatching materials). The cost of labour was to be divided equally between landlord and tenant. The rent accounts prepared for Edmund Southby in 1886 show that these stipulations were assiduously adhered to, with a carter's cottage being rented to house those living in one of the cottages which needed extensive work doing. In that one year repairs were made to cottages rented by Edward Sturgess, Sarah Sturgess, David Swatton and Mary Keel, the last of which needed new lead work.[4]

The 1891 census gives information about the number of rooms occupied by each household. There were seventy-three homes, the same number as there were in 1851, but two new houses, one opposite the church and the other next to the chapel, had replaced old ones. Just under half were either two or three roomed homes (ten per cent of the former) and fourteen per cent had five or more rooms (including the Manor House and farm houses). Four roomed houses were the commonest by far (forty per cent of all homes) which were presumably two up and two down. The recommended size agreed by the Rural Deanery meeting was, as we have seen, three up and three down indicating that many of the village homes were overcrowded. Large families, like Jonathan and Sarah Keel's with their eight children and his widowed mother all living in a four roomed house, would have been short of space. This gives weight to another observation made by an earlier meeting that, 'the crowded state of cottages where often there was only one bedroom for the whole family, or even if there were two, the limited accommodation was taken up by lodgers or double families', resulted, in their opinion, with an adverse effect on the children's education. The date of this comment coincided with the 1861 census which shows that there were eighteen houses in the village with double families at that time, but there were only two lodgers living in the cottages (and three in the pub).[5]

Bulford was well off for gardens. Bulford Manor had a large garden, as you would expect, where food was grown; in 1812, for example, a guinea was spent on three quince trees, six fine plums, two hundred scarlet Virginia strawberries and fifty new bearing raspberries to be planted in the gardens, along with radish, lettuce, onions, parsnips, parsley and potatoes. It gave employment to Sturgess the gardener, and to women who were paid for thirty-four days at six pence a day to work in the gardens from January to March that year. Thirteen stocks of bees were kept and pigeon houses supplied eggs. Watergate Farm had a walled vegetable garden constructed mid century but growing your own food was not only restricted to the upper echelons of Bulford society. Most houses in the village had an attached garden, or a garden area nearby, allowing some vegetables to be grown and even a pig to be kept. The clergy and lay consultees, though, thought that gardens were more important to the well being of labourers than just for growing food as,

> a healthy home with some more or less Garden ground near, if not attached to the house can be an almost inestimable boon to the labouring man producing contentment, a feeling of attachment to his house, and lessening the temptation to spending time at Public Houses.[6]

What can be said about the interior furnishings of a labourer's cottage? We have a fictionalised description of a shepherd's house on Salisbury Plain in the dying years of the eighteenth century which perhaps conveys a general impression. The shepherd, in this instance, was particularly pious:

> The furniture was very simple and poor, hardly indeed amounting to bare necessaries. It consisted of four brown wooden chairs, which by constant rubbing, were become as bright as a looking-glass; an iron pot and kettle; a poor old grate which scarcely held a handful of coals, and out of which the little fire that had been in it appeared to have been taken as soon as it had answered the end for which it had been lighted, that of boiling their potatoes. Over the chimney stood an old fashioned broad bright candlestick, and a still bright spit; it was clear that it was kept rather for ornament than for use. An old carved elbow-chair, and a chest of the same date which stood in the corner were considered to be the most valuable part of the shepherd's goods, having been in his family for three generations ... a large old Bible which

lay on the window seat, neatly covered in a brown cloth, variously patched ... On the clean white walls was pasted a hymn on the crucifixion of our Saviour, a print of the prodigal son,[and] the shepherds hymn ... .[7]

Diet

IN 1801 FORTY-ONE per cent of the population were employed in agriculture and thirty years later it provided employment for forty of the sixty-two families in the village (sixty-four per cent). More detailed analysis is possible with the 1851 census which shows that nearly half the adult population of the village were then either directly employed as labourers in the fields or else were carters; they worked long hours on the land or accompanied flocks on the downs for very little remuneration. William Cobbett saw through the contented veneer of valley life, realising that the agrarian prosperity represented by the number of hay and corn ricks he saw, was won at the expense of near the 'general extreme poverty' of the labourers and he forcibly argued to expose the true situation. He worked out a subsistence diet for the average labouring household consisting of 'a family of five persons; a man, wife, and three children, one child big enough to work, one big enough to eat heartily, and one baby', and then costed it, arriving at a yearly total of £62 6s 8d. He then went on to compare this with the actual income that such a family received:

'Why such a family as I have described is allowed to have at the utmost only about 9s a week. The parish allowance is only 7s 6d for five people, including clothing, fuel, bedding and everything. Even that only makes £31 8s a year, for ... everything, whereas I allowed £62 6s 8d for the bare eating and drinking; and this is little enough. Monstrous, barbarous, horrible as this appears, we do not, however, see it in half its horrors; our indignation and rage against this infernal system is not half roused, till we see the small number of labourers who raise all the food and drink, and, of course the mere trifling portion of it they are suffered to retain for their own use. [and later went on] ... the base wretches know well, that the common foot-soldier now receives more pay per week ... exclusive of clothing, firing, candle and lodgings; more to go down his own single throat, that the overseers and magistrates allow a working man, his wife and the three children.

William Cobbett went on to calculate that if the workers received a 'just reward' for their labour, the valley could produce five times its current population.[8]

The agricultural labourer's diet was very basic. Sunday lunch for the shepherd whose house was described earlier, consisted of 'a large dish of potatoes ... and a piece of coarse bread'. For a treat, 'a morsel of bacon' was used 'to relish his potatoes'. Beer was the beverage of choice, when they could afford it, and although the village had orchards and apple trees, Thomas Davis wrote in his survey of South Wiltshire that, 'The principle uses of apples are, however, puddings for the children of cottagers, and the table fruit for the other classes of society. Indeed the great predilection of the county is so strong for drinking beer that the want of cider is little felt in the district.' These contemporary quotes come from the first quarter of the century but twenty-five years later the situation had not improved. An enquiry into English Agriculture between 1850 and 1851 reported on the meagre diet of a labourer on Salisbury Plain:

> After doing up his horses he takes breakfast, which is made of flour with a little butter, and water 'from the tea-kettle' poured over it. He takes with him to the fields a piece of bread and (if he has not a young family, and can afford it) cheese to eat at mid-day. He returns home in the afternoon to a few potatoes, and possibly a little bacon, only those who are better off can afford this. The supper very commonly consists of bread and water. The appearance of labourers showed, as might be expected from such a meagre diet, a want of vigour and activity which mark the well-fed ploughman of the northern midland counties. Beer is given by the masters in hay-time and harvest, some farmers allow ground for planting potatoes to their labourers, and carry home their fuel – which on the downs where there is no wood, is a very expensive article in a labourer's family.[9]

Labourers' cottages lacked adequate cooking facilities, few had ovens and fuel was scarce. Most food had of necessity to be cooked before an open fire, boiled or fried. Prudence Sawyer, writing about the turn of the twentieth century, observed that 'every' cottage had a pig and that for villagers,

> Bacon was their only meat
> A ham was no unusual treat

> And butcher's meat to many
> Was practically unknown.

There was, as we have seen, a bacon curer who processed the villagers' pigs for them. Beer was the main drink.[10]

Beer was available from public houses, but the beer, 'given by the masters in hay-time' was almost certainly what they brewed themselves. Beer was drunk everywhere, even in the Manor House, where in three months in 1812 were delivered 102 gallons of porter, 72 gallons of 'old beer' and two barrels of 'table beer'. Farmhouses almost certainly had their own breweries – Lower Farm had a brewhouse with a fixed copper in it, and Watergate Farm had a cellar with two 'six and a half hogshead casks' and a quantity of cider and a brewhouse. It can be no coincidence that Nag's Head Farm, as will be seen in Chapter 6, also operated as a pub, and that James Aldridge Devenish, son of Matthew Devenish of Watergate Farm became a successful brewer in Weymouth giving credence to the statement that brewing was the most gentlemanly and least demanding of all businesses.[11]

Prices and income

AGRICULTURAL WAGES ON the Wiltshire chalklands were about six or seven shillings a week in 1794, but rose steadily during the Napoleonic Wars, peaking at about twelve shillings a week in 1814. With victory over Napoleon in 1815, prices started to collapse almost overnight and the government introduced the Corn Laws to keep prices artificially high, causing widespread hardship, and it was not until the middle years of the century that relative prosperity returned with the revival of the rural economy. Wages in 1817 fell back to seven or eight shillings and stayed at this level for the next twenty-five years. This post war depression meant that wages failed to keep up with price rises and conditions were desperate for many families. William Cobbett was writing during this depression and it is when the Swing Riots occurred. The mid century years saw greater prosperity return but all this was reversed in the last quarter of the century, when the agricultural depression began, not helped by the importation of corn from the American prairies and refrigerated meat from Australia and New Zealand. Between 1875 and 1896 nationally the prices of all cereals approximately halved, cultivated acreage shrunk by roughly a quarter as also did agricultural employment, and rents were reduced by a fifth. It is important to bear this mid century relative rural prosperity in mind when looking at the village as portrayed in the 1851 census. The village then contained seventy-six households headed by a married man and in twenty of these his wife went out to work as well. In six instances this was despite having a young family to support. The lucky few could find employment at home as a washer woman or a seamstress but there was little demand for either.[12]

A traditional source of income for wives and daughters in the locality was spinning yarn for clothiers. They worked for hard masters who were tough on those who failed to fulfil their quotas or make misrepresentations. 'The law against delinquencies of this nature are particularly severe, and the clothiers here [Salisbury] are determined to enforce them against all offenders with the utmost vigour' as the fate of villager Lucy Sturgess, shows; in 1790, she 'was committed to Fisherton Gaol, by the County Magistrates at the instance of a clothier of this city [Salisbury], for neglecting to finish her spinning work in due time, and not making a faithful return of the materials committed to her charge'. It was hoped that her punishment would have a salutary effect on others. Poor Lucy had other troubles. She had given birth to an illegitimate daughter, Priscilla, six years earlier. It was reckoned that 'a woman, in a good state of health and not incumbered with a family' can spin one pound of wool a day, 'and that is the utmost that can be done'. If, like Lucy, she had a family, the most that she could spin was two and a half pounds a week as opposed to the six pounds of the unencumbered woman. Income was therefore dramatically reduced from six or seven shillings a week, to just under three shillings. These figures were supplied in a letter written about Seend in 1796 by Sir Frederick Morton Eden as part of his enquiries into the state of the poor. His main point, though, was that,

> ... since the introduction of machinery hand-spinning has fallen into disuse, and for two reasons; the Clothier no longer depends on the Poor for yarn which they formerly spun for him at their own homes, as he finds that 50 persons ... with the help of machines, will not do as much work as 500 without them; and the Poor, from the great reduction in the price of spinning, scarcely have the heart to earn the little that is obtained by it. For when they used to receive 1s and 1s 2d the pound for spinning, before the application of machinery, they are now only allowed 5d.

Living Conditions

The earnings quoted above were at the higher rate, and these would be reduced to two and a half shillings and one shilling a week for the single and mothers with children respectively at the lower rate. Sir Frederic Morton Eden gives an example of a family budget of a labourer earning eight shillings a week, with his wife and elder daughter bringing in four and a half shillings (lower rate) which when supplemented by the parish outdoor relief makes a weekly income of fourteen shillings. This matches the weekly expenditure on bread, butter, clothes and other necessities.[13]

Although Seend is on the edge of the dairy farming area near Devizes, twenty miles from Bulford, the point is made that, 'In some of the neighbouring corn parishes, the reduction in the price of spinning has been more severely felt than at Seend'. William Cobbett a generation later observed that,

> The villages down this Valley of Avon ... used to have great employment for women and children *in the carding and spinning of wool for the making of broad cloth*. This was a very great employment for the women and girls, but, it is now [1826] *wholly gone*; and this has made a vast change in the condition of the people ...

It comes as little surprise, therefore, that the machinery used in the manufacture of woollen cloth at Figheldean was one of the targets for the 1830 rioters. In 1801 twenty-seven of Bulford's population of 228 were employed in 'Trade, Manufacture [and] Handicraft'. These would have included shopkeepers, builders and so forth, but also those employed in spinning. Thirty years later these trades were still important to the budgets of ten out of the sixty-two families then in the village. It was an uphill struggle, not only for the families dependent on spinning, but also for the clothiers who saw a decline set into their industry after 1815. About thirty per cent of Salisbury's population was involved in the textile industry in the eighteenth century, but this drastically reduced to about ten per cent by 1819, with very little manufacturing taking place.[14]

Not only in this instance, but also across agriculture in general, labourers saw their livelihoods threatened by the introduction of mechanisation. Bulford was not immune to this trend. One such machine was, 'A contraption for throwing grain for the action of the fan in the winnowing machine, and known as the Amesbury Heaver ... the invention of John Trowbridge a native of this [Amesbury] parish. He was a man in humble circumstances, but possessed an inventive and useful genius.' He was a carpenter by trade and one of his Amesbury Heavers appears in the auction of Thomas Croome's Bulford farm in 1825 at the 'Maidenhead Inn' in the village. It was sold for £2 4s 0d. Watergate Farm also had a heaver according to an inventory drawn up in 1872. The farms in the parish were not particularly large and so the farmers sometimes hired machines, as did Francis Stephen Long of Watergate Farm. In 1835 he hired from Isaac Watts of Amesbury a 'drill for sowing corn' with an operator who could earn ten shillings a week for sowing fields. A machine shed stood on the corner of Orchard Way, known by the children who liked to play there as the 'Sheen House', which was demolished when the post office was built in 1927. In response to mechanisation across Buckinghamshire, Wiltshire, Hampshire and Dorset, those who felt threatened ran riot in an orgy of rick burning and machine smashing for a few weeks in 1830, threatening their landlords and employers. These were the notorious Swing Riots and the degree that they affected Bulford is discussed below. It is enough at this stage to recognise that they were in part a panic reaction to the poverty which faced so many.[15]

Poverty

LAWS PROTECTING PROPERTY carried draconian punishment, with Frederick Weeks, for example, being imprisoned for two months in 1852 'for breaking down a dead fence'. Edward Macklin was hanged in March 1829 for burgling villager T. Sweet's house, and the thief who was found guilty of stealing a horse from Watergate Farm was sentenced in March 1835 to be 'transported for the term of his natural life'. He, though, may have thought himself lucky as an identical theft of a horse in the village from the stable of William Reeves a century earlier was punished by death. Robert Croome of Bulford, who probably farmed Lower Farm or Hindurrington Farm in 1790, felt it necessary to join the Sarum Association for the Prevention of Robberies which would indicate that he perceived that there was a threat of theft at that time. The Association had about a hundred members and during the course of the year it succeeded in bringing forward thirteen convictions. We have accounts of the Manor House at the time showing a similar concern for security. A 'Fancy key & Lock to Wine Cellar door' was purchased for seven

Living Conditions

shillings from Salisbury market in 1812, along with keys for the Harness Room and letter box, and a bill for a 'New key & Cleaning Lock.' Sir Edward Loveden was taking no chances and also bought '6 regulation swords at 7s with scabbards' to supplement his collection of guns. The establishment in the 1830s was scared by the spectre of revolution and, after the initial brutal reaction to the rioting, tried to ensure that it would not happen again by reforming the Poor Law. From Tudor times up to 1834 with the setting up of groups of parishes into Poor Law Unions, the care and containment of the poor was the responsibility each parish which was obliged to levy a rate and appoint an overseer to deal with problems. Paupers found wandering abroad were quickly sent back to where they were born to be looked after by that parish. Such an early instance was Joan Bakehouse, who in 1598, was punished for begging in Salisbury and given 'a passport to Bulford where she was born.'[16]

The village possessed no almshouses endowed by wealthy inhabitants although a onetime High Sheriff of Wiltshire left ten pounds in his will of 1651 to the poor of the village. This tradition continues with the widowed Lady of the Manor, Ann Duke, who in her will did 'give and bequeath ... to the poor of Bulford ... the summe of Five Pounds' to be invested and for her son Richard Southby to 'pay the interest annually to the poor.' She outlived her son, and so what happened to this bequest is uncertain. Perhaps this was paid 'into the hands of the Churchwardens and Overseers of the Poor' as she had stipulated in a similar bequest made to the poor of South Marston at the same time. It was left to private charity to bridge the gap between poor relief and destitution and this philanthropy continued after the reforms of 1834. The 1825 account of a shepherd on Salisbury Plain tells how his wife was poorly with rheumatism. He told how he left her in bed one morning and on his return, 'she uncovered the bed whereon she lay, and showed me two warm, thick, new blankets ... I had left her with no covering than our little old thin blue rug ... '. These had been donated, along with half a crown by a farmer who overheard the shepherd talking about his wife to the vicar after church. He went on to say, 'the rheumatism, sir, without blankets by night and flannel by day, is a bad job, especially to people who have little or no fire.' There must have been many cases like this in Bulford as is shown by the 1825 will of Thomas Croome. The paper reported that he left 'The sum of £18 in blankets, and clothing, [which] was last week distributed amongst the poor of the parish of Bulford.' The Blatch family, generous in their endowment of the chapel in Bulford with, among other things, three cottages at their disposal, were also active at a more individual level. When Sarah Blatch of Ratfyn Farm died, a eulogy written by her friend ran:

> If the poor and needy were sick, they knew where to look for advice and comfort. They were sure to meet the sympathy of those Christian matrons [her sister Elizabeth Devenish as well], whose eyes beamed with kindness, and whose hands were cheerfully stretched out for their relief. It was a delight to see all around them happy. They did good to all, but especially to them who were of the household of faith.

Her funeral on 20 August 1837 at Bulford chapel, where she was interred in the Blatch family vault, took place 'amidst the lamentations of nearly the whole village population.' When her daughter Sarah Blatch died in 1852 she too was remembered for her benevolence, although she lived across the parish boundary in Durrington. 'Her charity was diffusive; her chief pleasure seemed to be to mitigate human suffering, and to promote the glory of God.' Another remembered for her charity was the washerwoman Ann Smith, daughter of the village midwife and a property owning labourer, who died in 1889 aged sixty-one; her gravestone records that 'she was a friend of the needy ... '. Perhaps the attitude of those who were better off, often through no effort of their own, is summed up by the inscription (written by George Herbert for Bemerton) placed in the porch of the new vicarage on the corner of Milston Road by its first occupant, Rev. Cecil North Arnold:

> TO MY SUCCESSOR
> If thou shouldst find
> A house to thy mind
> Built without cost;
> Be good to the poor,
> Give them of thy store,
> Then my labour is not lost.[17]

Charity was not enough to alleviate village poverty. A quarter of the population of the parish received poor relief in 1802-1803: £164 8s 8½d being spent on materials for employing some, on regular out-relief for twenty adults and twenty-seven children up to the age of fourteen, and on occasional relief for a further eight adults. An average of £193 a year was spent between 1812 and 1815, with, on average, fourteen people relieved regularly and eight occasionally. In addition there were nine who were over sixty or 'disabled from Labour by permanent Illness, or other infirmity.' Some of the outdoor relief expenditure was given in the form of loaves; in January and February 1835, for example, between ten and twenty were given out each week at a cost of nine pence a loaf. Among the parishes of the Amesbury hundred Bulford spent more than average on the poor from 1816 to 1821, and then less than average between 1822 to 1834. Bulford became part of Amesbury poor-law union in 1835.[18]

The reform of 1834 radically restructured poor relief. The Amesbury Union was the largest in Wiltshire. Each Union was to have a workhouse, which in this case was built in Amesbury, to cater for the worst cases of destitution. Less severe cases were to be dealt with where they occurred through a system of 'outdoor relief' for which purpose the Amesbury Union was divided into three districts. Bulford was part of District One, grouped with Amesbury, Durnford, Durrington, Figheldean, Milston, Woodford and Wilsford and Lake. Poor Law Guardians were appointed to superintend each district and for many years this post was held by Francis Stephen Long. The accounts of the Board of Guardians show how each parish contributed towards the running of the Union, a cost in 1853, for example, running to £1,207 of which Bulford paid £45. Bulford's contribution decreased as the years went by reflecting that the worst cases were increasingly less frequent as the century wore on. Between 1850 and 1856, the village's contribution went almost exclusively on outdoor relief, occasionally on maintaining parishioners in the workhouse but never looking after lunatics. It would seem that Bulford escaped the worst of poverty but this, it must be remembered, is only a relative judgement. Villagers did end up in the workhouse euphemistically described as 'visitors' in the census returns. In 1851, for example, out of the eighty-one 'visitors', two were from Bulford: a forty year old man and a girl of fourteen, Mariah Batchelor.[19]

A strict puritanical regime prevailed in the workhouse but the inmates were at least guaranteed adequate nutrition and sufficient clothing. Tenders were sought for items such as cheese, oatmeal, potatoes, boiling peas, fagots, bread, coarse beef, mutton and suet on the diet side, and coarse materials, stout nailed and tipped boots and shoes, and crow hats on the clothing side. Inmates were given a subsistence diet and basic clothing which gives a good indication of the diet and dress of the poor in the village. Children unfortunate enough to find themselves confined in the workhouse had a strictly ordered day set out for them in the *Minute Book of the Board of Guardians*:

Boys   After breakfast to go into school from ¼ past 8 to 12
              To walk from ½ past 1 to 3
              To go into school again from 3 to 5
              To play from 5 to ½ past 6
              To go into school again from ½ past 6 to bedtime

Girls   After breakfast to go into school from ¼ past 8 to 11
              To walk from 11 to 12
              To go into school again from ½ past 1 to 4
              To play from 4 to ½ past 6
              To go into school again from ½ past 6 to bedtime.

Such was the daily timetable for Mariah and you can be sure that the adults were equally strictly regulated. There must have been time for relaxation and to develop personal relationships, for in December 1851 'Notice of marriage [was given] between Wilm Love of Bulford and Eliz Hayter of Salisbury.' Both were inmates of the workhouse. It would be naive to think of life in the workhouse as a pleasant existence; the three who broke out in 1852 obviously did not think so. One young pauper, Agnes Sainsbury, did not get very far as she broke her leg while getting over the wall but her two accomplices got as far as Salisbury before recapture, spending three weeks in Fisherton Gaol for their pains prior to being sent back.[20]

Outdoor relief was more important to the villagers than the workhouse, especially for families who had a pauper for head of household; one of the two of families in this position in 1851 were the Swattons – a family of four where three paupers depended on the wages of an elder sister, supplemented by poor relief. She was a farm servant and life must have been a long struggle to keep hunger and cold from the door. In the Weekes household John, a farm labourer, found it impossible to provide for his pauper parents without turning to poaching. He was caught in the act and 'charged with using a wire for the purpose of snaring game in the parish of Bulford' and was fined one pound and no doubt, not being able to pay this, would have been sent to prison for one month, leaving his parents in a worse state. A Gamekeeper Act was passed in 1831 to protect game birds by establishing a closed season when they could not be legally taken. The act also established the need for game licences and the appointing of gamekeepers. It listed the requirements for licensed gamekeepers and gave them power to seize 'such dogs, nets and other engines and instruments for the killing or taking up of game.' It was war as game was seen as a fair prize for anyone who could take it and poaching was seen as nothing wrong. Many agricultural labourers were driven to poaching by their acute distress after the collapse in wages after peace was declared in 1815. The years 1821 to 1822 were when this distress was at its most acute and poaching was consequently at its highest, tending to fall away around 1825 and 1826 when things got a little better. At times villagers took things into their own hands to find 'relief' by turning to petty theft as did George Knight who was gaoled in November 1825 for 'stealing a quantity of potatoes, the property of T W Dyke, Esq. at Bulford.' Another villager, Henry Kinsman, was sent to prison six months for stealing eight pounds (weight) of suet in 1852. Salmon could have graced the poacher's table because it could still be found in the river although it was becoming scarcer and causing concern. In 1790 a meeting was held to consider 'a means of preserving the Salmon' in the Avon between Salisbury and the sea.[21]

Every member of the family had to contribute to the household income as best they could. An account from beyond the village tells how,

> our little maids before they are six years old can first get a halfpenny, and then a penny a day for knitting. The boys who are too little to do hard work, get a trifle by keeping the birds off the corn; for this the farmer will give them a penny or two pence and now and then a bit of bread and cheese into the bargain. When the season of cow keeping is over, then they glean or pick stones ... .

Attention had to be paid to the bees; Jemima Swatton, for example, had to miss chapel to look after them. Others missed for attending to game birds reared on the manor, but these, unless poached, graced the tables of the gentry and not the labourers. A general picture is painted of the majority of villagers able, by the end of the century, to achieve a degree of self-sufficiency to cushion themselves from the worst of poverty. Even in the first quarter of the twentieth century Ann Sawyer tells of how, as a child, she used to collect mushrooms to sell for sixpence to earn extra money.[22]

Drinking

BEER FORMED AN important part of the labourer's diet. Returning to the hypothetical family quoted earlier from William Cobbett, he calculated that, 'they would want, on average, winter and summer, a gallon and a half of beer a-day.' The village's public house after 1844, the 'Rose and Crown', was frequently the scene of drunkenness and the petty sessions in Salisbury were littered with cases of drunken behaviour emanating from there; five labourers were reprimanded for placing a ladder from a house across the turnpike road; another was fined twenty-five shillings with eight shillings costs for 'assaulting Police Constable Willoughby, who was sent by the landlord to eject him', and the rag collector was fined five shillings for 'being drunk and using abusive language to the clergyman of the parish ... '. Failure to pay this fine would have incurred a spell of six hours in the stocks – quite an undertaking for a sixty-one year old. The local paper carried a report of a case of drunkenness in 1874 and recorded that 'Earl Radnor remarked that more cases of drunkenness came before the bench from Amesbury and the neighbourhood than from any other part of the division, and he thought it was high time it was put to a stop.' His action supported his views and villager John Sturgess was fined twenty shillings and had to spend one month in gaol for being drunk on the highway and 'challenging people to fight.'[23]

Drunken behaviour was a problem because beer drinking was both a necessity and one of the few forms of recreation. One person who agreed with Earl Radnor's call for action was Bulford's parish priest, the Rev Jacob Jehoshaphat Salter Mountain, who held pronounced ideas on the subject. Being a Canadian, he was well versed in the fate of the American Prohibition movement at that time which failed, in his opinion, because it aimed too high. He reported to his bishop that the existence of public houses, 'specially impedes my ministry' and are 'the greatest hindrance to the cause of religion and morality.' He then went on to provide statistics that within a radius of one and a quarter miles of the village there were eight drinking houses, two or three for every two or three hundred of the population. He saw 'the greatest evil of these licensed public drinking places' as being 'the allurement

Living Conditions

and facility thus presented to the young to acquire intemperate habits' and 'the rising generation ... becoming Drunkards.' His remedy, penned in 1873, was to prohibit Public Houses in country parishes from selling beer, except to travellers (of whom there were very few in Bulford), and establish

> instead one place for this purpose as central as might be for the supply of all villages within a radius of say 2 miles, under the management of a much respected and trustworthy person, where wholesome Beer ... could be purchased to be carried home. A central point for such a purpose exists here within 1½ miles of Amesbury, Bulford, Durrington and Milston.

The central point he alluded to was the Crossroads Brewery which was incorporated in the Stonehenge Inn on the edge of Durrington.[24]

This scheme was presented subsequently in a paper to the Amesbury Deanery in April 1874, prepared for their discussion on temperance. He was strongly of the opinion that the clergy were called to take a lead in this matter. Dr Mountain's 'long and carefully prepared paper' was favourably received by his fellow clergy at the Amesbury Deanery Meeting, although, 'it seemed however to be the general opinion of the meeting that it was impossible to make men sober by Act of Parliament. The Licensing Act of 1872 was a step in the right direction' with its limits to the opening hours of public houses which 'where they had been adopted have had a beneficial result in the morality of the people in our parishes', and that it was desirable 'that the number of public houses might well be diminished.' They did however resolve, 'That the Revd Dr Mountain be requested to print for general circulation his paper on the means of checking intemperance and that he be requested to send a copy to Paul Nelson the Chairman of the Committee and Temperance Society appointed by Synod.' On his return from a year's absence through illness in 1876, he was still fixated on the problem of drinking and had developed his ideas further. He reported to his bishop:

> I would beg to suggest a remedy as bold which is new and untried – namely – "That instead of having two or three Public Houses for every three or four hundred of the population or at least within easy reach of every village with that number of inhabitants, as is now I think the case in rural parts, the most central and convenient for each cluster of villages a Beer Depot

(which might or might not be itself a Brewery) from which good wholesome strength giving Beer (not like that nauseous drugged stuff which is sold by most of the Publicans) could be sent around, just as bread is, <u>daily</u>, the same time each day, thro' every village, to supply each family, at a regulated price, with the quantity required, and of such regulated strength and quality as prudence might suggest and the Authorities could then easily enforce. For what facilities would this plan afford for testing the nature of ale that was sold from Beer carts as they passed along the Highway (for <u>thus</u> only should it be dispensed, and not allowed to be sold upon the premises or carried away from thence by the buyer). Such establishments possessing a monopoly of the sale of Beer, each in its own District, could afford and should be able to pay as much <u>Revenue</u> as is desired.

These schemes, which totally ignored the social and recreational side of drinking, despite his efforts, got nowhere. (By coincidence, around this time the future Lord of the Manor, as we shall see, published a book on brewing). Nevertheless Rev. Dr Mountain's zeal for the cause was not totally wasted as a temperance association was formed in the village three years later, and in 1877 Bulford signed up to a petition to Parliament to close public houses on a Sunday. The relations between church and public house can hardly have been straightforward at the best of times as Mr Williams, landlord of the 'Rose and Crown', found when he was proposed for the office of churchwarden in 1831. The proposal was overruled, 'he being an ale-house keeper'. [25]

Villagers had easy access to drinking. There was a pub frequented by villagers just the other side of Bulford Bridge called the 'Nag's Head' which was in business by 1731. As well as serving drink, it offered entertainment and food. A 1784 newspaper report illustrates this:

> To be Shot for, at pigeons flying out of a box at twenty yards distance, on Friday 5th of November, at the Nag's Head, a SILVER BOWL, of four guineas value; likewise a SILVER PUNCH LADLE, of fourteen shillings value, for the person that shoots the second best shot – No rifle barrel to be allowed, or any longer than three feet ten inches in the barrel. The pigeons to fall within a hundred yards, or to be deemed no shoot – A dinner on the table at twelve o'clock, and begin shooting at one.

The pub was situated in the farmhouse of a working farm and perhaps it appealed more to the yeoman class that to the agricultural workers. Most farmhouses had their own breweries and so in many ways this was a natural extension of a farm's activities. The 'Nag's Head' went out of business between 1885 and 1898, no doubt suffering from the new pubs opened either side of it on the turnpike road, the 'Stonehenge Inn' in Durrington and the 'Rose and Crown' in the village. The 'Rose and Crown' was opened in 1844 (and rebuilt in 1896) and soon established itself at the heart of village social life. In all probability it eclipsed, perhaps literally replacing, the 'Maidenhead Inn' which had filled that role in the village during the early years of the century, certainly up to the 1820s.[26]

Health and insurance

ONE OF THE more basic constraints on the condition of life, good health or otherwise, must have been of major consequence before the days of the welfare state. By and large a labourer's prospects of a long life were surprisingly good once they had survived the hurdles of birth and childhood. We have already noted the high mortality rate of children in the decade after 1851, a time which coincided with a religious revival in the village. Medical support was rudimentary compared with today's standards but there was for a time a midwife in the village, Sophia Smith, who was known for her charity as 'a friend of the needy.' The incumbent of the Manor House for nearly half the century, Anthony Southby, was a doctor of medicine but to what extent he became involved in helping his tenants is impossible to know, especially as he was absent for long periods of time. It is hard to believe, knowing what we do about him, that he never used his skills when the need arose as he had after all practised as a doctor in Bristol and in Upper Canada where he often gave his services free. The location of the village at the confluence of two rivers makes, as already noted, for a damp environment, conducive to rheumatism and chills and it is noticeable that those who were able to, left the village for periods to recoup their health. The Rev. Mountain had a year away for health reasons as did the Pastor Williams's wife, though for a shorter duration. William Godwin went to London for medical treatment and the Rev. Protheroe left the village for a spell and was reluctant to return for health reasons. Villagers were at the mercy of the full range of infectious diseases, many of which are now inoculated against, as well as more serious diseases. Martha Hyatt (née Swatton) for example died at the age of twenty-eight in 1867 from tuberculosis after suffering from it for several years. It has been tentatively suggested that she might have contracted the condition, known then as phthisis, from working in the rag house of the paper-mill where she worked sorting rags.[27]

The nineteenth century saw a growth of insurance and friendly societies to see people through hard times and ill health. The gentry and upper echelons of society were well covered as we see in the case of Francis Stephen Long who, in 1852, lost a rick of wheat and one of vetches. There was a fire 'attributed to the carelessness of some women employed in the field couching, and who incautiously lit some straw under the shelter of one of the ricks, and the wind being high at the time, the flames caught the rick referred to, which was speedily in flames as well as the rick adjacent.' The report smugly concludes, 'It is satisfactory to add, that Mr Long was fully assured.' What is more significant, however, is that a sizeable section of the village society had protection of some sort. It was not just farmers, though, who insured themselves. There was a movement to set up Friendly Societies, mutual insurance groups which did much to mitigate the worst effects of harsh economic conditions for those who could afford to pay the small weekly contributions. In 1796 there were nineteen Friendly Societies in Wiltshire which by 1855 had risen to 292 responding to the needs of harsher times. In Bulford there was one such, unnamed, society registered in 1793 to meet at the 'Maidenhead Inn'. It had 70 members in 1803, and 112 (out of a population of 230) between 1812 and 1813 but was wound up in January 1882. This was either meeting alongside, or replaced by the Victoria Society which met at the 'Rose and Crown'. It in turn was wound up in 1889, when a letter was written by its vice chairman in August that year telling how,

> The Victoria Society came to grief last Easter. The members on Easter Monday had a supper to wind up the affairs. In the place of the old club a slate club has been started. All former members who are on the sick list have been excluded from it. All former sound members have been readmitted.

The vice chairman was Bulford's vicar, Rev. Cecil N. Arnold. He obviously had no qualms about meeting in the pub, unless of course they used the Reading Room. The decision to exclude sick members, though, rather goes against the inscription he had put in the vicarage porch quoted above. There had also been another unnamed Friendly Society which was meeting over the river in Durrington at the 'Nag's Head' in 1836. These were small scale, local friendly societies as opposed to those which operated on a countywide basis. [28]

The Wiltshire Friendly Society was one such countywide society, established in 1828 and by 1852 had no less than fifty members in the village which, being about one in six of the population, must have given a considerable degree of protection to the eighty-four households at that time, assuming that there was no more than one member per household. It continued to thrive and in 1866 the Lord of the Manor, Anthony Southby, was a member of its General Management Committee, paying his honorary subscription of £1 10s, and the same amount jointly from his two sons, the 'masters Southby'. Two of the village's farmers, Francis Stephen Long and John Robbins junior, also paid honorary subscriptions, as did the subsequent Lords of the Manor and successors at Watergate Farm. The Report of the Society shows that from 1866 to 1872 contributions from the villagers of Bulford were consistently around ten or eleven pounds per annum and payouts were made to sick members on each of these years. The 1866 total payout was £3 13s 9d to twenty-six villagers for an aggregated period of 182 weeks, and these payouts gradually rose to over £30 in 1871 and 1872. The number of people receiving the sick pay, though, reduced to fourteen in 1868, and then to three or four people for the subsequent years. The aggregated weeks paid out for the same period, however, after dipping, rose to 295 in 1871. More was being paid to fewer people. The Society must have viewed these figures with alarm because it paid out for a surgeon to visit the village at this peak in 1871, and again the following year, which resulted in a drop back to 114 aggregated weeks in 1872. The Society also paid out death endowments amounting to over £51 in 1866, and peaking at £58 pounds in 1868. This year was an exceptionally hot year and there was a bacillus scare in the river which accounts for this upturn in deaths. Over the next four years there were either no death payments, or merely one of £10. The Wiltshire Society was clearly of great comfort and benefit to villagers, but the Bulford branch was wound up in 1890 in the middle of an agricultural depression in which sheep and corn farmers were badly hit, especially on the lightest of light lands like the tops of the Wiltshire Downs. In its latter years, the number of policy holders in the village was eleven or twelve, rising to fifteen or sixteen in its final years, with sick payouts at ten or eleven pounds per annum. Why did it wind up? Perhaps the Society found itself unable to cope with the financial demands put on it, or those in need could no longer afford the subscription, or a combination of both. Or perhaps it was for the more prosaic reason that people could no longer be found to run it. During the 1880s, the local paid steward was William Love, with a committee made up of William Sturgess (chairman), James Macklin, Samuel Keele and William Dimer.[29]

Rural unrest

WE HAVE LOOKED as best we can at the physical constraints imposed on villagers' lives, and at how there were periods of deep agricultural depression. How did all of this affect their mindset; how much dissatisfaction was there and was any of this channelled politically? William Cobbett was appalled at the way that agricultural labourers were treated and wrote in August 1826 after travelling through the Vale of Pewsey and Avon Valley that,

> This state of things never can continue many years! *By some means or other there must be an end to it*; and my firm belief is, that the end will be dreadful. In the mean while I see, and I see it with pleasure, that the common people *know they are ill used*; and that they cordially, most cordially, hate those who ill-treat them.

Henry Graham, looking back at the same time fifty years later, wrote that,

> The distress caused by want of employment, and the very heavy burden of taxation, was further augmented by a cold wet summer, and indifferent harvest. The unsettled state of the continent, and the revolutions that occurred in France, Belgium, Spain and Portugal during the year, tended still further to disturb the minds of the disaffected and distressed, and there was a feeling throughout the country that, if something was not done speedily, the popular dissatisfaction generally prevailing might produce very serious disorders.

These feared disorders had materialised in Wiltshire with the Weavers' Riots of 1822, 'disturbances which, commencing among the manufacturing

Living Conditions

towns, and spreading in time to agricultural labourers, ultimately caused the deplorable riots of 1830.' 1830 was indeed the year that saw dissatisfaction come to a head. A new reign had begun and the Prime Minister, the Duke of Wellington, had scotched any ideas of electoral reform by declaring his intention to oppose any attempt at such reform on 2 Nov 1830. In that July, just prior to taking up his inheritance of Bulford, Anthony Gapper (Southby) was acutely aware of the general unrest and his brother-in-law responded from Upper Canada to one of his letters:

> I am seriously sorry for you all at home and am much afraid "the Devil has got amongst the Tailors" - ... but I can hardly think of England so near "an upset" as you seem to do – things are bad enough certainly and there is one class of people in England that certainly did not exist when the constitution was first framed and which in all its various modifications since have never been taken into consideration – I mean the labouring class – they are by their distress and numbers forcing themselves into notice – were they represented the Government would not have lost the fairest and best tax ever laid on the country – the income tax.[30]

The authorities prepared for further unrest. Magistrates in the South of England met to draw up precautions, special constables were sworn in and the Volunteer Yeomanry Cavalry told to be at the ready. Local militia regiments were the traditional mechanism to preserve law and order which was an issue dear to the hearts of those in society who owned property. The spectre of social revolution spreading across the channel during the Revolutionary War was very real in their minds and the formation of local militias took on a sense of urgency. Each parish was supposed to draw up a militia list of all men and then produce a militia enrolment list of those who were chosen to serve. During these years one such militia was based on Durrington in which Bulford's tenant farmers played their part. In 1799 Thomas Croome was a sergeant, not on permanent pay, and John Robbins, Joseph Mould and John Smith were corporals, and there were fifty-two privates in the troop. In 1796 a new force, Voluntary Yeoman Cavalry, was created by William Pitt. Wiltshire was divided into ten districts, each with its own troop, with Sarum and Everley being the nearest to Bulford. These troops superseded the militia which were disbanded by 1816. Troop numbers fluctuated, rising in times of crisis, but the Everley troop struggled, finally being disbanded in 1829. This then was the picture in November 1830 when the agricultural unrest, known as the Swing Riots, spread to the neighbourhood of Bulford.[31]

On 19 November farmers and labourers gathered in a field at Wallop to hold a wages meeting (*see Figure 5*). The going rate for labourers in the area was eight shillings a week. The farmers agreed to raise this to ten. The 20 November saw buildings destroyed at Collingbourne and Ludgershall during the night. Rumours were a rife, with William Jacob of Amesbury talking, on 21 November, about what was happening in the neighbourhood - fires and threshing machines being smashed. He told Sarah Wright that 'a mob was coming to Amesbury, and that half the town would be burnt.' That night at about half past ten a fire broke out in the rickyard of Mr Henry Self, of Countess Farm, Amesbury. At first it seemed as if the whole premises would be lost. Fortunately the fire was almost immediately discovered and the alarm was raised. The inhabitants, of all classes, instantly flocked to the scene to render assistance. The wind was also in their favour and continued

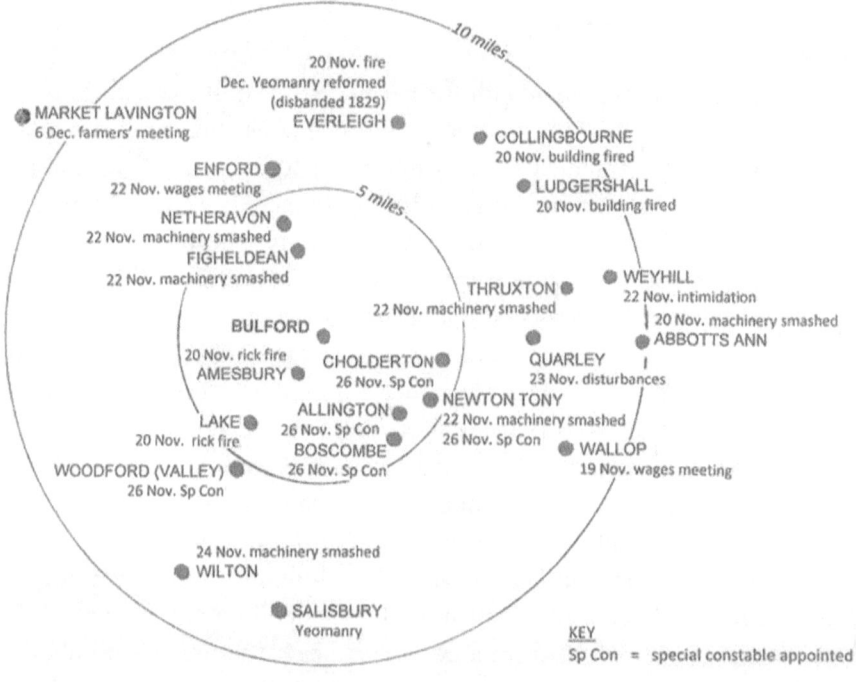

Figure 5 Swing Riots

to blow the sparks away from the other ricks. A small pea rick and a hayrick were destroyed. The fire was undoubtedly the work of incendiaries. Two strange men had been seen coming from the rickyard earlier that evening. They were dressed in snuff-coloured clothes and were seen heading towards the turnpike gate. A search was made for the men but they were not found. The next edition of the local paper carried a notice that, 'Mr Self, of Countess Farm, Amesbury, wishes to take the opportunity of acknowledging the sympathy and unwearied exertions of his Friends and Neighbours, of all classes, at the FIRE on his premises on Sunday evening, and begs to return them all his warmest thanks.' There were also nearby fires that night at Everleigh and Lake. There was a mob nearby causing James Judd of Newton Tony to send a pleading letter to the authorities reporting that,

> a mob has assembled this evening about 5 o'clock, they are mostly from adjoining parishes from Cholderon Wallop etc – I understand there has been several from Wallop today trying to excite our people to riot ... They also threatened to be here tomorrow with 5 or 600 ... My opinion is that unless we have the Cavalry or some troops to put a stop to it the consequences will be very bad ... .

The following day forty or fifty men arrived at Judd's farm. He tried to bribe them with the money and beer that they demanded but to no avail; they broke into his barn and smashed his threshing machine. [32]

Another group of labourers gathered outside a meeting held in the vestry by the overseers of Enford on 22 November, hastily convened to discuss agricultural wages. When the labourers were asked what they wanted, one said, 'We want two shillings a day. A gallon loaf and six pence, as it was in the paper.' This was agreed but one called out, 'But first we must break all the machines!' They then proceeded to the threshing machine workshop of Jonathan Smallbones, broke one machine, many parts of others, and several cast iron wheels with a sledge hammer. The mob then went on to break a machine at the farm of William Sweetapple, moving on nearer to Bulford. By the time the mob reached the farm of Charles Stagg at Netheravon, they numbered about a hundred. The threshing machine had been moved out of the rickyard as a precaution, but it was damaged in the process. The mob destroyed the rest of the machine. At about half past two they then arrived at farm of Thomas Jenner, in Netheravon, and broke the threshing machine in his barn using iron bars and sledge hammers. Moving on they attacked and destroyed machinery used in the manufacture of woollen cloth at Thomas Gaby's in Figheldean. Bulford was only three miles away, but the mob did not go on. Beside the panic, Bulford was beginning to be indirectly affected as Thomas Jenner also owned two cottages and a plot of arable land in Bulford, at 'Corner End' where the new vicarage was subsequently built. Disturbances reached neither Durrington nor Bulford which were like the calm at the eye of the storm as there were also mobs destroying property on the Bulford side of Andover (*see Figure 5*). On 22 November a mob of three hundred 'feloniously with threats' demanded and received divers quantities of beer and victuals from a doctor's house in Weyhill. His servant was put in bodily fear and she parted with the beer and victuals under the influence of fear of injury. The mob then moved on to Thruxton and a threshing machine was destroyed on the property of Sir John Pollen who had been pilloried by radicals for his strong support as M.P. for Andover of the legislation to keep corn prices artificially high and his condescending attitude to labourers. Perhaps he was deliberately picked upon. This incident must have been followed closely at Bulford Manor as Sir John Pollen was dowager Lady Charity Ann Pollen's stepson, and the property concerned was part of the estate of her marital home at Rendlesham. Lady Pollen had died on 30 July of that year, but her sister Mary Southby was still living at the Manor. The next day saw the disturbances move to Quarley, and a few days later the target was the woollen cloth mill at Wilton. On 26 November special constables were appointed in the area at Boscombe, Newton Tony, Allington, Cholderton and up the Woodford Valley. Robert Pinckney was appointed for Amesbury but none were for the Upper Avon Valley. As far as Bulford was concerned, the threat had moved away.[33]

Why did Bulford escape and what does this tell us about the village? For one thing it was not by then bound up with the clothing industry which had been undergoing a contraction since 1815, but why were no ricks set alight or threshing machines attacked? These machines were being introduced in a big way as a labour saving device which dramatically cut down the winter work for threshing. The village's winter unemployment between 1832 and 1835 was usually two able bodied men out of work (1 in 145 of the population), whereas neighbouring Durrington usually had four to eight out of work (1 in 78). The employment issue with the introduction of threshing machines does not seem to signify in Bulford. There were ninety-seven smashed in Wiltshire in a few days. Bulford's landowners could have been slow in the introduction of machinery, but this does not ring true. There was almost certainly a threshing machine on Watergate Farm in the village because there is evidence of one in 1841 which needed repair, and as the landowner rather than the leaseholder was concerned by its state it would suggest that it was a substantial piece of machinery. The region was not an agricultural backwater immune from the effects of the agrarian and industrial revolutions and, as we have seen in the account of the riots at Enford, Jonathan Smallbones had a threshing machine workshop. Wiltshire was in the forefront of the invention and introduction of new kinds of agricultural machinery and implements, with firms such as Robert and John Reeves of Bratton, Brown and May of Devizes, J. W. Titt of Warminster, and many others who produced improved ploughs, threshing machines, elevators and other implements, as well as steam engines both for threshing and steam ploughing. (We have a record, discussed in Chapter 7, of a portable steam engine by Brown and May on the Manor Farms in Bulford along with a steam elevator manufactured by Rawlings of Collingbourne.) These businesses, though, were insignificant compared with that of the enterprising Taskers. William and Robert Tasker, sons of the village blacksmith in Stanton St Bernard, near Devizes, moved to Abbotts Ann near Andover in 1806, and in 1809 took over the village forge. They were eager to embrace the latest technology and set up an iron foundry, the Waterloo Ironworks, which was only ten miles from Bulford, and started making cast iron ploughs, seed drills, rollers etc., which were stronger and more efficient than their wrought iron equivalents. The ironworks fell victim to the Swing Rioters who broke in on 20 November 1830, tore down walls, smashed windows, destroyed some half made ploughs and damaged the foundry crane and water wheel, promising to come back on Monday to finish the job. Special constables made thirty arrests on the Monday and charged fifteen of them who were subsequently condemned to death, only to have their sentences commuted to transportation to Australia for life. It is probable that Bulford's farmers had their products as in 1872 there were eight two wheeled iron ploughs and a corn bruiser made by Taskers on Watergate Farm.[34]

Low wages combined with high wheat prices were the underlying causes of discontent. A meeting at Lavington analysing the issues reported, 'That when the tenants first rented their land and tithes, they considered the weekly pay of their labourers was the price of a bushel of wheat; consequently, the labourers' pay has been generally regulated thereby for a great number of years ... ', but the magistrates' recommendation that wages be raised by two shillings a week 'adds 25 per cent to that price'. Landowners felt that they could not 'pay their labourers high wages, or to comply with the recommendation of the Magistrates, unless they be assisted by proprietors of land and tithes', and therefore demanded an equivalent reduction in the tithes. The same story is told in Wallop where 'The farmers agreed to raise this [8s a week] to 10s provided labourers help them to get their rent, tithes and taxes reduced'. Eight or nine farmers went to the house of James Blunt Esq., the proprietor of the great tithes, and demanded a reduction in tithes for this year. Mr Blunt agreed to reduce his tithes in proportion to the increased rate of wages the farmers intend to pay their labourers.' Tithes were not such an issue in Bulford as land was not subject to the great tithes as these had been owned by Amesbury Abbey and ceased with its dissolution. There is no evidence that consequently the tenant farmers paid any higher wages than the going rate but, as poor relief at this time in Bulford was below the average for the Amesbury Poor Law Union parishes, it might suggest that they were benevolent. There is indeed evidence that this was the case. The newly rebuilt chapel had opened two years before the riots, and the leaseholder of the largest farm in the village, the Devenish family, was a joint sponsor. 'The labourers, many of whom were in their employ, served good and kind masters [including the Blatches at Ratfyn], who remembered that they also had a Master in heaven. They did not forsake their servants, when disabled by infirmity or old age.' When Mrs Blatch died in 1837, her funeral was, as already seen, the occasion of 'lamentations of nearly the whole village population'. The chapel's influence was at this time growing rapidly and would have, almost certainly, steadied any disposed to become involved in the riots. The branches of many Bulford families were widespread in the locality and there were, for example, a Keel, an Eyres and a Ranger indicted for the riot in Netheravon, all local residents, and a Holmes at Allington. There are no obvious connections between villagers and any of those indicted, although there could have been through marriage which an examination of the registers might reveal. There is, however, the intriguing example of a Bulford born resident William Batchelor, a thatcher. His wife was born in Everleigh and would have been about eighteen when there were riots in her village. Was she related to any of them, a daughter for example? She later named one of her Bulford born sons Robespierre which could indicate that there was a radical tendency in her family.[35]

Henry Graham's judgement on the rioters was that, 'The active element in all the mobs was composed chiefly of men of artisan class, the labourers who followed them and gave weight to the movement seldom taking any active part in the proceedings.' Thomas Piggott who was convicted for acts of outrage at Netheravon was, for example, a chimney sweep. He could have been known in Bulford if he plied his trade up and down the valley in the houses of the gentry. The story of William Brackston, a rioter who was involved in destroying the property of Sir John Pollen at Thruxton, also supports Henry Graham's assertion. He had returned from a term of transportation in Australia for breaking open a fowl house at Foxcott, Andover, in 1820 and stealing fowl. On 22 November he was working on the turnpike road, which he had been doing for the last five and a half years, when a mob persuaded him to join them and bring along his stone hammer. They told him that all threshing machines were to be broken on orders from the government. At his trial he said, 'My Lord, I am no scholar. I can neither write nor read. There were several respectable tradesmen carpenters, and others in that mob, and when they told me so, I could not but believe them.' He even asked for payment once the machine had been destroyed. A further term of transportation was commuted to one year in prison. Perhaps another reason why riots did not occur in Bulford was that the village lacked an artisan class in any numbers who could lead any protest. One of Buford's papermakers, Lawrence Greatrake, confessed that he was at odds with the Tory establishment and supported the revolutionary cause of America and had a 'heartfelt preference ... for its laws, its government, and its manners'. He though, had moved to America by the time of the riots, and in any case would not have supported the destruction of machinery. The most that we can say about the political views of villagers is that the undercurrents that erupted in other nearby villages must have been present in Bulford as well.[36]

The story of the riots serves to remind us that life for the poor and dispossessed was hard. The heartrending plea to the judge of chimney sweep Thomas Piggott indicted for disturbances in Netheravon illustrates the harsher side of life. When he was sentenced to transportation for seven years he pleaded,

I beg you to permit me to take my child with me aboard, or, if this is not possible, could you recommend the parish authorities to care of it. The child is only eight months old and its mother died in childbirth. When I am gone it will have neither kith or kin to look after it.

The judge refused to acquiesce to either request saying that he should have thought about this first. Thomas then responded, 'God help my poor babe, she now has no one else to protect her.' The speed that rioters were apprehended and charged must have deterred further disorders; those from Netheravon were behind bars and special constables were appointed within the area within four days. Punishments were harsh, with death sentences handed out liberally in the first instance, most of which were later commuted to transportation. The first hanging at Salisbury for one of the Ludgershall rioters, Henry Wilkins, was on 22 March 1831. In December the Everley Troop of Volunteer Yeomanry Cavalry was reconstituted in response to the riots. It consisted of forty-nine men, including corporal Francis Long (of Watergate Farm) and private Sir Edmund Antrobus (of Amesbury). The troop was further expanded in January 1831 when the regiment of which it was a part was conferred with the title of 'Royal Wiltshire Regiment of Yeomanry Cavalry' in appreciation of its success in quelling riots countywide and the independent volunteers, Pewsey Troop, was merged with it. From 1837 to 1863 Sir Edmund Antrobus of Amesbury captained the Everley Troop, followed by his son Edmund. The troop was disbanded in 1870 with Bulford landowner, Henry Danby Seymour having served as its captain for the last seven years.[37]

The disturbances of 1830 provided a cover for common criminality as the case of Isaac Miller of Netheravon reminds us; he, along with others, threatened to set fire to James Stagg's house after 'obtaining beer and other things by means of intimidation'. When times are hard, the sight of those better off can make a poor man desperate and tempt him to crime – or did Isaac have a grudge? A later incident at Bulford probably fits this latter category of crime. On Christmas Day 1853, a time when those who could afford it indulged themselves, Squire Long happened to be away with most of his household and David Sturgess hoped to take advantage of this opportunity. The cook and a servant were left 'to keep a look out and see if there was anyone about on the premises' when at 'about nine o'clock they heard someone trying the kitchen window, and the cook observed a man looking over the shutters ... went out and saw' David Sturgess 'and four other men; he told them to go away and one of them did; but the defendant [David Sturgess] after asking what he had to do with it, followed him into the kitchen, using very abusive language, and pushed him, swearing he would beat his head off.'

It was reported as to what then happened but this tale serves to remind us that all was not idyllic, even twenty-three years after the Swing Riots. It was at his time that advertisements were appearing in paper encouraging 'married agricultural labourers, shepherds or herdsmen or women of working class' to emigrate to Australia and local 'charities' were clubbing together to pay their passage. It was not a new idea for as early as 1826 William Cobbett railed against the Emigration Committees 'sitting to devise ... means of getting rid of these working people, who are grudged even the miserable morsel that they get'. This was a period after the wars with Revolutionary France when returning troops added additional strain to a difficult employment market. There was a parallel situation after the First World War when the then owner of Watergate House, Allan Young, feared 'that the colonies will attract the experienced farm hands, and that is just the class of men who should be kept in the home country'.[38]

Emigration

During the 1830s thirty-five people from Netheravon and thirty-six from Durrington emigrated to Canada for a better livelihood. There is scarce evidence that there was a similar exodus from Bulford at the same time although several of the Durrington families were connected with the village either directly through family ties or indirectly through chapel attendance. One of the chapel preachers, Henry Gane, emigrated to Canada and one of his associates, James Errence, went to Australia. There was undoubted emigration from Bulford in the 1850s which, when one considers the connections above, was most probably to Canada. In 1829 it was noted in Mary O'Brien's letter back home from Upper Canada, that

> Labourers are much wanted and ... may therefore be sure of work. Wages are two shillings sixpence per day with keep, or three shillings and nine pence

without, and more for many sorts of harvest work. Living is about half what it is in England.

In 1851 the village population stood at 408 but ten years later it had shrunk to 383. It has already been noted that the census returning officer attributed the decrease 'partly to migration'. Significantly it was those elements of the population which were the most tempted and able to emigrate that left the village. In 1851 there were twenty-one agricultural workers aged between fifteen and twenty; ten year later this peer group, now aged between twenty-six and thirty, had been reduced to eight. It must have been these people who ended up carving new lives for themselves in the colonies, relieving the population pressure on the resources of the village. In 1861 Adam Pike was a carter but by the next census he had become an agricultural labourer. His thirteen year old son George was a farmer's boy but the lure of prospects in the colonies enticed him to emigrate when he was eighteen, arriving in New Zealand in March 1877. He died there at Wellington in 1930. It is only by digging into family histories like this that a fuller picture emerges.[39]

This emigration serves as a further reminder that all was not well in the lives of nineteenth-century agricultural workers. Incidences like the disturbances of 1830 were rare but this did not necessarily mean that all was contentment. As the century wore on, this dissatisfaction became channelled into the embryonic trade union movement which was given a boost by the onset of the agricultural depression in the 1870s. In 1872 the newly formed National Agricultural Labourers' Union was setting up branches in the county which hitherto had never been reached by rural trade unionism. In November a Union meeting was held at Netheravon, attended by 600 men, with 23 new members, and the following month a new branch with 93 members was formed. There was also a branch set up in Durrington described in March 1875 as a 'good Branch', and a union meeting was held at Figheldean in November 1873, attended by 300 with 17 new members. In January 1874 the Union's President, Joseph Arch, addressed a three thousand strong meeting at Swindon, and later a meeting in Salisbury. The Union demanded a fair wage of sixteen shillings a week for a nine and a half hour day. It also attacked the employment of women and children in the fields, and demanded a better education for village children. 1874 saw the farmers in eastern England locking out ten thousand agricultural workers and reports were reaching the Union of employers in Wiltshire reducing wages from twelve shillings to eleven despite an abundant harvest. It was a time of agricultural tension and this reached Bulford where there were Union members and passions could run high. In 1874, Charles Spreadbury, a former Agricultural Union representative, was had up for calling James Weeks 'a snake in the grass' and 'an old backslider' because he did not join the Union. Even at the end of the century, feelings could run high. In 1893 the first annual conference promoted by the Wiltshire General and Agricultural Labourers' Union was held at Trowbridge, attended by delegates from Netheravon, Figheldean and Bulford. The keynote speaker declared that they, 'had righteous demands for better treatment, and for a fair share of the wealth which labourers produced (hear, hear) should be accepted by those who profited by their toil (applause)'. This union activity gives us a glimpse into the everyday life of the villagers but the sources are just not there to give us a real insight other than a cryptic note in the records of Bulford chapel for May 1880 stating that weekly offerings 'for want of proper officer, have fallen considerably during the last few years. Those who in this office were efficient are either gone to Heaven or to more favourable parts of the earth'. The National Agricultural Labourers' Union supported emigration, and it is almost always those with most get up and go who take the plunge into the unknown. Some union members attending the Durrington meeting in November 1873, perhaps including George Pike, were preparing to emigrate to New Zealand and a locked out union man attending in March 1875 was about to leave for Canada.[40]

As the century wore on, more and more villagers left Bulford for reasons other than poverty and this topic is explored further in Chapter 11. This present chapter has been an attempt at penetrating the lives, in Hudson's words,

> of the humble cottagers ... who were rooted in the soil, and flourished and died like trees in the same place – of these no memory exists. We only know that they lived and laboured; that when they died ... they were buried in the little shady churchyard, each with a green mound over him to mark the spot. But in time these "mouldering heaps" subsided, the bodies turned to dust, and another and yet other generations were laid in the same place among the forgotten dead, to be themselves in turn forgotten ... humble unremembered lives ...

We can, however, occasionally get a glimpse of the hardships of village life, as in the case of Mary Ann Sweet (née Sturges). When she was orphaned at the age of eighteen, her grandfather Samuel Sturges and his employer, Francis Stephen Long, became her guardians - but only for a very short time as she married Noah Sturges when she was nineteen. They had seven children together, the last being born after Noah's untimely death at the age of forty. All her life she lived next door to her grandparents (whose house has since been demolished to build the Social Club), bringing her husband to her childhood home. One of her daughters married Thomas Truckle and their daughter Elizabeth, in due course, came to live with her grandmother in her widowhood. This snippet of family history shows the importance of family support in hard times. For some however, even this failed, and they ended their days in the Amesbury Workhouse. The 1881 census records as inmates born in Bulford William Sturges, widower aged seventy two, agricultural labourer, and Frank Sturgess, widower aged thirty-four, bricklayer, imbecile. William, the son of Samuel Sturges who played a prominent role in the chapel, was brought back to Bulford by the family to be buried in 1885.[41]

We may not know a lot about the villagers, but we do at least know their names. The 1851 census reveals that nearly every other woman was called Elizabeth, Mary, Ann(e) or Sarah in that order of popularity, whereas over half the men were called William, John, James, George, Thomas or Joseph – sixty-two people were christened either Elizabeth or William. There was a good sprinkling of Old Testament names, even before the 1860 religious revival, including Martha, Rachel, Abadiah, Elias, Aaron, Noah and Ephraim, and then one or two unusual names, like the thatcher's son who as we have seen was named Robespierre.

3
Horizons and Communications

Road communications

STUDY OF THE 1851 census returns reveals the stability of the village population; seventy-eight per cent of Bulford's inhabitants were born and bred there with a further nine per cent coming from nearby villages in the Avon Valley. This was a reflection, no doubt, of the bond of servitude encompassing the lives of agricultural workers in the nineteenth century, but also the result of the area's geography. All the villages and their surrounding cultivation nestled in the valley bottoms which converged on Salisbury. The valleys not only protected the village communities but also acted as highways of communication. Each village was a bead in a necklace, aware only of its neighbours and oblivious as to what lay on either side. Between the various strands of habitation lay the downs which were empty spaces, 'desert' even, inhabited only by sheep, shepherds and wild creatures. One of these shepherds who worked the downs nearby during the latter part of the century, reported that all he saw was turf closely cropped by sheep and innumerable rabbits; the only time he saw hedges, fences or people was when he descended from the downs to cross a river.[1]

The horizons of the majority of Bulford's inhabitants were bounded by downs either side, and the neighbouring villages up river and down river to the city of Salisbury. News, gossip and scandal travelled this route with the carters and local traders like Joe the coalman passing through the valley to and from Salisbury, keeping the village blacksmiths supplied.

He appeared periodically in the villages with his eight donkeys, or neddies as he called them, with jingling bells on their headstalls and their burdens of two sacks of small coal on each. In stature he was a giant of about six feet three, very broad-chested, and invariably wore a broad-brimmed hat, a slate coloured smock-frock, and blue worsted stockings to his knees. He walked behind the donkeys, a very long staff in his hand, shouting at them from time to time, and occasionally swinging his long staff and bringing it down on the back of a donkey who was not keeping pace. In this way he wandered from village to village from end to end of the Plain, getting rid of his small coal and loading his animals with scrap iron which the blacksmiths would keep for him, and as he continued his rounds for nearly forty years he was a familiar figure to every inhabitant throughout the district.

Another traveller down the valley, but this time very frequent and regular, was the local postman.

The nearest Post Office was at Amesbury; but there was a mailbox in the wall of one of the shops, where the Toll-Keeper lived. The postman used to walk from Netheravon to Amesbury every day, a distance of over 6 miles, collecting from the various mailboxes on his way. So punctual was he that the villagers called him 'The Eleven o'clock Postman' and many set their clocks by him.[2]

The more long distance travellers like William Cobbett also sought the protection and hospitality of the valley routes. He describes how he crossed the Avon fifteen or sixteen times in one day's travelling down the valley. Not all the main routes, however, hugged the valley floors but struck out across the downs. Most were neither well used nor easy to follow as an earlier traveller, Daniel Defoe, noted in the previous century:

There is neither house nor town in view all the way, and the road which often lyes very broad and branches off insensibly, might easily cause a traveller to lose his way, but there is certain never failing assistance upon the downs for telling a stranger his way, and that is a number of shepherds, feeding or keeping their vast flocks of sheep, which are everywhere in the way and who, with a very little pains, a traveller may speak with.

We can be sure that this situation remained true throughout the nineteenth century as a brigadier reported that his father travelling over Salisbury Plain in 1896 or 1897 said, 'It was lonely ... with hardly any traffic on the tracks that served as roads. Somewhere near Shrewton a shepherd came running across to him to pass the time of day, saying that my father was the first living person he had seen for the last two days.' The empty spaces of the plain in the early part of the century were home to highwaymen and dispossessed men, many demobbed from the Napoleonic Wars. Ella Noyes, writing in 1913, tells how up to about seventy years ago farmers from isolated villages never went to market without being well armed.[3]

Several roads passed through the parish. One was the Avon Valley route already mentioned, running north through Milston. Originally it entered the village along Church Path, but was replaced by a road running more to the east, the Broadway (the present Milston Road) which carried on to Salisbury or Amesbury via Folly Bottom. This revised route was turnpiked from 1761 until 1871. There was also a local route to Amesbury via Ratfyn. Both main routes are marked on the 1773 Andrews and Dury's map. Another road followed the Nine Mile River, originally leading into Water Street. This was known variously as Bourne Road or Bulford Droveway. At Sheep Bridge it joined up with the old Marlborough Road. Going west from the village, it crossed Bulford Bridge and headed along the Packway for Warminster via Shrewton. This section of road was also turnpiked between 1761 till 1871. This was a road that cut across the downs, deserting the valley bottoms and was a main drove-road. The drove-roads along which drovers moved cattle and sheep were very important in the economic life of the region until the coming of the railways, and this one came right through the heart of Bulford. The Marlborough Road which met it at Sheep Bridge, carried on through Amesbury past the sheep pound by Long's Pennings. This route had a sign post on it east of the village and the sixteen, seventeen and eighteen mile stones indicating the distance to Marlborough. This was no doubt the route that Sir Edward Loveden followed when travelling from Buscot in Oxfordshire, as he stopped to buy meat at Marlborough on his way to Bulford. It was never turnpiked or developed as a coaching route and as the century wore on carried less traffic. With the coming of the army at the end of the century, the local paper reported in August 1897 that, 'It is long since the old road from Salisbury to Marlborough ... was the scene of so much traffic since the cavalry camp was formed at Bulford.' Another cross country route from Hungerford to Salisbury clipped the south-east corner of the parish, but this was another route which changed course, bearing west and joining the Marlborough Road in the parish, north of Sheep Bridge. Like the Marlborough Road that it joined, it was never turnpiked or developed as a coaching route but the villagers were expected to maintain it, being summoned in 1833 to the quarter sessions in Salisbury for failing in their responsibility. This was for a two and a bit mile stretch which was expected to be 'in breadth twenty feet'. The cost of maintaining non turnpiked roads was borne by the church rates and county rates with Bulford's expenditure in 1803 being £47 9s. 10d. on highways and the militia combined. These downland roads were little more than tracks which became very muddy. A December 1829 dairy entry complaining about the muddy roads near Ontario in Canada says that the 'roads are worse I think I have ever seen them, as bad as any roads would be where there are no stones to make them firm, - as bad as the down roads about Bulford, not so bad as the droves over Sedgemoor'. [4]

Turnpikes

THE ADVENT OF turnpikes and long distance coaching caused a few main routes to develop which transverse the region regardless of the slow, bustling, valley routes; one such route known as 'The Great London Road through Andover', the present A303, passed along the southern boundary of the parish. They ignored local communities as they were essentially through routes. Even so, travelling these coaching routes, before the days of tarmac was still an ordeal, especially in winter. It was, in every way, an alien world which passed along that road which, by by-passing Salisbury, was a shortcut to the West Country, looking down on the tight-knit community below and occasionally tumbling down from the ridge to intrude into the life of the village. Such an unfortunate traveller was 'Thomas Strange, Lieutnt RN of HM Ship "Espair" [who] lost his life by upsetting of the Celebrity Exeter Coach. July 13th 1827. Age not known.' He had just crossed over from Ireland, waited on the Duke of Clarence at Plymouth 'under whose auspices he had just been appointed to the command of a vessel' and was on his way to London. Life must have seemed good to him but this tragedy left a widow back in Ireland and four or five children. He is buried in the churchyard. The route followed the prehistoric Harrow Way which skirted Stonehenge. It had always been a through route, cutting across local routes with important nodes of communication growing up where the two classes of route crossed. Amesbury, Bulford's larger neighbour, with its coaching inn was such an interchange between the, literally, two levels of communication, giving the villagers a window onto the outside world.[5]

The Amesbury Turnpike Trust was established in 1762 to improve the 'A303' route from London to Exeter and, to prevent local traffic from bypassing the Amesbury toll gates, several minor roads around the town were also turnpiked. Two of these roads, as already noted, ran through the parish of Bulford and through the village itself. One was the road from Beacon Hill, through the village and then on to Larkhill, and the other left Amesbury at Folly Bottom and passed through the village to Fittleton. There was a bar across the road at Folly Bottom as if to fend off invaders into the village, with a box, chains and charge boards, but the gatehouse was situated in the heart of the village between the Nine Mile River and the Avon, neighbouring the Manor House and opposite the church. For twenty years from 1780 the tollhouse was occupied by one Richard Sopp, an outsider with interests beyond the village. He was a salaried official of the Trust as the surveyor of all its roads and must have been an oddity of the village,

4 *Road over Beacon Hill. Photograph of the present A 303 after the Autumn Manoeuvres in 1900. (Wiltshire & Swindon Archives)*

5 Nine Mile River. One of the branches of Nine Mile River entering the Avon. (photographed by the author, 2011)

being closer to the gentry than his fellow villagers. He was a widower and in 1795 was married again to Ann Fricker of Bulford. Francis Stephen Long of Watergate Farm followed his father's interest in the improvement of road travel. Both were trustees of the Trust and the senior was one of the five trustees who, for example, called a meeting of the Trust in the George Hotel, Amesbury, in December 1830. His son brought a case in 1853 against John Smith of Durrington for recklessly driving on one of the Trust's roads in Durnford. Mr Long was returning from Bulford at a leisurely eight miles an hour between four and five o'clock when he met Mr Smith and felt it his duty to bring the case 'to put a stop to the prevailing practice of furious driving on market days'. The plaintiff was fined fifty shillings and costs.[6]

The traffic on the turnpike roads in the village was never excessive as the receipts at the Bulford gate show over a period of six years when the Trust was still vigorous:

1823	£22	2s	6d
1824	£16	5s	
1825	£5		
1826	£21	10s	

1827	£18	17s	6d
1828	£23	8s	

The income for 1825 was down because work had to be done on the bridge. In November 1823 it had been damaged by flooding and the following January proposals were agreed by the magistrates to repair and re-erect the bridge and, 'Work will start when the river level permits.' It was not until July that this started and in October the mason was still working on the piers, both of which needed rebuilding, with Mr Dyke providing the necessary timber. The bridge was closed until December 1825 when a public notice announced that 'the BRIDGE at BULFORD, which has lately undergone repair, is now in a proper state to be travelled on, and that persons passing that way will suffer no obstruction or inconvenience.' The tollhouse became absorbed into the local community. The 1851 census returns show it occupied by a local man, James Andrews, who is significantly described not as a toll keeper but as 'a carter'; the collection of tolls obviously took second place. It is not surprising, therefore, to find that when bidders were invited for the various gates of the Trust in 1852, none were sought for the Bulford Gate or the Folly Bottom Bar. The tollhouse had become just another house in the village, probably even serving as a shop at one time – but not quite. It couldn't escape the fate of the Trust's property and was sold in 1871, with its garden, along with its 'Gates and Posts', for £40 to George Melsome, Francis Stephen Long's successor at Watergate Farm. At some point, probably during the twentieth-century road widening, the house was demolished and no trace of it now survives.[7]

What did the village gain from the Turnpike Trust besides another house? It enjoyed outside financial help in the upkeep of two roads and local employment for their construction and maintenance. Most villagers depended on their own legs and carriers' carts to get about and most of the local 'roads' were little more than county tracks, many of which have since degenerated into country paths. At the beginning of the twentieth century even the turnpike road had deteriorated. It 'was very narrow. Grass and weeds grew between the wheel-ruts and wild roses formed a hedge on either side.' One advantage was the upkeep provided for the 'pretty little iron bridge' over the Avon. When the Trust was liquidated there was still a debt of £270 to be met for its maintenance and repair. The 'handsome iron bridge' survived the Trust by forty-three years despite some battering, particularly in its latter days, as this letter from the local constable to the County Surveyor shows:

> Bulford Station - Salisbury Div.
> July 1 1902
>
> Sir,
> I have the honour to report for your information that on Tuesday July 1st 1902, from the information I received from James Spratt, the Mill, Bulford, that some damage has been done to Bulford Bridge by a Traction Engine, about 6.15 pm, loaded with camp material. I at once examined the bridge and found that about six feet of the railings broken off and the two Pillar Stones shifted. I at once went and traced the Engine and found them at the Stonehenge Inn ... .

A new bridge was erected in 1913 and the old one was demolished. For a time the village was bridgeless and the old ford, which gave its name to the spot in Saxon times, was used once more. This bridge was subsequently rebuilt in 2011.[8]

Draw of Salisbury and Amesbury

THE BRIDGE BRINGS us back to the river again and the dominance of the Avon Valley on the life of the village. Ten miles downstream Salisbury provided a focus for the area's economy, which was described thus in 1910: 'It is the villager's own peculiar city, and even as the spot it stands upon is the "pan or receyvor of most part of the waters of Wiltshire," so is it the receyvor of all his accomplishes in his labourouis life, and thitherward flow all his thoughts and ambitions.' Its draw reached Bulford, and Prudence Sawyer reported how its villagers:

> ... once a year, when they held their club,
> Some would go into Salisbury Fair,
> But had to walk to get there,
> As there was neither train nor bus,
> Those who couldn't walk, well they didn't fuss.

There was a regular carrier service from Bulford to Salisbury run for many years by George Keele, leaving the village at about eight in the morning and returning the same day, on Tuesdays and Saturdays. By 1875, this had been augmented by an extra trip on Thursdays. Despite this contact, Salisbury made little impact on the social fabric of the village. For a villager, the size and vibrancy of the city would have seemed like another world with endless horizons, especially on market days, when:

> The one great and chief pleasure, in which all participate, is just to be there, to be in the crowd – a joyful occasion which gives a festive look to every face. The mere sight of it exhilarates like wine! The numbers – the people and the animals! The carriers' carts drawn up in rows on rows – carriers from a hundred little villages on the Bourne, the Avon, the Wylye, the Nadder, the Ebble, and from all over the Plain, each bringing its little contingent.

Passengers for Salisbury were probably picked up outside the 'Rose and Crown' and carriers from the Avon Valley tended to congregate at the 'Chough Inn' in Salisbury ready for the return journey. For most villagers, Salisbury would have been the limit of their horizons, although there could well have been some for whom this would have been too far. William Cobbett met a thirty year old woman with two children in Ludgershall who had never travelled further than two and a half miles in her life – but she was exceptional which caused him to comment on her. The greater impression was made, as one would suspect, by neighbouring Amesbury. Until the Post Office was established in Bulford the nearest office was at Amesbury; it was also the nearest coaching entrepôt with several inns. From 1835 it was the focus of the local Poor Law Union and home of the Workhouse where several villagers ended up when all other support failed. There was a wide variety of trades and professions established at Amesbury which were not found in the villages round about.[9]

You might have expected a considerable number of Bulford born to migrate to Amesbury with all its attractions but this is not the picture revealed by the 1851 Amesbury census returns. John Hedges and his wife had moved and brought up their family in Amesbury and Charles Sturgess, a labourer, had also moved there. Two women had moved when marrying from outside their village and the local post boy, David Andrews, 26, had moved for a job. In addition to these six people, there were a few temporary residents from Bulford: two lodgers working on Amesbury farms, two house servants and two children – Fanny Swatton living with her uncle, and Annie Robbins, daughter of one of Bulford's tenant farmers, who was described as a visiting scholar and probably attended an Amesbury school. This brings the total of Bulford emigrés to thirteen, including two confined to the workhouse.

Village insularity

THE 1851 CENSUS returns show that 315 of Bulford's 408 inhabitants were born and bred in the village and so it comes as no surprise to find that the majority of weddings at the parish church were purely village affairs. Nineteen of the twenty-seven weddings celebrated in the decade beginning in 1841 fell into this category. Six of the remaining marriages had the bride marrying an outsider and leaving the village and five had grooms settling in the village from elsewhere in the valley, and one from Shrewton over in the next valley. With intermarriage between relatively few village families being the norm, the dangers of marrying blood relatives must have been both great and restricting in the choice of partners. Perhaps it was no accident that the Table of Degrees listing the marriages forbidden between blood relatives went missing from the church. Over a third of villagers bore the surnames of Andrews, Kill (or Keele), Swatton or Sturgess – this last being the commonest, belonging to sixty individuals. Sturgess, or a slight variation of the name, had a long pedigree in the village. Two hundred years earlier, a list of fifty-three villagers contained six named Sturges or Sturgis and three others named Turgis or Burgis. Other common names were, and in many cases still are, Canning, Hedges, Truckle, Wittick, Thorn, Sawyer, Pike and Holmes.[10]

Decennial census returns in the second half of a century give some inkling as to the reasons for, and obstacles against, marriages to village outsiders. These tantalising snapshots can only be embellished by family histories, like that of the Sawyers. William Sawyer (born 1878), the youngest son of papermaker John Sawyer, went into service near Bath as a footman and met his future wife Prudence Howse who was also in service as the cook. She came from Latton, north of Swindon, where her father was a lock keeper on the North Wilts Canal, and her mother collected the tolls. William left service at Bath to work as a carpenter and conducted a courtship with Prudence for eight years by post. When his father died in 1901 and his mother became unwell, William married Prudence at Latton and then moved to Bulford in 1903 to look after her, living in Mill Cottage with his new wife, now Prudence Sawyer, whose writings have been used extensively throughout this book. She lived there until her death in 1979, aged one hundred.[11]

It is impossible to reconstruct how often short journeys to neighbouring villages were made in the absence of diaries, but they undoubtedly occurred. The fairs in Amesbury, relations living nearby and trips to markets would all take people beyond village bounds once in a while but with most of one's relations living in the village, the opportunities would have been few and far between. This is the picture reflected in a register kept by the Rev. William Williams of his congregation's attendance at chapel each Sunday between October 1835 and May 1840. All absences were noted and the reasons recorded. Two from the upper echelons of village society, Mr Godwin the papermaker and the pastor's own wife, were frequently absent in London and Taunton respectively for health reasons; but for others, very few visits outside the village were recorded – two apiece for Amesbury and Woodford, and three to Figheldean. The chapel was founded at Bulford to serve 'the surrounding villages, particularly Amesbury and Durrington' which makes the village a focus for the independents of the area, but even this pull, with the exception of one member who came from Cholderton in the neighbouring Bourne Valley, was restricted to the Avon Valley. Members came from as far as Haxton upstream and West Amesbury downstream.[12]

The horizons of gentlemen and yeoman farmers

THE TWO PROLONGED absences from chapel for health reasons are a reminder that not all in the village had restricted horizons. There were those who were not part of the village in a fundamental sense and looked further afield: the clergymen, papermakers and farming gentry. No matter how they controlled the village institutions as churchwardens, employers, trustees of this body and that, entrepreneurs and so forth, they were, with the exception the Lord of the Manor to a degree, a glossy veneer on the bedrock of village society, moving in a world unfettered by distance and labour. The Lord of the Manor Anthony Southby and his first wife came from Somerset and Bristol respectively; he was well travelled and cosmopolitan in outlook. Francis Stephen Long came from Boreham near Warminster and maintained close fiendships in the area, but it is a measure of the circles in which he moved that he found a wife, Anne Morlidge from Grosvenor Terrace, Westminster in fashionable London. The tenant farmers on the Manor estate, the Robbinses, were more local but alien to the valley. The papermakers, as we shall see in Chapter 9, were bound up in a wider economy and came from far and wide, as did the clerics who, for example, came from Canada, Yorkshire and Staffordshire.[13]

There were two degrees of tenant farmers in the village. There were those who, like Francis Stephen Long, leased the larger Watergate Farm on long term leases of ten or fifteen years and were part of County Society inhabiting a world of house guests and house parties. His wife Anne has left a domestic inventory which includes a dinner set for eighteen persons, including large, soup and pie plates, dishes, soup tureen and a cheese stand amongst other things. Drink was well catered for as well with fifty-seven cut wine glasses and twenty plain ones, a dozen champagne glasses, port and water glasses. Her recipe book gives us an idea of what they ate in addition to the meats, for example: carrot soup or green tea soup, gingerbread, blancmange, strawberry, orange or greengage jelly, potato pudding, macaroni, gateaux de pommes, common sponge pudding, sponge cakes, cheese or cabinet pudding, orange marmalade, damson cheese, cold cream and clarified lemonade. The inventory also lists an array of bed and table linen – in short all that was needed for a good house party with their social set. On the other hand, they integrated only superficially into the village. Their children were educated outside the village and married into what would now be called middle class families away from the village. They were mindful of their status and we have the echoes of this social divide in the twentieth century with 'Old Mrs Hill' who lived for a while at Bridgefoot Cottage after the Manor had been sold to the Secretary of State for War. Villager Ann Sawyer once visited her and described her as a 'scary lady who insisted on being addressed as "My Lady"' as Ann's mother Prudence did. The tenant farmers on the Manor estate, however, were a more localised group. They came from a nexus of local farming, property owning families in the village and neighbouring Durrington: the Smiths, Croomes and Haydens. When the Robbins family moved into the village to farm the two Manor Farms, they soon integrated into this upper echelon of village society. Joseph Robbins of Lower Farm married Elizabeth Croome and his aunt had married into the Haydens of Durrington, as did his daughter Emma. Joseph's sister-in-law, Mary Ann Croome who inherited Lower Farm from her uncle, married a farmer from out of the village, James Randall, but kept in touch with the village. The 1861 census shows her staying with her nephew John Robbins of Upper Farm with two members of her new extended family. John's wife, Elizabeth, was a Randall and her farmer brother John Self Randall was also visiting.[14]

It is a sign of the gentry's unwillingness to integrate into the village that they chose their domestic servants from neighbouring villages and not from Bulford itself. This worked two ways as some of the villagers were, in their turn, servants in Amesbury and Durrington. Rarely were servants brought to Bulford from very far away although a notable exception was Ellen Roberts whom Pastor Sleigh brought with him; she was born in Bethel, Anglesey. There was, however, one category of domestic servant drawn almost exclusively from the village itself; local girls between the ages of twelve and twenty taken into service as nurse maids. The overall picture, though, is of the tenant farmers and gentry keeping the village at arm's length to reinforce their authority and accentuate their status. The exception to this was the Lord of the Manor who in many ways was the village as he owned most of it. He had no need of this differentiation and it is interesting to note, in 1861 for example, that he was alone in employing two villagers as domestic servants; Mary Canning as cook and her sister Lucy Canning as a housemaid whose stories we will meet again. It was this clear distinction of class in the village which enabled both groups to inhabit different worlds with different horizons.[15]

Economic horizons

THE FARMERS AND landowners inhabited an economic world with its own horizons. Salisbury was obviously within this sphere but not as much as might seem apparent. The probate accounts of Thomas Croome show financial dealings with Salisbury and the towns to the north, like Devizes (where he banked), and even further afield like London. This is not surprising as Thomas Davis points out, 'South Wiltshire is the granary, not only of manufacturing towns within the county, but also those in the east part of Somersetshire; and it sends considerable quantities of wheat and barley to the cities of Bath and Bristol.' This picture is borne out from by 1809 trading data from Salisbury corn market which shows that the Avon Valley was hardly represented, as opposed to the other valleys converging on the city. In 1808 and 1809 Sam Sturgess had a quarterly standing at the Salisbury Fairs but from 1810 his name no longer appears. The records go up to 1819 showing that, if he had died, he was not replaced. By 1842 Devizes was one of the most important corn markets in England and it is here, and at Warminster that Bulford corn almost certainly ended up. Devizes opened a new corn exchange in 1857. It is perhaps significant that the principal farmer for much of the century came from Warminster.[16]

The main livestock in the village economy was sheep. Salisbury was a cattle market, as opposed to sheep, and so contacts were with sheep fairs elsewhere. Thomas Croome's 1820 and 1821 accounts of buying and selling sheep show that he attended the Andover fair, throughout the year selling over two thousand pounds worth, and buying nearly twice that figure. Over half his transactions were with farmers up and down the Avon valley from Durnford in the south, where he conducted a lot of transactions, to Netheravon in the north; a further quarter were with farmers in the Bourne Valley with particular emphasis on dealing with Mr Blatch in Cholderton, brother of Henry Blatch at Ratfyn. Further transactions were along the routes to Warminster and Devizes, at Maddington, Tilshead, West Lavington and (Winterbourne) Stoke. In addition he dealt with Mr Smith in Bulford and his sister-in-law, Mary Croome. All these business transactions were to the north of Salisbury and all were well within fifteen miles, a distance considered to be a reasonable day's return journey by cart. When Henry Seymour of East Knoyle twenty miles away leased the Seymour estates in Bulford to Matthew Devenish in 1801, he built in a clause in case his tenant failed in his obligations which allowed him to 'fetch and carry from any place or places not exceeding fifteen miles from Bulford ... all such timber and other materials' to make any repairs to the leased property at the tenant's expense. If twenty miles had been reasonable, he would have no doubt chosen that distance for the lease to allow materials to be brought from his own estate. Thomas Croome's reach for transactions involving sheep were well within this limit and sheep could be carried, or driven quite conveniently. The corn markets at Devizes and Warminster being nearer twenty miles away on the other hand, would have probably necessitated spending a night away. The economic horizons of villagers, therefore, would not have exceeded twenty miles and the rare instances of immigrants to the village for work, or marriage to 'outsiders' also reflects this as has already been seen.[17]

The most extreme example of someone dislocated from village society is provided by Sir Edward Loveden Loveden who occupied Bulford Manor in 1812-1815. His contacts with the village were by and large mediated through his relationships with the tenant farmers. He had an account with Mr Croome for faggots, coal and milk and he hired extra horses from him when they were needed. A butcher's account paid Mr Dyke for beef, veal and mutton pending his arrival at Bulford Manor and Mr Hooper was paid for pork and tripe. A month's bill with the local baker was for sixty-two gallon loaves and twenty-three pecks of flour. He had a garden account to pay Sturgess his gardener for fresh vegetables, three stocks of bees and to pay 'women weeding 34 days at 6d' a day. There was an account with the miller and one with Mr Six the apothecary, the latter in connexion with his dogs. A local carpenter, William Burton, made him a new ladder and bee stools, did some painting and put in six new gate posts. This was about the extent of his integration, along with hunting the Downs. We have details of his economic reach in the meticulous accounts that he kept. Basic necessities were purchased for him, mainly by James Hooper, at Amesbury. These were almost exclusively for kitchen use: besoms, dustpans and brushes, pots and pans, stone jars and quart jugs and such like. He regularly made purchases from Salisbury Market whilst in residence, buying from an R. Tuges, for example, '2 tin candlesticks, 2 iron snuffers, 1 plate warmer, cheese toaster, copper fountain, bread basket, japanned coal scoop, bush lanthorn, 2 horn lanthorns, dustpan, slop pail painted, 4 iron spoons, japanned hand candlestick', all for five pounds and seven shillings. Sir Edward also patronised Stevens and Gerrard of the City of New Sarum who were well known cabinet makers and upholsterers. He made purchases further afield, for example beds made by Fidell in Devizes. In all this, his outreach from the village was similar to that of any of the tenant farmers though his drink requirements no doubt were far more wide ranging than theirs. The basic beverages, porter, old beer and table beer were supplied through Whitchurch Co. of Salisbury but wines and spirits came from further afield with old port, Tenerife and Cognac Brandy (two gallons) coming from Perry and Murch of Bristol. Two cases of more refined liquor were sent down from London: 'Madeira 16 bottles, Port of 1788 34 bottles, Sherry 24 bottles, Port 55 bottles, Champagne 10 bottles and Claret 6 bottles' – quite a party! [18]

What made Sir Edward exceptional were his relationships way beyond the locality. He was an extremely wealthy individual, benefiting, as one biographer put it, 'from his own father's estate, inherited in 1787, the Loveden estate, and from three provident marriages'. He had built a grand country residence at Buscot Park in Oxfordshire from where he supplied Bulford Manor with most of the bed and table linen, all embroidered with his initials, along with items of furniture. He had an agent in London, Mr Chapman, who made purchases of furniture and luxury items on his behalf and had them transported to Bulford. In May 1813, for example, he sent 'a mahogany secretaire – with drawers inclosed under with doors & bookcase in 3 parts, a small bookcase with desk drawers, lower parts with drawers inclosed with folding doors in 2 parts, a mahogany corner cupboard and a Turkey carpet' at a cost of £37 7s 6d. Sir Edward Loveden also bought things himself at fashionable London stores. He purchased his table service, wine glasses, goblets and decanters from Spode & Co of Portugal Street, Lincoln Inn Fields, and other items, like a swan bowl, from the Derby China Warehouse. His plated silverware was made by Joseph Brasbridge (1743-1832) of 100 Fleet Street: cutlery, salt and mustard pots, sugar tongs, marrow scoops, soup ladles, waiters [trays], bottle stands and so forth, all engraved with his crest. Sir Edward Loveden was at the pinnacle of county and national society and his pretentions are best illustrated by purchases he made in July 1813. When Princess Augusta, the Duchess of Brunswick died in March, the contents of her house in Blackheath, London (where she had been living estranged from the rest of the royal family) were put up for sale. Sir Edward was there, paying ten guineas for 'an India Cabinet in 2 parts, an India book case in two parts, six India figures belonging to the above, [and] an India Chest on stand'. All these items owned by royalty were sent to Bulford Manor along with 'three fenders & three sets of fire irons'. This was a world as far away from the lives of the villagers as you could get and you only have to bear in mind that a woman, as we have seen, only earned six pence for a day's work weeding, which equates to three shillings for a six day week. She would have had to do this, every week for a year and a half to afford these purchases. The average agricultural wage at that time, as we have seen, was about seven shillings a week and so the men would have had to work thirty weeks to buy them.

Cultural horizons

THE YEOMAN FARMERS, gentry, clergymen and papermakers had a wider view of society and were aware of regional and national events through travel, newspapers and conversation. Wider family estates, Bath and London were all part of the gentry's social domain with London usurping Bath as the century wore on. You can see this in where marriage partners were sought and also in the few surviving letters of the Southbys. Ann Southby (1729-1795), for example writing from Bath asking her three daughters about their journey home to Bulford, and telling them how their ailing father was progressing: 'Dear Mr Southby mends every day he rode out 12 or 13 miles today with very little pain in his head tho he rode fairly fast and as soon as he gott of his horse was quite easy.' She tells them that at present, 'Your Father is at the coffey house', conjuring up images of Regency and Victorian Bath, returning whilst she was still writing and sending his 'kindest love'. The date of this letter must be about 1790 as her husband died in 1791 and she also enquires if they 'have heard anything of my poor [son] Edmund' who was to die three months after his father.[19]

Another illustration of the wider, intellectual world inhabited by the cultured gentry is provided by the joint Ladies of the Manor in 1796, Charity Ann and Mary Southby. They had an interest in romantic poetry and when Frances Greensted, whilst a servant at Maidstone wanted to publish by subscription a book of her poetry so she could support her aged mother, they were both 'liberal subscribers'. Her book was entitled *Fugitive Pieces* and in it the authoress gave particular thanks 'to those ladies and gentlemen, who, in addition to their own names, have generously procured those of their friends'. You can imagine the Southby sisters twisting the arms of the yeoman farmers in Bulford as the names of Mr Smith, Mr Swaine and Mr Robbins all appear in the list of subscribers along with the Rev. Mr Gilbert Gapper (their mother's relation in Somerset?). The sisters' heir to the Manor, Anthony Gapper, had wide cultural and intellectual interests as well, helping, for example, to conduct an autopsy on an Egyptian mummy at the Bristol Institution in 1824. William Swaine's successor but one at Watergate Farm, Francis Stephen Long was one of the partners of the Wiltshire and Dorset Banking Company, and when there was a 'Malignant Disorder among sheep' in 1862, we find him shouldering his civic responsibilities and chairing the public meeting in Salisbury, and following it up with a letter to *The Times*. There is an illustration of his countrywide view provided by the instance in 1835 when he had a dark brown gelding stolen from his stables at Watergate Farm. He 'had handbills printed [and] in consequence of information ... went to Saxmunden, in Suffolk, thence up to Uphill, to *the sign of the Bottle* [where] he found the gelding in the possession of Mr Moy, the landlord' and was able to recover his horse. There was no twenty mile horizon to the world of county society. He married Elizabeth Sophia from Bond Street in London and retired to Middlesex. George Melsome, Francis Stephen Long's successor at Watergate Farm, had his name published in 1874 as a supporter of Lord Henry Thynne and Viscount Folkestone in the election of that year. He was also, as we shall see in Chapter 10, active in the management of the village school, but he also had a wider involvement. Between 1880 and 1888 he regularly inspected Rose's Grammar School in Amesbury and wrote reports, and the *Log Book* records that 'Mr Melsome called at the school and looked over the premises' in 1890.[20]

National and international horizons

INVESTMENTS GAVE THE gentry a wider view of the world with Francis Stephen Long, for example having shares in the railways of this country and India, but this was a vicarious involvement. Anthony Southby became more personally involved in one great national event, the Indian Mutiny, which took the lives of his eldest daughter, Mary, and her surgeon husband, William Shaw. Mary was a victim of the boat massacre at Cawnpore on 27 June 1857, and her husband died at the siege of Lucknow a few months later. Anyone reading the memorial tablet in the church today might not be aware of the horrors of this incident which occurred in modern day Kanpur during what Indians call their First War of Independence. One thousand or so British residents were besieged throughout June, their numbers whittled away by disease, starvation and enemy sharp-shooting. Only a few hundred were still alive, including Anthony Southby's daughter when their commander managed to negotiate a truce so that they could be evacuated. However, as they boarded boats at Satichaura Ghat, to carry them to Allahabad, they were mown down by gunfire, and any survivors were put to the sword. When relief arrived a few days later, they found that two hundred imprisoned women and children had been butchered in revenge for previous British atrocities. When news reached Anthony

Southby, he can only have been grief stricken. The news would no doubt have percolated through to the villagers' awareness, especially as there was a national outcry, and some might even have had sons in the army at the time, but they would have remained ignorant of most national events unless they happened on their doorstep. Events like the Civil War skirmish back in June 1644, when 'The king's forces took 8 pack horses loaded with goods for London, at Bulford and carried them to Salisbury.' Anthony Southby was also vicariously connected to unrest in Canada which affected his sister and brother-in-law, this time without tragedy. This was the republican inspired Mackenzie Rebellion of 1837 to which the O'Briens and Gappers were naturally opposed. Anthony would have known, or certainly known of, the various players involved. Personal tragedy was also to hit James Ledger Hill whose son William Henry Tucker Hill, a Lieutenant in the 5th Lancers, 'fell in the defence of Ladysmith' during the Boer War. Some villagers undoubtedly had relatives involved in Imperial Wars as well. Back home, however, the Swing Riots and their aftermath in 1830 and 1831 would have excited both gentry and villagers, each looking at events from a different perspective. A retired soldier like James Grace from Downton who was father-in-law to Edward Sturgess, the bricklayer, and living in the village for the 1851 census would have plenty to tell of other events, but these would have already passed into history. He had been a groom in the 15th Regiment of Dragoons which had fought up through Spain in the Peninsular War and also at the Battle of Waterloo, for which he had a medal, when he would have been aged twenty-nine.[21]

The owners of Watergate Farm were the Seymours who, in the case of Henry Seymour senior and his son Henry Seymour junior, had very strong French connections, the latter being half French. They, however, were not resident in Bulford and these connections can hardly have impinged on the horizons of the village, except possibly in 1807-1808 when Henry Seymour junior was prevented from taking up his inheritance in Bulford being a political prisoner of the French at the time. This will be explored further in Chapter 5. The person with the widest horizons who was resident in the village, therefore, was indisputably Anthony Southby, Lord of the Manor from 1835 to 1883. His tragic colonial connection with India through his daughter has already been noted, but his internationalism went deeper than this. He was born Anthony Gapper in 1799, changing his name to Southby when he inherited the Bulford Manor as a kinsman of Mary Southby in

1835. Anthony Gapper was the third son of the Rev. Edmund Gapper (1753-1809), who was both Rector of Keinton Mandeville and Squire in the adjoining village of Charlton Adam in Somerset, and Mary née Barrett (1760-1834).[22]

Anthony Gapper/Southby

THE GAPPERS WERE a cultivated family for whom education was important, as Edmund Gapper's 1809 will shows, leaving 'all my effects for life [to his widow for] the maintaining and educating our children'. The two older boys (see Appendix 1a), Edmund Barrett Gapper, William Southby Gapper and the youngest, Richard Colston Gapper, saw active service in the Napoleonic Wars, the elder two in the navy and the youngest in the army, but Anthony stayed at home to qualify as a doctor at Edinburgh in 1822, and from 1823 to 1826 practised in Bristol (which is when he had helped with the mummy autopsy). Anthony had two elder sisters, Lucy Ann and Mary Sophia, who were well educated and well read. The Wars and agricultural depression depressed rural wages but increased the burden of the poor rates on landowners. The flood of books on settling in Upper Canada from 1819 and in full spate during the next decade, therefore, found a ready audience amongst both the gentry and reading public when peace broke out. The eldest boys Edmund and William, bought farms with their military half pay in the newly opened up Upper Canada at Thornhill and emigrated in 1825. This was pioneering country along Yonge Street, now part of Toronto. Edmund had recently married losing first his six month daughter and then his wife, Katherine Anne, who tragically died, at Belem, in Portugal, whilst making the Atlantic crossing. Anthony joined his elder brothers in 1826 and the experience was to give him a wide outlook on life. If he went to Thornhill the same way as his sister, he would have sailed to New York, sailed up the Hudson and then travelling overland across this frontier province by coach and canal.[23]

Anthony lived with William, helping out on the pioneering farmstead on Yonge Street, and he also practised as a doctor. His first love and passion, though was to roam around and study natural history in this newly opened up part of the Empire. They were joined by his sister Mary (1798-1876), brother Richard with his fiancée Fanny and their widowed mother Mary who sailed from Bristol in August 1828 to stay with William and his wife

6 *Engravings by Anthony Gapper (Southby). Illustrations for his 1830 paper* Observations on the Quadrupeds found in the District of Upper Canada extending between York and Lake Simcoe, with the view of illustrating their geographical distribution, as well as describing some Species hitherto unnoticed. *The bottom one is named after him –* Avricola Gapperi. *His description of it runs thus:* 'Meadow Mouse, with a tail more than half the length of the body; short round ears; the back and upper part of the head chestnut; sides and face yellowish brown; belly yellowish white; chin and throat ash-coloured.' *The editor's note says,* 'Dr. Gapper having left this new species unnamed, we take the opportunity of designating it by the name of the discoverer.' (Zoological Journal Vol V No XVIII Feb-June 1830) *(images courtesy of Biodiversity Heritage Library)*

Mary (née Hamilton) and help look after their newly born first child Lucy Mary. Anthony's sister Mary stayed in Canada, marrying her brother's friend and neighbour Edward G. O'Brien in 1830 and giving birth to a son they named Lucius Richard. Mary Gapper O'Brien was well educated, speaking fluent Italian and German, and is celebrated as a literary figure in

Canada as a result of the letters-come-journal she sent back to relations in England between 1828 and 1838 about her experiences in the new colony; each letter costing £1 1s to send home. This creative streak which was also found, as will be seen, in her brother Anthony, also flowered in her son born in 1832, Lucius Richard O'Brien. He gained fame as a landscape artist and subsequently founded the Ontario School of Art in 1876 and, in 1880, became the first president of the Canadian Academy of Arts. He came to Bulford, and in January 1869 spending some months on the family estate in the village, recording scenes round about. He returned briefly to England in 1883 and two of his paintings now hang in Buckingham Palace. This artistic streak was also evident in Anthony's future children. His daughter Claudia had at least one picture hung in the Royal Academy in 1874, which was given the number four. It is entitled 'Ducks in the New Forest' and is painted in water colours, with an oriental flavour, using bracken dipped in paint to depict the trees. This picture, given by Claudia to Mary Ann Knight, has been handed down through the family.[24]

Mary Gapper O'Brien was very close to her brother Anthony as they were living together on the eve of his becoming Lord of Bulford Manor. He was very active, helping his brother on the farm 'building a smoke house for drying bacon and hams of three pigs for the coming year', an ice house, and a sugar plant. He displayed pioneering practicality by, for example, helping his sister make mittens out of buffalo hide scraps and 'trying to make a dibbling implement' to plant mangle-wurzels but without success as 'the ground is too rough.' She also describes him visiting and treating his patients, for example in October 1828, 'Anthony was sent for in a hurry to put on some toes that had been cut off but could not succeed very well for want of instruments. It seems that he has many patients who would and could pay for his medical services if he would ask them.' It would appear from this comment that he didn't always charge for his services, doing what he could uniquely do in this embryonic community. When he had returned to England his sister wrote that, 'We want Anthony more often than I could wish for in his medical capacity.' Mary shared Anthony's love of natural history and helped him with collecting and pressing his plants. In December 1829, for example she wrote in her journal, 'I helped Anthony to arrange his beautiful flowers. He has collected a very large number, some very beautiful, and most with an air which we are accustomed to ascribe to garden flowers.' Anthony Gapper was in his element, and Mary's journals portray him as an excited, creative and self-reliant man totally at home in his surroundings. She came across him with his brother 'setting up their kettles.... so exactly did they look themselves twenty years ago building Robinson Crusoe houses'.[25]

Anthony Gapper was also a very proficient zoologist and she records one instance when he 'brought over a large snake (about as large as our common one [Grass snake]) which is not reputed to be venomous though his instinct and subsequent discovery of its fangs taught him that it must be so in some degree'. He went on expeditions of exploration and when he travelled north to the shores of Lake Huron, Mary begged him to keep a journal. The results of his fieldwork were to culminate in what Canadian naturalists have acclaimed as one of the most valuable early records of mammals in Upper Canada. Once back in England he published this as his *Observations on the Quadrupeds found in the District of Upper Canada extending between York* [later renamed Toronto] *and Lake Simcoe, with the view of illustrating their geographical distribution, as well as describing some Species hitherto unnoticed.* He had discovered four new mammal species which were then named 'Gapperi' after him. One was the 'Arvicola Gapperi', a small red backed vole, the capture of which was recorded by his sister: 'Anthony has at last succeeded in snaring a mouse, alias Hamster' on 12 February 1829. He eventually presented specimens of these new species to the Bristol Museum.[26]

In June 1829, Anthony abandoned a field trip and returned to England, much to the sadness of his brother and sister. He went to live, certainly for a while, at College Green in Bristol, before settling in Bridgwater, where he married and started his family. In 1831 he was elected physician to the Bridgwater Infirmary, and three years later he was elected Mayor. He could well have left Canada because Charity Ann Southby, Lady Pollen, was ill, dying in June 1830. She left her sister Mary Southby in sole charge of Bulford Manor and there is even a probability that Anthony helped Mary administer the estate after Charity's death as she had made him the sole heir of Bulford Manor. His sister implied this as she wrote that 'my Aunt's kindness has created circumstances to require Anthony to take up residence in England for the present'. He came into his new inheritance on the death of Mary Southby in 1835 as the new Lord of Bulford Manor, changing his own name to Southby. The story of Anthony Southby is now a significant part of the story of Bulford village. Once he settled in Bulford, Anthony

Southby displayed the same zeal for fieldwork, switching this time to flora. He gained a reputation as a biologist and catalogued plants in Somerset and Wiltshire which he sent to H. C. Watson, the 'Father of British topographical botany'. The latter acknowledged Dr Southby's contribution when he published his *Topographical Botany* in 1874, writing that he had checked his data against Dr Southby's lists of plants in Somerset and Wiltshire and that his 'Somerset list proved of much service to me years ago', although it had now been superseded. During the course of his fieldwork he identified a species new to the Bulford area, milk vetch, which was described as, 'An interesting addition to the Flora of Wilts, first observed….. by Dr Southby of Bulford'. He almost certainly became a familiar figure roaming his new estates and beyond and we have already noted his discovery of an extinct rhinoceros tooth. A description of him by his sister six years earlier, in Upper Canada, may well still have applied:

> Anthony's figure would amuse you. He wore a leather belt strapped around his waist, which confined his flower case to his back. On one side it sustained a small axe and on the other a large hammer the handle of which hung down below the skirt of his shooting jacket. Over this his shot belt was slung round him in the usual way. He had a gun on one shoulder and on the other his fishing rod bearing his bundle of needments.[27]

In 1845 he travelled through the High Pyrenees with the noted botanist, Richard Spruce, who recorded in his diary,

> On the 2nd Aug, [1845], accompanied by Dr Southby, a compatriot enthusiastic in the pursuit of Natural History, I crossed the central chain by the Port de Cauterets to the baths of Penticosa in Aragon….. In this excursion, which occupied four days, numerous interesting flowers, but scarcely any mosses were added to my collection.

They made new discoveries in their field trip and Richard Spruce named a new species, 'Southbya tophacea', after Dr Southby (to add to the 'gapperi' mammals he had discovered in Canada). They returned, landing in Brighton on 10 April 1846 and the results of this field trip were published by Richard Spruce in 1849, where he wrote, 'To no one can I with more propriety dedicate a new genus of Pyrenean Cryptogarnia than to Dr Southby, my companion in so many interesting excursions in those mountains, and a gentlemen accomplished in almost every branch of natural history.' In 1922 Anthony Southby's descendant presented to the Essex History Society 67 sheets of Australian marine algae and about 250 sheets of marine algae from Jersey which had belonged to him. It seems almost certain that he had collected the Jersey samples whilst visiting his younger son, Anthony Gapper Southby, who was living there in 1881 with his family and Bulford born servant Hannah M. Keel, and this then raises the possibility of him having travelled at some point to Australia where he collected the other specimens. This possibility is strengthened by the fact that his cook, Mary Ann Cannings, had travelled across the Sahara by camel which could well have been on the way to Australia before the opening of the Suez Canal. The sheets are undated.[28]

Natural history, however, was not his only accomplishment as he was a man of many parts, he was also a doctor and a craftsman who was into wood carving and papermaking (perhaps to supply his sister in Canada who had run out of paper and sent home to England for a new supply). Subsequent chapters will examine his involvement with the village church and paper-mill. Anthony Southby was not resident in the village continuously throughout his whole tenure as Lord of the Manor. The 1851 census shows him as a widower after the death of his first wife living with his family in Marylebone. He was able to take advantage of his wealth to live in the capital for a while, in all probability for the education of his five children aged between ten and eighteen who were all described as scholars; he himself was described as a 'physician not practising'. There could though be another explanation for him living in London at the time and that is that he was taking his family to see the Great Exhibition which would have appealed to his scientific bent and international outlook. If so, it must have been a prolonged visit as Bulford Manor was uninhabited at the time and he had taken his whole household with him to London.[29]

There is an intriguing connection between Bulford and the Great Exhibition in the person of William Williams and his Bulford wife Sarah (née Sturgess), eldest daughter of Thomas Sturgess, and their son Robert. The Great Exhibition was the event that triggered George Shillibeer to start the first omnibus service and William Williams shows the same spirit of enterprise. The 1851 census shows him living in Paddington and working as an 'Omnibus Proprietor' with his son Robert being one of his omnibus drivers – a job that he was still doing ten years later. The Williams family had placed villagers at the forefront of a social development in London. William Williams, the omnibus proprietor, was living in the village in 1827 when his son Robert was born and was still there six years later when another son, William, was baptised. He at that time was described as a 'labourer'.[30]

Bulford was never where Anthony Southby felt exclusively at home. His childhood home at Charlton Adam was no longer in the possession of his family but he had roots further west in Bristol where he first practised as a doctor. It is here that he returned when he left Upper Canada; it is here, at Clifton, that his brother Richard Colston Gapper settled on returning back to this country, and it is here that he found his first wife, Octavia Ibbotson. He courted her in the autumn of 1830, speaking enthusiastically to his sister Mary of 'a red haired lassie' and leaving her in no doubt that he was looking for a wife. She was very supportive, writing to him:

> May God grant you success in your search for a wife & give you one worthy of you according to my notions of your worth – it may be of less importance to me than it once was that she should also like & be liked by me but her suitability in every other respect I am equally anxious about. [At this point, he had not inherited Bulford Manor, and so she continues] You cannot tell how much we want you here ... – I used to make it part of my happiness to have you lodged with all your traps in a corner of my own house but since you must be married, the next best thing is to get you an estate amongst us.[31]

But this was not to be. Anthony married Octavia in Bath at Christmas time the following year and three years later he had an heir, Edmund Richard Southby, in Bridgwater where the couple were living. Octavia bore him two sons and three daughters in the seven years before her early death in June 1849. Anthony married again, taking Ellen Adam as his second wife. There were no further children. Anthony died aged 83 on 10 August 1883 bringing to an end his forty-eight year tenure as Lord of the Manor. Although he had not lived in the village all of these years there was enough time for him to remodel the Manor House with the addition of a bay window. We have seen an absence in London at the time of the Great Exhibition, and there are other documented absences besides the field trips abroad noted above. In 1852 to 1853 a Colonel Bradshaw was living in Bulford House, having probably moved in shortly after the 1851 census which shows the Manor House empty. The 1861 census shows the Southbys at home, and this was probably Anthony's main base until after his second wife Ellen's death three years later. The 1871 census has Bulford Manor House occupied by another military occupant, Captain John Taylor with his wife, two nieces and three domestic staff and he is still reported living there a year later. Anthony still returned to Bulford for the baptism of his granddaughter Violet Miriam in 1871. Now twice widowed and a free agent, 1874 sees him living at Bane Cottage, Lyndhurst before shortly returning to Bulford where he appears to have been in residence until his death in 1883. He regularly attended the Easter Vestry meetings between 1876 and 1881, and had three more grandchildren, Anthony Gapper, Edmund Hugh and Rupert, baptised in the church in 1876, 1877 and 1878 respectively. This last year saw him attend the Amesbury Deanery and Lay Representatives meeting with John Robbins and the 1881 census shows him resident in Bulford Manor with two daughters and a grandson. He was succeeded in Bulford by his elder son Edmund whose tenure of the Manor was short, ending with his untimely death three years later, aged fifty-three. At this point, Bulford Manor was put up for sale to be bought by James Ledger Hill for £24,000. It has been suggested that it was sold to pay off family debts.[32]

The village on the eve of the army 'invasion'

THIS BRINGS US to the closing years of the century when horizons of villagers dramatically expanded with the launching of their home on its new career as an integral part of the national picture. The railway mania of the nineteenth century hit the village, at first only in a small way, when the London and South Western Railway Company opened its line from Andover to Salisbury in 1857. In 1902 a line was constructed to Amesbury and four years later this was extended to Bulford. The Amesbury and Bulford line was constructed primarily to serve the military who by then owned most of the village and had established Bulford Camp at the foot of Beacon Hill. The consequences for villagers and their lives is the subject of Chapter 11. Before looking at these changes it is worth painting a picture of the village community before it was 'invaded'. The advertisement for the sale of the village on 10 July 1886 is worth quoting in full.

Sale of a most desirable Residence and Manorial Estate, comprising nearly the whole of the parish of Bulford, including a substantially-built, old fashioned Elizabethan residence standing in charming pasture grounds which extend to the River Avon, which affords nearly two miles of capital trout fishing; there is capital stabling, double chaise house, small farm, &. Pleasantly situate in the centre of the village is a small dwelling house, with capital gardens. The well-frequented public house, known as the Rose and Crown Inn, with Club room, stabling, outbuildings &c; also 49 well-built Tenements, with large gardens, several enclosures of accommodation lands, together with the upper and lower farms, on each of which will be found a superior residence and sets of home and down farm buildings. The entire property is tithe free, and embraces an area of 1,902a 2r 7p of sound arable and fertile meadows and capital down land, which with the exception of Bulford House, which is in hand, is leased to responsible tenants at reduced rental, together producing (estimating Bulford House and fishing at £200) an annual rental of £1,257 10s. The sporting incident to the property is first rate, and for variety unequalled. There is invariable a good head of game, and the coursing is some of the best in South England. Several packs of hounds are in very easy reach. Included in the sale is the advowson of the vicarage of Bulford.[33]

Two pillars of village society in the nineteenth century were the Lord of the Manor and the parish church, headed by the parish priest. Both Anthony Southby who had lived in Upper Canada and the first vicar of Bulford, Jacob Jehoshaphat Mountain, who was born and began his ministry there, brought a wider perspective to the village. It has already been noted how the Rev. Mountain's experience of the prohibition movement in America informed his views on drinking, and he must have been an 'exotic' influence on his parishioners. One can only imagine conversations that passed between the two men, and with those between the village priest and his new parishioners. A third pillar of village society was Mary Ann Knight, the schoolmistress from 1874, who had travelled the world before returning home to Bulford. She had been, as we have seen, in service at the Manor and as a young woman had been on a camel caravan across a desert either when travelling with her mariner husband or with the Southbys. Her lesson plans in the school log book indicate her knowledge of foreign goods, and villagers could not have grown up without being aware of the wider world beyond the village.[34]

We have to stray into the twentieth century for a postscript with the strong Canadian connection coming full circle. Bulford Manor was initially an Officers' Club at the turn of the twentieth century, but during the First World War when the No.1 General Hospital First Canadian contingent was stationed at Bulford, it became a convalescent home for wounded soldiers. The young twenty-nine year old chaplain, the Hon Capt George Lycester Ingles, who having 'succumbed to a dire contagious malady contracted in the discharge of his office', is buried in St Leonard's churchyard. He was born in Toronto in 1886, fifty-four years after Anthony Gapper left there to come to Bulford as the new Lord of the Manor.[35]

4
Full Circle of Ownership: Bulford Manor and the Village

The Inheritance of Bulford

BULFORD MANOR FROM Saxon Times was part of the demesne of the royal estate at Amesbury and its subsequent history shows it transferring in and out of royal ownership, finally being owned by the Crown again today. In 979 Queen Aelfthryth founded an abbey at Amesbury in contrition for the murder of King Edward and Bulford became part of the Abbey Estate, where the abbess held 720 acres in lordship for the Abbey. The Abbey, later refounded as a Priory, continued to own Bulford until it was dissolved by Henry VIII, and its estates, including Bulford, were taken back into royal ownership. James I settled the estate on his son, Henry Prince of Wales, and two years after the latter's death in 1612 the Bulford estate was bought by George Duke and was then in private hands. The Dukes maintained the Bulford estate, splitting it in half (moieties) to be enjoyed by various members of the family. One moiety was subsequently sold to Laurence Washington who in turn sold out to Sir Edward Seymour in 1678, and this half of the Bulford estate remained in the Seymour family into, and throughout the nineteenth century. The other moiety owned by the Duke family was split again between members of the family but by the end of the eighteenth century these had been reunited by inheritance under the ownership of Richard Duke. This estate, centred on Bulford Manor, kept the status of Manor and owned the small tithes from all other landholders, mainly the Seymours, until these were commuted into a money payment in 1838.[1]

Full Circle of Ownership

Between the death of Richard Duke without issue in 1757 and the succession of Anthony Southby in 1835, a period of three generations, the inheritance of Bulford Manor is an even more complicated affair. Anyone trying to track it in detail is faced with the challenge of repeated names; there are for example two Anthony Southbys, Richard Southbys, Charity Ann Southbys, Anne Southbys and two Rev. Edmund Gappers in succeeding generations and a sprinkling of Lucys. We are in the world portrayed by Jane Austen of county families socialising in their residences and at Bath. A world of intermarrying within their social set, of inheritance switching from one family to another with the widows having to either move back to their family homes or going to live with their daughters, a world of highly intelligent and articulate females proficient in languages, literature and the arts, and of double marriages between families. A gentle world with a strong philanthropic sense of duty, of militias, military service and a sense of Empire; these after all were the families living through the turmoil of the French Revolution, Napoleonic Wars and the burgeoning British Empire. All these attributes are documented at some point in the families of the Dukes, the Southbys and the Gappers, and all impinged on Bulford.[2]

These families were part of the bedrock of the establishment of which the Anglican Church was an integral part; for example in 1835 Anthony Southby had a brother-in-law, father, grandfather and a great aunt who were all either clergymen, or married to clergymen (see Appendix 1a). A recent description of the family values of Anthony Southby's sister, Mary O'Brien (née Gapper), which she took with her to Canada can be generalised across them all. They took for granted their position as members of the elite. It did not seem paradoxical to Mary O'Brien (Gapper) to be, on the one hand 'the nurse to the sick, the comforter of the miserable; wise discrete, loving, patient, adored by children, the embodiment of unselfishness' and on the other hand to declare: "We had a very pleasant party at Government House, the only house in the country where I care much to visit". It was an attitude consistent with the uniquely Victorian interpretation of noblesse oblige [where] the Victorian virtue of charity included this paternalistic attitude born of privilege ... Their faith, gentility and sense of responsibility, both towards the immediate community and to the Empire at large, dictated the course of their daily lives. These ideals of duty, leadership, discipline and hard work, accompanied but not diminished by an appreciation of European culture, were naturally communicated to their children.[3]

There are clues to help unpick the tangled relationships between the families: wills, an obsession to keep the family name, church memorials, and a tradition of giving the eldest son his mother's maiden name as a second name. Richard Duke's will proved after his death in 1757 split the estate between his sisters Anne and Mary. Anne had married Anthony Southby of South Marston who inherited his wife's moiety of Bulford Manor and the estate. He died in 1759 and when Mary in turn died without issue the whole estate was inherited by Anne's son Richard Southby junior, becoming the new Lord of the Manor until his death in March 1791. Before inheriting Bulford he had lived at the family estate of Highworth and married Ann Gapper of Charlton Adam on 26 December 1754. At what point he moved into the village is unclear although he must have done so because he is buried at Bulford. In November 1786, six years into his inheritance, Bulford Manor was put on the market:

> TO be LETT, BULFORD HOUSE, with the MANOR, TROUT FISHERY, and about fourteen acres of good pasture and water meadows adjoining the same. The House consists of two good parlours, a hall, kitchen, servant hall, butler's room, and other offices, five bed chambers, with ceiled garrets over them, two stables and stalls for eight horses, granary, large dove-house, and a garden, well planted with fruit trees. The premises are about one mile from Amesbury, and are particularly calculated for the Sportsman, as the Manor and Fishery are equal to most.
> N.B. Part of the furniture will be lett with the House, if required.

This advertisement makes it clear that the owners of Bulford Manor saw it as a desirable residence and that they had no interest in farming the estate themselves, leasing it out instead to tenant farmers and collecting the rents to support their lifestyle. Richard Southby died in 1791, his widow returning to Highworth. The Manor was inherited by their son Richard Duke Southby, but only for a few months as he died in December the same year. These double deaths, which robbed Bulford of a male heir, were tragedies for the surviving women of the family. The memorial they erected touched on a human story which was to influence the succession of the Manor in years to come:

> This monument is designed as the most expressive and effectual testimony now. alas! In their power, of a truly conjugal, filial, and fraternal regard and

Full Circle of Ownership

7 Bulford Manor House from the East. The crenellated bays were added by Anthony Southby in the nineteenth century to the original Elizabethan building which fronts the road. The striped flint and brick section is the extension built by the Dukes in the eighteenth century. The wing behind, protruding to the right, was added by James Ledger Hill. (Photographed by author in 2011)

affection, so justly due to them in their respective characters, and never to be collected but with the most tender and lasting regret, by an inconsolable widow and her three daughters, their mournful survivors.[4]

Under the 1791 will of Richard Southby the inheritance passed to Richard Duke Southby's two surviving sisters, Charity Ann Southby and Mary Southby, each having her own moiety (the youngest, Elizabeth, died in 1797). They lived at Bulford and depended on the local farmers to help with the management of their estate, paying in December 1801, for example, James Rose £5 9s 0d to plough, sow and harrow their six and a bit acres after deducting the cost of supplying their own horse valued at three shillings a day for the six days that it took to complete the work. In 1802 Charity Ann married Sir John Pollen whose first wife Louisa had died in 1793, but she was in turn widowed when Sir John died in 1814. Thereafter she lived in the Manor House as the Dowager Lady Pollen. She employed a Mr Fleet as her steward who, for example, was involved in negotiations with the County

Surveyor about damage caused to the wall of the Manor garden by flooding in November 1823. When she died in 1830, it left her sister Mary Southby in sole charge of Bulford Manor.[5]

Lady Pollen lived her married life with her husband Sir John Pollen, Baronet, at the 'ancient.....Mansion House called Redenham situate in the parish of Thruxton' inherited by him through his first wife Louise Holt. The estate was extensive, comprising the Manor of Fyfield and lands in Fyfield, Thruxton, Kimpton and Andover, which were always known as the Redenham Estate. Charity Ann and Sir John inhabited the same social world, their estates being in fairly close proximity. Once married, she was caught up in the social whirl of the high society inhabited by Sir John, going, for example, to a Handel concert in Salisbury Cathedral attended by His Royal Highness, the Duke of Cambridge 'and almost all the ranks and fashion of this and adjoining counties'. No doubt her sister Mary went to live with her leaving the Manor vacant, and this certainly was the case after 1812 when all the contents of Bulford Manor were moved out by Sir John Pollen with the letting of Bulford Manor to Sir Edward Loveden Loveden until 1815. Sir Edward was, until 1812, M.P. for Shaftesbury and, since 1807, the Vice President of the Board of Agriculture which he had helped to found in 1793. He was a wealthy man, having just built Buscot Park in Oxfordshire, and had earned the nickname of 'Old Father Thames' for presiding over the parliamentary committee of 1793 tasked with improving the Thames Navigation upstream from Staines, to Lechlade in Gloucestershire. He must have known the Southbys as Buscot Park was the neighbouring estate to the Dukes at Highworth, but why did he come to Bulford? The answer was for the hunting; he was a 'Sportsman' who would have fitted the 1786 advertisement. He was not the first as it can be deduced from the fact that a Mr Pickering had hired a field bedstead, a four post bedstead, a circular mahogany dining table, a dressing table, chairs and curtains for his stay at the Manor. Sir Edward bought these from Mr Norton the supplier for forty-seven pounds when he moved in after him.[6]

Edward Loveden's stays at Bulford were for several weeks at a time in the spring, summer and in the autumn, using the estate as a very well appointed hunting lodge. We know this by examining the detailed inventory and accounts for Bulford during his stays, and also from a letter sent to him in March 1815 which read, 'I hope you and Miss Theyer have had much pleasure and sport at Bulford and on the Downs'. He kept hunting dogs and had an account for their feed, for example '14 bushels of barley meal at 7/6' left by the previous occupant Mr Pickering. The documents also show concern for the welfare of his dogs. He bought bullock's liver, belly and lights for eight shillings, and also a cow for fifteen shillings and an old horse for a guinea from 'Mr Six apothecary for dog medicines'. He subsequently offset his costs by selling on the horse and cow kidneys for seventeen shillings and sixpence. He also jotted down a recipe for worms in dogs to make small balls of turpentine oil, hog lard and flour to be given night and morning. He also noted it was 'good also for man or horse in proper dose'! A cure for mange was to 'Strew the dogs fur over with Cream of Tartar'. Hunting was a social occasion and he had on one occasion to hire an extra 'horse to go with the Dogs' from farmer Thomas Croome for five days at five shillings a day. Sir Edward Loveden's interest in guns was demonstrated by his buying a 'seven Barrelled Gun' for £7 13s and the associated mould to make the 'seven shot'. This gun fired all seven barrels simultaneously and had been invented by James Wilson in 1779, to be fired from the rigging of Royal Navy warships onto the deck in the event of the ship being boarded by enemy sailors – what must it have done to any game he shot! He also bought 12 lbs of normal shot for six shillings.[7]

Sir Edward Loveden left Bulford for the last time on 27 March 1815, no doubt for Lady Pollen and her sister Mary Southby to return to their estate after the former's bereavement and the inheritance of her marital home by her husband's heir, Sir John Walter Pollen. Lady Pollen's estate had been kept separate from her husband's for inheritance purposes but her income from Bulford Manor was now supplemented by the four hundred pounds a year drawn from the rents of the Pollen estates 'for and during her natural life'. Her will left her sister Mary Southby free to enjoy the whole estate, uniting their two moieties 'without impairment' during her lifetime.[8]

The Southby / Gapper family links

BEFORE LOOKING AT the subsequent path of inheritance, we need to return to generation of Charity Ann and Mary Southby's parents (see Appendix 1a). Their father Richard Southby had married Ann Gapper but his eldest sister, another Charity Ann, also married into the Gappers. Charity Ann married Ann's brother the Rev. Anthony Gapper who combined his profession with owning the family estate, the Abbey at Charlton Adam

– this was the double wedding. Family ties between the Southbys and Gappers were naturally very strong, with Rev. Edward Gapper signing the register at his niece Charity Ann's wedding to Sir John Pollen in 1802 and he was also one of the two executors of Sir John's estates. Charity Ann and Edmund had two children, his heir Edmund Gapper junior who also was to combine his status of Lord of the Manor with that of being a clergyman, and Lucy. The children of the two marriages were very close cousins reflecting the strong family ties: Edmund, Charity Ann, Mary and Elizabeth Southby on the one hand, and Edmund and Lucy Gapper on the other. The links also extended to the next generation with Edmund's daughter Mary writing to her sister Lucy about the state of the downland roads of Bulford, long before her brother Anthony inherited the estate, showing that the Gapper children were no strangers to Bulford. The familiarity was at a personal level as well for when Mary had a daughter in Upper Canada in 1834 there ensued a discussion as to whom she resembled. It was suggested that she was like Miss Mary Southby, but Mary Gapper 'had before thought that she promised to be like either Lady Pollen or my Aunt Susan. She is a dear little fat thing.' The two families were close.[9]

With Edmund Gapper junior's death in 1809, the Gapper inheritance at Charlton Adam passed to the eldest son Edmund Barrett Gapper who sold the family estate in 1819 and passed on the assets to his wife when he died in 1829. This left Charity Ann's and Mary's cousin Lucy Gapper (the Rev. Edmund Gapper's unmarried sister, ten years his junior) homeless. She could have moved in with her nephew Edmund Barrett Gapper who died a year later, but instead it seems that she moved in with her maternal cousins Charity Ann and Mary at Bulford Manor. Lucy's niece had always calculated on her aunt living with Mary when Charity Ann died, envisaging the two spinsters moving Bristol way to live with another spinster aunt, Sophy Gapper, but this last part was not to be. Charity Ann died in 1830 leaving Lucy Gapper a legacy and a key role to play in sorting out the inheritance of her moiety at Bulford once her unmarried sister Mary died. There was a codicil added to the will which Lucy Gapper was called upon to verify in 1832. At this point she calls herself 'Lucy Gapper of Bulford' and states that she 'frequently saw her [Charity Ann Pollen] write and subscribe her name to writings whereby [she had] become well acquainted with her manner and the character of her handwriting' which clearly suggests that she was living at Bulford with Mary Southby her cousin, probably before Charity Ann's death.[10]

Charity Ann Pollen and Mary Southby were acutely aware that with their deaths the Southby line in Bulford would end and the elder sister's will goes to great lengths to mitigate this inescapable fact. The will was consequently based on two principles. The first of these was that the inheritance was to pass through the male line, of which there was only one option. Her mother's nephew, the Rev. Edmund Gapper (Charity Ann and Mary's cousin) had four sons (and two daughters) and it was to these that she turned. The eldest, Edmund Barrett Gapper was first in line then any sons he had who would inherit according to their 'respective seniorities in tail male', failing this the next son William Southby Gapper and his sons would inherit, failing that the third son Dr Anthony Gapper and his sons, and finally the youngest, Richard Colston Gapper and his sons. Failing all this it would go to the two daughters for their lifetimes and then through any male heirs. The second principle was that any male inheritor of the estate through 'tail male', or any husband of a female inheritor shall when they

> come into possession ... take upon himself and themselves respectively and bear the surname of Southby only and by the said surname of Southby continue to name stile and write ... in all deeds writings and instruments and upon all other occasions whatsoever and do and shall use and bear the arms of Southby as the same as are issued and bourne by me ... .

Anyone refusing to do this would be disinherited.[11]

These provisions, endorsed by Mary's will, were successful and the name of Southby remained at Bulford for two further generations. When Mary Southby died in 1835, Lucy Gapper, as instructed, swiftly oversaw the succession which passed to the third son, her nephew Dr Anthony Gapper. On the day after Mary's death Anthony wrote to his sister Lucy, 'Miss Southby died last night. I have not yet seen her lawyer but Tomy gave me a message from Miss S[outhby] – telling me that I am her heir and wishing me to take the name of Southby – and some other little requests that she had omitted in her will, I suppose.' He duly changed his name to Southby and inherited Bulford Manor. The *Gentleman's Magazine* reported, 'Dr Anthony Gapper, of Bridgewater, Somerset, in compliance with the will of Mary Southby, late of Bulford, Wilts, [was] to take the surname and bear the arms of Southby.' Anthony's two elder brothers were passed over as they left no male heirs when they died early aged forty and thirty-nine in 1829 and 1833 respectively. Anthony had moved to live with his brother in Upper Canada and owned no property and so Lucy passed the inheritance on to him. His family were always on the lookout for an estate for him to relieve his 'pecuniary anxiety' and for him to be able to keep a wife 'preserving her from the inconvenience of poverty'. All had now been resolved and it would appear that Anthony moved to Bulford in July and Aunt Lucy lived at Bulford Manor, with her nephew, until she died there in 1846, and her will looked after Anthony's youngest brother and sister. She left Anthony's wife, Octavia, her personal wardrobe and her 'broach which is set around with pearls'. Being the youngest of her generation and unmarried she played a key role in the flow of correspondence which kept the family, separated by the Atlantic, together.[12]

In the June preceding Lady Pollen's death, Anthony's mother, who had also moved to Upper Canada, was very anxious that he should be at home from an expedition to Pentanguishene after receiving news from England. He then set sail for England, his sister writing on 27 July that, 'It is now three weeks since Anthony sailed; It is not impossible but he may already be in England. God grant that he may be permitted to carry consolation if it be yet needed, I know not when.' It would appear that Charity Ann's health had taken a turn for the worst and Aunt Lucy had wanted Anthony with her to help manage affairs. He settled in Bridgwater and was certainly involved in managing Mary Southby's affairs because in March 1834, the year before she died, Mr Southby was levied six shillings church rate by the Easter Vestry. Later his sister Mary wrote in her journal that her 'Aunt's [Lucy's] kindness has created circumstances to require Anthony to take up residence in England', which he duly did. After Lady Pollen's death the family in Upper Canada pitied poor Miss Southby and awaited news from Anthony.[13]

Anthony Southby's heirs

THE RESULT OF all these various family histories, was that Bulford was divided almost equally between two landlords for all but the dying years of the nineteenth century: the Souhby/Gappers owning the Manor House and the northern half of the parish, including most of the village, and the Seymours owning Seymour/Watergate Farm and the southern half of the parish. There were, however, a few anomalies, mainly a small independent seventy-three acre farm and lands owned by the chapel which are considered in detail in Chapter 5. When Dr Anthony Southby died in 1883, Bulford passed to his elder son and heir Edmund Richard Southby until his early death aged fifty-two in 1886. Edmund and his younger brother Anthony Gapper Southby, followed in their father's footsteps into the world of science. Edmund, like his father, trained as a doctor in Edinburgh and became a Member of the Royal College of Surgeons but chemistry was his chosen field as opposed to botany and zoology, whereas his brother became a civil engineer. Father and sons evidently worked well together as will be seen. In June 1863, Edmund married a clergyman's daughter born in Somerset, Agnes Christiana Shaw who was living in Wilton in 1851. In 1881 the couple was living in London at Hampstead with Agnes's widowed father. Edmund worked as an analytical chemist at Gresham House, 46 Holborn Viaduct, and became a Fellow of the Chemical Society. His interests were focused on the process of brewing, publishing in 1877 a treatise entitled *Brewing: Practically & Scientifically Considered*. He later wrote that,

> In the introduction to my original treatise on brewing I promised my readers to give in conclusion a resume of the general subject from a more scientific point of view, so as to explain the relation between the most advanced theories, and their practical application, in such a form as to render them available to those who wish to assume the foremost position in the applied science of brewing.[14]

Edmund undertook extensive research work connected with his scientific analysis of the brewing process and had an article published in the *Country Brewers Gazette*, of 22 January, 1879, which 'proved conclusively that these sulphates do not prevent the solution of nitrogenous matters contained in the malt.' He travelled extensively looking at breweries, in 1880 for example, testing water in a brewery in the Isle of Man and 'made a careful series of experiments, on the manufacture of caramel on a considerable scale …'. Edmund became an 'Analytical and Consulting Chemist to the "Country Brewers' Society" of England, Consulting Brewer and Brewers' Engineer'. His work to publish a more scientific résumé of brewing as promised was, he later wrote, 'I fear very inadequately fulfilled, other engagements having prevented me from giving the time to the work which was necessary for the due elaboration of the subject ... '. This was the time of his father's death in 1883 and his taking over his inheritance of Bulford Manor with all that that entailed. Nevertheless he completed his book which was published in 1885 entitled *A Systematic Handbook of Practical Brewing: Including a Full Description of the Buildings, Plant, Materials and Processes Required for Brewing, All Descriptions of Beer, Both from Malt Alone and from Mixtures of Malt with All Descriptions of Unmalted Grain*, a work that went into at least two editions and has recently been reproduced as the editors believe it to be a 'culturally important' work. Edmund Southby was at the top of his game, but all this was dramatically cut short with his death in 1886, leaving his widow Agnes living on her own means. They had no children and his Bulford estate was put on the market (the advertisement has already been quoted in full in Chapter 3).[15]

What of his younger brother Anthony Gapper Southby and why did he not inherit Bulford Manor? When he was thirty he was granted a temporary patent in 1863 for 'Improvement of stills or retorts for the distillation of petroleum tars from coal or shale or the products thereof' and also applying for one to protect his work on 'Improvements in diverse lamps' describing himself as an 'Engineer' living at Bulford. Five years later he had turned his attention to papermaking, no doubt working with his father, taking out a patent in November 1868 for 'Improvements in operations and apparatus for drying down alkaline solutions of extractive matter obtained in preparing vegetable fibrous materials for use in the manufacture of paper, and in recovering alkali therefrom for re-employment'. He had worked on this with William Ibbotson who could well have been a relation of his mother Octavia, his uncle perhaps. A year later he refined his invention and took out a further patent with the wholesale stationer Henry Critchett Bartlett, of Garlick-Hill, in the City of London for 'improvements in paper making'. He was still giving Bulford as his residence but by 1871 Anthony was living at 51 Gloucester Road, London where he married Elizabeth Woodcock. They had moved to 10 Queen's Crescent, London where they were living when he took letters patent for 'improvements in the mode and apparatus for making ice, refrigerating, evaporating and desiccating' bearing the date 8 August 1877.[16]

It is clear that the practicalities of the manufacturing processes interested Anthony and so it is not surprising that he collaborated in 1884 with his brother over brewing. In his book Edmund acknowledges his brother's work in two areas of the brewing process, mashing and skimming. He wrote that Anthony

> Southby's new machine (1884 patent), is the simplest of all the Automatic mashers, and appears to be efficient as any. ... In Southby's new machine, the rows of jets are close together and are of such a form as to utilise the force of water to the uttermost.

And, when discussing the problems of skimming off the yeast, he reported that,

> A system of skimming by means of a pump delivering the yeast into bags, was patented by my brother in January, 1884. I have since that time introduced this system into many breweries, and with the most satisfactory results.

After his brother's death, he returned to the problems of refrigeration, issuing a petition in 1891 for the prolongation of his 1877 letters patent for the 'improvements in the mode and apparatus for making ice, refrigerating, evaporating and desiccating'.[17]

The careers of the Southby brothers illustrate changes in the fortunes of the landed gentry and help to explain why Bulford Manor was allowed to slip from the hands of their family. Dr Anthony Southby was a doctor of medicine and a naturalist who treated his estate as a means of generating income to allow him to pursue his interests – the estimated gross income that he received from Bulford rents in 1873 was, for example, £1,689. His sons turned their backs on the estate, moving to London, and in the case of Anthony Gapper, living in the Channel Islands in 1881. They were professional people, like their father, but unlike him they relied on their employment to fund their lifestyles, rather than their property. They had, along with many others, abandoned the land as a means of support at a time when the economic climate raised the spectre of being left with untenanted land. Selling up the estate and investing the money was a logical step as returns on rents were declining, the rent of Lower Farm, for example had been 'reduced to meet the times'. It was hard to make farms pay, as the sad case of William Dymer of Bulford illustrates. He was a 'farmer in the parish aged 47 ... who but recently commenced farming', but 'had not been very successful in his business, and had given way to depression'. He was 'found hanging to a plum tree in the garden' in April 1882. Returning again to the larger picture, there was, however, a contrary trend happening at the same time with successful businessmen investing their money in a country estate not to generate money, but for reasons of security and social status - and this was the case of Bulford's next Lord of the Manor.[18]

James Ledger Hill

THE ESTATE WAS bought by James Ledger Hill who became the new Lord of the Manor. Not being a member of the gentry, he was a break with social tradition and an example of the trend for successful business men to put their wealth into property. He was born 1839 in North Shields, the son of Dennis Hill, a draper and hosier. He received a good education, boarding at the Catterick Academy where he was taught classics and mathematics, before he entered the coal trade. By 1861 he had moved to Southampton where he lodged and pursued his occupation as a coal merchant and by 1871 had expanded his portfolio by becoming a ship owner, and had married Mary Alexander, a weaver's daughter from Trowbridge. His shipping interest grew, no doubt bringing coal down from Newcastle to Southampton, and his registered address for the 1880 *Lloyds Register* was

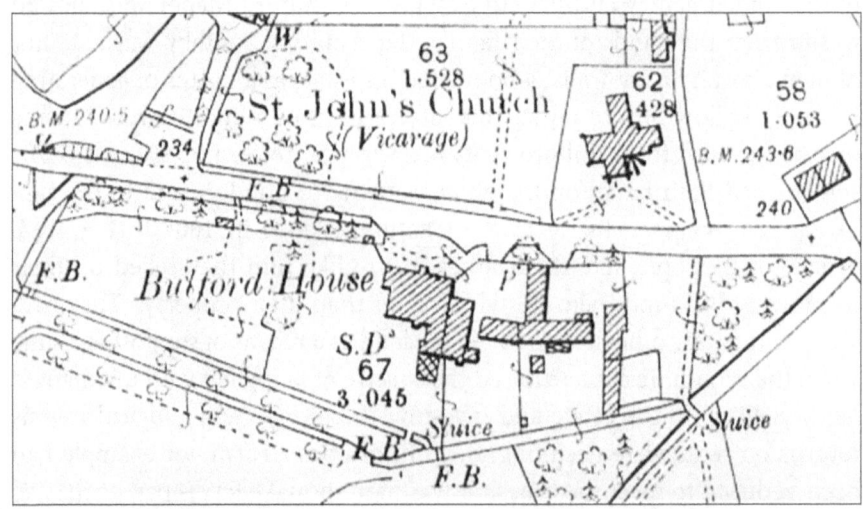

8 1897 OS Map. The map shows Bulford Manor House, its outbuildings and immediate grounds after James Ledger Hill's additions. The Church was yet to revert to its dedication to St Leonard. (courtesy of Ordnance Survey)

at Gloucester Square, Southampton. He at that point owned a 445 ton ship built in Hartlepool called 'Henry Brand'. His purchase of Bulford Manor no doubt suited him well as being halfway between Southampton and his wife's home at Trowbridge. James Ledger Hill improved Bulford Manor House by building a large service wing at the south-east corner of the eighteenth century range, employing the village builders, the Sturgesses. He also threw himself into village life, building the Reading Room next to the 'Rose and Crown' for village use. He gave the land for this, along with land for the new vicarage and new cemetery, he paid for a new stove in the church and put the grounds of the Manor at the village's disposal for fêtes and the celebrations, like those held to mark Queen Victoria's Diamond Jubilee. It is fitting that he has been commemorated in the name of Ledger Hill Close.[19]

The new Lord of the Manor's business interests, however, kept him away and he was 'only occasionally resident in the parish'. This is perhaps why he was reported as welcoming to the military when they started using the downs for manoeuvres and reviews, and was very co-operative in allowing the army to place 'noisy pumping engines' in meadows within earshot of the Manor House to pump water from the Avon to the cavalry camp on the downs in the very dry summer of August 1898. The cavalry camp was on the 1,917 acres of his estate that he had sold to the War Office in March 1898 for £36,800, no doubt making a profit on his recent purchase, and as the local paper reported on 10 August,

> The War Office have lost no time in taking advantage of acquirement by the Government of an extensive tract of land on Salisbury Plain, for the purposes of a military training ground and the past week has witnessed the encampment of the 4th Cavalry Brigade at Bulford. The camp.... is situated on Bulford Down about a mile and a half north-east of the village of Bulford and about twelve miles from Salisbury. Beacon Hill rises close to the eastern side of the camp.... and on the western side is Nine Mile Stream.

This area also included land of the Seymour estate on which the army had been granted an early possession prior to its sale in March of the following year. In buying up the Manor (and its fishing rights), the War Office took on his commitments of paying ten pounds a year to the parish for the 'Water Rights Rent for the watering of the Meadows on Upper Farm', and £8 a year to the church. Initially the War Office was only interested in purchasing the downs and farmland for military purposes but James Ledger Hill insisted that the village be included in the sale, and a price of fifty pounds per cottage was finally agreed. Excluded from the sale of the village were lands given to the church (the new cemetery and the vicarage built at a cost of £1,891 in 1893 on a plot at the corner of Milston Road and the Drove), properties belonging to the chapel, and the 'Rose and Crown' with a corner plot. There was one other part of the village excluded from the sale which was a field called the 'Coal Yard' (site of the present petrol station) which suggests that James Ledger Hill had an eye on developing the coal trade locally whilst at Bulford. The yard was no doubt sold as a business to Edward Pearce, a coal merchant living in the village in 1901 after James Ledger Hill had left the village. As soon as the sale was agreed, the Hills moved across the Avon into Bridgefoot Cottage, where Ann Sawyer as a little girl in the early years of the twentieth century could remember old Mrs Hill living. On leaving Bulford after his short tenure of the Manor, James Ledger Hill retired to Coombe Grove Mansion, Monkton Combe, near Bath, where in 1901 he is recorded in the census as a 'retired shipowner'. His memorial tablet at Monkton Combe reads, 'James Ledger Hill J.P., late of Bulford Manor. Nov. 9 1839 – Sep. 19 1912'.[20]

The Manor House was already vacated in 1891. With the closure of the paper-mill in the 1870s, the papermaker John Sawyer had become the gardener of the Manor House under Anthony Southby, and he carried on under Edmund Southby and James Ledger Hill. The 1891 census shows John Sawyer, living with his wife Elizabeth and occupying the Manor as the gardener and gatekeeper. He was also the caretaker of Bridgefoot Cottage. There is a photograph of this upright old craftsman pushing his wheelbarrow in the well tended Manor grounds *(see Plate 29)*. Bulford Manor House entered the new century as the Bulford Garrison Officers' Club, with nobody then living there although it was in occupation.[21]

The Farms of Bulford Manor

THE MANOR ESTATE was divided into two farms from 1659, Manor Farm and Hindurrington Farm. Both names are elusive and mutual boundaries are unclear. The name Hindurrington itself seems to be an earlier name for this settlement by the river. The Seymour farm is called Manor Farm as late as 1841 and was probably a survival from the days when the whole of Bulford was under a single ownership, but subsequently when the inheritance was split into moieties, the name 'Manor Farm' was probably transferred initially to buildings on the site of the Manor House, and Hindurrington Farm to farm buildings north of the church, the old centre of Hindurrington. Richard Duke's will indicates that the old farm house stood north of the churchyard; it had a Home Orchard and the Hindurrington Farm rick-yard was just north of the church. If this is a correct interpretation, it bears out Thomas Davis's statement that farms 'are crowded together in villages, for convenience of water and are therefore frequently very badly situated for the occupation of the lands'. The Dukes obviously thought this too, because they reorganised the farming of their demesne in the eighteenth century by resiting one of the farmsteads in new buildings to the north of the village close to the border with Milston. This was known as Manor or Upper Farm, as opposed to the still existing Hindurrington Farm. An 1880 map shows Upper Farm's lands starting just north of the church, enveloping The Park of the Manor House, and incorporating all the land between the Avon and Milston Road, as far as Milston. Then there is a swathe of arable land extending to the downs between the parish boundary and the present line of copses on Bulford Fields. The farm land formed an L-shape with the new Upper Farm house and yard situated in the angle of the L, making for greater efficiency in farming the northern part of the demesne. Its situation on higher ground also made for more efficient exploitation of the higher arable land by making transport to and from the farmstead easier. The remaining acreage of Lower Farm (960 acres) is the same as that given for Hindurrington Farm in some of the 1838 documentation. This means that the eventual farm buildings for farming the rump of Hindurrington Farm, after Upper Farm had been created, were those which came to be known logically as Lower Farm. The 'old pennings' near Sheep Bridge were probably those used before the Manor demesne was divided in two, or even predating this to a time when the whole of Bulford was a single entity before Watergate Farm was created. The 'old pennings' no doubt continued in use with the new pennings being created on the Seymour lands on the edge of the present day Bulford Camp. After enclosures had taken place, pennings were given names to reflect the names of the farmers who owned them, and these were known variously as Tidworth Pennings or Robbins Pennings after the tenant farmer at the time and Melsome's Pennings, the new name for Longs Pennings when the tenancy of Watergate Farm changed.[22]

When we enter the nineteenth century the names of the two demesne farms had by and large settled on Upper Farm and Lower Farm, replacing the Hindurrington Farm, with its still extant farmhouse located in the village away from the Manor House and church. This farmhouse was operating as a farm in the late seventeenth to early eighteenth century when a dairy was built to the rear of the kitchen. It was no doubt one of the copyhold or leasehold farms that took on a new role as the Manor's Lower Farm. We have a detailed picture of the Farm dating from 1881. The Farm House was described as being,

> Situate in the Village of Bulford, fronting the high road, is built of brink and flint and tiled. It contains ENTRANCE HALL, DINING ROOM, DRAWING ROOM, FOUR GOOD BEDROOMS, Two Attics, Kitchen, Dairy, Washhouse, and Cellar, with necessary Offices. There is also a small Conservatory and a large partially Walled Garden. Contiguous is a brick built and slated NAG STABLE (Two Loose Boxes and a Stall), COACH-HOUSE and HARNESS ROOM.

The attached buildings of the Home Farm comprised 'a Large BARN of Six Bays, Range of COW PENS, STABLING for Twelve Horses, CHAFF PEN, Range of Open and Enclosed CATTLE SHEDS and PIGGERIES' which enclosed the farmyard. The adjoining rickyard was walled in and contained 'a Rick House, Six-bay Cart Shed, Piggeries, and Poultry House'. The other side of the High Road, on the corner of the present Orchard Way was 'an ENGINE and MACHINE HOUSE with Store over, brick, flint and weather-board built and tiled', and on the other side of the road, beyond the 'Rose and Crown', was 'another set of Farm Buildings, viz, Barn, Stabling for Six Horses, Drill House, Cattle Shed, Cart Shed, Granary on Staddles' and an enclosed farmyard and a rickyard. There was, in addition, another farmyard next to Sheep Bridge, and a field barn with a cattle shed and yard next to the farm's boundary with the fields of Watergate Farm. The tenant farmer had twelve cottages with gardens for his labourers, ten in the village and two by the Sheep Bridge farmyard. He was also responsible for letting three more substantial cottages in the village.[23]

Upper and Lower Farms are the names used from now on in this chapter although in 1901, after the War Department owned the whole estate, the Lower Farm House was replaced by Manor Farm created by developing and extending Manor Cottage (*Figure 2, no.6*). This was in effect a revival of the obsolete Home Farm site of Hindurrington Farm and was for a time called Church Farm. The farmhouse itself was the two back rooms of the 1960s enlarged house which had had its roof raised, plus a store room and a place for milk churns. Opposite was a wooden shed. The two rooms have thick walls, one of which has the remains of a bread oven. At the foot of the garden were fields with pens for the pheasants.[24]

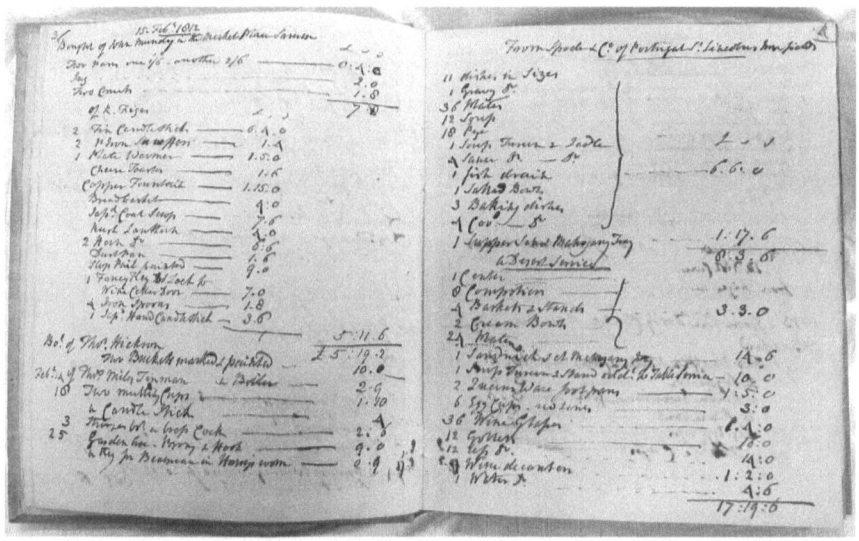

9 Bulford Manor House Accounts. February 1812 accounts of Sir Edward Loveden Loveden showing items that he brought to Bulford. There are everyday items like tin candlesticks bought at Salisbury market, and fine china bought from Spode & Co of Portugal Street, Lincoln Inn Fields, in London. (Berkshire Record Office)

Lower Farm was almost certainly the 'late Mr Croome's Farm', occupied in 1829 by Mary Croome when it was valued at £423 6s 8d for the parish levy. This estate, unlike the Seymour estate farmed by Mr Devenish, had no tithes to pay to the Lord of the Manor, making it part of the manorial demesne. Mrs Croome, in addition was levied for the mill, orchard and gardens. There is a useful list of churchwardens culled from the *Church Books* and registers in the papers of the Rev. Rhys-Hughes. The wardens, either People's Wardens or Vicar's Wardens, are almost exclusively tenant farmers, certainly up to 1896, with all of them serving a term or terms with the exception of Matthew Devenish, who as will be seen owed his loyalties to the chapel, and William

Bailey who lived in the next parish and was tainted by being an alehouse keeper. This list shows that Mary Croome was People's Warden in 1800 and 1802, with Thomas Croome serving the following year implying that the Croomes farmed Lower Farm from the beginning of the century.[25]

It is a bit of a puzzle to unwrap the exact relationships between the Robert Croome of Bulford who in 1790 was a member of the Sarum Association for the Prevention of Theft and paid the parish rate in 1801 and Mary Croome. Mary paid the church rate and appears in Sir Edward Loveden's 1811 and in 1812 Manor accounts, supplying him with oats, beans, sainfoin hay and coal, as well as leasing a horse and transporting house contents for him. It is almost certain that Mary was Robert's widow, taking on the lease of Lower Farm after his death sometime after 1801 (see Appendix 1c). Mary was succeeded by Thomas Croome who was Robert Croome's brother, possibly in 1812 when the Loveden accounts feature 'Mr Croome's Stable Account'. His will tells us that he had no heirs and so he passed his inheritance to Robert's elder daughter Mary Ann Croome, with her younger sister Elizabeth as the next in line. Probate papers filed with Thomas Croome's will show that he was actively farming Lower Farm (although this is not mentioned by name); these are discussed in detail elsewhere. Meanwhile Mary was T. W. Dyke's tenant of Orchard End house and garden in 1819. Thomas probably supported his sister-in-law in running Lower Farm before taking it over in his own right until his death without issue in 1825, leaving his niece Mary Ann Croome to inherit as laid down in his will. Mary Croome paid the parish rate for the 'late Mr Croome's Farm, Mill garden & orchard' in 1829. How she ran the farm is uncertain as all the farming stock and equipment had been auctioned on Thomas Croome's death, but in any case she married James Randall of Wilton and must have moved out of the village to take up married life. It would appear that her younger sister Elizabeth had something to do with the farm. She had married Joseph Robbins, elder son of John Robbins of Upper Farm in 1825 and two years later Lady Pollen was paying his gamekeeper's licence implying perhaps that he was working for her on the Lower Farm, supporting his new wife. There is an entry in the *Church Book* in 1834 of Mrs Croome paying the parish rate for the farm, paper-mill, house and garden. As both the Croome sisters had married and changed their names, this can only have been Robert Croome's widow Mary. Four years later all becomes clearer.[26]

Full Circle of Ownership

By 1838 Joseph Robbins had become the tenant of Lower Farm which then consisted of 460 acres of arable and 500 acres of pasture and meadow. The 1851 census shows him employing nineteen men, eight women and seven boys. The next census in 1861 shows that the tenure had passed to his nephew, John Robbins, the eldest son of his elder brother, Thomas, who was the tenant of Upper Farm. The acreage had increased by 160 acres to 1,100 acres, farmed by a slightly smaller workforce of twenty men and five boys. There were no women employed on a permanent basis although they would have still worked on a casual basis, for example 'couching'. His tenancy continued to at least 1875. In all probability it lasted until 1877 for in that year a new churchwarden was appointed, Gilbert Miles. The 1881 census has John Robbins living as a retired farmer at New End Corner in Amesbury with his wife Martha. Having had no children to take over the farm, a new tenant had to be found. His successor Joseph Gilbert Miles's tenure was short, three or four years, for in 1880 Joseph Gilbert Miles, handed Lower Farm over to James Hooper. Joseph Gilbert Miles was born in Maddington and his father farmed 680 acres in Durrington (1851). Joseph did not follow his father straight into farming working for a while as a banker's clerk in Calne. His tenure of Lower Farm was short, possibly as short as two years which was the term of a subsequent lease issued by Anthony Southby. The census in April 1881 must have taken place during the change over period with the next tenant as it describes Joseph Miles as, 'Formerly Farmer 1000a'. It would appear that the responsibility of running a farm was too much for him, but he stayed in farming, and is recorded ten years later as the farm bailiff on Newtown Farm at Boldre in Hampshire.[27]

The Robbins family were a local dynasty of farmers in the nineteenth century, farming both Lower and Upper Farms. They came to Bulford from nearby Tidworth (Tedworth) and remained local in outlook, marrying into families from Bulford, Milston, and Durrington (see Appendix 1c). The first member of the family to appear in the records of Bulford was a John Robbins who was Vicar's Warden from 1799 until 1818 and died in 1824 aged seventy-three. 'Farmer Robbins of Bulford' let a small house in neighbouring Milston in 1812 which would indicate that he was the tenant of Upper Farm, next to the Milston boundary. He was very possibly the first tenant of this newly built farm, and was succeeded by his son Thomas Robbins who served as People's Warden in the parish from 1826, which as has been noted was an office held by the tenant farmers in the nineteenth century. In 1833 he was described as 'the tenant of a farm-house, and about 800 acres of land in the parish of Bulford, formerly belonging to Lady Pollen, and now the property of Miss Southby', confirming that he had taken over from his father after his death in 1824. John Robbins's widow Ann, and her two sons, Thomas and Joseph Robbins, all signed his probate documents. Thomas Robbins was Joseph Robbins' elder brother and he married Bulford girl Hannah Jackman in 1815. The 1838 tithe commutation confirms Thomas as the tenant of Upper Farm, farming 470 acres of arable land and 340 acres of meadow and pasture. He carried on at this farm to at least the 1851 census which shows him employing sixteen men, six women and seven boys. Thomas Robbins of Bulford ... Gentleman', subsequently downsized his farming by taking out a fourteen year lease on a 310 acre farm at Hursley (Hampshire) in 1858. The 1861 census shows that he had moved to Hursley to run his new farm leaving his elder son John Robbins to take over the tenancy of Upper Farm. After his death, Thomas Robbins' widow moved to Southampton with two of their children Sarah and William, both unmarried. The 1871 census shows Sarah and William running a Registry Office for Servants, perhaps even finding positions for young women from Bulford. Meanwhile back in Bulford we now have both the Upper and Lower Farms run by a John Robbins. The younger Robbins at Upper Farm was distinguished from his cousin by the epithet 'the sidesman' as opposed to churchwarden in the parish record. Under him the Upper Farm's acreage was unchanged but he worked it with only eleven men and eight boys in 1861, a reduction of ten employees, amounting to a cut of thirty-four per cent, which was no doubt due to an increase in mechanisation over the middle years of the century. His tenure at Upper Farm was long, lasting in all probability until 1888 when he had progressed from being 'the sidesman' to being Vicar's Warden.[28]

Consolidation of farms

THE PROCESS OF consolidating smaller farms into larger units as leases and copyholds expired during the course of the eighteenth and nineteenth centuries as has already been noted. This process continued in Bulford. The century opened with four farms in the village (Watergate, Upper, Lower and the Nag's Head/Orchard End Farms) which by the time that the War Office bought up the land had been reduced to two. The Manor's lands were equally divided between the Upper and Lower Farms

Full Circle of Ownership

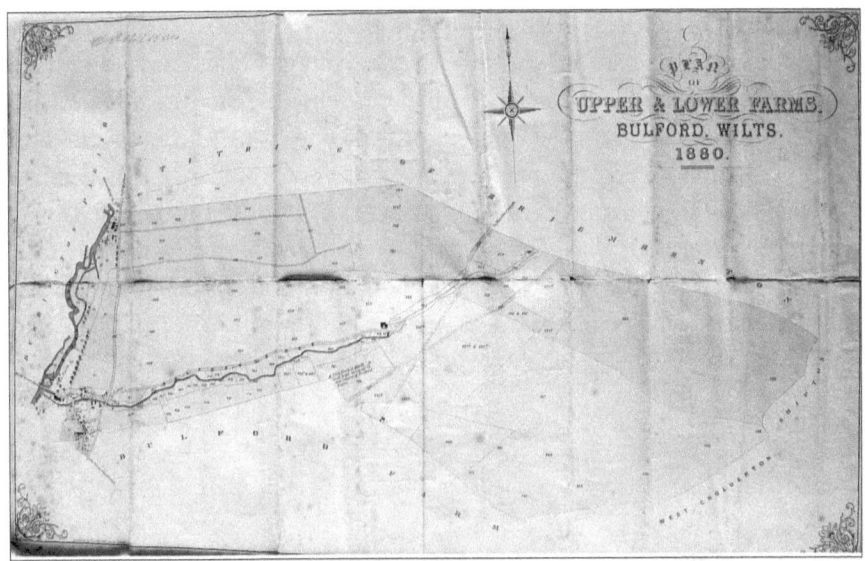

10 *Upper and Lower Farms in 1880. 1880 Map of the two farms of Bulford Manor. Upper Farm consists of the land between Milston Road and the river and the northern portion of the parish. This map post-dates the 1871 exchange of lands and shows the strip of land bordering Brigmerston tithing lost to Upper Farm, whereas Lower Farm includes the lands along Nine Mile River which were given in exchange. (Wiltshire and Swindon Archives)*

until 1871 when the exchange of lands between Charles Edward Rendall of Brigmerston and Anthony Southby (discussed in Chapter 6) altered this balance. Lower Farm stretched from Nile Mile River to the later line of copses in Bulford Fields and Upper Farm extended from this line to the parish boundary with Milston. The meadowland between Milston Road and the River was part of Upper Farm. The absorption of the Rendall lands in Bulford into the Manor was at the expense of the Upper Farm lands along the parish boundary so that the two farms were now unequal. The rent of Upper Farm must have been reduced although we have no documentation to reflect this until fifteen years later when the rent for Upper Farm was £410 per annum, whereas that for Lower Farm was £550.[29]

The Rendall lands, the Orchard End Farm, appear to have been leased out initially as an independent small farm by Anthony Southby, no doubt keeping the same tenant at the time of the exchange. An 1878 Directory lists a George Parkins as a farmer and he most probably tenanted this farm. In 1880, however, when Anthony Southby took on James Hooper of Maddington as his new tenant for Lower Farm, he took the opportunity to widen the lease 'together with twelve cottages and Farm Buildings formerly belonging to the small farm (late Rendalls)' for the term of two years from Michaelmas 1880 at a rent of £500 and £550 'for the second and every subsequent year' thereby creating a further imbalance between the two farms - Lower Farm having 1,048 acres as opposed to Upper Farm's 800 acres. The logic was leading to the two farms being farmed as one, especially with the fast progress of mechanisation, and it was James Hooper, as will be seen, who achieved this.[30]

11 *Lower Farm. The Lower Farm of Bulford Manor (FIG 3, no.12) which replaced Hindurrington Farm in the nineteenth century. It was a pre-existing farm, no doubt one of the copyhold farms absorbed into the Manor by the Dukes. (Photographed by author in 2011)*

With the tenanting of Upper Farm by James Hooper, the long association lasting nearly a century of the Robbins dynasty with Bulford came to an end. James Hooper, though, was also a member of a local farming dynasty. He had been born at Imber in 1840 where his father Henry farmed 800 acres. In 1871 he was living with his brother William, thirteen years his senior, who was farming the 960 acre Browne Farm at Imber, which could well have been their late father's farm. James needed his own farm, and in 1881 he had a 516 acre farm, Bourton Farm, at Maddington. He was at that time a bachelor, but after his marriage to Alice Pile, a farmer's daughter from Upper Woodford, he moved to Bulford, (no doubt to be near his widowed mother-in-law who still ran her late husband's farm,) to take on Lower Farm, and eventually Upper Farm as well.[31]

It is possible to trace the evolution of the Manor farms in detail with the survival of a series of leases between James Hooper and the successive landlords of the Manor. The 1881 lease with Anthony Southby was renewed by his son and successor, Edmund Southby, in 1885 on the same terms and conditions and the same rent of £550 per annum. The rent of Upper Farm at this time was £410 with the landlord paying, in addition to the usual Land Tax, the Water Rights Rent for the watering of the meadows on Upper Farm. Between 1886 and 1889 Upper and Lower Farms were farmed as one by James Hooper. The policy he took out with the Liverpool and London and Globe Insurance Company for £7,000 'insured farms only situate and known as Upper and Lower Farms Bulford and Brigmerston Salisbury all worked as one farm' but it would appear that he was not the tenant of Upper Farm at that time. We have correspondence 7 September 1893 in which James Ledger Hill, the new owner of Bulford Manor, discusses James Hooper taking over the leases of both farms. He wrote,

> I herewith enclose your particulars of the Upper Farm as set forth in the conditions of sale under which I purchased the property and which may be taken as practically correct and in accordance with the schedule attached to the January agreement – I am prepared to cancel your present agreements for the Lower Farm and issue a fresh agreement for the Upper and Lower Farms together on a 2 years tenancy from October 11th next at the Rent of £650 per annum or practically 7s an acre 2/3rd of the Rent payable by Mr Bewick (Viz £26-13-4) to be yours also ... excepting in regard to the piece of cover (viz bushes) on the Upper Farm on the downs which I propose to enclose. I also reserve to myself the rights of taking 25 acres if I require it in the Church Field and a strip between the Upper and Lower Farm for planting purposes by allowing you 20/- per acre for each and every acre taken ... next year I am at liberty to have possession of the Farm Building close to the present Vicarage House [Orchard End] – giving in exchange the buildings attached to the

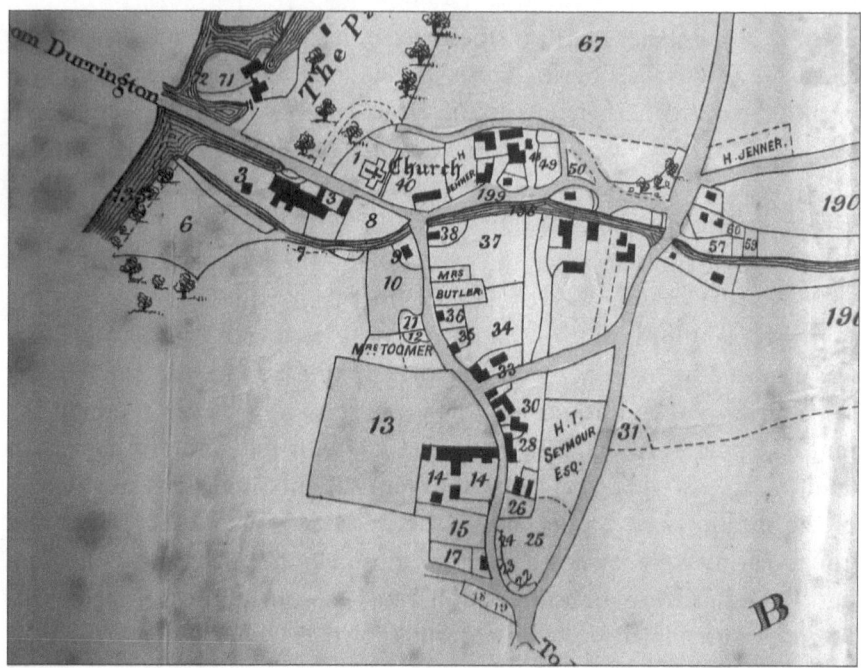

12 *Lower Farm tenancies. Map accompanying 1881 lease of Lower Farm. It shows the tenant of Lower Farm (no.14 on the map) and the properties owned by the Manor. Those owned by others are not shown. At this point, after the 1871 exchange of lands, Mr Jenner and Mrs Toomer of Durrington own property. Neither the Chapel properties are shown, with the exception of those owned by Mrs Butler (née Blatch), nor those owned by the Seymours at Watergate Farm. The site of the future coal yard, though, is shown under the ownership of the Seymours. The buildings either side of the road (no.33 on the map), are additional farm buildings belonging to Lower Farm (see FIG 5). The map shows the Park attached to the Manor House and marks the Summer House by the 'P' of Park. (Map accompanying 1881 lease of Lower Farm, Wiltshire and Swindon Archives)*

present Rose and Crown Inn. Land Tax to be paid by me also Water Rights Rent for the watering of the meadows on Upper Farm.

James Hooper's response must have discussed the rent and terms of the lease as James Ledger Hill's next letter on 16 September said that 'you can have Farms on 2 years tenancy at £650 per annum with an allowance of £50 for 4 years or you can have them at £600 for 4 years'. Payment for the purchase of stacks and crops on Upper Farm was set at £3,000 - £1,500 in cash and £1,500 in promissory notes on demand at 3½ per cent if required. The letter ended with 'As I have to see Mr Robbins this evening I should like to have your answer in writing or I can see you at 6 o'clock.' This last statement implies that John Robbins still held the lease and owned the 'stacks and crops' with the implication that James Hooper had been farming both farms under some sort of agreement which needed to be regularised with a new lease. Negotiations were concluded and a new joint lease was issued in 1895, with effect backdated to October 1893, for a farm of 1,848 acres. We can see the strength of James Hooper's negotiations as the term was extended from four to seven years, with two years' notice on either side, at a rent of £600 per annum. James Ledger Hill was not slow in creating the new plantations dividing the lands of the two farms and he stipulated that 'the lessor shall keep down and destroy so far as may be all rabbits in the new plantations which are now being made'.[32]

James Hooper vacated the Lower Farm house at some point and moved into the Upper Farm house, retaining responsibility for letting the former. When this happened is not clear but in October 1895 Rose's Grammar School in Amesbury admitted a pupil who was 'son of Mr William Parsons of Upper Farm, Bulford'. In 1901 William Parsons was living at The Farm in Milston when James Hooper, farmer, was living at 'The Hill'; Lower Farm at that time was 'unoccupied'. ('The Hill' was the name given at the end of the century to Upper Farm House, before being called Hooper's Farm.) William Parsons was from a farming family, described by a lodger in 1900 when they lived at Milston Farm:

> The Parsons were farmers of the yeoman type, rooted, through many generations, to the soil, and with every reason to be proud of their ancestry. Mrs Parsons was strong and calm, with a broad brow above clear, kind eyes and a firm, resolute mouth. Her husband, an elderly man, with a short reddish beard, had a more nervous highly-strung disposition. Young Mr Parsons, their only son, was about twenty-three years of age. I used to hear him early in the morning loading up the milk churns into the dog-cart, and starting off for Salisbury. He was tall and sunburnt. Two elder daughters helped their mother with the household duties, and two younger attended the local school. Such were the people we had come to live among; kind and wholesome, peaceful and generous.

William was the son of Arthur Parsons who had a small farm of 150 acres at Pitton (1861) and in 1881 William farmed in Newton Tony. His younger brother, Edwin G. Parsons, farmed Countess Farm in Amesbury at the turn of the twentieth century.[33]

Ownership by the Secretary of State for War

THESE CONFUSING DETAILS about Upper Farm refer to the time after the Secretary of State for War had become the landowner of the farmlands in the village and beyond. When he leased and tenanted the farms, traditional farming units and boundaries were often ignored to suit the restrictions imposed on farming practices needed to accommodate military needs. This can be seen in the village where the 1901 census shows Manor Cottage inhabited by a James Hann who had moved up from Sherborne to be the gamekeeper of Bulford Manor. It was he who subsequently developed the property by extending it and adding a farmyard to create Manor Farm, farming land leased from the War Office. This, though, did not include Upper and Lower Farms which remained with James Hooper well into the twentieth century. Robert Melsome's lease of Watergate Farm expired in 1901 and so it was land that he had farmed that James Hann probably took over (see Chapter 5).

The Secretary of State for War bought the Manor in 1897 and set out drawing up and tendering new leases. James Hooper responded that he was 'willing to become the tenant ... and occupy the messuages and lands mentioned in the First, Second, and Third schedules annexed hereto, and from the eleventh day of October 1897 for the term of three years.' The schedules encompassed Upper and Lower Farms, but were divided into three to accommodate military use of the land which was dovetailed into the agricultural needs. The land between the Avon and Nine Mile River was Schedule 1 land which James Hooper was free to farm as he pleased. A strip of land along the Nine Mile River bottom was Schedule 2 over which the military had absolute right of use between 1 May and 30 September. The Schedule 3 land extended over the downs where the camps were situated and over which the military had complete control at all times. Other terms of the lease mirrored previous civilian leases but a clause was added that, 'All hedges shall be neatly cut and all ditches scoured and cleansed once at least every year' to keep the property neat and tidy as befitted the military. In addition, the tenant had to 'keep insured the houses, cottages and buildings from loss or damage by fire in some insurance office of repute in London

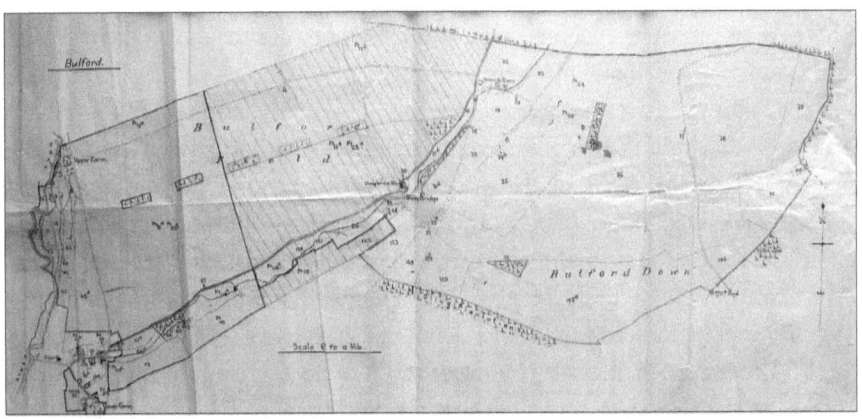

13 *1897 map of Upper and Lower Farms. This map shows both farms being farmed as a single unit. The row of five copses was planted by James Ledger Hill along the old Upper and Lower Farm boundaries. The farmland is divided into the different scheduling after the 1897 revision which increased the area (cross hatched) under total control of the War Office. (Wiltshire and Swindon Archives)*

or Westminster to be approved by the landlord'. (The insurance stipulation applied to all their properties in the village. Lucy Sturgess, for example, was required in 1899 to have £250 insurance cover for Spring Cottage (*Figure 2, no.37*).[34]

The three year lease did not, however, run its full course as James Hooper received a letter from land agents for the War Office on 26 September 1899 informing him that,

> The Secretary of State for War has decided that a large area of land forming part of the War Department Property which is now arable some of which is in your occupation shall be sown to grass not later than 1901, so that it may be in pasture in 1902, and that the Military shall after July 15th in that year, when the Hay will have been stacked, have the right of use without paying compensation. ... we reluctantly conclude that it is advisable to send you a formal notice to quit which we enclose forthwith.
>
> At the same time we are to express the desire of the Secretary of State for War, and likewise our own anxiety, that you will be disposed to treat for, and that terms may be arranged for the continuation of your tenancy under altered conditions, in which case we have much pleasure in cancelling the notice to quit sent you.

The new terms were accepted and James Hooper continued to farm Upper and Lower Farms, insuring them again in 1907. Along with the letter there is a map showing the changes made. The Schedule 1 land which the tenant was free to farm without restriction had been more than halved, ending in a line dissecting Bulford Field before the third plantation from the Avon, and then, even on this land, 'troops and military forces of any description' had the right to manoeuvre at any time, without compensation except for any claims for damage which were agreed. The effects of this militarisation on farming will be looked at in more detail in Chapter 11.[35]

The tenant farmers throughout the century were all on much shorter leases on the Manor Lands than on the Seymour Estate (see Chapter 5). The Lord or Lady of the Manor depended on his or her farms for income and the will of Charity Ann Pollen is very clear in putting obligation on the executors of her estate to set up leases for 'any term or number of years not exceeding sixteen years' and at the expiry of a term to charge 'the most and best improved rents that can be reasonably obtained' and further to keep strict control of any new building and the management of timber resources. Details of lease terms do not survive until, as we have seen, 1881 when Anthony Southby set up James Hooper's lease of Lower Farm 'for the term of two years from Michaelmas' 1880. Two years was the norm, with the 1885 lease for the same farm requiring two years' notice before quitting, the assumption being that it would be automatically renewed. In 1893 this arrangement, though, was given a period of seven years before it was to be renegotiated and the rent reviewed, well within Lady Pollen's stipulation of sixteen years. James Ledger Hill's approach was slightly different, as we have seen above, offering a choice of two or three year terms, and giving himself more income security by offering a reduced rent over the longer term. When the War Office took over, they followed the three year pattern at a reduced rent of £400 reflecting the shrinkage of land controlled by the tenant.[36]

Cottage tenants

THE TENANT FARMERS of the Manor were, as the name applies, tenants. Their 'leases determinable by two years' notice' in 1880 laid down the rights and responsibilities of both parties and we can gain a glimpse of these from a set of accounts drawn up for Edmund Southby in

1886. They show that he paid the Land Tax and Income Tax for his tenant farmers of Lower Farm and Upper Farm, Hooper and Robbins. They in turn had the responsibility for the tenants on their farms which they shared with the Lord of the Manor. The 1885 lease, for example, has the landlord supplying materials to maintain and repair the 'tenement cottages', except for the thatch, leaving the leasee responsible for transport within five miles to collect materials and half the labour costs. The 1886 accounts show that the costs for six days work at a cottage and the repair of a well were divided equally between the Lord of the Manor and tenant farmer, and that repairs were made to cottages occupied by Edward Sturgess, Sarah Sturgess, David Swatton and Mary Keel – the last being for new lead work. Every dwelling in the village was owned and, either occupied by the owner, or leased out to tenants. The vast majority were owned by the Lord of the Manor which were described in 1838 as 'Sundry Cottages or Dwelling Houses and gardens also belonging to the said Anthony Southby in the occupation of Labourers as Tenants at Will ... exempt from payment of Great Tithes only'. After the exchange of lands in 1871 (see Chapter 6) brought twelve more cottages and a farm house with farm buildings at Orchard End under his ownership, Anthony Southby owned even more of the village. He passed on responsibility for all these newly acquired properties except Orchard End House to the tenant of Lower Farm, James Hooper. The sale of the Manor in 1886 was for '49 well-built Tenements with large gardens, several enclosures of accommodation lands ... ' and also 'Pleasantly situate in the centre of the village is a small dwelling house [Orchard End] with capital gardens ... '. All these properties, and the thirteen or fourteen cottages on the Seymour estate, were subject to the small 'Tithes of Lambswool, Cows, Pigs, Poultry, Gardens, Orchard and Clover Seed'. This reflects the days when most houses were copyhold, farming the common fields, but now that the landlords had consolidated and enclosed their estates, residents were the employed labourers and craftsmen that supported the agrarian economy, paying money rent as opposed to paying in kind. Some residents were allowed to live in the houses as grace and favour tenants without paying rent, such as clergymen. Orchard End House posed a problem because it was too big for agricultural workers and was now superfluous as a farm house. Anthony Southby gave it to the parish priest as a grace and favour residence, but the latter found it too small for the needs of his large family and moved into the newly built vicarage. At the turn of the century it found a potential role for accommodating officers moving into the new camp, but it was by then run down and unsuitable for a home of status. Its role was then as a hostel for tradesmen working on construction of the hutted army camp. In 1901 it was called the 'Old Vicarage' and was run as a boarding house by Jane Strange with a clientele of three carpenters, four joiner/carpenters, an electric fitter, a civil engineer and a Church Army Missionary at the time of the census.[37]

Some properties in the village were owned by the chapel as will be seen in Chapter 8, and George Melsome of Watergate Farm had bought property. He bought the old toll house and garden for £40 in an auction on 30 October 1871 of the assets of the wound up Amesbury Turnpike Trust, and he also owned a garden on the corner of Watergate Lane, which was probably the plot of land owned by Mr Jenner of Durrington in 1841 (occupied by John Maton), and another on the side of the 'Rose and Crown'. We have already seen two houses in the High Street owned by a Durrington blacksmith but to all intents and purposes, though, when the Secretary of State for War bought Bulford Manor, he bought the whole village. When this purchase is combined with that of the Seymour estate (save for Watergate House and its surrounding land), the ownership of Bulford had turned full circle. It had emerged into written records in Anglo-Saxon times as part of an estate which provided sustenance to the King when he travelled around his Kingdom, and retained this role until the king gave it away to the newly founded Amesbury Abbey in 979. It returned briefly to the Crown after Henry VIII had dissolved the Abbey (then a Priory) but was treated as a financial asset to be sold back into private hands in 1612. It remained private property until the dying years of the nineteenth century saw it returning once again into royal ownership, in the guise of the War Office, to play a critical role in the security of the Crown embodied in the State. It was the end of a journey, a second full circle of ownership.[38]

5
The Seymour Estate and the Leaseholders of Watergate Farm

Inheritance of the Seymour Estate

THE MANOR OF Bulford incorporating the whole of the present day parish was split in half in the seventeenth century with Sir Laurence Washington purchasing the southern moiety (half). This estate was subsequently sold to Sir Edward Seymour, Speaker of the House of Commons, in 1678 marking the beginning of the Seymour's long association with Bulford. In contrast to the reduced Manor estate owned by the Dukes (the other moiety), the Seymour estate in the south of the parish was, until the final years of the nineteenth century, farmed as a single unit. Its boundary followed the River Avon south of the Manor House until it reached the boundary with Amesbury and Ratfyn Farm. Following the Amesbury boundary as far as the Cholderton boundary beyond the ridge of Beacon Hill, it then followed this new boundary to incorporate part of Beacon Hill ridge before cutting down through the Sling plantation in the present Bulford Camp, where it met the lands of Bulford Manor, towards Nine Mile River. It then followed the river towards the village and cut back to the farm buildings which in the nineteenth century were called Watergate Farm. The name of Manor Farm was sometimes linked with the farm probably reflecting that it was once the home farm of Bulford Manor before it was split into moieties. During the period covered by this book, this estate was part of the wider estates owned by a branch of one of England's pre-eminent land owning aristocratic families, the Seymours of East Knoyle.[1]

As the century opened, the owner of the Seymour estate in Bulford was Henry Seymour senior, until his death in 1807. He, in common with great landlords, was interested in land primarily as a unit of ownership, income yielding with rent paying occupants. He was not, as such, a farmer although there was a home farm of 368 acres at East Knoyle which he farmed directly mainly to supply his household with fresh produce rather than to sell on the open market. He no doubt grew plenty of asparagus to which his son was partial, eating fifty shoots a day. This was mirrored at Bulford Manor with its partially walled garden and eight acres of arable land farmed directly by the Southbys. Legal developments in the eighteenth century had enabled estates to be used as collateral for long term mortgages enabling landowners to finance their life styles. Estates could carry permanently a very high load of debt from one generation to another and there is evidence to support this being the fate of the Seymour estate at Bulford. This debt burden gave a particular incentive for the landowner to improve his estate so that its productivity rose and higher rents could then be charged. The choice of good tenants to farm the estate and efficient stewards to keep them up to scratch were the key to maximising income from their estates. In February 1785 Henry Seymour senior was indebted to banks to the tune of £5,200 which he cleared in July by selling superfluous, non-paying properties. That Bulford was not sold, indicates that it was a profit making concern for the Seymours and the lease he drew up in 1801 with his new tenant Matthew Devenish shows his concern to keep it that way.[2]

Henry Seymour senior's father Francis Seymour had a very poor opinion of his son, describing him as 'a scoundrel of a son, a grasping disrespective fellow if ever there was one'. He cut him out of his will so that when he succeeded to the estates in 1761 he had to fight his half sister for his inheritance. Money was always a problem for him which he needed to fund his lavish lifestyle in Paris where he bought a house, had an affair with Louis XV's mistress Mme Du Barry and later married the Comtesse of Panthou. He had to flee L'Isle d'Adam, his Paris home, in 1792 with his wife and half French son, Henry Seymour junior, when his house was confiscated by the Revolutionary Government. He returned to live in Knoyle and manage his estates. His son and heir returned to France in 1801 after the Peace of Amiens to try and recover the family's French estate, but without success. Henry Seymour junior lived a dissolute life and when the Peace broke down he was imprisoned at Verdun and then confined in Melun (near Fontainebleau).

The Seymour Estate

When his father died in 1807, his will described his son as being 'tyranically held prisoner in France'. For the best part of a year, therefore, the owner of the Seymour estate in Bulford was a French political prisoner, and the estate was administered by his executors which no doubt included William Seymour who is recorded as running the estate in 1808-09.³

On his return to England, Henry Seymour junior settled at Knoyle House situated in its 1,284 acre estate, preferring England to France and feeling that he owed a duty to his tenants on whose earnings he lived. Not only did he have to support his lifestyle at Knoyle, he also owned a London house at 39 Upper Grosvenor Street. Money was always tight but he did what was expected of landowners by marrying into wealth when in 1817 he took Jane Hopkinson of the Royal Crescent in Bath as his wife. She was the heiress to a £100,000 fortune. He raised two sons, Henry Danby and Alfred, and led a contented family life. The whole family enjoyed travel abroad, spending two or three months a year on the continent, particularly Paris. It was an extravagant lifestyle although he skilfully managed to gain considerable compensation for the loss of L'Isle D'Adam at the Restoration of the Bourbons as Kings of France. He had strong links with the Bourbon-Conti family and his Parisian mistress from that family gave birth to a daughter Henriette Félicité Seymour. Henry Seymour junior supported his illegitimate daughter and in 1827 arranged for her to marry James Tichbourne, a long standing friend, giving her a £6,000 dowry which strained his finances further. He, however, was considered to be a man of excellent judgement possessing keen business acumen and after his term as High Sheriff of Wiltshire in 1835, his neighbours said that never was there a High Sheriff with so firm a grasp of realities. He was not over wealthy when he died in Bath of dropsy in November 1849.⁴

The estate passed to his elder son Henry Danby Seymour who became the new owner of Watergate Farm on the Seymour estate in Bulford. He was in business, sometime Chairman of Lloyds and a partner in Robinson, Brooking and Garland, a London firm involved in the Newfoundland trade. Things had gone sour for him in 1838 with the crash of the Imperial Mercantile Finance Company leaving him owing £24,000, with a further £16,000 worth of debt about to be called. As a local Poole paper put it, 'To avoid difficulties arising out of these calls, Mr Seymour went abroad', and resigned as M.P. for Poole. When he inherited Bulford eleven years later, he was still unable to support his lifestyle without having to raise money from the banks and he used his Bulford estate in 1873 as collateral for a twenty-five year loan from the Land Loan Enfranchisement Company, paying back £97 a year. Two years later, he took out a further loan paying back £22 for a further twenty-five year term. Together, the loan company was paid back £2,992 including interest at 3¾ per cent. It is inconceivable that this was the first time that the Bulford estate was used as collateral for a loan as it was a large estate, being 352 acres larger than the main estate at East Knoyle, and over twice as large as the 791 acres that the Seymours owned at Stapleford. It is almost certain that it was used as surety under Henry Seymour senior when he was indebted to the banks as has been noted earlier, and the fact that he did not dispose of the estate would indicate that it was paying sufficiently well under his tenant William Swayne to bring him income over and above any loan repayments, as well as providing excellent hunting.[5]

On Henry Danby Seymour's death in 1877, the Seymour estates passed to his younger brother Alfred Seymour. He had a naturally jovial disposition and he was loved by his tenants as much for his genial manner as for his actual kindness. He had served as Liberal M.P. for Totnes and his 1865 election address shows him in favour of

> an extension of the suffrage to those persons who give proofs of their fitness to enjoy it; and who by their industry, intelligence, education, and thrifty habits of life, show themselves equal and not inferior to those to whom is at present entrusted the Election of Members to carry on the business of Empire in Parliament.

If Alfred's own thrifty habits were the standard he was thinking about, it was a pretty low bar to cross! A window was put in East Knoyle parish church after his death as a memorial to him from 'his tenantry who loved him'. Alfred Seymour was heavy handed with money and spent a fortune on his obsession of remodelling and improving Knoyle House. He was unable to raise more loans and had to sell off half his estate to keep his creditors from the door which had already started under his brother. The Knoyle House Game Book was also used as a scrapbook for newspaper cuttings relating to the Seymours and amongst these are accounts of the sale of some of their properties in 1876 and 1877. Once again the Bulford estate was not one of these as it was a good source of income, and could well have been one of the jewels in his crown. When Alfred died in March 1888, his widow

The Seymour Estate

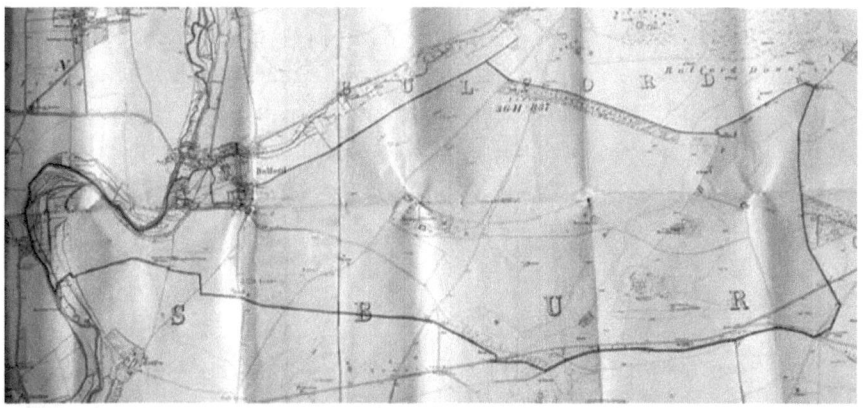

14 *The Seymour Estate at its maximum extent of 1628 acres. This map was prepared in 1897 as part of the negotiations with the War Office to take over 751 acres for military purposes. A letter dated 19 March 1897 which accompanied the map read: 'I have shown on the plan the whole of Miss Seymour's Estate as it formerly stood.' The Eastern portion, of 382 acres, had been sold to H. F. Stephens Esq., MP. The central section, of 751 acres, was proposed to be purchased by the War Department, leaving the remaining 494 acres to Miss Jane Seymour. The sitting tenants of the four cottages at the Pennings were the first villagers to be transferred to the new landlord, the War Office. The hutted camp was built on this area. A further 288 acres were purchased by the War Office two years later, leaving Miss Seymour 207 acres with Watergate House and the Home Farm buildings. (Wiltshire and Swindon Archives)*

Isabella as executrix of his will, passed the ownership of his Bulford estate to their daughter and only child Jane Margaret Seymour (who retired to Bournemouth and died in 1943). By this time, interest in Bulford as a farming business had declined and so Jane Margaret Seymour was quite happy to sell 751 acres in March 1898 for £7,500 and a further 288 acres in 1900 for £9,000 to the War Department. She had already sold 383 acres over Beacon Hill for £2,500 to H. C. Stephens to add to his Cholderton Estate. Altogether she had realised £19,000 for the sale of 1,422 acres, and was left with an estate of 288 acres centred on 'Watergate House' as the farm house stripped of its farm became known. The Seymours never farmed their Bulford estate themselves but leased it out to a series of farming gentry who lived at Watergate Farm, which was also known as Seymour Farm or Bulford Manor Farm – not to be confused with Manor Farm owned by the Lord of the Manor. The tithe commutation survey in 1838 describes it as,

All that messuage and lands called Bulford Manor Farm belonging to Henry Seymour [junior] Esquire in the occupation of Francis Stephen Long and his undertenants containing eight hundred and fifty-five acres by estimation of land cultivated as Arable land and seven hundred and forty acres by estimation of land cultivated as Meadow pasture and Downland and thirty-eight acres by estimation of land cultivated as Woodland and Plantations.[6]

Leaseholders of Watergate Farm

THE CENTURY OPENS with the death of the leaseholder William Swayne and a new lease being drawn up in 1801 with the next tenant being Matthew Devenish, yeoman in the County of Dorset. The lease was for sixteen years with a rent payable of £800 per annum, increasing to £850 after five years, perhaps reflecting the contemporary opinion that it 'must be a good farmer indeed, or [he has] very good luck, who (on land fairly tenanted), can do more than save his own in the first four years of his term.' Henry Seymour senior was planning to maximise the return on his land. The lease was drawn up in great detail because as an economic unit there is no single cut off point. The handover period lasted from October 1801 to July 1802 allowing the outgoing tenant, or his heirs in this case, to literally reap what he had sown. What had to be handed over and in what state the new tenant had to leave the estate at the end of his tenure was laid out in detail. Thomas Davis remarked that everything had 'by all means to be positively settled previous to a tenant's entry. Nothing but this can prevent the quarrels which are continually happening between a going-off tenant and coming-on tenant in this district.' The dwelling house, barns, stables, pigeon house, fences, walls, hatches etcetera, all had to be left 'in good and sufficient repair'; this included the 'glass lead and iron windows of the dwelling house'. Beyond these expected conditions, with provision for the landlord to step in if the property was not being properly maintained, Matthew Devenish was not to have total control of the estate. Henry Seymour senior reserved the usual mining and quarrying rights with rights of ingress and egress, but in addition he reserved ownership rights over, 'Game and fish at anytime hereafter to be found on the premises with the liberty to hunt hawk sett shoot and catch the same'. He also reserved ownership rights over 'the parlour and chamber over the same and the Hackney Stable part of the premises hereby demised to and for his own use only during the season of hunting shooting

The Seymour Estate

and fishing.' The East Knoyle Game Book considered in the opening chapter is evidence that these rights were fully exercised, with for example, Henry [Seymour junior], his staff and guests hunting on 6 and 7 September 1837 and his two heirs Henry Danby and Alfred Seymour hunting the estate ten times between 1852 and 1883.[7]

Watergate Farm, as it became known (perhaps a distant folk memory of the prehistoric road from Durrington Walls which joined the Avon on the further bank), on its southern border was contiguous to land in Amesbury parish which was farmed by Henry Blatch (1768-1821) of Ratfyn Farm. He and Matthew Devenish were married to sisters, Elizabeth and Sarah Aldridge and the relationship between the two men and their father-in-law, James Aldridge, was a close one as the history of the chapel will show. Matthew Devenish ran the farm until he 'injured vertebra in backbone after falling from his horse' in 1811. He died seven weeks, three days later, aged 40. His widow Elizabeth kept on the farm being his 'heirs and assigns' as stipulated in the lease. The lease must have subsequently been renewed by the Devenishes as the 1829 parish rates for repairing the church have Mr Devenish, Matthew's heir also called Matthew, eligible to pay £700 for Manor Farm. Matthew Devenish senior's two children, Matthew junior and James Aldridge, were born in Bulford in 1830 and 1831 implying residence at Watergate Farm up to the latter date. Assuming that the original 1801 lease was renewed for a further fifteen years in 1816, this would also bring us to 1831. This is the year the evidence suggests a new joint lease was drawn up between Henry Seymour junior, the new owner, for Francis Stephen Long and his eldest son of the same name. The change of tenancy is confirmed by Francis Stephen Long junior obtaining the vote at Bulford as the tenant of Manor Farm (an old name for Watergate Farm), although he was residing in Amesbury at the time. The evidence that it was a joint lease is supplied by a draft lease in 1841 between 'Francis Stephen Long of Amesbury ... and Francis Stephen Long the younger of Bulford' and Henry Seymour for Bulford Farm 'formerly in the occupation of Matthew Devenish and now of the s^d Francis Stephen Long and Francis Stephen Long the younger as tenants ... ' It reads 'for the term of 10 12 years' at a yearly rent of £1,200 (a fifty per cent rise since 1801). It was a draft renewing a lease which left a choice of either ten or twelve years open for the term. The parish rate for the farm in 1829 was paid, as we have seen, by Mr Devenish, implying that the lease being renewed in 1841 must have been over a ten year term, bringing the Amesbury Longs to Bulford in 1831.[8]

Francis Stephen Long senior owned several farms: his freehold inheritance at Sutton Veny, leasehold farms at Longbridge Deverell (owned by the Marquis of Bath), at Overton and finally the farm he 'cultivated and managed' himself at Amesbury. This was Red House Farm in Amesbury which was part of the Antrobus estate situated on the west side of town between Boscombe and the river. Francis Stephen Long senior was sixty in 1841 and was planning provision for his five sons. His will left the Red House Farm to his son William Long, and other properties to other sons, and then stated,

> and whereas my eldest son Francis Stephen Long is now resident and I have established him on a farm at Bulford in this county as an agriculturalist and the entire stock both live and dead on such farm I sometime past gave absolutely to him and the same now belongs to him and is his own entire property goods chattels and effects.

William Long is recorded as occupier of Red House Farm in Amesbury in 1841 which implies that the terms of his will had been activated on his father's death that year which would also indicate that the lease for Bulford passed to the survivor as stipulated by the lease. In any case, the father lived in Amesbury and the son lived at Bulford Farm (Watergate Farm) which was known as his farm. *The Times* reported in March 1834 that 'Francis Stephen Long – Has a farm at Bulford' from whence he had a horse stolen, and the 1838 tithe commutation quoted above, states that the farm was 'in the occupation of Francis Stephen Long and his undertenants'. This last reference was a legal document naming only one tenant implying that Francis Stephen Long had given the farm over absolutely to his son very early on.[9]

The large map of Bulford Farm belonging to 'H Seymour', dated to about 1820, could well have been drawn up when the Devenish lease was renewed for a second term, and gives an accurate representation of the farm on the eve of Francis Stephen Long's tenancy. It was an undertaking to produce it but the Seymours took great interest in knowing the state of their estate and 'improving' it. The 1801 lease had stipulated that Matthew Devenish would be allowed 'the sum of Two Hundred and Thirty pounds out of the first years rent towards the expense of improving the water meadows [and] inclosing part of the Down called the Pennings or any other improvements' as long as he produced receipts. The Pennings were enclosed by 1820, no doubt as part of this arrangement. In addition he was adamant that the estate preserved its corn producing productivity, which was the economic focus of the farm. The Napoleonic Wars had seen a boom in corn prices which triggered 'the rage there has been of late years for ploughing up sheep downs'. This was achieved by preparing the downland for tillage by,

> "Paring and burning land", or as it is called in Wiltshire, "burn-beaking" ... The wood was cut off, most of the roots were grubbed, and then the rough grass and moss, and the whole surface of the land, were chopped up with a curved-cutting mattock, and burnt to ashes, and thus the land was prepared for sowing. This mattock was called a "beak", and the operation was, therefore, and is still frequently, called "beaking and burning".

The ash which resulted served as 'manure' for several crops in succession, but then the land became exhausted and unproductive. Land on the Seymour estate had been burn-beaked and the lease sets out in detail that the 'old Burnbeaked arable land' be farmed on a six year cycle, five years of pasture to support the sixth year of crops. 'In the first year of the last six years' the tenant had to 'sow a sixth part of the old Burnbeaked arable with grass seed', repeating the pattern in the succeeding years so that when the lease was renewed, or a new tenant took over, he could sow a sixth of the area and expect a good crop of corn. Whether the previous tenant William Swayne was guilty of exploiting the downs for short term arable gain, or whether Henry Seymour senior was just being prudent is unclear but what is certain is that he judged the balance between arable and pasture needed to be maintained. The deterrent was that Matthew Devenish would have to pay an extra £20 an acre rent 'for any greater or lesser quantity of meadow pasture sheep down or land ... which have not been in tillage or ploughed within fifteen years last past' if it 'be eared ploughed spitted digged or converted to tillage or garden'. Another stipulation was that he should 'keep and depasture on the premises so great a stock and number of sheep as may be conveniently depastured and supported thereon'. Sheep stock was, as Thomas Davis put it,

> the basis of Wiltshire Down husbandry [as] carriers of dung, in situations where the distance from home and the steepness of hills almost preclude the possibility of carrying it by any other mode ... The sheep stock of South

15 *North barn of Watergate Farm. The extant south doors and five bays of the north barn in the original farmyard of Watergate Farm. The tiled roof of 1829? has been replaced by corrugated iron. (Photographed by author in 2011)*

> Wiltshire has been for many years decreasing ... on the downland part of the district, where the sheepfold is indispensibly necessary to the production of corn, a diminution of sheep stock is a serious evil.

Henry Seymour senior knew all this as did his son who drew up the 1841 draft lease for Francis Stephen Long, father and son.[10]

The 1841 lease follows the same structure as the 1801 lease, reserving the landlord the same set of rights and exemptions, but being more specific at times, for example, Henry Seymour junior had use of the same parts of the premises in the seasons of hunting, shooting and fishing, but extended its use to 'their friends gamekeepers and servants to hunt shoot sport and fish'. He also was even more vigorous in preserving the timber assets of the estate, adding that the tenants 'will keep from injury by cattle or otherwise all timber ... trees spires saplings hollies shrubs and pollards standing and growing', and extended the age of trees to be harvested from four to twelve years. Henry Seymour's aim to maximise his rent from good tenants is still the bedrock of the lease. The annual rent had gone up fifty per cent in forty years from £800 to £1,200 per annum, and the extra rent for converting downland to tillage or garden had similarly increased from £20 to £30 an acre. There was a more rigorous economic consideration given to the tenant by example, compensation for any land taken out of agriculture by the landlord being recognised with an adjustment in the rent. Responsibility was shared for the repair and maintenance of

> all aspects whats[r] the thatching and rafters of the Barns and other Outhouses now covered with thatch and the groundwalls of the Barns Stables and other buildings and the glass lead and iron of the windows of the Dwelling House and Pigeon House ... and keep the thrashing machine and all gates stiles hedges ditches underwalls mounds bounds bridges and small hatches

with the landlord providing 'sufficient rough timber Bricks and Lime' for the repairs as long as the tenant picked it up, at his own expense, from within a fifteen mile radius. The Seymours actively managed their estates.

16 Site of water wheel. The north doors of the barn with the bridge over the leat leading to the rickyard and new farm yard. (Photographed by author in 2011)

There were, for example, plans in 1827 to refurbish a room at the farmhouse, taking out the dado and papering the walls down to the skirting, taking out an old fireplace and substituting it with a 'plain Marble Chimney Piece' for a cost of eight pounds, and 'an alteration in fitting up the Cupboards in the Same Room' for a further five pounds. This was at a time when repairs were being carried out after a fire and the plans were submitted to Henry Seymour's steward, James Still, who visited the house three months later to 'examine the carpentry work at Bulford', and again a few days later to examine more work being done. They also kept responsibility for maintaining the Hatch House and Great Hatches which were critical for controlling the water meadows. The 1801 lease had stipulated improvements to the Pennings and water meadows, and in 1841 new stipulations were written in to improve the farm infrastructure. The 1820 map shows a field barn complex on Beacon Hill and, separated from it, an isolated building, which was probably a cottage. The Longs were instructed to 'remove the cottage situate at Beacon Hill to the Field Homest"d' nearby. This must have been part of the Pennings which according to an 1897 description 'consisted of 4 old cottages, a Barn, Yard etc which are also old. There is however a new shed very substantially built in brick and slate'. In addition the Longs had to make changes to the main farm complex at Watergate Farm which are considered below in more detail.[11]

    Francis Stephen Long farmed the estate after the Devenish lease expired up until 1871 as he was Vicar's Warden from 1857 to 1871, with his successor, George Melsome, taking on the post in 1872. In July 1871 his daughter Annie married Nicholas Charles Browne of Upper Tooting and Francis Stephen Long also moved, perhaps prompted by the marriage of his daughter, to the Home Counties where in 1881 the census records him as a widowed retired farmer and landowner living in Middlesex. Throughout his tenure of the farm its acreage remained unchanged, but the workforce showed the same shrinkage, although to a lesser degree, than that already has been noted for Upper Farm in Chapter 4. The workforce employed on Watergate Farm in 1851 stood at fifty-one: twenty-six men, twelve boys and thirteen women. Ten years later it had shrunk by eighteen per cent (as opposed to thirty-four per cent on Upper Farm) to just thirty men and twelve boys; again, women had been cut out of the employed workforce other than as casual labour for tasks such as couching. We know that Francis Stephen Long used machinery as early as July 1834 when he hired a seed drill to work his fields, and there was a threshing machine on the farm

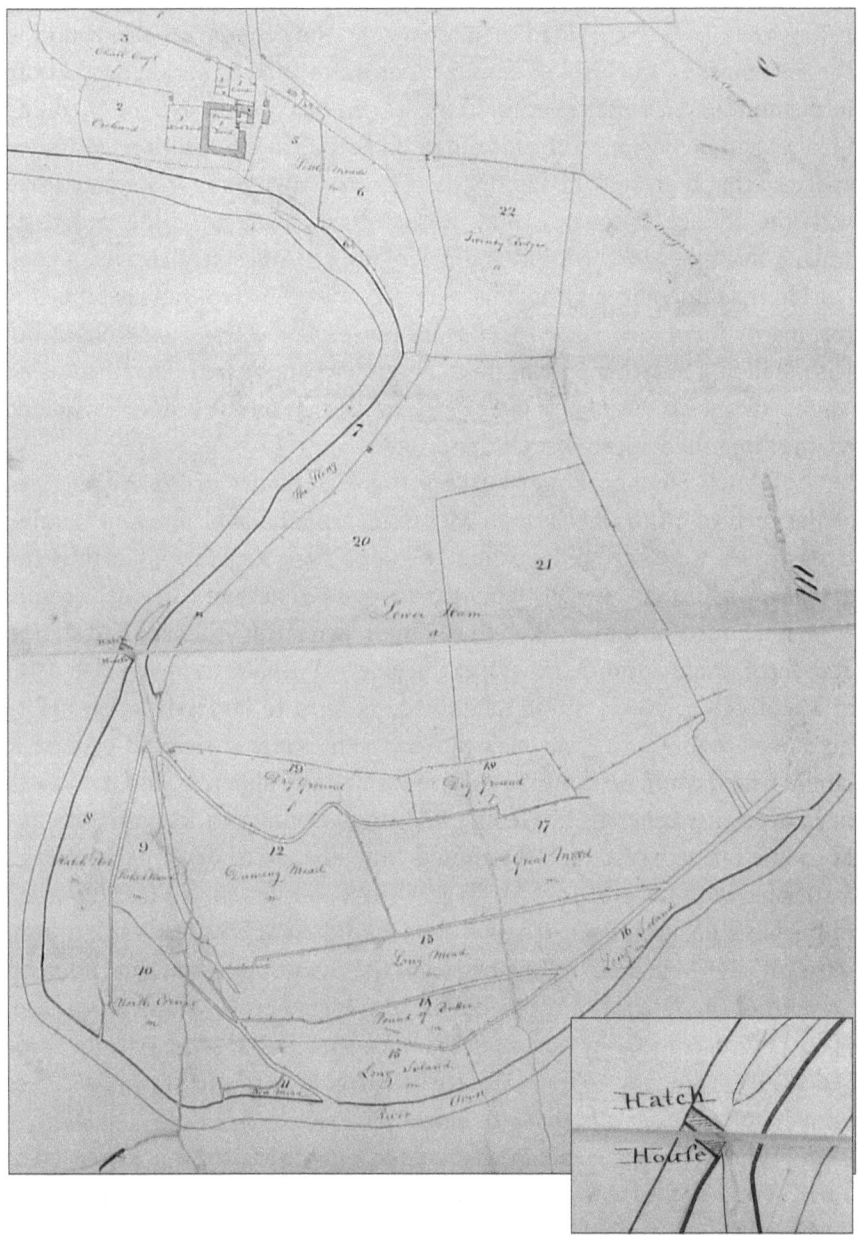

17 Water meadows. Detail of the 1820 Map of
Seymour Farm showing the water meadows at the western end in the loop of the
River Avon. The Great Hatches spanning the Avon fed the water into the network
of channels used to drown the meadows. With enlarged detail of the Hatch House.
(Wiltshire and Swindon Archives)

before 1841 (when it needed maintenance). The economic background to these changes in the level of employment was a time of agricultural boom in the middle years of the century. As the century progressed, the shedding of labour in favour of more efficient and cheaper mechanisation continued apace so that by 1871 when an inventory was drawn up of Watergate Farm with the change of tenant, there was a broadcasting machine and three sowing machines, two winnowing machines, an Amesbury Heaver, a chaff cutting machine and a Crosskills reaper powered by two horses replacing reaping by hand (see Plate 19). Steam power was soon to make its debut with William Blanchard living in a labourer's cottage and described as an 'engine driver' in the census of 1881. Lower Farm on the Manor estate had its 'machine shed' located at Orchard End.[12]

Francis Stephen Long's successor as leaseholder of Watergate Farm at the turn of 1872 was George Melsome, a member of another farming dynasty. He was born on his father William's 1,300 acre farm, North Farm, at Oaksey in c1832. He had a younger brother Richard and an elder brother William, both of whom went on to run their own farms. Richard had a 1,130 acre farm at Stockton in 1871 and the eldest, William farmed 1,000 acres at Maddington (1881) in the neighbouring farm to James Hooper, before he moved to Bulford. Farmers moved in the same social and economic circles which could no doubt foster friendships and alliances, and could well have been instrumental in George Melsome's coming to Bulford. George Melsome farmed Watergate Farm and immediately took on parish duties associated with his position in village society. He served as Vicar's Warden in the parish church from 1872 till 1876, and then as People's Warden from 1881 till 1898. He died in June 1899 and the school closed an 'afternoon on account of the funeral of one of the School Managers G. W. Melsome Esq'. His son Robert took the post of People's Warden in the same year for three years. His widow stayed on at Watergate Farm, living there in 1901 with her French domestic servant Jeanette Bataille.[13]

When Watergate Farm was leased to George Melsome, it consisted of 1,628 acres. The lease was renewed in 1894 at a rent of £500 per annum but it was reduced to £450 when Jane Seymour sold 383 acres on Beacon Hill in 1893 to H. F. Stephens M.P. whose Cholderton estates abutted the Seymour lands. The 'low rent was submitted to rather than allow Mr Melsome to leave as it was felt that having regard to the large area of land in hand in the neighbourhood Miss Seymour would be very unlikely to relet such a huge occupation'. Negotiations leading up to the first sale of 751 acres of Seymour lands to the War Office show that a sale price was agreed at ten pounds an acre. This included about 570 acres of down, droves and roads and about 182 acres of 'thin arable land on the chalk'. It also included the Pennings complex which the War Office did not really want but was included in the sale as it would otherwise 'simply be a "white elephant"' to the farm once shorn of the downs and hill arable. After the sale, George Melsome continued to pay the £450 rent for the remaining 495 acres. Mr Rawlence, who was responsible for Miss Seymour's interests, was

> confident that with Railway accommodation in the district we shall let the residue of the farm for quite as much as Mr Melsome is now paying for the whole viz: £440. The character of the Farm and indeed the whole neighbourhood will be altered and I do not see how a large flock can be maintained but with 20, or 30,000 soldiers in the district all Summer the demand for milk and Dairy produce must be very great so that I should lay out a Farm for a Dairy of 40 or 50 cows.[14]

George Melsome's son Robert had inherited the tenancy by the time of the second sale on 30 January 1901, 'subject to the tenancy there of ... Mr Robert Francis Melsome expiring on the twenty-ninth day of September One thousand nine hundred and one at an entire yearly rent of Three Hundred and fifty pounds ... '. Watergate Farm had been reduced to 495 acres in January 1897, and now a new era had begun where the War Office rented out farm lands on a piecemeal basis which ignored the historic moieties of Bulford. George Melsome, for example, also farmed Ratfyn, as well as a farm at Maddington. The Seymours' two hundred and twenty-three years' association with village agriculture had in essence come to an end as only Watergate House and the Home Farm buildings set in 207 acres still remained in their possession, passing to Jane Seymour's cousin in 1943 before being sold to another private owner in 1985. It was, and still remains, one of the village's grand houses.[15]

Gentrification

THE HISTORY OF Watergate Farm needs to be put into a wider social context, starting with the views of contemporary observers. The polemicist William Cobbett, writing in the first quarter of the century, looked back romantically to the time when a farmer would,

> sit at the head of the oak-table along with his men, say grace to them, and cut up the meat and pudding. He might take a cup of *strong beer* whereas they had none and that was pretty nearly all the difference in their manner of living…. [But now there are] *wine decanters* and *wine glasses* and 'a *dinner set*', and a '*breakfast set*', and '*desert knives*'. …. [There is now] a Mistress within, who is stuck up in a place called a *parlour*, with, if she have children, the 'young ladies and gentlemen' about her …. the house is too neat for a dirty-shoed carter to be allowed to come into…. The children…. are too clever to *work*: they are all *gentlefolks*. Go to the plough! Good God! What 'young gentlemen' go to the plough! They become *clerks*, or some shimy-dish thing or other. They flee from dirty work as cunning horses do from the bridle.

Richard Jefferies writing in the third quarter also observed the process of gentrification of the tenant farmers. He was writing about the role of women in the farms.

> The house is full of servants, and need be, to wait upon these people. …..It is part and parcel of the wide-spread social changes which have gradually been proceeding. But the tenant farmer's wife who made the butter and cheese, and even helped to salt bacon, where is she now? Where are the healthy daughters that used to assist her? The wife is a fine lady not, indeed, with carriage and pair, but with a dandy dog-cart at least; not with three-guinea bonnets, but with a costly sealskin jacket. The 'civilisation' of the town has, in fact, gone out and taken root afresh in the country. There is no reason why the farmer should not be educated; there is no reason why his wife should not wear a sealskin jacket, or the daughter interpret Beethoven. But the question arises, Has not some of the old stubborn spirit of earnest work and careful prudence gone with the advent of the piano and the oil painting? While wearing the dress of a lady, the wife cannot tuck up her sleeves and see to the butter, or even feed the poultry, which are down at the pen across 'a nasty dirty field.'
>
> Today, if you call at such a country house, how strangely different is the reception! None of the family come to the door to meet you. A servant

The Seymour Estate

shows you into a parlour - drawing-room is the proper word now - well carpeted and furnished in the modern style. She then takes your name - what a world of change is shown in that trifling piece of etiquette! By-and-by, after the proper interval, the ladies enter in morning costume…..Then a touch of the bell, and decanters of port and sherry are produced and your wine presented to you on an electro salver together with sweet biscuits. It is the correct thing to sip one glass and eat one biscuit……

You cannot blame these girls, whether poor or moderately well-to-do, for thinking of something higher, more refined and elevating than the cheese-tub or the kitchen. It is natural, and it is right, that they should wish to rise above that old, dull, dead level in which their mothers and grandmothers worked from youth to age. The world has gone on since then - it is a world of education, books, and wider sympathies. In all this they must and ought to share. The problem is how to enjoy the intellectual progress of the century and yet not forfeit the advantages of the hand labour and the thrift of our ancestors? ……. They have shamed them out of the old rough, boorish ways; compelled them to abandon the former coarseness, to become more gentlemanly in manner. By their interest in the greater world of society, literature, art, and music (more musical publications probably are now sold for the country in a month than used to be in a year), they have made the somewhat narrow-sighted farmer glance outside his parish. If the rising generation of tenant farmers have lost much of the bigoted provincial mode of thought, together with the provincial pronunciation, it is undoubtedly due to the influence of the higher ideal of womanhood that now occupies their minds. And this is a good work to have accomplished.

Watergate Farm has the best documentation of all the farms in Bulford during the nineteenth century and consequently we are able to see the social changes in the status of farmers as the century wore on. The changes made to the layout of the farm reflect this process of gentrification, of the civilization of the town taking root in the country, as Jefferies put it.[16]

At the end of the eighteenth century the farmhouse on the Seymour estate was a simple stone structure, with two downstairs rooms either side of a central smoke stack, built in 1618 by Sir Laurence Washington. The house faced east and alongside the southern side of the house was a long, detached structure according to a map in 1773 (see *map, p.5*). This must have been a range of farm buildings probably incorporating stables, a dairy, a cart shed and so forth, or even a barn which was repositioned when the farmyard was developed. Whatever it was, the nineteenth century witnessed an upgrading of the farmhouse to make it a more desirable residence for a country gentleman in an age when fashion and style were becoming important to those who aspired to a position in society, epitomised by the tenant of the farm from c1831 to 1871, Francis Stephen Long. This change is reflected in the two leases for the farm, the first in 1801 and the second forty years later. The former is with Matthew Devenish described as a 'yeoman' and the latter describes Francis Stephen Long as a 'gentleman' and an 'agriculturalist'. In about 1800 the addition of a block on the western side, mostly of stone and flint, made the house square, and a south entrance front, of chequered flint and ashlar, was made across both the old and new parts. The aspect of the house had swung ninety degrees and now faced the detached range of buildings which was an undesirable situation. It is at this time that they must have been either entirely, or partially, demolished as maps in 1820 and 1838 show that they had been replaced by two smaller structures, identified below as a cart shed and a granary. The present owners have seen the foundations of the original range in dry weather, situated under the lawn opposite the south facing front door. There was also a detached building nearby to the south-east which was probably, 'The old cottage used as a Store Room' which in 1827, 'should have the Tyling repaired so as to secure the inside from further decay'. Work had also to be done to maintain the original structure built by Laurence Washington because smoke was leaking occasionally into Mrs Devenish's closet through 'some fissure of the chimney'. There was a 'slight fracture in the ceiling' of her bedroom and in the servant's room above, 'one of Principal Timber of the Roof' was 'fractured' and required 'an Iron Cramp to secure it'. [17]

 The 1801 lease also describes a 'parlour and chamber over the same and the Hackney stable part of the premises' along with 'Dairyhouse and Chamber over the same with one half of the Carthorse Stable and Meadow Ground', which cannot have been part of the freestanding range as the description is repeated in 1841, long after the range had been demolished. This 'part of the premises' was most probably part of the extended house being two storied. Alternatively it was situated to the north of the house, but demolished when the L-shaped servants' wing was built on to the house. This now joins on to the new service wing and stables built in mid nineteenth century, but after 1841. There is an intriguing piece of the jigsaw to fit in, and that is the whereabouts

18 Watergate Farm granary. (Photographed by author in 2011)

of the stable which was the scene of the theft in 1835 of one of Squire Long's horses. The newspaper report tells how witness James Thorn's

> bed-room window lies in such a way that a person must pass by it to the stable ..... There are two doors opening into his master's stable – the first fastened with a spring latch, the second has a common finger-latch. There is no padlock or pull-latch; the stalls are on the left-hand side; four stalls and two horses; one tied and the other in a loose box.... saddle was hanging on a saddle-tree, and the bridle on a pin.

The stable in question was probably demolished with the building of the new L-shaped service wing mid century. The old wing must have incorporated accommodation where James Thorn was sleeping, and could well have been the site of 'the parlour and chamber over the same and the Hackney Stable' which the Seymours had access to for hunting, shooting and fishing. It was probably the stable near the old skilling which, we will see, was demolished to make way for a new carriage way. The survey conducted after a fire in 1827 which estimated the repairs and 'securing the chimney' at an estimated cost of nine pounds and sixteen shillings, also looked at other issues with the property. The 'angle of the door leading to a room designated as Mr Seymour's' was caused by 'rotting of the Timbers at the foot on Ground Floor' level. This was the door of the parlour and chamber with the rotten timbers being in the hackney stable below. The general condition of this wing of the building was wanting. The floor joists and some of the floor boards in Mr Seymor's room were rotten, as was a 'considerable portion' of the wainscoting. The survey found that the 'outside walls of this wing are somewhat defective, they are built of flint and many cracks are apparent, these though not at present of much consequence, should be repaired and occasionally looked to'. The days of this wing of the building were numbered.[18]

The demolition of the old service accommodation and the building of the new L-shaped service wing was a major remodelling to cater for increased domestic staff and must have been the time when the walled garden was created to the east of the service range. The new service wing incorporated the dairy with '50 feet of shelving, head well in floor', and probably the Back Kitchen with its 'table, 2 coolers and stand, mesh tub and stand, stool and stirrer, 2 coppers, small copper and steamer, force pump and cistern to supply boiler, quantity of piping, plate rack, pair of steps, pot cupboard, 2 shelves and hooks, plate rack' described in the 1872 inventory of the farm. The well in this range has been reopened by the present owners. The inventory also describes a Wine Cellar with 'steps, barrel horsing' and a second cellar with '2 six and a half hogs head casks, bull, 1 small cask, barrel horse, meat safe, [and a] quantity of cider'. The whereabouts of these is unknown and problematical as the water table is very near the surface at the farm, and no doubt was even higher before the days of water extraction from the river for the needs of the Bulford Camp. The Manor House had a wine cellar with a locked door but this was merely an enclosed space, with a step down to get in, under the main staircase of the original house. Perhaps 'cellar' at Watergate Farm was equally too grand a description.[19]

Major features of the farm not recorded on the Andrews and Dury map of 1773 were two barns in an L-shape to north-west and south of the farmhouse, forming the two sides of the farmyard with the house in its south-east corner (unless, as suggested above as a possibility, the structure of 1773 to the south of the house was one that had been relocated). The barns have been dated from the seventeenth and eighteenth centuries and

The Seymour Estate

appear on the first Ordnance Survey Map of 1810. Barns were relatively easy to dismantle and re-erect elsewhere and so they could also have been field barns subsequently moved to the home farm. They were timber framed and weather boarded with thatched or tiled roofs, the tenants having to 'maintain and keep the Thatching and Rafters of the barns and other outhouses now covered with thatch and the groundwalls of barns stables and other buildings' in good repair. These were structures that needed constant maintenance as is illustrated by the main barn on the north side of the farmyard. Its roof timbers were sound in 1827, except for 'the bay over the barn doors to the southward' where 'the head piece which forms the plate is completely decayed and must be replaced' along with some of the rafters. The roof was tiled and required considerable repairs (as with roof over the stables), and 'about two squares of Tiling must be stripped and relaid'. 'Great mischief has occurred by suffering the moss to grow on the tiles' which needed to be cleaned off. The 'Barn Doors are also in a very bad state' and 'some portions of the Eaves where the Board has decayed' required replacing. Now, nearly two hundred years later, the central and west sections of barn on the north side of the farmyard are still standing with a cart way in the fourth bay, entering from the south and leading out of the north side, across a leat to the rickyard. Adjacent to the third bay there is a weir in the leat, dug out between 1838 and 1887, where a water wheel was situated, surviving into the middle of the twentieth century. Village memories recall 'the old water-wheel.... turned by water from the little side stream which set the grinding-machinery in motion'. What machinery precisely is not recorded but what is clear is that water power was used in the barn. The 1841 lease contains a clause that the tenant 'will put into good and substantial repair being allowed sufficient rough timber for the purpose….. in the manner afs[d] the Thrashing Machine'. This must have been situated in the barn and the third bay next to the cart way would have been an ideal position. The reaped corn could be brought in one door, thrashed, and the straw then being carted out the other door, across the leat to the rickyard. The threshing machine could have been water powered, with the Nine Mile River being diverted at the sluice, down the leat, to drive the water wheel connected to the threshing machine when needed. The 1790 Andrews and Dury Map shows this in fact to be the course of Nine Mile River. Thomas Davies had written as early as 1811 that threshing machines saved a serious part of the expense of new barn floors and that these 'machines are now constructed at about 60 l.[£], to thrash with two horses two sacks of wheat perfectly clean in one hour.... It is of course desirable that works should go by water, if possible, as the least expensive process to the tenant.' Water power was possible at Bulford and was used to cut down on expenditure. It could not have had much power and so could have only driven small scale machinery, and the machinery connected over time could have been changed. A small threshing machine was conceivable. The south-west barn in the farmyard is no longer extant, being replaced by a new one over the leat to the west of the farm house where it still stands at the entrance to 'The Dovecot', situated in the old rickyard. Both these barns are shown standing in the 1887 map.[20]

The process of gentrification went on further as the century wore on with a cast iron veranda being erected along the front of the farmhouse where the outlook was still marred by the two small buildings situated outside the front door. In 1841 Henry Seymour junior put a clause in the draft lease for the tenant to

> .... remove the Cart House and Granary now standing near the Dwelling House h"by demised to the rickyard belonging to the s^d farm and shall and will rebuild .... such cart house and granary in a substantial and proper manner and also shall and will at his and their own costs and charges make a carriage road of convenient width from the Farmyard where the present old skilling near the stable of of the s^d demised premises now stands....

What we are witnessing here is a process of closing down the old farmyard by the house, and moving it westward, over the leat, out of view of the house. The granary still stands but the cart shed no longer exists, although it could well have been the structure shown in the 1901 map between the granary and the new farmyard which was demolished in the twentieth century along with a greenhouse. The nucleus of the new farmyard was the old dovecote which predates all the buildings in the new complex, the new brick built cart shed, for example, being abutted against it. The dovecote is not marked on any maps prior to the 1901 Ordinance Survey map, but we know that a pigeon house existed as far back as 1801 when the tenants were charged with keeping the 'Pigeon house part of the premises hereby demised in good sufficient and necessary repair'. The pigeon house could have either been incorporated in the old farm buildings, as at the Manor, or it could have

The Seymour Estate

referred to the extant freestanding dovecote. Between the new service wing and the old barn, there is a bridge 'of convenient width' and strength over the leat to link the old and new farmyards. This is where 'old skilling [a lean to structure or bay of a barn] near the stable' once stood, being demolished to build the road. The map evidence bears this out. The 1838 map of the farm shows an unbroken line of buildings around the old farmyard saving for the entrance by the house, whereas the 1887 map shows a break for access to the new bridge.[21]

There is an intriguing sketch of Bulford drawn in April 1869 by Lucius O'Brien which can only be a view from Watergate Lane towards the present day 'The Dovecot'. It shows the pigeon house, granary and other structures which indicate that the alterations stipulated in the 1841 lease were indeed carried out. The present day access road to 'The Dovecot' does not appear to be portrayed, and in any case would not have been needed as a new access road from the old farmyard had been created. The new farmyard with the pigeon house in the corner is not shown, indicating that it was not built until after 1869. And this was indeed the case as the evidence from 1897 tells us that the 1873 loan raised from the Land Loan and Enfranchisement Company by Henry Danby Seymour was used in 1873-1874 to build 'the new Cart Shed with a Granary over' at the Pennings 'together with some new buildings at the Home premises'. These new buildings were undoubtedly the cart shed abutted to the dovecote and the ranges of buildings forming two sides of the new farmyard. These were now described as 'the Home Buildings near the Farmhouse', and are shown on the 1887 map. It was at that point that the new access road must have been built now that the working part of the farm was totally divorced from the farm house. The residence became known as 'Watergate House' as opposed to the farm house of Watergate Farm. The process of gentrification was complete. The second sale of land at Watergate Farm to the Secretary of State in 1899 was the logical final chapter of the story. The farming land had all but disappeared leaving the Seymour Family with the farm buildings, Watergate House, and 288 acres including the water meadows that the house overlooked. The newly developed farm buildings were now obsolete as there was no farm to speak of, and subsequently they were sold off and developed into what now is 'The Dovecot'.[22]

A description of the farm house in 1871 tells of an entrance hall with a floor cloth, with two baize doors and a servants' board with eight bells. There was a dining room with a shelved closet, a drawing room and a breakfast room. There were two kitchens; the main one had a range, an iron stove, cupboards, a hanging table and a dresser with shelves and drawers. In addition there was a bacon rack, five rails with hooks and pins, and two coffee mills. The back kitchen was more of a scullery with a table, three coppers, a steamer, a force pump and cistern to supply the boiler, a plate rack, a pot cupboard and shelves. The larder had butter making equipment, slate shelves and facility for salting meat. Below there was a wine cellar and another cellar with barrels for beer, a meat safe and a quantity of cider. In addition there was a dairy with fifty feet of shelving and a well head in the floor; there was a coal hole and a servants' closet. Upstairs there were six bedrooms, a toilet and a dressing room. Outside was a newly built veranda. All living rooms had fire grates, several had mantle pieces and were equipped with roller blinds and sunshades. Outside was the pigeon house with its coppers and boiler, bees and beehives, gardening tools, a garden roller, sets of cucumber lights and finally a double back iron garden seat. All in all, it was a desirable country residence. The 1851 census records a domestic staff of five looking after Francis Stephen Long and his wife Elizabeth, with their quartet of children under four years old. The staff consisted of a cook-come-house servant, a housemaid, two nursery maids and a nurse. There was also a visitor. Ten years later one of the nursery maids had been replaced by a governess and Francis Stephen Long's London nephew was living with him, no doubt taking advantage of her service. In 1871 the governess and nursery maid had disappeared to be replaced by a stable boy living in the service wing. He also employed Michael Stone 'for many years ... acting as Coachman to Mr Francis Stephen Long' but he lived with his wife in the groom's cottage.[23]

6
'Nag's Head' and the Third Estate

The Nag's Head

It is a challenge to unravel the picture of the ownership of Bulford and the succession of tenant farmers, especially in the early years of the century. There were the two estates of the Manor and the Seymours which divided the parish in half, but sandwiched between them was an independent estate farmed as a separate unit or units. Associated with the farmland were Orchard End and its cottages, and in some way, Bulford Mill. The farm is thought to be a continuation of Chafyn's Farm owned by William Staple in the seventeenth century as its acreage is the same as that owned by T. W. Dyke in 1825-1826, namely seventy-three acres. The exact history of this farm has always been elusive but we can get further in unravelling its story by looking at the 'Nag's Head', just over the Bulford Bridge, in Durrington. Some of the questions to unpick are these? Who owned this third estate? Who were its tenant farmers? How does the 'Nag's Head' fit into the picture? Where was the farmhouse associated with this estate? We are presented with a kaleidoscope of shifting patterns with fragments of information which at times seem to conflict with one another but a picture does emerge from piecing together certain key facts.[1]

The ownership of the 'Nag's Head' and the seventy-three acre farmland in Bulford parish was intimately entwined with land ownership in Durrington. The West Manor of Durrington was bought in 1399 by St Mary's College Winchester and remained in their ownership until into the twentieth century. From 1604 to 1718 the entire West End Manor was leased to the Poore family who also owned leases in the neighbouring

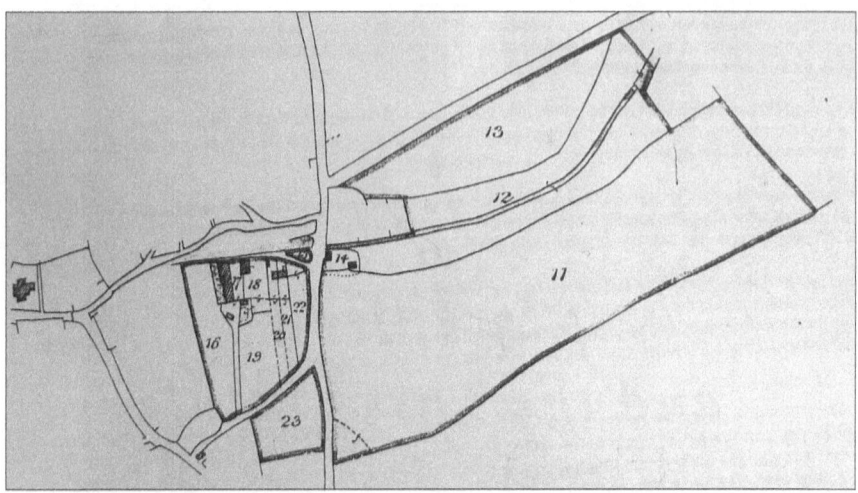

19 *The 'Third Estate'. Property in the village which formed part of the 'third estate' acquired by Anthony Southby in 1871 in an exchange of lands with Charles Rendall of Brigmerston. The Church is shown to the left. 17 and 18 are the farm buildings of Orchard End Farm, with Orchard End House at the top left hand corner of plot 19. 19, 20 and 21 are all orchard. 16 and 22 are pasture and 23 is paddock. 13 is Bourne Field, 12 is pasture and 11 is Steal Pease. (Courtesy of The National Archives)*

East End Manor. As lessees, the Poores granted nearly all the land they controlled by copy to members of their own family. Winchester College sold the leasehold for part of the estate for twenty-one years to the Dean and Chapter of Sarum. The lease was renewable in the usual manner with the lessee empowered to grant the land as copyhold for three lives. Winchester College also directly sold other parts of the estate as copyhold for three lives. The Poores and the Dean and Chapter of Sarum were in dispute, with the former being accused of letting copyholds deliberately fall into disuse by unscrupulous treatment of tenants, and absorbing land into the Manor demense thereby extinguishing the copyhold. The picture that emerges from documentary evidence for Bulford is the century opening with the Poore family in the person of Edward Poore as landlord of the 'Nag's Head' and the seventy-three acre farm associated with it, which in 1832, and again two years later, was described as Dyke's Farm. Edward Poore died in 1838 but his trustees still owned the 'Nag's Head' three years later and in that same year, 1841, Winchester College is recorded as the owner of the 'Mill, Mill Acre meadowland and the Haskett' under the occupation of John Cooe. Although there was a mill in Durrington north-west of the church, the fact

Nag's Head and the Third Estate

that the name of Charles Edward Rendall is recorded in association with this property along with John Cooe points to it being Bulford Mill as we know that he owned property in Bulford in 1871 (see below). The web of leases and copyhold in Durrington, which is a subject beyond this book, clearly extended over Bulford Bridge into the village.²

In 1745 the 'messuage or tenement and Inn commonly called or known by the name or sign of the 'Nag's Head' together with the Barns Stables Backsides Gardens Orchards Outhouses and Appurtenances thereunto belonging' was leased to Thomas Jennings of Durrington, Innkeeper, by Edward Poore of The Close, New Sarum. The lease included fifty-three acres of arable land and three acres of pasture and meadow land in Durrington. A subsequent lease was drawn up with the new tenant, Benjamin Haydon of West Lavington in 1762, which included 'also all those seventy-seven acres of arable land meadows and pasture ground hereunto belonging now in the possession of John Andrews' which he now rents from Edward Poore. This was the land in Bulford, that remained under the ownership of Salisbury landlords for at least another ninety years. It was leased in conjunction with the 'Nag's Head' which was occupied in 1790 by James Rose (whom we have seen being paid to look after the Manor's fields in 1801) and the registration of places of Nonconformist worship shows that he was still a property owner in 1805. Although situated in Durrington, the 'Nag's Head' was very much part of Bulford Village with *Kelly's Directory* including it in the village. The 'Nag's Head' was a public house from at least 1731 and continued as such until between 1885 and 1889. It was situated in an old farm house but it is certain that the premises had a dual role as public house and farm up to the middle years of the century at least.³

The Poore family, as we have seen, owned extensive lands in the area particularly at Figheldean based on Syrencote House. Another Figheldean gentry family was the Dykes, and it appears that the two families intermarried judging by the name of the 1851 incumbent of Syrencote House, Edward Dyke Poore. He probably followed the convention of the time and took his mother's maiden name as his middle name. In 1804 a seventy-three acre farm in Bulford was owned by William Dyke, through his connections with the Poores, and it remained with the Dyke family as shall be seen until at least 1830, after which date the name of Dyke disappears from the village records. In all probability the family had been associated with the estate from at least 1767 when money was raised so that the incumbent of Bulford

Manor could pay off a £1,300 debt to Mr Dyke. No doubt the Poore penchant for granting copyhold to family members included the Dykes in the extended family. In 1812 William was able to supply beef, veal and mutton to the tenant of Bulford Manor ready for his arrival, indicating that he was actively farming his estate at that date. When he died, aged seventy-four in 1818, he was described in his obituary as 'William Dyke, esq, of Syrencot, Wilts, many years one of his Majesty's Justices of the Peace for that county. He was an active, intelligent, and truly upright man'. It would appear that he had been granted the copyhold and lived at Syrencote House as Edward Poore lived at that time at Rushall. The estate was then passed on to William's son(?) Thomas Webb Dyke who in 1819 was entitled to vote in Bulford as he owned a house in the village, tenanted by Mary Croome, and land in Bulford. The house in question was not the 'Nag's Head' which was still the property of Edward Poore, and in any case was not in the village, but it could have been Orchard End House before the leasehold was bought by William Williams (see below). Thomas Webb Dyke himself lived at Laverstock and was an absentee landlord owing, by 1826, back payment of four years' parish rates. He attended the vestry meeting at Bulford that year, settled his debts of 13s 11½d, and then from 1828 till 1831 served as Vicar's Warden implying perhaps that he had moved into the village which enabled him to play an active part in parish affairs. He had probably moved in by 1825 when it was reported that a George Knight had been committed to gaol for 'stealing a quantity of potatoes, the property of T. W. Dyke Esq. at Bulford'. His son(?) William also became involved, chairing vestry meetings in 1829. The Dykes probably moved into the farmhouse at Orchard End vacated by Mary Croome just prior to May 1825 (see below). Their association with the village ceased between 1831 and 1833 with the passing of ownership of the seventy-three acre farm and the 'Nag's Head' to Richard and John Cooe who by 1838 had leased the farm (and the Inn) to William Bailey. Thomas and Richard Cooe also owned a 490 acre farm in Laverstock in 1838 which could well have been Thomas Webb Dyke's property of 1819, and bought at the same time as the land in Bulford – or more probably inherited. Richard owned a further 106 acres at Salisbury, St Martin which is where the brothers lived.[4]

On 24 April 1833 there was an auction held at the 'George Inn', Amesbury, of land owned by Mr R. Cooe, of Milford near Salisbury, successor to the Poore/Dyke estate. The seventy-three acre farm in Bulford was included in this auction. The new leasehold was to be for twenty-one years and the dates fit what we know of the occupation of the farm. We can be sure that the ownership of the farm changed at this time, ending the Poore association, because the tithe commutation for Bulford in 1838 has William Bailey as tenant of a seventy-three acre farm in Bulford owned by the two bachelor brothers living in Salisbury, Richard and John Cooe. The earlier Electoral Register drawn up in 1833, the year of the auction, has William Bailey with his 'abode' in Durrington called 'Cooe's Farm' (although the 1833-1834 Electoral Register still has the property known as 'Dyke's Farm', but thereafter it is consistently known as 'Cooe's Farm'). He is qualified to vote as he pays a rent of over fifty pounds, which has to include all the seventy-three acres of farm land in Bulford he rented from the Cooes. The Cooes had bought the leasehold auctioned at the George Inn 'for investment' rather than 'occupation' as the advertisement had put it. This Durrington abode described as a farm has to be the 'Nag's Head'. William is described as an innkeeper in the Durrington census of 1841 and the tithe commutation of the same year confirms him as the occupier of the 'Nag's Head', garden and orchard. Seven years later his wife Susan (Susannah) is named as the landlady of the 'Nag's Head' in *Kelly's Directory*. In 1841 William Bailey also paid the parish rate for Steal Pease, owned by the Cooes, which is part of the seventy-three acre farm. In 1851 after William's death, his widow (the landlady) is described in the Durrington census as a farmer of seventy-eight acres, employing five men and two boys. The increased acreage over the seventy-three acres owned by the Cooes in 1838 can be accounted for by the meadow and pasture land connected with the 'Nag's Head' farm, held as copyhold under Winchester College in Durrington, which would not have been included in Bulford's figures. The year before his death William is described in the marriage registers as an 'innkeeper'. Perhaps as he became frailer, he swapped roles with his wife. In 1827, a William Bailey was selling up as tenant of the 'Anchor and Hope' in Winchester Street, Salisbury, 'declining the public business on account of ill health'. If this is the same William Bailey, as is probable, he would have been about thirty-four at the time indicating that he had long standing health problems. He appears to have invested his money for security as the 1870 chapel accounts have an income of five pounds from 'Mr Bailey's charity arising from a quarry, thro Mr Wells, one of the Trustees at the Quarry'. After he died about the age of fifty-seven, his widow continued to run the farm for a further three years until February 1854 when the freehold expired (see below).[5]

The uniting of the 'Nag's Head' with the seventy-three acre Bulford farm as a single economic unit came after a period when there appears to be a linking up of the Bulford lands with the Lower (also called Middle) Farm of the Manor. This latter farm was worked by Thomas Croome until his death in 1825 which coincided within months of the death of Robert Smith who was almost certainly the tenant of the seventy-three acres owned by William Dyke. Robert Smith was People's Warden in 1801, and again from 1804 till 1825, and he was a farmer who bought 100 lambs for £107 from Thomas Croome of Lower Farm in 1820. The names of the tenants of all the other farms in the parish are known, and so Robert Smith must have farmed the Dyke farm. Mary Croome continued to lease and run Lower Farm after her husband's death and also took on the lease of the Dyke's farm for a while for in May 1825 she had to pay Thomas Webb Dyke's £20 7s 6d for 'delapidations to the house, barn, stable' and walls and fences after vacating the premises. In 1829 the church rate that she paid suddenly jumped. Until that point it had been roughly equivalent to that paid for Upper Farm, but it then jumped to nearly twice as much and included the mill, garden and orchard, and it was the same in 1834. What is clear is that she farmed the lands of both Lower Farm and the Dyke's estate, but the picture of where she farmed these from is confused. Thomas Croome's accounts of 1820 show that he sold lambs and ewes in September with the 'mark of Mrs Croomes of Bulford' on them. This would suggest that she actively farmed her late husband's estate, probably with her brother-in-law, described in 1824 as a 'corn-dealer', but there was a separation in their businesses. In 1825 Mary's daughter Ann had married Joseph Robbins, son of John Robbins of Upper Farm, and she could have taken on the lease vacated by Robert Smith's death for her daughter and son-in-law to farm. In 1829 he was living in a house and garden in the village, paying the parish rate. He had status as a tenant farmer and was proposed for the position of churchwarden two years later, but he was 'not seconded it appearing that Mr Joseph Robbins not being an inhabitant [of Bulford parish] was not rated to the last poor rate and consequently not elected'. Perhaps he at the time was living at the 'Nag's Head' farm in the next parish. By 1838 he had taken over and moved into Lower Farm. We have already noticed that Thomas's widow Mary Croome was the tenant of a house with land leased from Thomas Webb Dyke In 1819. Was this Orchard End House? [6]

20 Orchard End. Orchard End House (FIg. 3 no.58) Owned by the Dykes, lived in by Mary Croome and Godwin before becoming the farmhouse inhabited by Henry Pearce. In 1872 it became the vicarage. (photograph by permission of Jonathan Stone)

Orchard End

THIS BRINGS US to next part of the jigsaw, Orchard End House itself, which by 1851 had become the farm house associated with the seventy-three acre farm, but at the beginning of the century there was no such connection. The 1838 tithe map shows that the ownership of the buildings of Orchard End with its gardens and orchard was divided equally between John and William Williams with both in occupation. The freehold was owned in 1839 by John Williams who perhaps had bought the copyhold from the Dykes when they left the village explaining the poll book entry of 1819 noted above. John had moved out by 1839 and with his wife Elizabeth (née Gilbert) was living in one of two leasehold houses in the High Street owned by the Durrington blacksmith James Toomer (see 1880 map, and *Figure 2, no.9, 10 or 11*). Orchard End at that time was occupied by his tenant Henry Godwin, the papermaker. John Williams' will left his widow the freehold of a house 'with gardens thereto belonging at the back and front now in the occupation of Henry Godwin'. On her death (or remarriage) this property was to pass to his nephew William Williams' son John. The property also included an orchard which John gave separately to his nephew's son another John Williams. This property was Orchard End House with its orchard on which Mr Williams paid the parish rate in 1829. After John's death in 1839, his widow Elizabeth paid the rate for the 'Orchard End' orchard whilst continuing to live in the High Street as provided for by her late husband's will. By 1841 she had moved into Orchard End with her High Street house being occupied by James Toomer (*Figure 2, no.9, 10 or 11*).[7]

The years 1851 to 1855 were key dates in piecing together both the histories of the seventy-three acre 'Nag's Head' farm and Orchard End House. The last reference of Susanna Bailey at the 'Nag's Head' farm is in 1854, and 1851 has both Cooe brothers absent from any census returns. They would have been seventy-two and seventy-three years old and presumably had died bringing their ownership of part of Bulford to an end. 1855 has Henry Pearce as the new farmer and he lived in Orchard End House, marrying his daughter Thyra from there to Thomas Draper, a yeoman farmer in Netheravon (1856). 1854 was the expiry date of the leasehold of the seventy-three acre farm auctioned at the 'George Inn', Amesbury, twenty-one years earlier. There was also a sale in February of that year of 'the whole of the LIVE AND DEAD FARMING STOCK and other effects of Mrs Susanna Bailey, who is relinquishing agricultural pursuits' now that her lease had expired. Henry Pearce was no doubt the new tenant of the seventy-three acres, but there is no evidence to show that he was also associated with the 'Nag's Head'. This would suggest that the 'Nag's Head' became detached from the farmland in Bulford, requiring a new farmhouse to be found – Orchard End. Whether or not he held the farm as freehold or leasehold is unknown but circumstantial evidence would suggest that Charles Edward Rendall had bought the freehold after Elizabeth Williams had died sometime after 1841. As he owned the whole estate, including Orchard End House, in 1871, this would have made Henry Pearce a leaseholder.[8]

Light is shown on the ownership of this part of Bulford by a case heard by the Vice-Chancellor at the Court of Chancery, and an appeal against its ruling heard on 27 July 1852 by the Lord Chancellor. The case was brought by Thomas Webb Dyke's widow Elizabeth against a Mr Rendall, presumably Charles Edward. When the Dykes were married in 1810, Elizabeth gave up her right of dower on 'an estate situate in Bulford' owned by her husband in a settlement by which her husband agreed to set up a 'bond for payment of 2,000 l. [£] and interest within six months after marriage [which was] to pay the interest after the death of her husband to Mrs Dyke and her assigns during her life, with the remainder to her children'. Thomas Webb Dyke was unreliable when it came to financial affairs as we have seen with his failure to pay the parish rate, and so it comes as no surprise that he failed to set up the bond which, it was argued meant that his widow therefore still had the right of dower against the estate which had 'since his death become vested in the defence [Rendall] by purchase'. She won her case but Rendall appealed against the judgement and the decision was overturned as it was not Rendall's fault that Mrs Dyke's husband had 'failed in performing his covenant'. What this case reveals is that by 1852, if not earlier, Charles Edward Rendall had purchased the estate which had previously been owned by Thomas Webb Dyke. The Cooes had almost certainly bought the estate prior to its purchase by Charles Edward Rendall, but the case was brought against him as the owner at the time of the court action. He owned Orchard End by the time of the exchange of lands in 1871, and so at some point he had also acquired the house from the Williams family and by 1855 it was tenanted by Henry Pearce.[9]

Henry Pearce was brought up on his father's farm at Enford with two sisters, the elder of whom, Meliora, was the parochial schoolmistress. In 1851 Henry was described as a grocer before he moved to Bulford and married Londoner Emily Adlard at Islington in April 1856. The public notice decribes him as living in Bulford. They brought up their young family at Orchard End with the help of two servants. Their fourth child George was born in the village in 1862 but their fifth was born in Hampshire in 1864 so it is between these dates that Henry Pearce left Bulford. Soon after leaving, Henry was widowed and moved to the London area where he worked (1871) as a carpet salesman. 1859 Henry Pearce had served his term as churchwarden and the 1861 census showed that he had expanded the farm to 100 acres, employing three men and a boy. It is likely that he was succeeded by James Hayden (perhaps related to Benjamin Haydon and Robert Hayden mentioned earlier) who married Jane Jenkins at Bulford in 1864, recorded as a farmer, and he is again recorded as a farmer at Bulford the following year. He was a Durrington man who had been a farm bailiff at Chute and it is likely that he was running the farm for its new owner who is recorded in 1871 as Charles Rendall. Orchard End farm finally ended its days as an independent economic unit in 1871 with the Lord of the Manor Anthony Southby acquiring it, thereby consolidating the village in his Lordship, in exchange for a strip of land along the northern boundary of the parish with the parish of Milston, consisting of meadows either side of the Avon and fields extending eastwards on to the downs. The owner of Orchard End farm at that time was Charles Edward Rendall of Brigmerston. As the century was drawing to a close the land along the northern edge of the parish was still owned by the Rendall family after Charles Edward's death in 1872. Rachel Frances Rendall, wife of Shuttleworth Rendall of Brigmerston, owned the deeds when the land was sold to the Secretary of State for War, having changed her name to Pinkney in 1877.[10]

Exchange of lands and the wider picture

THE 1871 LAND exchange documents include maps of the farm estate. They show Orchard End House and two adjoining cottages, a farmyard attached opening on to orchards and pasture. Over the Orchard Way, in an area which remained unbuilt upon until the 1970s, was the Paddock. The other side of the Salisbury Road were two tenements and fields extending down either side of Nine Mile River: Bourne Field next to Bourne Road, and Meadows either side of the river, and a larger field to the south called Steal Pease (where the late 1960s estate was built). There was another detached field called Moore's Leaze further up the river towards Sheep Bridge. Detached again, to the east are two fields of down arable either side of the Salisbury Road and a small field barn. Unless there were arrangements with his larger neighbours, it is unlikely that the farm had many sheep as access to open downland had been denied. Access to common pastures, when they existed, was important as Thomas Jennings' 1745 lease of the 'Nag's Head' farm makes clear as it included rights to 'ways paths passages easements' giving access to 'all commons and common pasture' in Durrington. The purchasing of a hundred lambs by Thomas Smith in 1820 would indicate that he enjoyed the access to common pastures guaranteed by the 1745 lease, but the transfer of the farm from the 'Nag's Head' to Orchard End meant this access to the Durrington pastures was now denied making the farm less of a viable unit. It is perhaps significant in the exchange of lands in 1871 that the then owner of the farm swapped it for lands which contained the full range of fields <u>and</u> downland, and at a time when sheep were fast becoming a more important part of the local farming economy. In many ways the farm's survival through the changes brought about by enclosure and consolidation of small farms into larger, more efficient units, only delayed the inevitable. Without common pastures, the farm was ultimately doomed. The list of items to be sold by Mrs Susanna Bailey when she left the farm hardly paints a picture of a flourishing farm. The most prominent lot was a 'Team of three valuable young cart horses' along with a dairy cow and a calf, and '2 fine sow pigs in farrow'. The only machinery for sale were a small wagon and spring cart, three dung carts, a two wheeled land presser and various small items of equipment. The farm was hardly a thriving concern although there are plans for a new barn of six bays with the leases of the 'Nag's Head'. It is perhaps significant that the remodelling of Orchard End's windows and the building of a cob wall around the garden were done in the early years of the century, probably by the Dykes before it assumed the role of farmhouse under Henry Pearce. Even at the end of the century it was judged to be 'an impressive house', though much neglected by then.[11]

This portrait of the Bulford estates and tenant farmers, excluding the Seymour estate which was the subject of the previous chapter, needs to be put into context with an overview of trends at the time. Thomas Davis wrote his *Report of the state of agriculture in the County of Wilts* in the early years of the nineteenth century and the section on South Wiltshire provides a general picture of the agrarian communities in the region.

> The common Meadows of which the greatest part are watered immediately adjoin the river; the houses are small enclosures as near to it as possible. Next follows the arable, until the land becomes too steep or too thin to plough, and then the sheep and cow downs, and frequently the woods at the extremity of the manor, and adjoining the downs or woods of the adjoining manor.

This is an accurate reflection of Bulford except that the common meadows no longer existed. It was a period of agricultural change and Thomas Davis felt that his report or enquiry was 'particularly necessary at a time when a great part of South Wiltshire is emerging into a new system, by the extinction of lifehold tenures, and the abolition of common-field husbandry'. He argued the need for farms to be consolidated into larger units in full control of their fields and downland pasture through enclosures to allow necessary agricultural improvements. It must be remembered that this happened against the background of an agricultural depression. The Lord of the Manor who died in 1757, Richard Duke, concurred with Thomas Davis' views and was ahead of the game. He directed his successors not to renew the tenancies of leaseholds and copyholds for lives when they ended, but to absorb the lands into the Upper and Hindurrington Farms, both in his demesne. In 1744 there were sixteen separate farms in Bulford, the farmsteads crowding the village and the houses in Water Street are thought to be the remnants of some of these, as we have already noted.[12]

One of the farmers who were squeezed out was undoubtedly John Grist who describes himself as a yeoman of the parish of Bulford in his 1797 will bequeathing his remaining estate to his niece Jane Castleman, and should she die first, then to his brother James Grist. John died in 1799 and Jane inherited her uncle's property, paying the parish rate for the house and garden valued at £4 13s 4d from 1801 until 1829. She was sole executrix of the estate and appears to have passed on ownership of the property to John's brother James (probably her father) who in the 1818 and 1819 Poll Books had a vote in Bulford as he was the freeholder rated for Land Tax on the property occupied by Jane Castleman, although he lived in Buckinghamshire. Jane died in 1832 leaving no heir as she was a spinster. A slightly higher valued rate than that of 1829 was paid in 1841 by James Jarman for a cottage and garden in the High Street and he may well have been the new owner of the property. The property in question is probably the present 41 and 43 High Street (*Figure 2, no.23*) which were originally a single house built in 1769 as a farmhouse for John Gast. The documentation supporting this, such as the 1781 will of John Gast, were copied documents and Grist and Gast looked very similar in the script of the time. The Grist family had been in the village since the seventeenth century.[13]

7
The Agricultural Heartbeat of Village Life

Climatic influences

EVERY PERIOD OF history is a time of transition and the nineteenth century was no exception. The focus of this chapter is agriculture, the industry and way of life that underpinned village life, and indeed was the reason for the village's existence. At the start of the century, the country was emerging from the agricultural revolution and coming to terms with its consequences. The end of the century saw a rural economy cushioned from crop failures and famine by international trade and a revolution in transport which enabled produce to be moved quickly and over vast distances. In an even wider context these changes were set against fluctuations in climate. The lives of tenant farmers were, like all villagers in an agricultural community, governed by the weather and seasons which drove the agrarian economy. There was a time to plough, to sow and to reap; a time for lambing and market; a time for haymaking and rick building. These were the imperatives which were the reality of village life.

The eighteenth century experienced the depths of the Little Ice Age with a growing season five weeks shorter than at the turn of the twentieth century, due to a generally cooler climate. This helps to explain the imperative placed by farmers to lengthen the growing season at either end by crop improvement and by the technological innovation of the water meadow. The remarkable transformations in English agriculture came during a century of a changeable, often cool climate, interspersed with unexpected heat waves. As farms grew larger and more intensive cultivation spread over Southern and Central Britain, famine episodes gave way to periodic food dearths, where more deaths came from infectious diseases due to malnutrition and poor sanitation than from hunger. Villagers were less vulnerable to climate-triggered crop failure, even during sudden climate swings. Agriculture had diversified so that failure of one crop could be compensated by other crops doing better. William Cobbett observed, for example in August 1826, that in the Avon Valley early turnips had nearly all failed but Swedish turnips were doing well, oats and pulses had failed but the rickyards showed that overall the corn harvest was very good, especially wheat, potatoes looked well enough and this year trees were well-loaded with fruit.[1]

The Little Ice-Age, which lasted until about 1850, was characterised by cold winters and sudden heat waves. William Cobbett, for example, said of 30 August 1826 that, 'Today has been exceedingly hot. Hotter, I think, for a short time than I have ever felt in England before'. 1805 till 1820 were cold years with white Christmases common after 1812, and these were years when there were at least three major volcanic eruptions that lowered temperatures through volcanic dust in the stratosphere. 1816 was a catastrophic year, a year without a summer, a year of abnormally low temperatures and heavy rain. *The Times* reported on 20 July that 'should the present weather continue, the corn will inevitably be laid and the effects of such a calamity and at such a time cannot be otherwise than ruinous to farmers, and even to the people at large'. This was indeed the case. The wheat yields that year were the lowest between 1815 and 1857, grain prices rose rapidly, employment opportunities shrank, and there were typhus and relapsing fever epidemics. These were the years, as has been noted in Chapter 1, that infant mortality was high in Bulford and acted as a trigger for the religious revival; typhus may well have been to blame for children's deaths. The middle years of the century saw the climate generally warm. 1868 was exceptionally hot with many days over thirty degrees centigrade and a record high of thirty-eight degrees was recorded at Tunbridge Wells on 22 July. The following winter was very mild and warmer years followed during the 1870s except for the occasional cold Februarys and very wet summers from 1875 onwards. 1879 saw another cold snap with weeks of below freezing temperatures, and January 1881 was also exceptionally cold. 'Terrific snow storm, intense cold' and 'severe frost' were recorded at Amesbury and the roads were blocked 'and communication with adjoining villages extremely difficult'. The cold spring in 1880 was followed by one of the wettest, coldest summers ever recorded, triggering two years of poor corn yields. This coincided with a time of general agricultural decline when British markets were flooded by cheap North American wheat from the Prairies, tipping the rural economy into a full grown agricultural depression the effects of which can be seen in the price of wheat. In 1847 it was selling at seventy shillings a quarter, falling to forty-six in 1870, and then to twenty-four in 1896. This drastic drop in prices hit hardest the farmers on the chalklands of Hampshire, Wiltshire and Dorset. 1895 then sees the beginning of fifty years of climatic warming which takes us out of the nineteenth century.[2]

Cycles of the farming year

CHANGING WEATHER CONDITIONS impacted on the lives of villagers in a way unimaginable today; they lived closer to nature and were at the mercy of the elements all the time. It is against this background that the farming cycle unfolded year on year. Within the farming calendar, there were several interlocking cycles to manage. There was that of the water meadows and that of rearing sheep both of which were subservient to the cycle of growing crops. The main crop of the village in terms of acreage was barley (although wheat came a close second and in fact superseded it in 1876) and this had to be sown by the beginning of May. The old Wiltshire proverb went, 'barley will do if it have a *May* dew'. This put pressure on the whole agricultural system as the fields had to be ploughed and manured ready for sowing by then. This meant in turn that the sheep needed to be ready to manure the fields and their ability to do this depended on an early crop of meadow grass to feed them. The key to this was the water meadows. The 'drowner' who managed the water meadows, spent the autumn repairing any damage to the drains, ditches, banks and hatches and 'making all necessary reparation and amendments whatsoever' ready for the first heavy rains of the autumn. All the 'thick and good' accumulated muck on the roads, tracks and fields was washed down to settle on, and enrich the meadows. The hatches were opened to flood the meadows for a period of two or three weeks and then closed again for two or three days to allow the ground to dry out between soakings. This 'first soaking is to make the land sink and pitch close together; a circumstance of great consequence, not only to the quantity, but to the quality of grass and particularly to encourage the shooting of new roots which the grass is continually forming to support the forced growth above.' The fundamental rule was 'to make the meadows as dry as possible after every watering; and to take the water off as soon as any scum appears upon the land which shows it has already had enough' water. Water was allowed back over the meadows as soon as growth began to flag. The drowner's work was skilled. In general water was allowed to cover the meadows for about three weeks in November and December, and two weeks in February and March. 'A water meadow is a hot bed for grass' and the flowing water protected the early shoots from frosts. Its 'value ... is almost beyond computation' because it meant that the meadows were ready for the ewes and lambs as soon as they could travel from their winter pennings down to the water meadows, about mid-March. It also helped with the challenge of feed for sheep early in the year, enabling larger flocks to be overwintered and thereby improving fertilisation of the arable land. The real profit from investment in water meadows emerged in the improvement of corn crops. It was reckoned at the turn of the century that the yearly expense of managing water meadows if the hatches were well maintained was about seven shillings an acre.[3]

When the ewes and lambs used the first crop of grass on the water meadows, they were brought down to feed from about ten or eleven o'clock in the morning, and then at about four or five in the afternoon they were driven up to the newly ploughed fields to be penned overnight and manure the land – the primary purpose of keeping sheep.

> 'Five hundred ewes with their lambs, will fold a tenantry acre [(about ¾ of a statutory acre)] well in one night; and none but those who have seen this kind of husbandry can form a just idea of the value of ewes and lambs coming immediately on the fallow land with their bellies full of quick young grass, from a good water meadow, and particularly how much it will increase the quantity of the barley crop. The increase may be fairly stated as a quarter of barley per acre'

Whilst the ewes and lambs were feeding, the hurdles of the temporary penning had to be moved for a fresh part of the field to be manured each night. Farms needed a good supply of hurdles; Watergate Farm, for example had 160 dozen wooden hurdles and fifty-five iron ones in 1872. A 1793 report stated that, in general the size of the hurdle is about four feet six inches long and three feet six inches high, made chiefly of hazel, with ten upright sticks, and fifteen dozen of them, with a like number of stakes and wriths, to confine them together, will inclose a statute acre of ground, and will contain twelve to thirteen hundred sheep therein very commodiously.

The laborious process of moving the temporary penning lasted on average from 15 March to the 25 April, allowing the fields to be sown in time for the 'May dew'. By then, the meadow grass was eaten, and 'the summer field (especially if it be sown with ray grass) is ready to receive the sheep'. The water meadows were flooded if necessary for a couple of days in April and May to bring on a second crop of grass to be turned into hay after about a six week period, which was enough in June 1872 to make four ricks of 'water meadow hay' on Watergate Farm. The sheep stayed in their summer pastures on the downs until shearing time and then the rams were put to the ewes in about mid-September. During the summer months, the sheep were still penned at night on any newly ploughed, or recently sown arable land to improve fertility and consolidate the soil. The farmer's next concern was to get his flocks through the winter when food was scarce and the sheep had to 'dig for the wither'd herb through heaps of snow' unless they are brought down from the downs to the pennings for shelter and winter feeding. An eighteenth century poet exhorted the shepherds, 'to your helpless charge be kind, baffle the raging year, and fill their pens with food at will; lodge them below the storm, and watch them strict'. The work of the shepherds was constant, day and night. They lived with their sheep and away from home in a 'shepherds house on four wheel carriage' (1872) which could be trundled across the downs and fields to keep up with the sheep. The critical time of year was the lambing season in April and May and these were the months when George Peck's Sunday absences were regularly recorded at the chapel for 'shepherding'.[4]

The Pennings in Bulford were sited in sheltered spots where the sheep could overwinter and be cared for and 'covered lamb troughs' were there for early lambing. The flocks had to be reduced first before the winter with the old ewes and wether lambs (castrated males) being sold off at markets about Michaelmas (29 September). Lower Farm, for instance sold a hundred at the beginning of October 1820. The reduced flock was wintered, feeding off the barley stubble, and when that was exhausted, eating turnips, especially

Swedish turnips, which William Cobbett noticed were prevalent in the Avon Valley when he rode down in August. We know Swedish turnips, and indigenous turnips were grown in equal amounts on Lower Farm in the 1820s judging by the sale of seed when the farming assets were sold, but the former, as the name implies, could tolerate colder temperatures which extended the growing season, making it more useful as winter fodder. There is also a list of other seeds used for sowing the pastures: ray seed, Dutch clover, broad clover, hop seed and black and white seed. Hop and ray grass was what was termed 'artificial grass' to be sown on the summer pasture. It was ready for sheep to graze earlier than native grasses and is again an indication of how important it was to get any early start to facilitate early planting of crops. Thomas Seymour stipulated in the 1801 lease of Watergate Farm that 'into every acre ... two bushels of good Hop and Ray grass seed was to be sown with the Lenten crop of barley on the old arable land' to establish pasture when the field was left fallow the next year prior to change of tenant. The new tenant could then use any seeds 'Broad Clover in and with the Barley excepted'. This then was the routine of preparing the arable fields which was common practice in the Wiltshire downlands. Details have survived of payments by the Lady of the Manor for work on the Hams in 1801. Ploughing was costed at fourteen shillings an acre, with an extra four shillings for sowing and harrowing. Horses for the work were costed at six pence a day.[5]

    There were extensive water meadows on Watergate Farm with field names such as 'Long Mead', 'Dancing Mead', 'Picked Mead', 'Little Mead' and 'Hatch Plot'. This last was next to the Hatch House which spanned the river where the Great Hatches which controlled the flooding of the meadow were situated. As has already been noted, Henry Seymour made provision against the first year's rent to improve the water meadows. There were also extensive water meadows north of Bulford Mill on the Manor demesne, constructed in the seventeenth century; these were all on Upper Farm – Lower Farm had none. There were also limited fields either side of Nine Mile River which the Orchard End farm no doubt used as water meadows, certainly as pasture. In 1871 these became absorbed in to Lower Farm and might well have been an incentive for Anthony Southby to agree to the exchange of lands which brought this about. Matthew Devenish's lease stipulated that sheep be penned and folded on the summer fallow from 12 May, that is once the barley had been sown in time for the 'May dew', and that the sheep 'shall be driven to some Fair and Fairs' and sold between 21 September and the 10 October (this was extended to run from 10 September in 1841). We have already seen evidence of Thomas Croome visiting the Andover Fair, and no doubt this was common for all the farmers of the parish.[6]

Livestock

IT IS IMPOSSIBLE to give accurate numbers for sheep in the parish during the first half of the century but some idea can be gathered from various sources. The first is the accounts of Thomas Croome who in late summer and autumn of 1820, for example, sold 926 lambs, 727 ewes, 100 wethers and 60 nondescript sheep. One hundred of these lambs were sold to a Mr Smith of Bulford. This totals over 1,800 sheep that he shed to keep his over wintering flock to a viable size. Interestingly, though, he bought over 3,200 sheep prior to that in July and August indicating that he could not sustain all year round the number of sheep that he needed to manure his crops, a consequence maybe of not having water meadows on his farm (see Chapter 4). The second source is the tithe valuation for Watergate Farm in 1838 revealing that Francis Stephen Long kept 1,100 ewes, 900 lambs and 400 tups, a total of 2,400 sheep. Summer sheep stock for the whole parish could well have approached 5,000 sheep in the early years of the century. By 1872 the Watergate Farm flock had reduced sixteen per cent to 2,016, including eleven rams. There were between 300 and 350 each year of ewes aged between one and three, and a further 317 old ewes ready for sale. They produced 299 chilver lambs (females) to be kept for breeding and 370 wether lambs (castrated males) ready for market. These figures enable us to see the structure of a farmer's flock. Two thirds of the flock were ewes, three quarters of which were in prime breeding condition (two, four and six teethed) producing double their number of lambs each year (a third of the flock), and the remaining quarter were the four year old ewes past their prime ready to be sold at the autumn fairs along with the wether lambs. The chilver lambs (female) were overwintered and kept to join the breeding stock the following year as two teethed ewes. Each year a third of the flock, wether lambs and four year old ewes, were sold off leaving two thirds to be over wintered in the pennings. It is safe to double the number of sheep on Watergate Farm to give a conservative estimate of sheep numbers in the parish. In 1883 the tenant of Lower Farm's lease obliged him to keep either

700 dry sheep or 500 ewes with lambs, and when the Upper and Lower Farms were combined in 1895, these figures had risen to 1100 or 1000 respectively. The 1820 Lower Farm figures could indicate the changing of its flock's genetic makeup with the breeding of Merino or 'Spanish sheep' which is considered below. Numbers of sheep on the downs were about 3,000 in 1867, rising to about 4,500 in 1886 which would have been about thirteen sheep for every inhabitant of the village. Numbers peaked at about 4,700 in 1896, before dramatically decreasing as the military took over more and more of the down land for the Camp – in 1906 there were only about 1,600 sheep left on the downs.[7]

Arable

ARABLE FARMING WAS the mainstay of village agriculture, with barley and wheat being the main crops. 'The climate, and a considerable portion of the soil (the flinty loams) [being] particularly favourable to the growth and the quality of this grain, and the water meadow and sheep fold system are well adapted to its cultivation.' Of the three main elements of the farms, downs, arable and meadows, arable had the greatest area. In 1838, 54 per cent of Watergate Farm was arable field, the Upper Farm was 58 per cent and Lower Farm 48 per cent. The total arable was 1,836 acres, being 53 per cent of the total area of the parish. As the century wore on, changes in farming reduced this proportion, with about a third of the parish being arable land in 1867. The decline in the agricultural workforce between 1851 and 1861 has already been noted and this reflects the decline of the arable, the most labour intensive part of farming. This does not automatically mean that the yield of the land dropped as a consequence; the growth of chemical fertiliser usage, seed improvement and mechanisation, combined to make farming more efficient and productive. There was, for example, an advertisement in 1878 for 'a labourer to drive a steam threshing machine' in nearby Figheldean. And it was these same developments that saw water meadows generally go into decline at the end of the century although Upper Farm was still paying its Water Rights Rent for its water meadows in 1893. Artificial fertilizers and the increased use of machinery to consolidate the land usurped the crucial role of the flock. Sheep were now kept for the quality of their wool and meat, and the increase in dairy farming in response to cheap grain imports made demands on pasture land. Skilled

The Agricultural Heartbeat of Village Life

labour to maintain and operate the water meadows was expensive and these tasks could not be mechanised. All these were factors in the demise of water meadows so that in the early twentieth century Frank Sawyer could write,

> the irrigation system is a thing of the past – an almost forgotten art ... everywhere is a scene of neglect. The carriers, which in by-gone years brought life-giving water to the meadow vegetation, are now dried up ditches - drains have been trodden flat with countless hooves of cattle. Bridges, arches and bunny holes have all collapsed, hatches lie rotting by their structures, or are suspended high and dry in their sockets, while the crumbling wingings of wood and brickwork of the hatchways now rest amongst dried mud and other rubbish ... .[8]

The 1801 lease for Watergate Farm gives a detailed insight in to how the arable fields were managed, and the approach was no doubt consistent across all the farms. An article written in 1913 about Allan G. Young who owned a farm based on Watergate House, gives a retrospective insight into some of the changes that occurred as the century progressed which will be looked at in due course. The best arable land was the lowest dry land near the river and farm buildings. These were 'the three enclosures commonly called the Hamms or Hitchland Fields': the two Lower Ham fields separated from the water meadows by a narrow strip of dry pasture, and the Home Ham field next to the farmyard on the village side. Hitchland, also known as Hookland was originally part of the open fields too good to lie fallow in the four year crop rotation cycle which, as Thomas Davis puts it, is a waste of land

> too good to lie still for two years; instead, therefore, of sowing the whole of the barley field with clover, they have reserved one third, or one fourth of it for vetches, peas, beans; and of late years for potatoes ... but taking care to have it ready to come in course with the rest of the field for wheat. This part of the field is called *hookland* or *hitchland* field.

Their location was the best place for wheat and during the take-over period at the end of the term of the lease, the outgoing tenant could take three loads of wheatstraw but had to leave enough for thatching. He could also take 'pease or vetches' from 'thirty acres of the old arable land and ten acres of the Hamms' by 20 September by which time the acres concerned were ready to be sown with wheat. The expectation was to sow the lowest and strongest land with wheat every third year. 'Peas and beans [were] only grown in small quantities in the hookland [hitchland] fields'; (in 1876 there were only ten acres of beans and eight of peas in the entire parish). The Seymours laid a further stipulation in 1841 that 'at no time during the said term less than a third part' was to be 'in artificial grass or green feeding crop' emphasising the importance of this area for feeding livestock. Hitchland was not restricted to Watergate Farm as the 1830 inventory of Lower Farm shows with a 'tub of hitch quality rudder' itemised. The snapshots of farm crops in the Board of Agriculture's returns show turnips and swedes to be the main root crops, increasing from about 300 acres in 1867, to about 400 acres over the next thirty years, with mangold adding a further 30 plus acres at the end of the century.[9]

The majority of arable land on Wiltshire downland farms followed a four field system with a cycle of wheat, followed by barley with clover, followed by clover on its own which was mown for feed, and in the fourth year of the cycle this was ploughed up ready for the wheat again. The 1801 lease stipulated that all the arable was to be divided, except the 'Hamms or Hitchland fields and such part the said arable land as was formerly burnbeaked as near as maybe into four equal parts or fields each of which ... shall be together and be in one intire piece of ground'. The tenant, in each of the last four years of his term, 'was to sow a fourth part of the said arable with grass seed till the whole shall successively in a proper method of four fields be laid down to grass and so that two fourth parts shall during the last four years of the term ... alternatively rest unploughed and be sown down to grass as aforesaid and in the third year ... .' The next tenant could use any pasture seed, except broad clover in with the barley. The variation on Thomas Davis's ideal was to grow oats and barley as opposed to wheat and barley. Sowing wheat, after a field had been put down to vetches, was 'generally ... immediately after the first rains in September' but a second fall of rain was desirable. The soil needs to be left to settle after ploughing to 'get as close as possible before sowing'. If sowing happens too soon, grubs and wireworm are likely to eat the seeds. Lower Farm followed suit growing barley, oats and wheat and leases of Upper Farm, then of Upper and Lower Farms as a single unit, make it clear that the 'usual course of good husbandry as practised in the neighbourhood' applied across the parish. The 1895 lease stipulated that the tenant was 'not to crop more than a moiety [half] of the field arable (after deducting sound sainfoin) in any one year to white corn or pulse, or to have more than two white straw crops in succession' – this was a four year rotation. The Directories variously stated that 'the chief crops are wheat, barley and oats,' and this is borne out by the Board of Agriculture surveys.[10]

The poorest soil for growing crops was the high downland. It could be used as arable but 'pulverising by repeated summer ploughing [of] land in high exposed situations, whose principle fault was that of already being too thin' destroyed its fertility. It was marginal arable land and these were the lands that were 'burnbeaked' on the Seymour estate during the Napoleonic Wars. These lands, the black lands due to the burning process, when over exploited had reduced in value '(after the heat of the fire had been exhausted) by two or three crops, to a mere bed of dust, without tenacity or cohesion, and thereby rendered by a series of years totally unfit for vegetation, corn or grass'. It was land that was hard to manage and, if for example, it was sown at the time of ploughing it became vulnerable to weeds, especially poppies, choking the wheat, and if ploughed fields were subject to strong March winds, particularly after a frost, the wheat would be "hung by one leg" or 'knee sick', yielding little grain. To give this thin, high, exposed soil the capacity to grow a satisfactory crop, it had to be farmed on a six year cycle. The 1801 lease stipulated that the tenant was, in the last six years of his term, to divide all burnbeaked arable into six contiguous parts and each year to sow one of the six parts with 'a good and sufficient quantity of grass seed till five fields be sown down to grass', making sure that the seed was harrowed 'in a good husbandlike manner'. The 1841 stipulation was that at least half of the arable land was in grass and that 'cornpease pulse or vetches standing to seed', crops of increasing importance, should not at any time exceed fifty per cent of the acreage. In the district generally oats were 'seldom sown in large quantities except in such soils and situations as are not applicable to barley, particularly in the black light soils of new broke downs'. The Seymour lease talks of sowing oats or barley and Lower Farm kept stocks of oat seed equal in value to barley seed, and this was a farm where no down land was burnbeaked during the wars. A noticeable feature of the 1841 Seymour lease is that in many ways it is less prescriptive than the one thirty years earlier. All the constraints on the four year cycle for arable land were replaced by the simple statement of an obligation to 'manure and cultivate the arable land'. Thomas Davis had highlighted the trap that many landlords fell into of being too prescriptive in agricultural requirements which stifled the tenant farmer from adopting improved practices which would lead to increased profitability of the farm. It appears that the Seymours avoided this trap and the little evidence there is points to a positive encouragement for improvements with the reconfiguration of the farm buildings being actively pursued as we saw in the previous chapter.[11]

In 1872 Seymour Farm was valued at £10,280 16s 7d and the inventory supporting this figure gives a snapshot of the farm in June of that year. There were fields of barley, wheat, oats, rye and peas in that order of value. A twelve acre wheat field was ploughed and dunged, part harrowed and rolled ready for cereal sowing. A field for swedes was 'water drilled, couched' and seeded as was a field for turnips. Wheat fields and turnip fields were 'raftered and harrowed', that is ploughed in furrows wide enough apart for the turned sod to be upended between the furrows, and then harrowed. There were also fields of rape, mangold and vetches (which followed after turnips). Vetches were cut up to feed the horses and there were fields of meadow grass. Fields on the Down and Salisbury Hill were being put down to grass with rye grass being sown. The root crops were growing on the Down, Beech Bottom, Salisbury Hill, Twenty Ridges and in the Hams. Turnips were grown as feed for the sheep, those in Beech Bottom by Nine Mile River, for example, were sown in 1870 and had been fed off by the sheep. There were stocks of clover seed. June was a time when the growing season was in full swing and bills were presented for hoeing and beer for the labourers. The picture of the farm was one geared to growing cereals for sale at market. Sheep were vital for this so fields had to be set aside for feed, both root crops and meadow, and feed was grown for the working animals, nineteen cart horses and nine 'working oxen'. Dairying was non-existent other than for local domestic use, there being only three dairy cows. On the other hand there were forty piglets being kept, the offspring of a boar and five sows, again for local domestic consumption. A survey of Upper Farm in September 1893 by the landlord James Ledger Hill as part of the negotiations for the valuation for a new tenant, gives a similar picture of the importance of root and fodder crops. There were thirty-one acres of swedes, fifty-six of rape and turnips, and forty-four of sainfoin. He observed that 'the root crops are <u>very</u> healthy they only require a ram to make them go ahead' and valued 'the whole of the Stock, Crops, Tillages and Implements' at £3,000.[12]

Sainfoin is a deep rooted perennial legume which grows well on calcareous soil too dry or too barren for clover; these were chalk, marl and limestone soils. Chalk outcrops occurred throughout the parish and field names on Watergate Farm bear testimony to calcareous soils: 'Chalk Pit Furlong' and 'Marble Stone Furlong'. Sainfoin is highly palatable to sheep and cattle and 'Its herbage is said to be equally suited for pasturage or for hay' and consequently was mixed in with hay for feed. Watergate Farm had two ricks of sainfoin hay in 1872 and a sainfoin shogger as we have already noted. Unlike other crops, sainfoin was a long term undertaking which 'usually attained its perfect growth in about three years, and begins to decline towards the eight to tenth on calcareous soils'. Upper and Lower Farms had a stipulation in their joint 1895 lease that they were to have in the last year of a term, forty acres of 'sainfoin roots which shall not have been cut more than four times' and not 'to sow more than one sixth of arable lands to sainfoin. In 1893 there were forty-four acres of sanfoin on Upper Farm. Watergate Farm had five or six year old sainfoin growing on Beacon Hill in 1872 valued at twenty-one pounds, and a further ten pounds worth of one year old roots to come into 'perfect growth' to replace the older roots once they became too old. The long term nature of the farming cycle of sainfoin meant that it had to be taken account of in the lease. The 1841 draft lease of Watergate Farm stated that 'in case ... there shall be any quantity not exceeding 150 acres of S^{t}foin roots under the age of 5 years left' the outgoing tenant 'will pay for such S^{t}foin roots a fair and reasonable price'. There had been no such provision in 1801 suggesting during the intervening years it had become a more significant crop on the farm.[13]

Changes in farming

HOW HAD ARABLE farming methods changed by the end of the century? Allan G. Young had taken over Watergate House in 1903 and run a small farm from it. He then acquired a further 1,200 acres and then the farm was augmented to 4,500 acres by land leased from the Crown who then owned the majority of the Seymour estate, before shrinking back to about 2,500 acres when the army required more land. Forty per cent of the land was arable. When he took over, the farm was still running on a six year course, as follows:

First course:	Potatoes, mangolds or Swedes, with a preparation of thirty tons of dung to the acre.
Second course:	Wheat or clover, and grass mixtures. No dung used, but four to five hundredweight of artificial manure to the acre. The soil of the fields is analysed, and the manure prepared to suit its conditions.
Third course:	Hay is cropped from second course sowings.
Fourth course:	Hay again, with twenty-five tons of dung.
Fifth course:	Hay, after which the ground is ploughed up.
Sixth course:	Oats.

Plenty of manure was used every three years, but Allan G. Young had plenty of this. He had a contract to clear manure from the camp and amassed 4,500 tons of it. When he tried to auction it, he only got three pounds for it all which must reflect the progress that had been made in the area by artificial fertilisers. His experiences of downland farming reinforced what Thomas Davis had written a century earlier. When he ploughed up twenty acres of downland and sowed oats straight away, the crop was decimated by wireworm. When subsequently he ploughed a further forty acres of downland with a steam plough which also had a furrow presser, and then left it for the grass to rot before sowing, there was no wire worm and a good crop. He was acting like 'the best farmers [who a century before] have made a point of getting their lands clean ploughed by Midsummer, and treading it as firm as possible with the sheepfold a long time before sowing'. The technology had changed but the principle that Thomas Davis identified remained true. Allan G. Young went on to explain that pressures of the First World War with its necessity for increasing the area of land under cereals, caused the six year cycle to be abandoned and replaced with a four year cycle of potatoes, followed by wheat, followed by seeds or barley and then oats in the fourth year which was exhausting the land. He said, "Our land will not stand this for long, but long enough, I hope, to get over the scarcity." This was 'burnbeaking' and over cropping in the Napoleonic Wars all over again and, as it has already been noted in chapter 2; the threat of labour emigrating to the colonies was also repeating itself.[14]

One part of the downs on the summit of Beacon Hill has a different geology and soil. There are two patches of Reading Beds, the larger on the end of the ridge where the gun end was located, and the smaller on the

The Agricultural Heartbeat of Village Life

summit above the Sling plantation. Reading Beds, were alluvial in origin and supported a soil which was seasonally waterlogged fine or coarse loams over clay, making it a heavy soil capable of supporting a mixed pasture of arable crops, and which benefited from 'chalking' to improve its fertility. Chalk was available from the nearby outcrops and although there was a chalk pit on the edge of the village, this was too far away to transport and was used, no doubt, for building the cob walls of farmyards, and for houses. The Reading Beds are the 'red strong land on the high level parts of the Downs, which were once woodland, and sometimes expressly called "wood-sour land", [and] is astonishingly improved by chalking' to make it sweet. Autumn was the best time for chalking which required 160 cart loads of chalk per acre costing about two to four pounds. 'The red land being capable, with proper management, of remaining in tillage', did not require the six year cycle. Left to its own, it became covered with furze and thorn bushes. Beyond the larger area of Reading Beds, Watergate Farm had a well developed field system 'Over Beacon Hill' which exploited these lands for arable and it is significant that this was the site, from at least 1820, of a yard of three field barns enabling the farmer to manage these fields without having to trek up hill and back from the main farmyard by the water meadows. This is where sainfoin was being grown in 1872.[15]

The 1820 probate inventory of Lower Farm and the one in 1872 for Watergate Farm give a detailed picture of the equipment that was needed on an arable farm. They also document the progress of mechanisation over half a century. Starting with the preparation of the fields for planting crops, Lower Farm had '2 wheeled ploughs' and an old 'iron plough', and '3 harrows'. All these were dependent on horse power, of which two were itemised in the inventory. Watergate Farm had eight 'two wheel iron ploughs and tackle by Tasker', which were forged iron and much stronger, there were six plough sledges to transport them to and from the field being worked and sixty-six ploughshares, reflecting the punishment that the flinty loams did to the ploughs. There were also several bits of machinery to firm up the ploughed soil to counter erosion and wireworm: two three-wheel pressers, four cast iron rollers and a Cambridge roller. Then there were the harrows to break up the tilth, Lower Farm had three whereas Watergate Farm had two zigzag harrows, a chain harrow, three wood drags and twenty-two wood harrows and tackle. It has to be remembered that Watergate Farm had double the acreage of Lower Farm, but even so the impression is of a mushrooming of equipment and machinery in the middle years of the century. There is an absence of seeding machinery on Lower Farm indicating that broadcasting seed by hand was the practice, although the absence of machinery does not necessarily mean that it was not used. Machinery could be hired as was the case in March 1835 when a seed drill and its operator were hired from Amesbury to work on Watergate Farm. By 1872, however, the Watergate Farm inventory lists a broadcasting machine, a corn drill with steerage and three seed machines and a horse rake, much more efficient and labour saving. Temporary labour, mainly women, was traditionally used for couching and weeding the crops, but even this process was being mechanised, with implications for rural employment. There is an 1895 diagram drawn up for James Hooper showing him how to set the blades on a horse drawn machine to hoe five rows of a crop at once. Watergate Farm had two horse hoes in 1872.[16]

Harvesting was another traditionally labour intensive phase of agriculture and again the lack of any specialised equipment in 1820 points to harvesting by hand. A picture of men harvesting is painted by Jefferies:

> The reapers were at work in the wheat, but the plain was so level that it was not possible to see them without mounting upon a flint heap. Then their heads were just visible as they stood upright, but when they stooped to use the hook they disappeared. Yonder, however, a solitary man in his shirt-sleeves perched up above the corn went round and round the field, and beside him strange awkward arms seemed to beat down the wheat. He was driving a reaping machine, to which the windmill-like arms belonged.

In 1872 Watergate Farm possessed a Crosskills Reaper. This was a reaping machine pushed by two horses in harness, making hand reaping with a sickle redundant except in pockets inaccessible to the reaper. Once harvested, rick making was an occupation for the farm labourers and thatchers and, then throughout the winter, threshing the cereal crops by hand was a major source of employment. By 1841 Watergate Farm possessed a threshing machine probably situated in the main barn which, as has been argued in Chapter 5, could have harnessed water power to drive it by the end of the century. Lower Farm had a 'chaff cutting machine' (as also did Watergate Farm), '4 barley chumpers' (an instrument for cutting off the beards or awns of barley), and as already noted, an 'Amesbury heaver' which part

The Agricultural Heartbeat of Village Life

21   Crosskills Reaper. *The 1872 inventory of Watergate Farm shows that Francis Stephen Long owned one of these machines to work on Watergate Farm.*

mechanised the winnowing process. There were also a 'bean mill', corn bins and countless sacks. Watergate Farm had a chaff cutting machine, two winnowing machines, an oil cake crusher and a shogger to dig up sainfoin. Towards the end of the century, we have a glimpse of the machinery used on the farms when in 1889 a thirty pound insurance was paid, 'On machinery worked by power' on Upper and Lower Farms, 'Excluding Engine, Thrashing machines and Elevators'. The power source was undoubtedly a portable steam engine, no doubt similar to ones insured in 1907. There were then, two on the farm. The more expensive premium of £150 pounds was for 'a portable Steam Engine … manufactured by Brown and May of Devizes and numbered 6,588'. The high premium no doubt indicated that it was an old, more unreliable machine when compared with a premium of only £30 on the more modern (?) one 'manufactured by Tasker and Sons of Andover, and numbered 48'. In addition James Hooper paid a £100 premium for a threshing machine 'manufactured by Nalder of Wantage', and £25 for a steam elevator 'manufactured by Rawlings of Collingbourne'. This 1907 policy stipulated that the machinery insured was covered 'whilst out on hire on any Farm within a radius of ten miles' of Upper and Lower Farm which warns us that although we might lack evidence of machinery elsewhere, the certainty is that it was being used, either owned or hired.[17]

Farm infrastructure

BARNS WERE ESSENTIAL with their winnowing floors and storage facilities, and it was generally reckoned that a separate one was needed for each type of grain. By having separate field barns, as there were 'Over Beacon Hill' and the 'Sheepbridge Barn' at Sheep Bridge, transport costs were dramatically reduced. All the products of the harvesting and winnowing processes, and indeed all the by-products of farming, were utilised and needed storing, either in barns or in the 'backsides' of the farm buildings. As the 1801 lease stated, the tenant was to 'put in barns and rickyards ... all the corn ... [and] all the Dust Straw Chaff Fodder Compost Soil and Dung which shall yearly grow on or arise from the produce on the premises ... in a good husbandlike manner for the better improvement thereof'. The stubble left in the fields was used for feeding livestock, the sheep and cattle. Farmers stored their straw and other crops in ricks. There were hay ricks, straw and vetch ricks, and in the Lower Farm inventory, a 'sanfoin hay rick'. In 1872, Watergate Farm had '9 working oxen' which could well have been kept for, amongst other things, driving the threshing machine. They could also have been used for ploughing for they trampled the fields more than horses and helped to compact the thin soils of the higher land, especially 'burnbeaked' downs, and the presence of '7 set of ox harnesses' would support this, as does an observer in 1900 who saw 'three teams of shorthorn cattle tilling the ground just over the brow of the hill [Beacon Hill]'. They were also no doubt used to pull carts. [18]

Both farms owned fleets of carts, Lower Farm had six of various sorts: broad wheeled and narrow and a 'tipping caravan' with the necessary 'wagon jack and grease pot', and Watergate Farm had twelve wagons, five dung carts and an old chaff wagon. All the field machinery was pulled (or pushed) by horse power. Lower Farm had two horses itemised in the inventory. Over the whole parish there were twelve carters identified in the 1851 census and this number remained constant ten years later, a period when the overall numbers of farm labourers declined. Richard Jefferies describes the carter as,

> a man of much importance on a farm. If he is up to his duties he is a most valuable servant; if he neglects them he is a costly nuisance, not so much

from his pay, but because of the hindrance and disorganisation of the whole farm-work which such neglect entails.... [He] has to be up while the moon casts a shadow.... to feed his team very early in order to get them to eat sufficient. If the manger be over-filled they spill and waste it, and at the same time will not eat so much. This is tedious work. Then the lads come and polish up the harness, and so soon as it is well light get out to plough. The custom with the horses is to begin to work as early as possible, but to strike off in the afternoon some time before the other men, the lads riding home astride. The strength of the carthorse has to be husbanded carefully, and the labour performed must be adjusted to it and to the food, i.e. fuel, consumed. To manage a large team of horses, so as to keep them in good condition, with glossy coats and willing step, and yet to get the maximum of work out of them, requires long experience and constant attention.

Thomas Davis reckoned that a farmer needed at least six horses for carrying corn to market. Watergate Farm had nineteen cart horses and a nag mare – more than enough. We have already referred in Chapter 6 to the list of equipment auctioned at Nag's Head Farm in 1854, but it is noticeable that the prime asset for sale was a 'Team of three valuable young cart horses (2 grey, 1 roan)'. When the Board of Agriculture started to record the number of horses used for agriculture in 1876, there were fifty-three in the village, with the number increasing to sixty-five in 1896 before falling away again with the shrinking of agriculture caused by the arrival of the army. These figures remind us that although steam power was being used, the heavy engines, threshing machines, elevators and so forth were all portable and needed horse power to move them into place, creating a demand for more horsepower. [19]

The village blacksmith had an important role to play with on the farms. The smithy was situated behind Lower Farm and the chapel, and we have records in the village of William Toomer, described as a 'blacksmith and farrier' in an 1830 Directory, and paying the parish rate in 1834 for a house he owned in Main Street (*Figure 2, no.9, 10 or 11*), not far from the Smithy. In the latter years of the century Robert Lake was the blacksmith, living in the 'Blacksmith's Cottage' with another blacksmith, Charles Hicks, boarding with him in 1881. We have already seen in Chapter 1 that he was also a shopkeeper.[20]

Sheep were worth more to the farmer than solely being the muck spreaders and field tramplers needed to prepare the arable for sowing, they also produced an income for sale as meat, and from the sale of wool. 'Great numbers were sold off yearly, to be fattened elsewhere, chiefly in the eastern counties for the London market.' Thomas Croome, for example sold 926 lambs and 100 wethers in one year (1820) along with 787 ewes to obtain an income of £2,021 10s. The ewes being the older ones past lambing, and the wethers were not needed for breeding and would be dead weight over the winter. Shearing took place in summer and the fleece of the traditional breed of South Wiltshire horned sheep sold at the beginning of the century at fifteen to twenty shillings a pound, and as a sheep carried about two to two and a half pounds of wool, each sheep would bring in about three shillings and sixpence for its wool. It was moderately fine wool and particularly useful for super broadcloth. Farmers looked for profits and two events combined to cause them to make changes to improve their flocks. The first was that the stock of sheep was deteriorating from inbreeding and suffering from 'goggles' or rickets, and the second was a consequence of the Peninsula War in Spain. 'This state in that peninsula [(Spain) was] not allowing our manufacturers to depend on the stock of wool hitherto received, [and] many speculative men in this district ... are now breeding Spanish sheep, as stock for general farming purposes, from the flocks lately imported by His Majesty.' In 1794 George III had procured Merino rams from Spain and distributed them through the Marquis of Bath (Thomas Davis' employer at Longleat) to improve the quality of Wiltshire stock. Thomas Croome was one such speculative man as he kept Spanish sheep, selling 170 lambs in 1820 at Andover fair at £1 each. Merino sheep carried much more wool than the Wiltshire sheep and were good walkers, but there were downsides. They did not crop the turf so closely with a result that the downs could not support so many sheep and they would 'starve on the same kind of land on which the old sort of sheep lived so well'. The value of their wool had to be balanced against the extraordinary care they needed during the winter months. [21]

Economics of farming

THE MAIN BREED that all but took over Wiltshire downland farming was the Southdown sheep. Their wool was as good as that of the Merino, and they produced as much as the old breed but it fetched up to a shilling a pound more. They ate the turf closer, enabling the downs to support more sheep; they were quieter in the pens and were good nurses to their lambs which were of equal value. All in all, the farmer could double his profit from sheep and the number of sheep at Bulford in c1886, as we have seen, was about 4,500. As the century wore on, artificial fertilizers diminished the need for sheep as dung carriers to the ploughed fields, and so the sale of wool and marketing for meat gained greater significance. Experimentation kept happening, and still does. In the early years of the next century, Allan G. Young was still searching for a suitable breed of sheep for the downs. He tried Cheviots and Scotch crosses 'but they were too wild; a troop of soldiers or a gun would send them at full speed all over the downs'. His final choice was Exmoor sheep which were quiet by nature, good mothers and not scared of artillery. The produced excellent mutton and very fair wool – walking and dung carrying was of little consequence by then.[22]

> Although milch cows have paid very well of late, and milk and butter are indispensibly necessary, the rage for keeping "fine sheep" has almost driven cows out of the district; and were there not a necessity of keeping them to feed the water meads in the autumn (when they are not safe for sheep), and to eat barley straw, and to make manure in the winter, there would soon be very few cows in South Wiltshire.

Thomas Davis's fears expressed in 1811 seemed to be true of Bulford. On Watergate Farm in 1838 there were only seven cows and there was a 'Dairy house' and one of the water meadows called 'Pound of Butter'. Even though the value of dairy produce had increased by a third from before the Napoleonic Wars, the boom for wool production was the stronger economic force. Sheep were the main livestock until the end of the century when the army took over the downs, and sheep numbers decreased with a reduction of the area of sheep downs, whereas dairy herds increased. There were only three dairy cows on Watergate Farm in 1872 but by the early years of the twentieth century this had expanded to a sixty strong dairy herd, but this was reduced because the milch cows did not do very well on the water meadows, and although they showed a profit, arable farming and hay brought in more. Allan G. Young said that it was, as it had always been, important to, 'Keep accounts and know what everything costs, that you may discontinue unprofitable items.' He, as you would expect from this comment, did well out of farming and when he retired as churchwarden in 1917 it was recorded that he 'practically saved the dear old Church, collecting and spending large sums (about £1,300) on its restoration. The church, the tower, and the bells had all been restored'. Returning to farming, across the farms of the parish as a whole, you can see the same flirtation with dairying. Between 1867 and 1886, the number of cows and calves rose from thirty to sixty-four, and then doubled in number by 1906 before falling back to fifty-two in 1916. No doubt Allan G. Young's fellow farmers had similar experiences and came to the same conclusions. There were other animals which were part of the farm, pigs (between eighty and a hundred in the parish), and poultry. In 1886 there were over 500 chickens, nearly 50 turkeys, 10 geese and 125 ducks on the farms altogether. Doves were also kept in the Pigeon Houses at Watergate Farm and at the Manor and no doubt on all the farms.[23]

Trees

FURTHER ECONOMIC ACTIVITY of the farm was centered around the woodland – timber was an important crop. Wood was essential both as fuel and as a raw material for making all sorts of necessary implements: ash poles were used, for example, to make handles for rakes, spades and picks; hazel for sheep hurdles, spars for thatching, pea and bean sticks; alder and birch for rafter poles, clogs and pattens and fencing rails. In addition, trees and woodland were essential for game and rookeries. Bulford had its rookeries, like the one mentioned at Bulford Manor Farm in 1876, and its eggs were an important source of protein for the villagers' diet. All along the rivers, willow and alder, especially, were farmed and harvested, and the farms and richer houses were surrounded by trees. Wood was a valuable resource, so much so, that Henry Seymour kept total control of it on his estate, as did the Lords of the Manor, specifying in 1801 that 'all timber and other trees whatsoever germines plants and springs likely to become timber which now or hereafter shall be standing growing or being' belonged to him to be managed as he thought fit as opposed to being managed by his tenant. What is more, he went on to stipulate that he, or his heirs, could 'plant or cause to be planted any sort or number of trees either for use of ornament or pleasure upon any part of the premises ... as he or they [his heirs or assigns] shall think fit without the let denial or interruption'. The growing cycle of timber took it out of being properly managed by short term leases. He also wanted to avoid overharvesting by stipulating that the tenant 'shall not nor will not shroud [thin by pruning] or cause to be shrouded any of the witheys [willows] growing on the premises until the shrouds of the same witheys shall be of four years growth'. By the end of the century, the neglect of managing the willows and alders by the Avon was lamented by an old drowner. He recalled (in dialect),

> Ah ... they medders wir tinded thin, in us used to cut thay withey pollards en they ashes fir faggots, spars en vincing posts. None of em wir lowed ta git like they be now. All they withy bids wir planted zinc I kin mind, en us used to keep em cut. Zum of em wir used to mik edges ta kip in tha ship en tha lambs. Thin thir be thay alder bids. I elped plant zum a they – varmer wir gwine to use em fir brumheads or zummit, bit twer niver done. [Ah ... those meadows were tended thin, as we used to cut those willow pollards and those ashes for faggots, spars and fencing posts. None of them were allowed to get like they are now. All those willow beds were planted in my memory, and we used to keep them cut. Some of them were used to make hedges to keep in the sheep and lambs. Then there are those alder beds. I helped plant some of them – the farmer was going to use them as broom heads or something, but it was never done.] [24]

The 1767 accounts of Bulford Manor estate give a hint of the importance of timber costs to the landlord. Richard Duke took out a thirty year loan of £5,192, of which £1,130 was needed to cover the cost of timber. Lady Pollen's will was also attentive to the timber resources of the Manor making it clear to 'not otherwise to cut Timber with the exception of such trees as may be deemed ornamental or for shelter as well as for necessary repairs to the hereditaments ... and for the erection of any new building'. If trees are cut down in other circumstances, the perpetrator would be 'subject to impeachment of waste' which no doubt helps to explain why she was so reluctant to cut back overhanging trees which 'very much darkened and injured for want of sun' the parish church. It is hardly surprising, therefore, that at the turn of the eighteenth and nineteenth centuries, there was an 'amazing spirit of planting that for some years has been diffused through every part of [the County]', and there needed to be as there was a 'serious want of wood' on the plain. We can see this happening at Bulford. Laburnum, weeping willows, alder, fine plums and three quince trees were all planted at the Manor in February and March 1812 at a cost of £1 2s 6d, but these were not to redress the 'serious want of wood' in the same way as later planting. Between 1820 and 1838, 'thirty-eight acres by estimation of land cultivated as Woodland and plantations' were planted on the downs above the Nine Mile River, the 'Sling Plantation', and in c1877, there were further plantations established on Beacon Hill and north-east of Nine Mile River utilising the potential of the Reading Beds. Trees were planted around the Seymour estate Pennings by 1901 and a copse had been established at the corner of Watergate Lane to supplement that already in situ at the junction of the Old Coach Road (was this the village rookery?). The line of copses on Bulford Fields along the old boundary between the Upper and Lower Farms was being created in 1895 and planting continued into the twentieth century with, for example, a plantation created in the 1960s behind the houses in Milston Road. The village was also well treed with orchards, the largest was at Orchard End, extending across the two tenement cottage gardens as well. In 1900 this orchard was 'a mass of pink in the summer dusk' and is still remembered by the name of the road, Orchard Way. Watergate Farm also had a fair sized Orchard. Fruit yields were affected by invasive grubs and insect life before the days of insecticides. The traditional method of controlling this 'latent foe' was described by a poet:

> To check this plague, the skilful farmer chaff
> And blazing straw, before his orchard burns;
> Till, all involved in smoke, the latent foe
> From every cranny suffocated falls.[25]

Farm management

THE HEARTBEAT OF the village was dictated by the agricultural and livestock cycles of the farms, and by the weather. Within these bounds, the farmers or their bailiffs dictated the exact timing and pace of the work performed by the villagers. The relatively small size of gentry estates meant that the owners were more intimately concerned in their management than aristocrats like the Marquis of Bath, who relied on his steward Thomas Davis who has been much quoted in this chapter, although oversight could be put into the hands of a local attorney without much agricultural knowledge. In 1824 the Ladies of the Manor, Lady Pollen and Mary

The Agricultural Heartbeat of Village Life

Southby both had stewards, Mary Tredgold and Fanny Sture respectively, who would have managed their employers' households but would not have had any agricultural responsibilities – the focus of this section. Lady Pollen also employed a Mr Fleet as her steward, who was concerned with the repairs to the garden wall after flooding in 1823, and he may well have had a wider brief. A similar situation is found on the Seymour estate with their steward James Still supervising the renovation of the Watergate Farm house in 1827. [26]

The national picture with regard to agricultural management sees various combinations of bailiffs, farmer bailiffs, owner agents and part time solicitor superintendents used to manage farms. As the nineteenth century progressed the general picture is of the landed gentry becoming more like the aristocracy in their degree of detachment from their landed estates. Richard Duke employed a bailiff, Richard Cox, for his estates at the end of the eighteenth century but no other mention is made of a bailiff at Bulford until the end of the nineteenth century when Harry Lawrence is described in 1881 as a bailiff living in the 'Bailiff's Cottage' and another bailiff, Edward G. Philps, was a lodger at the school house. Both were Dorset born men. In 1891 and 1901 George Andrews was the sole bailiff, living in 'Briary Cottage'. The latter census entry was the next entry to 'The Hill' (Upper Farm) and so it would appear that he was employed on Upper Farm first by John Robbins and then by James Hooper who then combined both the Lower and Upper Farms in 1895. Both George Andrews and his wife Caroline (née Holmes) were village born. George was an agricultural labourer before his promotion to bailiff and Caroline's father Joseph Holmes was similarly employed. George's local knowledge, abilities and personnel skills must have been considered assets by James Hooper.[27]

The Lords of the Manor did not farm directly, as is clearly illustrated in the lease drawn up between Anthony Southby and James Hooper in 1881 which contains the following statement: 'This said lease shall contain the usual agricultural covenants which shall be agreed upon between Mr Frederick Charles Ellen of Andover Estate Agent on behalf of the said Anthony Southby and James Hooper himself or his agent ... .' Five years later his heir was still employing Frederick Ellen & Son of Andover to keep his rent accounts, and in August of that year the firm was 'favoured with instructions to SELL by AUCTION' in London the Manor and its estate after Edmund Southby's death. When the War Office were negotiating with Miss Seymour for the purchase of her land in the village in 1897, the land agent involved thought it 'desirable that some independent expert should see the property and say that £10 (Ten pounds) per acre is a fair price to be paid. I would suggest Mr Fred Ellen of Andover as a proper person for this'. The firm of land agents concerned was founded by R. Rawlence and E. P. Squarey, who both actively farmed very large estates in South Wiltshire, and were concerned with fostering and financing agricultural improvements. Their firm was behind securing a loan from the Land Loan and Enfranchisement Company to build the new farmyard on Watergate Farm. Ernest Rawlence's subsequent advice to Miss Seymour for the farm after the War Office had bought the downland, already quoted in Chapter 5, was to switch to dairy farming. Their expertise was economic and this would not have affected the day to day working life of the farm other than in the broader strategic sense. Their views, for example, were put into practice by Allan G. Young who as we have seen was to keep a dairy herd sixty strong.[28]

Farming was the life force for the vast majority of the village inhabitants, but all were ultimately dependent on its health and profitability. The parish was 'exclusively agricultural' as the vicar wrote in 1870, but the last word, however, ought to go to Prudence Sawyer who looked back at these times in the village from the turn of the twentieth century:

> Three farms and plenty of men for hire ...
> There were shepherds, cowmen, carters too,
> Who always found plenty of work to do,
> From early rise till set of sun,
> A farmer's work was never done,
> Ploughing and sowing, reaping and mowing,
> Mangold pulling, or turnip hoeing.
> Hedging, and ditching, spreading and pitching,
> And a hundred and one jobs in between.
> There was animal breeding and poultry feeding,
> And many more things that were unforeseen.
> The women worked in the fields all day,
> Picking up stones or making hay,
> Or washing the milk pails, pens and churns,
> And doing the Farmer's wife many good turns.[29]

8
Church and Chapel

Clerical provision

THE INHERITANCE OF Bulford Manor has been looked at in detail for the late eighteenth and nineteenth centuries in Chapter 4 and, as has been noted, the right of advowson (the right and responsibility for nominating a curate for the parish church) went with the inheritance. The past ownership of the village by Amesbury Abbey, later Priory, meant that there were no resources within the parish to support the work of the church, other than the church building itself. There was no house for a clergyman, nor any glebe land to support him. The tithes which went to many churches as a source of income, went instead to the Lord of the Manor who, in return, paid an annual endowment to a clergyman. The Lord of the Manor was 'only entitled to the small Tithes of Bulford Farm, that is to say the Tithes of Lambswool, Cows, Pigs, Poultry, Gardens, Orchards and Clover Seeds' and when these were commuted to a money payment in 1838, they amounted to £98 per annum which was a tenth (tithe) of the assessed value. Bulford Farm at this time, as we have seen, was divided between the Manor estate, the Seymour estate and the land owned by the Cooe brothers, and as the payment went to the Lord of the Manor (Anthony Southby at the time). The payment was for the two latter estates. If the small tithes had been levied over the whole parish, they would have amounted to double the amount. This income would have gone to the clergyman were he the rector, entitled to the small tithes, but this was not the case with Bulford where it went to the Lord of the Manor who then had the responsibility and right of advowson. The advowson at Bulford was 'presentative' which placed on the Lord of the Manor as patron of the village church the responsibility of providing a clergyman for the cure of parishioners' souls (hence the term 'curate' in the documentation) whom he then presented to the bishop for approval. The quality of clerical cover was left to the patron and the legacy of monastic domination was, as will be seen, detrimental to the religious life of the village from the point of view of the Established Church. Before looking at the provision we must note the confusion over the church's dedication. It was dedicated to St Leonard, but in the course of time this changed to St John; the nineteenth century saw it revert to St Leonard once again and has remained as such until today.[1]

There is no list of clergy who administered to the needs of the village for the first part of the century, but by looking at the signatures of registers and other parish documents, a list has been put together by Rev. Rhys-Hughes (see Appendix 4a). This reveals a total lack of continuity for the villagers with, for example, four different clergy signing the registers in 1804. By and large clergy of adjoining parishes took Bulford under their wing. From 1813 till 1817 this was Rev. Allan Borman Hutchins who was appointed the curate of Shipton Bellinger in 1812 and then moved to Allington in 1814 but as the parsonage was unfit for residence he lived at Porton. He moved to Kimpton and Grately in 1818 into a parsonage with a rise in income leaving Bulford to be cared for by his successor at Shipton Bellinger and Allington, the Rev. Wilson Becket, who again had to live out of the parish, this time in Amesbury. A year later the Rev. George Thomas Rudd, the newly ordained priest at Shipton Bellinger, took Bulford under his wing until 1821. The care of souls in Bulford then moved to the clergy of Durrington for the next nine years until 1830. First was the Rev. Fulwar William Fowle and then the Rev. Richard Webb, born in Hungerford and ordained in 1821. Though curate of Durrington, the latter was required to live in Amesbury where he married a local girl, Mary. He served many years in the area, becoming Rector of Milston from 1850 to 1862. Although Rev. Richard Webb was still a curate in Durrington in 1830, the care of Bulford transferred to the Rev. Walter Blunt, stipendary curate at Cholderton who lived in the Rectory on £60 a year. He served Bulford for the next five years. In 1835 Richard Webb's predecessor as Rector of Milston, the Rev. James Watts Ellaby, took over the care of Bulford and introduced an element of stability until 1851.[2]

The Rev. James Watt Ellaby's association with Bulford seems to have been a turning point in the church life of the parish because it emphasised the need for more than just someone to carry out the legal duties of celebrating marriages and registering baptisms and deaths. The surviving minutes of the church vestry meetings during the first half of the century fail to record the presence of any clergyman. What was needed was a clergyman to become immersed in village and church life, and perhaps the Rev. James Ellaby was able to do this to a degree as Milston and Bulford were very closely connected, both geographically and economically. He is described as 'Incumbent of Bulford' in the marriage announcement of his daughter in 1847. The weak position of Bulford, with its greater population compared to Milston, is thrown into stark relief. The Lord of the Manor gave a peculiar stipend of £85 per annum compared with the £80 that the Rector of Milston received, but in addition the latter had a Rectory and its tithes, garden and an office as well. A Parliamentary survey of Bulford in 1650 thought that the logic of this position, even then, was

> that the parishe of Bulforde be vnited to Milston and Brigmiston and that the Church at Milston be scituate fittly and made convenient to receive the whole congregation of the Three Hamlets but it is prayed by the Inhabitantes of Bulforde which is a through fare to the West that the Church may stand and that the Minister of the whole united Parishe doe preache there once every Lordes day att least there beinge the greatest number of Inhabitantes

It was an argument that carried on until the nineteenth century and beyond with the grouping of churches extending even further today. Before this, though, the momentum was for Bulford to have its own incumbent.[3]

Resident Parish Priest

THE YEAR 1852 was significant as it saw the first clergyman to be inducted as 'incumbent' at Bulford on a stipend of £85 per annum (although as we have seen, not the first to be called such). This was the Yorkshireman the Rev. Thomas Darnton Millner who retained his post as perpetual curate until 1867-1868. He had initially to reside outside the parish as there was no glebe house, but there is evidence of his activity within the parish, taking a wedding in 1853 and attending the vestry meeting to appoint Francis Stephen Long churchwarden. He, though, held other positions, notably as Chaplain to Rt Hon George William Frederick Howard, 7th Earl of Carlisle KG, PC, Lord Lieutenant of Ireland between 1855 and 1864 which inevitably took him away from the parish. He emphatically failed to fulfil the 275 days' residence prescribed by law. Perhaps expectations had been dashed giving rise to complaints, or perhaps he failed to do the required paperwork, but in any case his absenteeism got back to his bishop who wrote to him on at least two occasions. He took a heavy line as his second letter clearly shows:

> To the Reverend Thomas Darnton Millner, Perpetual Curate of Bulford in the County of Wilts and Diocese of Salisbury.
> Whereas it appears to us Walter Kerr Hamilton by divine permission Bishop of Salisbury that you the said Thomas Darnton Millner are absent from your benefice of Bulford without our license to be absent therefrom and without legal cause of exemption from residence thereon – That you have been admonished by Us to proceed to your said Benefice and to reside thereon and to make a return to the such monition and that you have made an insufficient return thereto Now we the said Walter Kerr Hamilton by Divine Permission Bishop of Salisbury pursuant of the statute 1 and 2 Victoria Chapter 106 Do hereby monish and require you forwith to proceed to and reside upon your said Benefice and perform the duties thereof within thirty days after the due service upon you of this order.
>
> 30th November 1859

This 'monition' appears to have had the desired effect, for a while at least, as the 1861 census shows him residing in a private house in the village which he shared with a groom and his wife, David and Elizabeth Swatton, and he attended the Amesbury Deanery Meetings between October 1856 and October 1861. The 1851 census map, interpolated ten years later, has the Rev. Bowman's name by the church but locates the 'parsonage' in a newly built house which was to become the headmistress's house attached to the new village school (*Figure 2, no.24*), and then, ironically the chapel manse in 1962. The Rev. Bowman represented Bulford in Amesbury Deanery Meetings between May and October 1862 although the Rev. Millner was still perpetual curate of the parish. He was once again an absentee clergyman and in 1867 his return to his bishop was sent from Bristol. He described himself as 'non resident', with another curacy in Cornwall, leaving three neighbouring clergymen with the care of his Bulford parishioners' souls. The Post Office Directory of that year declared that the 'living is now vacant'. The three clergymen were the Rev. Edmund Burkett Bowman, John James Scott and Christopher Salter who between them covered for him from 1861 till 1869. The situation was akin to that castigated by William Cobbett complaining that 'A journeyman parson comes and works in three or four churches of a Sunday; but the master parson is not there'. One can sense the frustration felt by the parishioners of Bulford with Francis Stephen Long proposing to the Deanery Meeting in November 1868 that 'the clergy of each parish be requested to attend ... in order to consider the present position and future prospects of the united Church of England and Ireland as by law established'. The dream of a resident vicar in the parish was still to be realised and religious life of the church remained skeletal.[4]

The description of church life in 1783 when Rev. W. Copley, curate at Boscombe who was living in Amesbury and covering Bulford, responded to questions from his bishop must paint an accurate picture for the whole of the period considered so far. 'The parish', he reported, 'consists mainly of labouring people and except on Christmas Day and Good Friday or a general fast and thanksgiving no service is performed on weekdays'. On Sunday however, 'The service at Bulford is generally performed at eleven or one but never twice on the same Sunday', and in response to the bishop's query as to why not, he reported that 'it has never been customary'. The congregation are instructed in the catechism in Lent and 'The sacrament is administered at Christmas, Easter, and Whitsuntide' to between six and ten communicants. There were no church collections, charity schooling, or as far as he was aware, no Dissenters. Churchwardens were appointed to conduct the business of the church, one by the minister and the other by villagers at the Easter Vestry meeting. Despite this minimal service, his view was that 'Few country churches are better attended'. Nevertheless, it is not a picture of a vibrant church community, leaving a vacuum in the religious life of the village.[5]

Neglect of the Parish Church

NEARLY HALF A century later, in 1826, William Cobbett presents us with a picture of a decaying church, both morally and physically. He was ecstatic about the agricultural vistas he viewed on his ride down the Avon Valley, but not so with the state of the church.

> There are no less than *nine* parishes, out of twenty-nine, that have either no *parsonage-house*, or have such as are in such a state that a Parson will not, or

cannot live in them. Three of them are without any parsonage-houses at all, and the rest are become poor, mean, falling-down places.

22 Parish church 1869. St Leonard's Church, called St John's at the time, from the north in about 1869. This photograph was stuck in Lucius O'Brien's sketch book, next to his April 1869 sketch (page 7 above). It shows a girl walking in The Park along the path from the Bulford Manor which connected with the end of the Old Coach Road. (see Fig. 3)

Bulford was one of the three with no parsonage. He appears not to have been exaggerating for we have already seen how the local parsonages at Allington and Berwick St James were both deemed unfit to live in. Bulford church itself was in poor condition. Three years later it was inspected by the Rural Dean whose office had been revived in 1807 by the bishop to remedy deficiencies in the parishes. He ordered extensive repairs to be made to the fabric and fittings: the bells, font cover, nave seats, gallery, belfry loft and church roof all needed repairing. In addition the inside walls needed whitewashing, a bier was needed with a black cloth for burials, a Table of Degrees (of relationships where marriage was forbidden by law) was to be set up in the porch and a Book of Homilies needed to be procured. The outside walls of the church had, in places, five or six feet of earth piled against them and Lady Pollen of the Manor turned her horses into the graveyard to feed.

Church and Chapel

To their credit, the vestry in their 17 July meeting 1829, set to putting these matters to rights and,

ordered	That the clapper of the bell be repaired.
ordered	That a Bier with a Black hearse cloth be provided as soon as possible.
ordered	That a Book of Homilies be procured.
ordered	That a covering for the font be procured.
ordered	That a Notice be given to the several persons to whom the sittings of Pews out of repair belong, that they do forthwith cause them to be repaired.
ordered	That the roof of the Church be repaired and that the Churchwardens do employ some competent person to inspect the same and report to them with an Estimate of the Probable expense of doing the same properly and also an estimate for repairing the Ceiling and whitewashing the inside of the Church that they may lay the same before the next vestry meeting.
ordered	That a small seat in the North aisle be removed and that part of the said aisle be paved with bricks.
ordered	That the Churchwardens do cause the gallery to be examined and the necessary repairs done thereto forthwith.
ordered	That the same be done to the loft of the belfry.

In November of that year, the vestry then levied a parish rate of 7½ d in the pound, bringing in an income of £48 12s 6d to pay for the repairs. The vestry meeting a year later placed the roofing contract with Joseph Scott of Salisbury and reported that all the other work had been completed except the font cover which was in hand. They went further than the Rural Dean's demands with the Chairman T. W. Dyke being instructed to make an application

> to Lady Pollen and Miss [Mary] Southby requesting them to cause, at their earliest convenience, the windows of the Chancel to be repaired; the Thorn hedge on the east side of the churchyard to be so cut as to be out of the way of the Footpath and the Boughs of the Trees hanging over the churchyard to be shortened that the Church may be more benefitted by sun, air and light than at present ...

These were all matters that were the responsibility of the patrons, hence the application. [6]

When the churchwardens met the Rural Dean the following year, they were able to report that, 'We present the Parish Church and Chancel of Bulford in the County of Wilts in good repair, excepting two bells which for many years past have been broken and become useless; and we desire to be directed concerning them.' The roof work had been carried out despite a dispute with the contractor who had made repairs not in the contract and had not finished plastering the outside walls. They went on to list several items that they were turning their attention towards, such as repairs to the church door and raising certain floor levels to keep the ever present damp at bay. It was probably in conjunction with the latter that a trench was dug outside the building but Lady Pollen sent one of her employees to order part of it to be filled in again. (Perhaps she was worried about injuring one of her horses.) She was a Lady not to be pushed around by her inferiors and the 1830 vestry meeting noted that their request for the overhanging trees to

23 *Parish Church 1895. Photograph of St Leonard's Church taken in c1895 by Canon Ruddle of Durrington.*

be cut back had not been acceded to and 'the church is very much darkened and injured for want of sun'. They also noted that 'A part of the Fence of the Churchyard [was] out of repairs and the Graves of the Churchyard [were] much injured by the horses of Lady Pollen being turned there to feed and in consequence the Churchyard is made in a very indecent state'.

Growth of Dissent

THE MAINTENANCE OF old buildings is an ongoing headache and further work was done in 1865. There is no doubt that a great deal of effort was expended in bringing the fabric of the church into good repair but this did not alter the spiritual doldrums that the church was experiencing. The lack of consistent and local ministry left a religious vacuum just waiting to be filled and during the first half of the century the Established Church lost the initiative as religious minded villagers, perhaps despairing of the neglect that they were suffering, began to look elsewhere to Dissenting congregations coming together in the area. Looking back to these times thirty years later, the local clergy including the Vicar of Bulford, could plainly see what had gone wrong:

> ... the chief cause of Dissent in the Deanery had been the absence of church ministrations. This was notably the case with Bulford. For many years there was no certain provision even for the Sunday Services. When Sunday came the parishioners could not reckon upon any services at all nor could they anticipate, upon the chance arrival of some clergyman, whether the service would be at this hour or that. The ringing of the Church bells was the first notice they had that a service was about to be performed. As for the visitation of the sick or any personal intercourse between a clergyman and the people, these were almost, if not quite, unknown in the Parish. It was no marvel therefore that a desire sprang up for a change of some kind. Nor can anyone who is mindful of human infirmity be surprised, that the wealthiest inhabitants moved by impatience exhibited a disregard for the doctrines of a church which had left them in so deplorable condition.

They went further, citing that 'our grandparents had a dread of innovation, believing that it might lead to irreverence', or

... revive the religious troubles of former days. And the mere teaching of morality in which the clergy had taken refuge, had produced a coldness which was sad and distasteful to ardent spirits. Their dissatisfaction with the present and the opposition that was offered to any proposed innovation drove many an earnest man to the ranks of Dissent.[7]

In 1783 the Curate of Bulford had complacently reported to his bishop, 'I believe all the inhabitants of Bulford are of the established church', but twenty-five years later this could no longer be said. As this statement was being written, there was an explosion of non-conformity in the manufacturing centres around Calne and Devizes and it soon spread into the Avon Valley with Salisbury becoming a centre of Baptist activity under Pastor John Adams. Under him the Scots Lane chapel in Salisbury was enlarged in 1791 and it is said that he trained fifty to sixty Dissenting preachers who streamed out from Salisbury each Sunday to preach in surrounding villages. There were complaints that in consequence it was impossible to hire a horse on a Sunday. Be that as it may, the outreach of Scots Lane chapel reached Bulford and its surrounds with several Dissenters from the neighbourhood attending. An account of what happened next is preserved in the opening pages of the *Chapel Church Book*.

> In the year of 1805 Mr Henry Blatch of Ratfyn near Amesbury in the County of Wilts, - and Mr Matthew Devenish of Bulford in the same County, being of the Society of Protestant Dissenters, assembling in Scots Lane, New Sarum, and formerly under the pastoral care of the Rev. John Adams, with a view to their spiritual benefit and the spiritual benefit of the surrounding villages particularly Amesbury and Durrington, where the population is considerable, invited the Rev Francis William Dury of Oakham in the County of Rutland to preach to them with a view to settling among them. They subsequently invited him to preach the Gospel in the village of Bulford which invitation he accepted and accordingly came there with his family in the month of October (1805) and in his house public preaching commenced the tenth of November.

This house was undoubtedly the newly built house, the property of Mr Rose, which was registered on 17 March 1805 and rented to be fitted up for Dissenting worship in preparation for Rev. Dury's move. Mr Rose was James

Church and Chapel

Rose of 'Nag's Head' farm (1790) who had extra income from 'ploughing sowing and harrowing' six acres of Manor land at eighteen shillings an acre, bringing in an income of £6 7s 10d in 1801. He must have been doing well and hence the new house. The army deeds mark the site of a chapel on the corner of Salisbury Road and the High Street, opposite the junction of Watergate Lane where the present chapel is situated. This could have been the site of Mr Rose's house which to all intents and purposes was used as a chapel (*Figure 2 no.22*). Dissenters at the end of the eighteenth century were suspected of having sympathies with the French Revolutionaries and of anti-monarchy and dissident views and in consequence the establishment kept close tabs on them, requiring them to register their meeting places and chapels. Mr Rose's house was registered by Henry Blatch, James Rose, Matthew Devenish, William Sturges, James Chalk (the unfortunate shoemaker) and George Harrison. The registers show that four months later there was a certification of a second house in the village occupied by Samuel Mould which was registered, again by Henry Blatch, Matthew Devenish, James Chalk, George Harrison with the addition of Samuel Mould and Robert Gale who was described as 'Minister'. It would appear that attendances were too much for one house and the documentation supports this, as

> The attendance of the inhabitants of Bulford and the surrounding villages during the winter and spring was so great, and the general aspect of things so encouraging that Mr Blatch and Mr Devenish were induced to erect a chapel; they accordingly purchased the site of ground on which the present Meeting-House stands, together with a House and Garden, and built the Meeting-House which was completed in the summer of 1806 and publicly opened on the 30th July.[8]

Before considering the erection of the purpose built chapel we need to backtrack a little. Samuel Mould, whose house was registered as a second place of worship was the son(?) of Thomas Mould. Back on 9 January 1781, 'the House of Mr Thomas Mould Papermaker adjoining to the paper-mill and being one with the same situate in the Parish of Bulford aforesaid as and for a Place of Religious Worship and Assembly of Protestant Dissenters ... under the denomination of Methodists' was registered by Thomas Mould, James and John Rattew and Thomas Lawrence (*Figure 2, no.3*). In all probability the second meeting house registered in 1805 was a re-registering of the Mill House after a lapse of twenty-four years. The links between the papermakers and Dissent will be looked at in more detail in the next chapter but it is sufficient at this stage to note that the 1781 registration shows that Dissenters had reached the village well before the end of the eighteenth century and before the arrival of the Devenish households in 1802. The Blatches at Ratfyn, on the other hand, could have been involved as they were a locally based family.[9]

Henry Blatch's father was Amesbury born (Ratfyn?) and his younger brother James farmed at Winterborne Dauntsey. After Henry's death in 1821 his widow Sarah took on the lease of Ratfyn Farm in her own right until 'sickness disabled her' after 'she was visited by a paralytic seizure from which she never wholly recovered' before her own death in 1837. In widowhood, she,

> Though possessed of a most affectionate heart, did not pass the rest of her life in unprofitable lamentation, but looking with compassion on the moral wants of the neighbouring village of Durrington, and thinking that a regular place of worship there would prove a valuable appendage to Bulford, erected a very neat Chapel

on property that she owned, which was opened in September 1824. Their son Henry then took over the tenure of Ratfyn Farm which did not expire until Michaelmas 1840 and was still 'holding over' a year later whilst a new tenant was being put in place. He then retired in 1841 to live in Durrington on a small property which he owned, with his two sisters Sarah and Elizabeth. Henry and Sarah remained single but Elizabeth, who had married a solicitor E. R. Butler, lived with them on what looks like a permanent basis with her daughter, another Sarah. Both Henry junior's and his sister Elizabeth's deaths in 1870 marked an end of the Blatch association with Bulford chapel other than the legacy that the family left.[10]

Matthew Devenish, on the other hand, was a Dorset man living at Alton prior to moving to Bulford with his wife and two daughters in 1801 or 1802. He had two sons and three more daughters whilst living at Watergate Farm before his untimely death from a riding accident in 1811. His wife Elizabeth carried on with the farm until her elder son Matthew took over the reins. Matthew junior and his wife Catherine had two boys whilst running

Watergate Farm, another Matthew and James Aldridge. The year 1841, just as at Ratfyn Farm, sees all change at Watergate Farm as well. Henry's widow Elizabeth was living in Salisbury with her four unmarried daughters and younger son James Aldridge until her painful death later that year whereas Henry junior had moved back to Dorset where he pursued a career as a wine and spirits merchant in Dorchester. James Aldridge Devenish too went into the drinks industry as a brewer. He appears to have been supporting his mother in Salisbury in 1841, in conjunction with running the Devenish Brewery he had founded in Weymouth three years earlier. The brewery thrived, employing 115 men in 1851. He married and brought up his family near Weymouth and became an alderman. In 1851 Matthew and Elizabeth's three surviving, unmarried daughters Sarah, Hannah and Ann moved to Romsey in Hampshire but still supported the work of Bulford chapel. With their deaths, like the Blatches, the Devenish association with Bulford was at an end except for their legacy left to the chapel.[11]

Founding of Bulford Chapel

'THESE TWO FAMILIES [the Blatches and Devenishes] being like-minded in their religious opinions' were very close and it appears that this bond was forged at the Scots Lane chapel in Salisbury where the two farmers could well have first met. They married two sisters, Elizabeth and Sarah Aldridge and it was probable that Henry Blatch suggested that Matthew Devenish take on the vacant lease of Watergate Farm which was next to his at Ratfyn. Matthew Devenish Junior wrote that,

> My Uncle Henry Blatch of Ratfin who married my mother's only sister and my Father who went to live in Bulford in 1802 used to worship at Scot's Lane Congregational Chapel Salisbury. When it became inconvenient for my father to take his family to worship in Salisbury, my Grandfather Mr James Aldridge gave a piece of land for a Chapel on which my Uncle and Father at their own expense built the first Chapel at Bulford.

This account differs slightly from the one quoted earlier of the chapel's foundation. Was the land for the chapel built in 1805 purchased by the farming brothers-in-law, or did their father-in-law, James Aldridge, give the land?[12]

The land and the buildings where the chapel and Chapel Cottage now stand were owned as a leasehold in 1763 by Wlliam Andrews and his wife Sarah which was sold to 'Silas Burges ... thenceforth for a term of one thousand years Subject only to a yearly rent of two pence ... ' The ownership of the lease subsequently passed to Joseph Mould who was a papermaker at Bulford Mill in 1810 and his family, as we have seen, were associated with the registration of Dissenting meeting places. He was no doubt an eager accomplice to the sale of the leasehold and in 1805 it was 'assigned unto and became legally rested' with Matthew Devenish and Henry Blatch 'for all the residue of the said term of one thousand years equally to be divided between them as Tenants in Common'. Matthew Devenish and Henry Blatch then,

> at their joint expense pulled down the said Messuage and certain other Buildings then standing upon the said piece of Ground and erected thereon the Chapel or Meeting House now standing thereon with the vestry a school Room attached thereto and converted the remaining part of the said Land or Ground immediately adjoining the said Chapel or Meeting House into a burial place or ground for the interment more particularly of Members of the said Society and they also permitted an individual who had the care of the said Chapel or Meeting House to reside in and occupy part of the said leasehold hereditaments consisting of a Cottage and Garden rent free.

This legal account of the transactions does not say who put the money up for the purchase of the leasehold. An explanation which would reconcile the differing versions is that the two farmers jointly bought the leasehold but the money for this transaction was put up by James Aldridge.[13]

James Aldridge was a prosperous gentleman living at East Wellow on the Andover side of Romsey. He took on several leases in the area and served as Romsey's mayor four times between 1813 and 1831, delivering the borough's congratulations to George IV on his accession to the throne. He was no stranger to the village as an 1813 newspaper report has a Mr James Aldridge being verbally abused by Sir Isaac Pickering whilst they were out shooting together. Although there are no links with Bulford in the report, Sir Isaac Pickering was an associate of Sir Edward Loveden, the then lessor of Bulford Manor and having in fact occupied the Manor before him, making it safe to assume that it is the same James Aldridge and further that the incident happened on the Manor estates. Matthew Devenish appointed his

24 *Bulford Chapel. The two chapel cottages on the corner of Watergate Lane (Fig. 3, nos. 16 and 17) with the 1825 Chapel behind.*

father-in-law as one of his executors when he drew up his rushed deathbed will in 1811. In 1847 when the deeds of the chapel were regularised, 'James Aldridge of Romsey' was one of 'the surviving trustees and executors' of the will, who together with all the parties with an interest in the original setting up of the chapel, put it on a firm footing. This became necessary as, although 'Matthew Devenish and Henry Blatch both deceased did during their lives altogether devote and appoint the same leasehold Hereditaments to the use and for the purpose of the Society of Protestant Dissenters denominated Paedo Baptist Independents assembling at Bulford', there was a problem in that Matthew Devenish's will of 1811 made no mention of the real estate of the chapel and to complicate matters further, 'Henry Blatch died intestate'. They had both agreed during their lives 'the absolute purchase of the freehold Hereditament ... for the sum of one hundred pounds which said sum has been duly paid ... but no conveyance thereof has ever been executed'. All this was put to rights in the 1847 document putting the deeds of the chapel and the other properties involved on a secure footing with seven Dissenting Ministers being party to the agreement, including John Protheroe of Bulford.[14]

The chapel begun in 1805 'was completed in the summer of 1806 and publicly opened on the 30th July in the same year' with a long service at which sermons were preached 'by the Rev. Messrs Berry of Warminster, - Bennet of Romsey, - and Griffin of Portsea'. The new chapel and the work of the pastor had great influence in the village and beyond, and the sponsors were 'pleased that the villagers received so favourable an impression' but 'The chapel at Bulford, though erected so recently ... , owing to some defect in its structure, was considered to be unsafe for public worship, and it was therefore deemed expedient to take it down and to build one more substantial and commodious in its room', opening 17 September 1828. This new chapel 'implied a heavy expenditure' which was met principally but not exclusively by the Blatch and Devenish families'. There was also a public subscription.[15]

This redeveloped chapel that we see today was by itself an important legacy of the Blatch and Devenish families but, in many ways, they left an

25 *First Chapel Manse. Avondale School. The central portion of this house, minus the attic extension, was built by Henry Blatch as the Chapel Manse. This is where John Protheroe lived. (Fig. 3, no.34).*

even greater legacy. They also helped to provide the economic basis for provision of a permanent pastor living in the village. 'The first Minister's house belonged to the Devenish family – they gave the old house and land'. A likely scenario is that the old house was knocked down, after all it was an 'old house', when the Blatch family built the new Manse, part of the present day Avondale School, which with the chapel was invested in the hands of the trustees. The census map marks it (*Figure 2, no.34*) as built since the last census, meaning between 1841 and 1851 (or possibly 1851 and 1861). It was a well appointed house with a drawing room, dining room, kitchen, scullery and pantry. There was an entrance hall and passage leading to the stairs and upstairs there was a 'Best Bed Room' and three other bedrooms. In 1874 'A New Water Closet' was created upstairs (at a cost of £33). Outside there was a stable and coach house. It was later to prove too large a building for the financial resources of the chapel and in 1962 a prefabricated bungalow was erected adjacent to the original Manse for the pastor prior to acquiring the old school house and school buildings in 1977 as the present Manse, Godfrey Room and Lawes Hall (the old village school). The challenge to the founders, however, had been to secure their legacy to the chapel. The 1876 Report of the County Union was effusive about what they had achieved, stating that,

> A noble example has been furnished by Misses DEVENISH late of Bulford, of the way in which provision may be made for maintaining the gospel in a village, when its wealthy supporters have been removed. These excellent ladies were natives of Bulford, and their family built the chapel and maintained the ministry while they lived there; and now that none are left but the labouring poor, they have given the Treasurer of our Union £700 in trust, to be invested and the interest to be employed in maintaining an evangelical ministry in their native village. The interest of £600 is employed, under the control of the Union, in augmenting the salary of the minister. A good manse and some cottages are also provided, and the interest of £100 to keep the property in repair.[16]

The Misses Devenish of the report were Sarah, Hannah and Ann who had moved to Romsey, their grandfather James Aldridge's home, after their mother's death. The pastor felt, however, that the report was inaccurate and the record needed putting straight by adding that the Blatches had also built the chapel, and then went further in saying that it was 'built principally by Miss Blatch'. This was Sarah Blatch (1801-1852) and she does seem to be one of the driving forces behind the work of the chapel. She, as we have seen, ended up living in Durrington where she was committed to deepening the impact of the work of the Bulford chapel. It is clear that the ladies of the two families played a major role in securing their joint legacy as the chapel accounts in c1870 reveal. The minister enjoyed a stipend of eighty pounds a year, of which £25 was provided by the Devenish family, and £34 10s by Elizabeth Butler (née Blatch). The remainder was made up by the £9 6s balance of the rent, after deductions, from the four cottages given to the chapel by Matthew Devenish, weekly offerings and 'Mr Bailey's charity arising from a quarry'. When Mrs Butler died in 1870 her donation ceased and John Protheroe noted that his other major source of income was only secure 'while the Devenish family are alive'. The education work and support for the County Union and Missionary Society were also supported by Mrs Butler to the tune of £9 8s 6d out of a total budget of £26 10s, which also ceased on her death. In total, sixty-five years after the foundation of the chapel, just over sixty per cent of its budget still came from the two families.[17]

Chapel influence on the village

WITH THE CHAPEL firmly established, financially independent and nurtured by a minister resident in the village, Bulford had a strong and active focus for its religious life which was bound to have an effect. The seven original members of the chapel, the pastor and his wife, the Blatches, Devenishes and Rebecca Peck, were soon augmented by a further seven from Ablington who were 'admitted to occasional communion with the Church at Bulford'. Chapel members endeavoured to meet together once a month for communion and to attend the Friday evening prayer meeting. New members could only apply to join if they were sponsored by a member and endorsed the founders' Covenant. This required a commitment amongst many things, to 'make a visible Profession of religion' as 'we know that the eyes of the world are upon us' and a promise 'not to be absent from the Lord's table at any time except on a Journey or in Illness, and [to] bear the welfare of the Church in our Hearts continually and pray earnestly for its Prosperity'. The number of members who attended the monthly communion fluctuated between sixteen and twenty-four during the years 1835 to 1838 but by 1848 this had risen to thirty-four members on the books with a further thirty in attendance. The chapel had become, as the founders intended, a focus for the district with twenty-two of the 1848 congregation, nearly a third, coming from outside Bulford. The local chapel-goers were drawn from over a quarter of the village households – a state of affairs which worried the Established Church. [18]

For thirty-seven crucial years during the build up of the chapel congregation, the pastor was a Welshman from Carmarthen, John Protheroe. He trained at Newport Pagnell and was an earnest, conscientious, self-critical man who devoted all his energies to his work. His letter of acceptance clearly shows that he wanted to make an impact in the village.

> Bretheren! [he wrote] need I remind you that a man and not an angel is coming amongst you, - a man who needs your prayers and your sympathies ... it shall be my study affectionately, faithfully, and fearlessly, to preach the everlasting Gospel, - to give saint and sinner his portion of meat in due season, - to promote the peace and prosperity of the Church and Congregation, - and lead you in the way that leads to Heaven.

He seemed to be an emotional character who could easily become depressed as his letter written to a fellow clergyman in April 1875 from Bulford towards the end of his ministry shows. He was being chased for money owed to the County Union and writes that 'I have however regular payment to make and must be met, in addition to those which like so many clouds have been and still are hanging over my head. You know dear Brother to what I refer – the European Arbitration – and God only knows when it will terminate.' He became Bulford's minister in 1840, but in 1847, suffering from ill health and despondency about his effectiveness, he decided to leave. His congregation was upset and met on 30 May and it was reported,

> That this meeting deeply sympathises with their respected Pastor, in his protracted indisposition, and that the members of this church would deeply regret his removal, which has been intimated as necessary. Instead of this they respectfully propose that he should leave his charge for a period, to be limited only by himself, and that, should his health be restored – which by the blessing of God in answer to prayer they hope it will – he will again resume his labours among them.

John Protheroe did leave, first for London and then Plymouth where he was still afflicted by illness. He kept in contact with Bulford by staying for example with Henry Blatch in 1841 but in 1853 he returned to be pastor once more and stayed until 1877. On his return he found a cure for his ailments by marrying Ellen, (née Godwin) the widow of the Amesbury miller Joseph Olding who had just moved back to Downton; we hear no more of his ill health. His wife sadly died only two years later and finding married life so agreeable, he soon married his deceased wife's sister, Sarah Godwin who 'too, like her sister is eminently pious; and maintains daily converse with her Father in heaven.' As the marriage of a deceased wife's sister was forbidden by English law, the couple had to trek to Gretna Green to be wed in September 1856. He returned to his 'sweet home in Bulford on the 3 October grateful to our Heavenly Father for all His mercies' believing 'that God will render our Union not only a source of enjoyment to ourselves but a blessing to others'. His marriage was blessed with the birth of two sons: John Godwin in 1858, and Edward William three years later. [19]

John Protheroe's second term in the village was distinguished by a remarkable upsurge of religious fervour which trebled his congregation within the year 1860-1861. Looking back over the year, he wrote in the *Chapel Church Book* in enthusiastic detail about the revival and it is worth quoting extensively in detail to give an insight into the religious life of the village.

> The first indications ... became visible about the end of November last and were observed in the great stillness which pervaded the congregation ... – in the extraordinary spirit of prayer which was poured out upon the people and their faith in the efficacy of prayer – and in some mysterious influence almost irresistible which I felt on my own mind by which for some time before the Revival 'broke out' I was all but impelled to preach to my people from certain subjects ... Duty became a pleasure ... This happy state of things had been preceded by ... a great amount of self denying labour on the part of the Sabbath-School teachers, with the addition of a prayer meeting immediately at the close of school in the afternoon – by the establishment of a meeting for members exclusively for Christian fellowship and prayer ... Even at <u>one</u> of our church meetings, lately held, I had the unspeakable pleasure and amor to give the right hand of fellowship to twenty on their admission into

the church, and to propose, at the same time, ten more as candidates for Christian Communion ... The awakening at Bulford has been very general – among young and old – among persons of every character ... For the last four months, meetings for prayer have been held almost every night in the week, and are not only numerously attended, but generally crowded. The effects of the present awakening on our young people are remarkable ... they pray not only for themselves, but for their relatives and friends and the unconverted in the village and neighbourhood ... There is no loss for words, no hesitation as generally is the case with young converts when they begin to pray. Their language flows on apparently without any let or hindrance ... Even little children now pray ... Indeed all pray ... And when on a Sabbath or on week evenings the regular service is over – a service of perhaps of more than two hours duration, and sometimes three – a great number then linger about, as if unwilling to leave, and then return to pray, and continue to late ... A large a proportion of the candidates for Church fellowship are found among the young, some few of whom, before their conversion and while in the Sabbath School, were almost unmanageable by their teachers. Now they are in their right mind and pray ...

A happy change has come over the village, and everywhere around its influence is felt. The police officer, located in our neighbourhood, referring to this happy change, one day remarked that, in his walks thro' Bulford, instead of trifling conversation, he could only hear the voice of prayer and praise ascending to God, from cottages of the poor ... And the young people instead of frequenting as formerly they did the public house now abstain altogether from intoxicating drinks and derive their chief delight from the service of God. The fields, too, present a very different aspect from what they ever had before. Here and there, during the dinner hour you may see and hear groups of persons while resting speak of things touching the King [God], and perhaps, one of their number reading to the rest some religious book ...

The present revival at Bulford is distinguished more by deep inward solemnity than by external manifestation:- there is no physical prostration – no outward extravagance – no religious bustle ... We had long been praying for this revival – crying long, but believingly and patiently ... It is now come ...[20]

Response of the Established Church

EVEN IF WE allow for any overstatement due to John Protheroe being at the centre of this expression of popular devotion, the happenings of 1860 to 1861 were not to be ignored by the Established Church (nor by the landlord of the 'Rose and Crown'!). The parish church was still the focus for most farmers and gentry but fundamental changes were inevitable to prevent the mass of the population from going over to the chapel. How could any headway be made without a resident Church of England curate in the village? The reason for the chapel's success was all too evident to Rev. John James Scott when he wrote in 1864 that,

> The Independent Meeting House, Endowed, and its resident Minister; who professedly administers Baptism, and the Lord's Supper, [has been] to the detriment of the Church. He has been living in a house especially built for the Dissenting Minister, for the last twenty years in Bulford, and from this one circumstance alone possesses considerable influence in the village, while there is no parsonage, or any house fit for a clergyman to reside in. [Just what William Cobbett said thirty-eight years before!] Remedy – A parsonage, in order to secure a Resident Clergyman, and one likely to be permanent. I would recommend that the clergyman incumbent in Milston, be invited to accept the Curacy, being resident within a mile of Bulford Church.

This was a view endorsed in 1873 when there were,

> 44 heads of families (counting both man and wife) decidedly Dissenters (Independents). Such owing to former neglect of the parish and the irregularity of church services. Many more have got into the habit of attending church and chapel alternatively; and in several cases husbands belong to one, the wife to the other.

In 1870 a Wiltshire vicar lamented 'the prevailing habit of our people going to church in the morning and to the Meeting in the evening, so that the Church itself is half Wesleyanised'. This seems very apposite to the situation in Bulford. The church in Wiltshire was slow to catch on to the convenience of evening services to an agricultural population, whereas in the chapels evening services were the rule rather than the exception, and in Bulford they were not begun in the parish church until about 1895. A further indication of the relative followings of church and chapel can be gleaned from the following figures. In 1864 the parish church had sixty-six communicants and an average Sunday attendance of one hundred at the 11 o'clock service and fifty at the 3 o'clock, whereas the chapel commanded the loyalties of about one hundred and twelve villagers. The community was split between church and chapel with the latter increasing its hold at the expense of the former which was static, if not decreasing – no candidate came forward for parish confirmation that and the previous year. [21]

One of the reasons given for the rapid inroads of nonconformity at this time was that it was an age of missionary activity when The London Missionary Society, CMS, SPG and SPCK were all founded. The Dissenters also had a new interest in overseas mission to convert the heathen which prompted the question, "Have you not heathen enough at home to warrant your attention?" In Bulford, the enthusiasm and commitment of a resident clergyman in the village, ready to put all his energy into mission, had borne great fruits. Being resident, the times of services and meetings could be held in the evenings which suited villagers as opposed to in the middle of the day which suited a clergyman having to travel to and fro to the village. This is supported by chapel statistics in 1884 which showed that seventy or eighty attended evening services as opposed to fifty or sixty during the day. Although this was down on the figures from four years previously which were a hundred and twelve and eighty-five respectively, the pattern was still the same. Being resident also enabled him to motivate villagers to assist him in his work. When Pastor John Penn was appointed in June 1884, his contract stipulated,

> Special Requirements as to the Bulford Station
> 1   That the Mission Pastor shall conduct two public services in the Chapel and at least one service during the week together with such visitation and attention to the Sunday School as may be desirable.
> 2   Bulford being but a small village the Mission Pastor will be expected to visit all the villages within reach to preach the gospel, distribute tracts and promote the Salvation of Souls in every practicable way and report the same in the periodical journal.

This clearly illustrates how central mission remained to the raison d'être of the chapel right through the century and beyond. In 1906, for example, a visitation was concerned with the effectiveness of the chapel's mission in Bulford Camp, reporting that, 'We understand that [the current minister] Mr Farr's status and influence with the soldiers would be increased if he were formally recognised by the Military Authorities and we recommend that application be made to the War Office for such recognition'. This, though, is jumping ahead. Returning to the situation before the army arrived, it was clear that the Established Church had to respond to the challenge posed by the chapel in kind and it rose to the challenge by appointing the first resident vicar of Bulford in December 1869 with the patron giving him Orchard End House as his vicarage and an increased stipend of £100. The appointment they made was a Canadian born clergyman who was one of the curates in Milston between 1858 and October 1862. He represented that parish at the Amesbury Deanery meetings from 1860 until 1862. It is worth looking at his career and personality in some detail to try to assess his impact on the village. [22]

Bulford's first Parish Priest

THE REV. JACOB Jehoshaphat Salter Mountain was a member of a dynasty of Church of England clergymen who moved from Thwaite in Norfolk to Canada in 1793 and within a century produced two bishops and eight priests both in England and Canada, and what is very noticeable is the ease in which they travelled regularly between the two countries and held benefices in both. Jacob Jehoshaphat Mountain's great uncle Jacob Mountain, and grandfather Jehosaphat Mountain emigrated, the former becoming the first Anglican bishop of Quebec and his brother Jehoshaphat, a priest in his diocese. The bishop's son George Jehoshaphat became the third bishop of Quebec and his cousin Salter, Jehoshaphat's son, became Rector of Christchurch, Quebec, before moving to become Rector of Trinity, Cornwall (Ontario) to nurse his health. It was in Cornwall that Salter's wife Anna Maria (née Scott) gave birth to Jacob Jehoshaphat Salter on 2 October 1824. Quebec had not long been in English hands and Bishop Jacob has been described as the 'Founder of the Church of England in Canada', founding the bishopric and Bishop's College, Lennoxville from where Jacob Jehoshaphat Salter graduated. This was the time when the Gappers, Mary and her brother Anthony (Southby), were involved with the church in Ontario. She wrote in her journal that, 'Mr Thorne has just sent a letter of Mountain's (quite a large book) in answer to somebody's narrative of his conversion to the Roman Catholic Faith but I have not yet had time to look into it.' Three days later she wrote, 'I have read some of Mountain's letters and liked much the spirit.' The mission of the Church of England was to make headway in a Catholic country, as well as with the settlers from England and with the Native Americans. In 1836 Jacob Jehosaphat Salter's uncle George became the third Suffragan Bishop of Quebec and as bishop, he was faced with the task of creating a sense of diocesan unity in a country where communication was a major challenge. Throughout his career he methodically and indefatigably toured his diocese injecting a new spiritual life into his people. He had begun this journeying as an archdeacon and on all his tours the living conditions of the people, the state of religion and education in every settlement at which he stopped were his prime concerns. The Gappers, who were staunchly Anglican, in all probability met him and certainly knew of his work and reputation. To all practical purposes the bishop had pastoral care of their parish in Upper Canada, although this was technically under the Bishop of London. The relationship is illustrated in 1830 when the Gappers had plans afoot to make one of Anthony Gapper's brothers-in-law a professor of divinity and classics in Upper Canada. It was reported by Mary Gapper that 'probably Mountain had mentioned him [to the Governor] as he promised to do'. [23]

26 *Rev Dr Jacob Jehoshaphat Salter Mountain.*
Rev Dr Jacob Jehoshaphat Salter Mountain (1824-1910), the first Vicar of Bulford. This was taken in his old age in Cornwall, Ontario. He wanted a memorial window portraying Moses whom he said that he resembled.

Jacob Jehoshaphat Salter Mountain was no doubt influenced by his uncle the bishop's example, combined with that of his parents. He later wrote of his mother's 'life of influence in the parish that has never been surpassed'. He went to Cornwall Grammar School and then, with this pedigree, there was only one possible career for him; the church. He was one of the first graduates of Bishop's College, founded by his great uncle, and then went on to King's College, University of Windsor, Nova Scotia where he obtained his BA and DD, and probably met his Nova Scotia born wife to be Annie Gilpin, the daughter of an archdeacon. He married her in Toronto in 1847 and in the same year was ordained deacon before embarking on two years as a travelling missionary in the backwoods of Canada. These must have been formative years in his life as a commitment to mission work was a constant aspect of his life. In his will he made a bequest to set up a Mission Fellowship at Bishop's College, where the Bishop of Quebec was to appoint a 'a clergyman of the Church of England in Priests Orders', to work six months in the year 'to conduct parochial missions in the Diocese of Quebec or Montreal'. The remainder of the year he was to be college-based, lecturing students and to 'conduct annually or oftener a 'Quiet Day' or 'Retreat' for the benefit of the inmates of the college'. The fellow was to be selected for literary attainment and teaching quality, as well as an ability to extemporise in delivering his message. He needed 'such personal gifts of spiritual mindedness as may, in the bishop's judgement, qualify him to deepen the spiritual life of his brethren'. These were the qualities needed by the Vicar of Bulford and it is fair to assume that Jacob Jehoshaphat Salter Mountain thought that he possessed them, and the evidence is that he did. He certainly had the academic attainment, having a BCL and DCL and was known as 'Doctor Mountain' in Bulford. He was a deeply religious man and his piety was matched by that of his wife who published a book of poems in 1873 entitled *A Wreath of Rue, for Lent and the Sacred Lake*. This was a collection of devotional poems and reflections upon divinity for the weeks of Lent, followed by verses appropriate for reading on Good Friday and Easter Eve. The couple were both involved in teaching evening classes in Bulford twice a week for villagers, along with the school mistress. A missionary way of life obviously appealed as a letter from his nephew's wife recounts. When he returned to Canada, after Annie's death in 1882, 'every now and again he went off on some tour in out-of-the-world places, as much of his journey on foot as possible.' He was also, in his personal life, modest and stipulated that he wished his funeral 'to be as plain as possible, *and no expensive flowers even*, in order to set a much needed example in this repect'. This spirituality, modesty and devotion to expanding his beloved Church of England, very suited to his ministry in Bulford, was as we will see, just one strand in his complex character and when Jacob Jehosophat Salter Mountain's name came up to become the first resident Vicar of Bulford village, Anthony Gapper (Southby) who was by then the Lord of the Manor and patron of the church, certainly knew a lot about his background and would no doubt have been enthusiastic to appoint him. They might even have known each other as there were links between Thornhill in Upper Canada where Anthony lived and Cornwall, where Jacob Jehoshaphat was born and educated. The clergyman in the former was reportedly taking over in the latter 'in place of Mr Mountain'. What is more, Jacob Jehoshaphat Salter Mountain also had the experience of running a parish at Coteau du Lac, East Quebec from 1849 till 1857 after his being ordained a priest in Montreal. A catalyst for a more settled life was probably the birth of his son Jacob in 1849. [24]

Doctor Mountain was appointed to the incumbency of Bulford in December 1869 upon the resignation of Rev. Millner and held it until April 1878. He took up residence in the house provided by Anthony Southby (Orchard End) and enjoyed the enhanced income of one hundred pounds. He appears to have been diligent in his duties being resident, in 1873 for example, the required 275 days of the year. The remaining ninety days could have seen him travelling, either to visit relatives in this country, or else crossing over to Canada and America where he owned property and had a deep and enduring commitment to the parish of his birth, Cornwall, Ontario. He must have made an impression in the village and appears to have been an ideal choice to win back the church congregation; attendances and numbers coming forward for confirmation both increased and in 1870 he could report that '¾ of the families of the labouring population ... are members of the Church of England; of the other families, some send their children to the Church of England Sunday School ... '. He appears to have thrown himself into village life and reached out to villagers but he wrote that the eight drinking houses within a one and a quarter mile radius of the village 'specially impedes my ministry'. This was a challenge for him. His nephew's wife later wrote of him that he 'was great at making elaborate and sometimes remarkably successful plans'; and he had one for this problem. As we saw in Chapter 2, he proposed delivering good quality beer straight to

27 Mary Anne Knight. This is almost certainly a portrait of Mary Anne Knight, née Cannings, (1835-1915) probably taken in about 1860, when she was cook to Anthony Southby. She later travelled the world with her mariner husband before being widowed and becoming the first village schoolmistress in 1875.

the door of each house, ensuring that the labourers drank good healthy beer, and were not drawn into drink-induced unruly behaviour. This scheme never got off the ground but it illustrates that he was concerned with all aspects of village life, and not just the formalities of services, births, deaths and marriages. [25]

The ability to analyse and tackle a challenge was also evident in Dr Mountain's response to the 1870 Education Act which put an obligation on the parish to provide education (not free at this point) to all children. As head of the parish, he had to make the case for the building of a new school to accommodate sixty children, which was way beyond the existing provision. He was successful in this with the new school being opened in 1874 and he was no doubt supportive of the appointment, as its first mistress, of Mary Ann Knight who had just returned from America. His commitment to education, which was a family tradition back in Canada, as we have seen, went beyond the setting up of a new school. He was involved in teaching evening classes twice a week, recognising the need to reach out to an agricultural population at a time convenient to them. His wife Annie helped in this venture reflecting that not only did the village now posses a resident Church of England clergyman, it was also blessed with a clergyman's wife, alongside the Dissenting minister and his wife. Religion and spirituality could no longer be ignored in the village. Doctor Mountain's health suffered (from overwork?) causing him to take a sabbatical year in 1875 but the parish was not neglected as the Rev. Charles Amfill moved into the Vicarage to cover his absence. Even so, on his return he reported to his bishop that he was sorry to find that attendance had 'decreased very much during my absence, partly owing to preaching in the neighbouring parishes of the so called Evangelists'. Once back in Bulford, he wrote a letter about his family to the Canadian press and signing himself off as 'Formerly of Coteau du Lac, Canada, now Vicar of Bulford, England. BULFORD VICARAGE, Amesbury, Salisbury, May 30, 1877.' The following June he witnessed as Vicar of Bulford the will of Michael Stone, 'for many years past resident at Bulford'. The will was also witnessed by 'Jacob Mountain junr, son of the above of Queens College Oxford'. Jacob junior followed the family tradition, becoming Vicar of Hampton Poyle and Barford St Michael, Oxfordshire, before his sudden death in 1899. In November 1877 Dr Mountain attended his last deanery meeting at Amesbury prior to relinquishing his incumbency of Bulford. [26]

His time in Bulford must have been some of Jacob Jehoshaphat Salter Mountain's happiest years – family was important to him and all seemed to be going well, but it was not to last. In 1881 he and Annie were living at Brading in the Isle of Wight where she was to die the following year. He spent the rest of his life split between the Isle of Wight and Ontario, marrying a second time in Shanklin and dying in 1910, widowed for a second time and with no descendants. He was proud of his family and even, like Lady Pollen, left money to a nephew if he changed his name to 'Mountain'. These sad bereavements help to explain why he devoted so much energy to creating memorials to his family. He centred his love and attention on building the Church of the Good Shepherd, known as the Mountain Family Memorial Church, in Cornwall, Ontario in 1893 and his work was recognised with the title of Honorary Canon of Ottawa Cathedral in 1897. Much of the impetus and cash to build this church came from the Rev. Canon Jacob Jehoshaphat Salter Mountain and he 'gave its beautiful chime of 9 bells'. His will requested that three memorial windows be created, one for his mother, one for his first wife and the middle one for himself, stating that, 'I should prefer that the light on which Moses is represented should be selected for the last named purpose as I have been said to bear some slight resemblance to him for which character I have always felt the greatest admiration'. It was done as he asked, including the picture of Moses. A photographic portrait of Jacob Jehoshaphat Salter Mountain in his latter years shows a saddened, strong looking face with flowing white beard, indeed like Moses. He had outlived two wives, a son and two daughters, had no grandchildren and had not achieved his ambition of becoming a bishop or even of his family church becoming the seat of a bishopric, nevertheless he had achieved a lot, including a revival of parish life at Bulford. He is buried at Brading, Isle of Wight. [27]

The pattern had been set at Bulford. Doctor Mountain's successor for a brief time was Rev. Robert Liston Johnson under whom a partial restoration of the church took place in 1879. The seats in the nave and transepts were lowered and 'turned into open seats', and the pulpit was placed in its original position. A new reading desk and lectern were provided for which George Melsome of Watergate House gave a prayer book. The pews were moved without a faculty (permission from the diocesan authorities) because of the 'attitude of patron and his family, who appears to wish church matters to remain as they were a century ago'. In 1880 the incumbency was taken over by the Rev. John Gray Goodrich until his death in 1886 and burial in Bulford churchyard. He was then succeeded by the twenty-seven year old Rev. Cecil North Arnold who saw the century out with a twenty-one year stint as Vicar of Bulford and it was under him that several changes in the parish took place. He had been made a deacon in 1882, serving as curate of Stour Provost in Dorset and in 1885 was ordained a priest before moving to Bulford two years later. He died in 1908 and is buried in the New Cemetery. He moved into Orchard End, called 'Bulford Parsonage' in the 1891 census which shows him living with his wife Sarah and five and a half month daughter Ruth, a visitor and two servants. It appears that a second daughter Hannah had died in infancy, but the following year they had another, Dorothy. The family found the parsonage too small and damp for their growing family with the domestic staff they needed. [28]

Status and lifestyle of incumbents

THE NINETEENTH CENTURY was a time of large gentrified vicarages and rectories suited to the aspirations of the incumbents who were often men of means, the Rev. Jacob Jehoshaphat Salter Mountain, for example, leaving an estate of $79,000 on his death. Some idea of the living style of a nineteenth-century cleric, most of whom had living-in domestic servants, can be gained from the Independent Minister Samuel Sleigh. He was involved with the Scots Lane chapel in Salisbury, coming to the village in the break between John Protheroe's two ministries, and when he left in 1852 auctioned the contents of the Manse. It must be said that he was relatively wealthy and his previous congregation at Wavertree were beholden to him for personally liquidating the debts on their new chapel. This advertisement appeared in the *Salisbury and Winchester Journal* on Saturday 4 September 1852:

> EXCELLENT NEAT AND MODERN HOUSEHOLD FURNITURE AND OTHER EFFECTS FOR SALE
> MR. H.P.EWER will sell by AUCTION, on the premises at BULFORD, Wilts, on Wednesday, September 22, 1852,- The whole of the superior and Neat and Modern HOUSEHOLD FURNITURE, and other Effect, the property of the Rev. Thomas Sleigh, who is removing to a distance; comprising mahogany and birch four-post, tent, and French bedsteads, straw palliasses, hair and wool mattresses, feather beds, bolsters, and pillows, blankets, counterpanes, double and single washstands with ware, mahogany and painted chests of drawers, dressing tables, mahogany frame swing glasses, mahogany pedestal night commodes, mahogany centre table on pillar and claw, mahogany pedestal sideboard as fitted up with three drawers, cellaret and cupboard, 8 mahogany chairs with hair stuffed seats, mahogany easy chair covered with morocco, sofa, with hair and swab cushions, Brussels carpet, 15 by 15, hearth rug, drugget, pair scarlet moreen curtains, with pole, rings and holders, fancy cane seat and other chairs, mahogany study table with 10 drawers and cupboard under, easy chair, study ditto, blue and white figured damask moreen window curtains with pole, rings and holders, mahogany Pembroke table, mahogany butler's tray and stand, gold, green and white tea service, consisting of 60 pieces, china tea and breakfast service of about 80 piece, glass, sundry dinner and tea ware, 24-hour clock, fenders and fire irons, with kitchen and culinary requisites, &c. &c.
> The above furniture has been new within the last four years, and is in an excellent state of preservation.

This list does not, of course, include his personal effects which he took away with him. In neighbouring Milston the Rectory had recently been rebuilt (c1870) to support this kind of lifestyle and now it was turn for Bulford's vicar to have a new vicarage. We have a description of Orchard End from 1900 after it had relinquished its role as Bulford's Vicarage:

> ... the Old Vicarage, which we saw to be an impressive house, overshadowed by trees ... Once it must have been comfortable, but it had fallen into disrepair.

> The woman caretaker gave us [Mary Hamiltion and her officer husband] an unappertising meal in a sitting room overladen with half-mouldy furniture. Upstairs the beds were poor, the door handles loose, the carpets worn, and the wallpaper shabby. Outside was no better ... [except] the orchard was there, its blossom a mass of pink in the summer dusk ... [29]

In 1893 a new, larger vicarage was built on the corner of Milston Road on land donated by the new Lord of the Manor, James Ledger Hill. The site was owned in 1838 by Jenner, occupied by John Maton in 1841 and was known as 'Corner End', but had since been absorbed into the Manor lands. The new Vicarage cost £1,891, with the money being raised by subscriptions and grants from the Ecclesiastical Commissioners and the Trustees of Queen Anne's Bounty, a fund established in 1704 for the augmentation of the incomes of the poorer clergy. There was concerted village support behind this project with inhabitants buying bricks at two pence each, and the bricklayers of the village giving their services for free, giving weight to the inscription in the Vicarage porch which reads 'built without cost'. The Arnolds moved in and in 1901 we find them settled with their four children, two daughters and two sons ranging in age from one to nine years old, a twenty-five year old school governess from London and local teenagers Alice Keel from the village and Alice Waters from Winterbourne Stoke as housemaid and nurse respectively. The village now had a resident vicar in a purpose-built vicarage with an endowment, since 1884, of £75 7s 6d. It was everything that had been asked for over the years but the truth of the matter was that the village had overstretched itself and did not have the wealth to support it all. The new Vicarage was sold to a private individual in 1978 and four years later the benefice of Bulford was united with that of Figheldean with Milston. Today it is part of the even larger Avon Valley Team Ministry comprising of Bulford, Enford, Figheldean, Fittleton, Milston and Netheravon. The last years of the nineteenth century and the early years of the twentieth, therefore, saw the parish of Bulford at its self contained peak. The church had a new organ in 1890, costing £150, a thriving choir and a new stove, paid for by the new Lord of the Manor, James Ledger Hill, and an undisputed role as the focus of the community; but changes had begun with the 1894 Local Government Act. [30]

Parish governance

SINCE THE CLOSE of the Middle Ages, the church vestry had been the unit of local government in the village. It had wide responsibilities for overseeing the poor, controlling vermin, moral conduct of villagers as well as duties associated with the parish church. Churchwardens had wider responsibility; for example they could instruct the police constable in his duties. The rise of religious Dissent had weakened this bond between Established Church and villagers and, when combined with a more secular approach to local government in which all villagers could play a part, was the catalyst for the changes in 1894. The Local Government Act established elected parish councils in rural areas and reformed the boards of guardians of poor law unions. Each parish was to have a parish meeting with each elector having a single vote on all matters raised, including the election of parish councillors who would have a one-year term of office. The parish council was to assume all powers exercised by parish vestries except those dealing with the church or ecclesiastical charities. Examples included the maintenance of closed burial grounds, ownership of village greens and recreation grounds and it could also take on powers under various statutes relating to, for example, street lighting.

The first parish council meeting on 13 December 1894 was held in the Reading Room with the Lord of the Manor, James Ledger Hill as chairman and George Melsome of Watergate House as vice-chairman who, along with James Hooper was appointed overseer of the poor. In terms of personnel, nothing much had changed in the governance of the village, but their first act was to use the new powers by voting unanimously that, 'The village should be lighted with Parafin or other Oil lamps to be placed in such positions as the council should think best', and seeking tenders 'for the required number of pillar lamps complete also the required number of bracket lamps complete. Tenders to be asked from Mr Merchant of Amesbury and Mess[r] Woodrow Wilton Lloyd and Wilkes of Salisbury'. On 10 July 1891 a new cemetery on land given by James Ledger Hill was consecrated by the Bishop of Salisbury allowing 'the old graveyard [at the church to] be closed strictly for burial purposes on the consecration of the new burial ground', which thereby allowed the local authority to take on responsibility for maintaining it under powers subsequently granted by the 1894 Act. The new parish council also negotiated with the War Office to allow their tenant James Hooper to sublet land to create a recreational ground in 1901. The old role of the parish priest being the undisputed head of the village community was changing, but this perception did not change overnight. Four years after the parish council was set up, a 'circular letter to Mr Arnold was read on the subject of the Pewsey and Salisbury Railway' showing that the parish priest was still perceived to have a role in local government. [31]

The church was still a very important part of the establishment with Christianity seen as the cement of village society which was reflected in the parish council setting letting charges in 1898 for hire of the Reading Room (at 2s 6d to cover cleaning and so forth) 'for the benefit of parishioners at large and for missionary and philanthropic and Christian work'. And we must not forget that the church controlled village education and the Managers could use the school for church purposes as the following extracts from the log book illustrate:

> A whole holiday given on this day on account of the Sunday Scholars' Tea.' [13 Jan. 1898]
> a half day holiday given in the afternoon to enable some of the scholars to attend a tea meeting.' [3 Oct. 1899]
> opened school at 1.10 pm to enable the children to attend Divine Service at 3.30 pm.[16 Oct. 1899]

The church was still at the centre of established life in the village and when, for example, the villagers marked Queen Victoria's Diamond Jubilee, it played a central role in the celebrations.

> On Sunday special thanksgiving services were held in the parish church. The evening service was fully choral, the anthem, "The Lord is loving unto every man" (Caleb Simper), being well rendered by the choir. The Bulford brass band played a selection of sacred airs both before and after the evening service. On Tuesday the village was prettily decorated with flags, and a general holiday was given in the afternoon. A procession, headed by the band, was formed at the Reading Room and proceeded to the Park, kindly lent by Mr J. L. Hill. A cricket match between married and single, ending in defeat of the single by one run, was played. At 4.30 a meat tea was partaken by the women and children, and later on a supper by the men. The

proceedings terminated with dancing and a visit to the Bonfire on Beacon Hill. A short service was held in the church at 6.30.

Four years later with the Queen's death, the parish was saddled with a 'large deficit .... accounted for by exceptional expenditure in connection with the late Queen's death and funeral', debts which took several years to pay off.[32]

Church and Chapel relationships

TO BRING THIS survey of religious life in Bulford to a close, it is worth considering the relationships between church and chapel. Rivals they were but not altogether hostile or aggressive to one another. Matthew Devenish, the chapel co-founder, was a regular attender at the Easter Vestry meetings in the parish church and when he died in 1811 after a fall from his horse, a memorial plaque was put up to him in the church. Many villagers looked to both church and chapel and 'got into the habit of attending church and chapel alternatively; in several cases the husband belongs to one, the wife to the other'. We can see how one individual, Jane Tinham, went from one to the other. In 1807 she attended chapel and applied for membership but she returned as a communicant to the church. She finally became a full member of the chapel in 1822 and remained as such until her death fifteen years later. The two churches saw each other as fellow Christians and the 1862 chapel resolution against marriage with unbelievers and against the will of Christ as 'such marriages have generally been productive of the greatest miseries, and woeful defections among Christians', did not apply to marriages between church and chapel goers. Indeed Samuel Sleigh, Pastor of the chapel, saw his daughter Elizabeth marry a surgeon from Daventry in the parish church. Perhaps the clearest indication of the closeness of the two churches was provided by William Williams, Pastor of the chapel from 1831 to 1840, who left Bulford to become a Church of England priest. Looking back in 1887 at the reasons why Dissent had taken such a hold in the village, the local clergy, including the incumbent of Bulford felt that,

> The absence of all bitterness of feeling would appear to indicate that it was not so much the doctrine of the Church of England which produced the original breach, as her manner in teaching and enforcing it. One circumstance will at least show that the churchmen of Amesbury did not regard the Dissenters

as those who separated on serious questions of doctrine. For when the chapel, originally founded in 1806, was a few years afterwards enlarged and improved, among the subscribers was the Incumbent of the Parish and Sir Edmund Antrobus [of Amesbury].

Relationships could however still be strained as the following incident shows. In the burial register of the chapel the death of the eighty year old John Mundy, a retired police officer, of 'senile decay' on 14 January 1897 is followed by this comment:

> John Mundy was the first person buried with Nonconformist service in Bulford Parish grave yard. The first part of the service was held in the Chapel. The vicar was much aggrieved, and his friends made many unkind reflections on the officiating Minister. [Rev. Cecil North Arnold?] The tolling of the bell was refused, but no harm resulted. [33]

Parish Clerk

FINALLY, THIS CHAPTER has looked latterly at the role which the institution of the parish played in the governance of Bulford Village through changing times. The parish clerk was crucial in keeping the parish functioning, especially in the days before Bulford had its own incumbent. During the last quarter of the eighteenth century the post was held by Samuel Sturges, who died in 1788. At the beginning of the nineteenth century (1804) the office was held by another Sturges, Sam, who could well be the Samuel Sturges who went on to play such a active part in the life of the chapel after being admitted in 1813. This would have made him the nephew of the previous parish clerk Samuel Sturges. 1833 and 1834 see John Kinsman holding the 'freehold office [of] parish clerk' which entitled him to vote in parliamentary elections. 1835 sees Robert Hedges as parish clerk, beginning of a fifty-four year tenure of the office by the Hedges, father and son. The father Robert Hedges, who was born in Enford and worked as an agricultural labourer. In the 1861 census his son James was the parish clerk with his widowed father living with him 'who for many years was clerk before him'. He had been in domestic service for a while to a farmer of 130 acres (to whom he appears to have been related) in Portbury, Somerset, before taking over from his father. He married Orah who was a member of the Durrington branch of the Sturgis clan and worked as a dressmaker. The parish accounts have Robert Sturgis receiving payment as the clerk in 1843; perhaps he was covering for Robert Hedges? When James in turn retired from his office after holding it for thirty years, the vestry marked the occasion with a vote of grateful thanks on 25 April 1889; he was still a man of status in the village as there were still five years to go before the 1894 Local Government Act diminished the post's responsibilities. He lived to see these changes, dying in 1897. [34]

9
Bulford Paper Mill and its Papermakers

The River Avon flowing past,
Kept the millwheels turning fast,
Inside the tanks came tumbling and splashing,
And washed the rags for paper maching.

Prudence Sawyer [1]

Early paper making at Bulford

FROM THE SIXTEENTH century onwards, papermaking was a widespread industry in Wessex where chalk streams were ideal for the mills. There were paper-mills at Bemerton, Downton and Bulford, clustering around Salisbury which also had its own mill at Grey Friars. Salisbury provided a market for paper as well as for its chief raw material – rags. Another paper-mill was situated further east at Andover. The River Avon provided, according to an advertisement for Bulford Mill in 1790, 'a constant supply of water, of a quality for making the best papers', and so it is not surprising that a paper-mill should have been set up in the village once the necessary capital and enterprise had been brought together. Existing watermills could easily be converted for papermaking as an advertisement for the sale of Upwey Mill, Dorset, asserts: 'N.B. The mills are eligibly situated for, and at small expense, easily converted into Paper Mills'. Bulford's paper-mill occupied the site of the present Mill House and was certainly one of the two watermills mentioned in the Domesday Book; the other mill could have been situated further downstream at Watergate Farm, or else the two mills

Bulford Paper Mill and its Papermakers

were in one building. Up until the 1950s traces of a wheel could still be seen alongside the barn on Watergate Farm, which was certainly not connected with a mill, or if it was, it had a later role (see Chapter 5 above). [2]

The earliest evidence of papermaking at Bulford comes from the records of the Sun Fire Insurance Company. Wingfield Hillman and Thomas Noyce were insured as papermakers in 1765. In 1781 the mill was registered as a Nonconformist meeting house under papermaker Thomas Mould, marking the beginning of a thirty year association with the family. It would appear that William Mould (Thomas's father?) was also working at the mill with Thomas as he was described as being 'of Bulford Paper-Mill' when his estate was wound up in 1875. He probably died in 1784 when Mary Mould, almost certainly his widow, insured her stock as a papermaker, no doubt taking over the business from her late husband. Although the Moulds worked at the mill, it appears that the leasehold or copyhold was held by Mr Noyes (or Noyce), who in 1786 advertised,

> TO be LETT or SOLD, a valuable leasehold PAPER MILL and DWELLING HOUSE, with offices adjoining, and all other requisites for carrying on the Paper Trade in an extensive manner, all new built within these twenty years, with about an acre of meadow ground ...

This would indicate that when the stock was insured in 1765, it was the beginning of the paper-mill's history at Bulford. The advertisement went on to stress the good communications with Amesbury, Salisbury, Devizes, Marlborough and Andover, near where Mr Noyes was living at the time in Westover. It then sang the praises of the mill as, 'The engine, chest, and vat, are completely leaded, and there is an excellent never failing stream of water, which has a peculiar tendency to make Paper of a beautiful white colour'.[3]

The next we hear of the mill is when Isaac Brodribb was insured as the 'master papermaker' and he is the first person to emerge from the records as more than just a name. He leased the mill from 1786 until his bankruptcy in 1790, when he was described as a 'papermaker, late of Durrington'. During the term of his lease, he had spent a 'considerable sum to bring the premises into repair'. There was at least one other papermaker working under him, Thomas Mould, and it would appear that the Noyes connection with the paper-mill continued up until 1817 when *The Times* reported in its bankruptcy notices, 'H Noyes [Thomas's son?] Bulford,

Wiltshire. Papermaker, to surrender Mar 28, 29, May 3 at the Public Rooms, New Sarum'. [4]

It is difficult to gain a full picture of the papermakers and papermaking until the decennial census returns give a clearer picture of the business. Isaac Brodribb had other business interests besides papermaking and it is these that might well have made him bankrupt, forcing him to sell the mill. (We have a record dated 23 November 1789 of him, along with his elder brother Abraham, a clothier in Shepton Mallet, and two Bristol men, one a maltster, leasing a property in the city to a distiller.) His advertisement, which lasted for seven weeks, read:

> To be lett and entered immediately for the remainder of the lease of which 10 years are unexpired the 24th June last [1789], the PAPERMILL and DWELLING HOUSE at Bulford, in the county of Wilts, with three quarters of an acre of rich meadow land. – The Mill and Premises are in compleat repair, there having lately been a considerable sum expended thereon; a constant supply of water, of a quality for making the best papers; the coming-on tenant will be quite easy, and the Mill may immediately be set to work at little or no expense; the coming-in tenant to take the utensils at a fair valuation ...

The sale of the utensils and the, by then, nine remaining years on the lease was made to Lawrence Greatrake who duly insured the utensils and stock in Bulford Paper-Mill and a warehouse at Andover in 1791, and two years later he was described as a papermaker of Bulford. [5]

Lawrence Greatrake

LAWRENCE GREATRAKE, LIKE Isaac Brodribb, also had a Bristol connection. His grandfather was a shipping merchant trading with colonial America, but of more interest to the history of Bulford was his father Roger, born in Cork as was Lawrence in c1760, marrying Elizabeth Cottle in Bath, and then settling in Kings Langley, near Hemel Hempstead, where he managed and perhaps part owned until the late 1790s Apsley Mill, a corn and paper-mill. He was insured as a papermaker in 1778 with Sun Fire Insurance and his son, Lawrence was described as a 'paper maker' on the 1781- 1785 militia list. Roger Greatrake died in 1799 and a year later Apsley Mill was registered with George Stafford. It was at this mill and

Bulford Paper Mill and its Papermakers

some adjacent mills that the machine made papermaking industry was established soon after Roger Greatrake's death, and this is where Lawrence Greatrake grew up. In 1790 he then bought the lease of Bulford Mill and probably saw out the lease before emigrating to America. He almost certainly met Joshua Gilpin who visited England from America between 1795 and 1801 to update himself on the latest papermaking technology, visiting the Lawrence Greatrake's mill in 1796. This is when he no doubt persuaded Lawrence to emigrate to America and manage his papermaking mill in Delaware. Lawrence emigrated in September 1799 (the year the lease of Bulford Mill expired) and arrived in Philadelphia in May 1800 after a 'seven month and twenty-six day voyage from London' which included a five month repair stop in Lisbon after being attacked by a French warship. He settled in Wilmington, Delaware, where he became manager of the Gilpins' Brandywine Paper-Mill, Delaware's first papermill. He ran it until his death from 'a short but severe illness, occasioned by an attack of Gout in the Stomach' in June 1817. [6]

A recurring theme in this chapter is extensive links between the papermaking and cloth industries, but in Lawrence Greatrake we have a papermaker who specialised in the trade. Whilst living in Bristol he and the later to be famous papermaker John Dickinson were apprentices together in the firm of Richardson and Harrison, stationers to the East India Company. He, later in his life, described himself as 'devoting my whole time, thoughts and attention to the promotion of useful and valuable manufactories ... ' and his papermaking career shows him playing an important role in the development of mechanised papermaking in America. He returned to England to deal with a disputed inheritance, and then again in 1815 - 1816 when he was instructed by his employer at Brandywine, Thomas Gilpin, to acquire designs of the latest papermaking machines in England. He made a surreptitious drawing of Fourdrinier's machine at Apsley Mill where he worked when his father owned the mill, but more importantly, his old associate John Dickinson let him make drawings of his invention of a cylinder papermaking machine, patented in 1809. He sent these drawings back to Delaware and took his knowledge back with him to America where in 1816 Thomas Gilpin patented a cylinder machine for the manufacture of paper which closely followed Dickinson's machine. It was the first papermaking machine in America, and Lawrence Greatrake played an important part in its development. [7]

The papermakers in Bulford were independently minded and in this Lawrence Greatrake was no exception. He was at odds with the Tory establishment, later writing that he 'was known both here [America] and in Engand as a most notorious WHIG ... who supported the revolutionary cause of AMERICA from its commencement to its termination' and during the war with England became a naturalised citizen of America. He had gone to America 'from a heartfelt preference ... for its laws, its government, and its manners'. His independent mind also extended to his religious beliefs and this is an area where Bulford might well have influenced him during his association with the village in the last decade of the eighteenth century. Thomas Mould, working as a papermaker at Bulford with Isaac Brodribb, could very easily have also worked with Lawrence Greatrake and influenced his religious thinking. When the law was changed in 1781 the paper-mill was licensed by Thomas Mould as a nonconformist meeting house. Shortly after he first arrived in Philadelphia Lawrence Greatrake was licensed to preach in the Second Baptist Church of Baltimore and it has been suggested that he may have preached in England prior to his immigration. He could well have preached in Bulford and helped to establish nonconformity in the village at the end of the eighteenth century. He was obviously a dynamic personality who could lead and influence others. His son, another Lawrence, followed him as a papermaker before being ordained as a Baptist minister in Pittsburgh, and then became, as the Minister of Pittsburgh's First Baptist Church, an influential figure in American religious history. [8]

Papermaking at its zenith in Bulford

CENSUS RETURNS SHOW that there were five or six papermakers working at the mill from the 1841 census up until the one in 1871, the last before it was disbanded. The six in 1841 cannot have constituted the entire workforce as only the heads of each household had their occupations recorded in that year. Ten years later when every inhabitant's occupation was recorded, there were a further three people described as 'working at the paper-mill' at jobs other than papermakers: an eighteen year old boy and girl, and a boy of thirteen. One of the youths, John Sawyer, later went on to become a papermaker and then rose to become joint proprietor of the business by 1867, a position he retained until the business was folded up. His early work at the paper-mill must have been a form of apprenticeship.

A description of a paper-mill in 1813 describes how one apprentice, who was generally the son of one of the regular workmen, was allowed at each of the papermaking vats. There were two further jobs at the mill differentiated by the census returns: a 'paper stripper', Ellen Godwin (John Sawyer's elder sister), and a 'paper layer', Thomas Truckle, but these will be considered later. There were at least six jobs dependent on the paper-mill in 1841, nine in 1851, eleven in 1861 before sinking to eight in 1871. Looking at the business in a different way, it provided jobs for nearly five per cent of the working population of the village in 1851, rising to over six per cent in 1861. 1861, therefore, marks the peak of papermaking (on the evidence available) in terms of numbers employed. There were five papermakers, a paper stripper, and three other workers. These statistics also include Jane Cooper, who as a dealer in rags, was certainly dependent on supplying the mill for her livelihood. This aspect of the business was in the hands of Thomas Cooper in 1851 and his wife carried it on after his death. The Coopers were a Durrington family and ten years earlier it was William Cooper of Durrington who was the rag man. There are no other rag men in the census returns of Amesbury and the nearby villages for these years and so the Coopers must have been a familiar sight collecting rags for the mill throughout the district. The economic influence of the mill in the village could have extended even further if it provided any business for the thirteen carters resident in the village providing transport for materials and the finished products, but this would have been unlikely as they would have been fully occupied by work on the village's farms.[9]

Characteristics of the papermakers and links with cloth industry

THE PAPERMAKERS WERE enterprising craftsmen who linked Bulford to the wider national economy. They came to Bulford from afar, and after a few years some moved on again without rooting themselves in the village, in a way that no other group did except the tenant farmers and clergymen. Both Mary and Thomas Mould plied their craft in the village in the 1780s and it appears that their son Thomas followed them, and then another son (or grandson?) as we find a Joseph Mould, papermaker at Bulford, renting the Carey paper-mill (Dorset) in 1810. He appears to have moved from Bulford as he turns up six years later working at another

Dorset paper-mill in Wimborne. There is a postscript to this story when in 1852 a Harriet Mould was admitted to the Bulford chapel from the Scots Lane chapel in Salisbury. She and her husband, Edmund Mould, lived in Alverstoke (Hampshire) at the time and he is described in the census of that year as being rich and living off private means. Perhaps their fortune was made in the papermaking business and she was returning to her husband's family roots. A similar migrating pattern of the papermakers is presented by the Hyatt family. William Hyatt, a papermaker at Bulford in 1841 and 1851, came from Bungay (Suffolk). His eldest son was born in the village in about 1825 and so he could well have been working at the paper-mill from that date, or even earlier as his wife Eliza (née Sturgess) was Bulford born. Two of his sons William and James followed him into the business as papermakers at Bulford Mill in 1851 and 1861 respectively whereas his middle son married an Imber girl and moved to Hampshire to work as a railway porter. James married Martha Swatton from the village but then left the village becoming a domestic coachman in Hove (Sussex). Perhaps both boys left papermaking as the writing was already on the wall for the handmade paper industry. [10]

Papermakers displayed the same characteristics as the master craftsmen of medieval times and indeed Isaac Brodribb was described as a 'master Papermaker'. John Sawyer's school copybook is still kept in the family and shows the sure touch of a craftsman in its beautifully executed copperplate writing and meticulous layout of mathematical tables (*Plate 32*). As a social class papermakers were sandwiched between the tenant farmers and agricultural workers along with the other businessmen of the village – the carriers, bricklayers, blacksmith and shopkeepers. They were in the middle class of village society who on the one hand enjoyed a standing with the village gentry as is illustrated by the Lord of the Manor, Anthony Southby, working in the mill as a papermaker, and on the other hand they had contacts with those beneath them. William Hyatt's two youngest sons worked as agricultural labourers at Bulford although, as we have seen, James later became a papermaker in his own right. William Kinsman, a papermaker in 1861, was a ploughboy ten years earlier in an agricultural labourer's household and he married Eliza Andrews who was a farm servant. They were both probably working on the Upper Farm because by 1871 William had returned to working as a labourer, living in one of the Upper Farm cottages. He probably got his papermaking job at

Bulford Paper Mill and its Papermakers

the mill through family connections. The papermaker William Godwin had married Elizabeth Kinsman and a generation later their eldest son, Henry Godwin, married Charlotte Kinsman. On the whole, however, they stuck with their equals. Henry Godwin's son Alfred became the village shoemaker and his daughter Ann was, for a time, the village schoolmistress. [11]

Along with the Hyatts, the Godwins were more unusual in that, unlike most papermakers, they stayed put in Bulford and became deeply involved in the fabric of village life – especially the chapel. There was a strong link between Bulford papermakers in general and religious Dissent. This was not just limited to the Moulds and Lawrence Greatrake (who was described at one point as a Quaker). Over half of the fifteen papermakers listed in the census returns from 1841 till 1871 attended chapel and two members of the wider Godwin family, sisters Ellen and Sarah, married the chapel pastor, John Protheroe. [12]

The Godwins of Bulford were almost certainly a branch of the family centred on Bradford-on-Avon and found in the north-west of Wiltshire, for example at Steeple Ashton and Calne. Godwins were also papermakers at Downton and a Benjamin Godwin is the first known papermaker of the mill at Alton. In 1816 Samuel Godwin of Avoncliff, near Bradford-on-Avon, was one of the first three men in Wiltshire to be described as a 'millwright'. Twelve years earlier, however, he was described as a 'clothier' in a patent he took out for 'machines for carding, scribbling, and brushing woollen cloth'; machines designed to reduce the water power needed to drive them. It is not surprising to find a man described as both 'millwright' and 'clothier' as rural industries before the age of steam depended on water power for an efficient source of energy. Mills needed careful management and it was an advantage for the industrialist to be able to do this himself. Clothiers were forbidden by law to take a personal part in the process of cloth making except for the final stages of fulling, scouring and stretching. These were carried out in the fulling mill, often by the clothier personally, and so as a result his business was based at the mill, so much so that cloth was sometimes described as being 'made at the mill'. Fulling consisted of beating woven cloth to matt the fibres, a process not so completely different from 'maching' rags at the paper-mill, so there existed a natural link between fulling and papermaking. Both demanded the skill of operating a waterwheel to drive trip hammers for beating fabrics. [13]

Clothiers led an active life necessitating travel to their markets, to their sources of raw material, to the scattered properties that they managed and to their outworkers. It was one such visit that must have led to the spinner Lucy Sturgess being sent to gaol in 1790 as has been already noted. It would present no difficulties for a clothier to have interests in papermaking and during the 1850s, when demand for paper dramatically increased, it would be natural for enterprising clothiers to try their hand at papermaking. This diversification of enterprise can be seen in the Brodribb family who, like the Godwins, came from around Bradford-on-Avon. In 1639 Henry Brodribb of Freshford leased two fulling mills at Limpley Stoke between Bath and Bradford-on-Avon for at least ten years. One of his descendants, Isaac, was papermaker at Bulford in the 1780s but when he went bankrupt, he returned to Shepton Mallet, describing himself as 'Mr Brodribb, clothier, Shepton Mallet'. As we have seen earlier, his elder brother Abraham was a 'clothier' who lived there as well. There could possibly have been a further connection between the clothiers of Shepton Mallet and the Bulford papermakers, this time involving the Hyatt family. William Hyatt, a Bulford papermaker between 1823 and 1851 at least, could have been part of the wider Hyatt family in the area. A clothier, William Hyatt had a factory for sale in Shepton Mallet in 1836, worked by an iron wheel and including a dye house and store. [14]

It may seem that a case is being made for papermaking as an offshoot of the cloth industry and although this may have been an important connection in the West of England where the chalklands were suitable for sheep rearing and papermaking, the picture is not complete. The papermaking expertise came initially from France as the activities of the Huguenot émigrés around Andover clearly show, but Bulford papermakers have deep roots in the technological centres of the cloth industry. The one locally produced entrepreneurial papermaker was John Sawyer (grandfather of the famous fisherman) whose family have been traced back in the village to the beginning of the seventeenth century. He started work as an employee at the mill and worked his way up to becoming the foreman papermaker and then went on in partnership with Thomas Godwin in 1867 to run the business. He lived in the Mill House whilst a papermaker and then moved across to the Mill Cottage when the paper-mill was pulled down and he retired, ending his working life as a groundsman for the Lords of the Manor (*Plate 29*). His family still live in Mill Cottage, providing a last link with the papermakers of the nineteenth century, and have in their possession some of the paper manufactured at the mill. The samples have been cut from

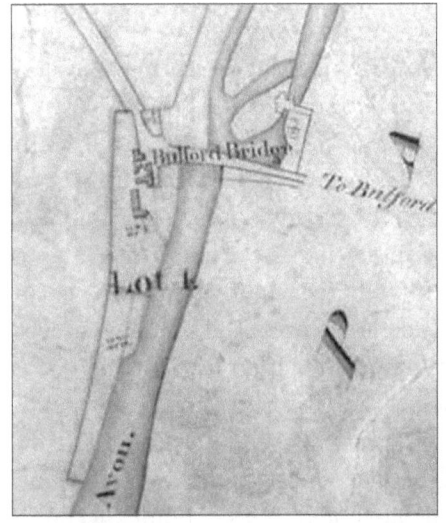 

28 Bulford Mill. *This map (left) was drawn up for the 1833 sale of the Poore Estates in Durrington. Lot 1 was for the copyhold property of the Nag's Head and its farm buildings. Interestingly it also has a plan of the paper-mill, spanning the mill leat which, as it is the only building in Bulford which was mapped, could indicate that there was a relationship between the Nag's Head and the paper mill. Conversely, it could indicate that the mill was considered to be part of Durrington as the detail (above right) from the 1840 tithe map for Durrington would indicate. (Wiltshire and Swindon Archives)*

a book leaving a gap down the centre of the watermark which shows the Prince of Wales' feathers with '*B M 1823*' underneath – the BM standing for Bulford Mill (*Figure 8*). John Sawyer's school copybook is watermarked and the paper was almost certainly produced at the mill. None of the marks give any indication of where and when the paper was produced, although it must have been used in the 1840s. They follow the same patriotic theme as the 1823 sample: two versions of Britannia, one seated in a field with '*PRO PATRIA*' inscribed above, and a crown with '*G R*' below – could this be George IV and thus dating the paper to 1820 – 1830? If so, the school was using old stock which could well have been the case as Anthony Southby was said to have made a book for every child and would probably have used up surplus paper. [15]

The ownership of Bulford Mill

THE OWNERSHIP OF Bulford Mill is bound up with the complicated pattern of land ownership in parts of Bulford and in Durrington and the boundary between the two, which at times, seems confused. The Moulds were associated with the paper-mill for a period of thirty years which could indicate three leases of ten years, with Joseph Mould then renting the Carey paper-mill in Dorset just before the third term expired. A similar lease for ten years can be seen with Lawrence Greatrake. (see Appendix 4). Nearby 'Nag's Head' farm is an integral part of the picture. The 1807 survey of lands owned by St Mary's College, Winchester shows a kaleidoscope of leaseholds, copyhold occupied by the copyholder or else tenanted by another, and lands leased and then sublet. Names associated with the history of Bulford pepper the record: Cooe, Mould, Jenner, Hayden and Rose. The survey, however, does not mention a mill. The 1841 tithe commutation for Durrington, as we have seen in Chapter 6 however, does. The Mill, Mill Acre meadowlands and the Haskett are all owned by St Mary's College Winchester with the leasehold(?) held by Charles Edward Rendall, and occupied by John Cooe. The picture that emerges from the settlement of Thomas Croome's accounts as part of the probate, however, clearly indicates that the Manor owned, or possibly leased, the mill. In November of that year, his executors 'Received of Mr Thomas Croome the sum of twenty-two pounds and ten shillings for half a year's rent for Bulford Mill due to Lady Pollen and Miss Southby at Michaelmas last old style for whose use and by whose order the rent is paid me'. The ownership of the mill is not identified in the 1838 tithe commutation clearly indicating that it was part of the Manor. Ten years earlier the parish rate of 3s 4d was paid by Mrs Croome for the Mill, orchard and garden as a separate item from the rate that she paid on the Lower Farm and was still paying it in 1834. The conclusion seems to be that that Bulford Mill was owned by St Mary's College Winchester and leased to the owners of Bulford Manor before they fully owned the mill. The Manor leased the mill to the Croomes who played an active part in its affairs as Thomas Croome's probate accounts show. There is a bill to settle with the rag collector Thomas Cooper of 10s and bills of £2 8s and £2 4s for paper sold to a Mr Ashton and a Mrs King of Devizes. They also show that he borrowed from the mill money. His accounts are all clearly watermarked with the figure of Britannia, and the chances are that he was using paper manufactured at the mill. [16]

Anthony Southby, Lord of the Manor in 1835, was to play an important part in the history of the paper-mill. In 1861 he was described as 'landholder and papermaker' and it is obvious that this latter role was taken seriously as he appears to have been responsible for running the mill and employed five men, five women and a boy in this connection. In 1865 he was described as a 'Paper Manufacturer' with Mrs Godwin as his 'Paper Maker' (papermaking was obviously a craft practised by women as well, as the example of Mary Mould also indicates) and a year later he insured the business in his own name. It could well be that this time of active involvement in the mill was a catalyst for the land exchange of 1871 which then gave him the ownership of the mill. [17]

Papermaking must have been an unusual occupation for a country gentleman but then Anthony Southby appears to have been an unusual character. He was a medical doctor with some reputation as a naturalist and he had an active interest in the crafts as is evidenced by him personally carving the oak font cover in 1841, still to be seen in the parish church. He appears to have had a yearning for the ways and achievements of the past for, in 1879, he insisted that the pews be removed from the church as he wished things to remain as they were a century ago and, as patron, his wishes were met without the necessary permission being granted. He would have fitted comfortably in to William Morris's Art and Crafts Movement (except for its association with radical politics); he made etchings to illustrate his

29 *John Sawyer. After retiring from being Foreman Papermaker at the Mill, John Sawyer (1833–1901) became the gardener and caretaker of the Manor. (Courtesy of Ann Sawyer*

papers, made a weathervane for his local church in Upper Canada, and made implements for his brother's farm. It was probable that his interest in the traditional craft of papermaking kept the mill at Bulford in production for longer than most and in 1860 he registered a patent for the invention of 'improvements in the manufacture of paper'. The mill's closure roughly coincided with his old age and death at the age of eighty-three in 1883. He was sixty-one when he was first known to us as a papermaker but he soon handed over the management of the business as he was often absent from the Manor. The resident papermaker brothers-in-law Thomas Godwin and John Sawyer ran the business in 1867 but by 1871 Joseph Hobday, born in Midhurst (West Sussex), took over as the undisputed entrepreneur. He is described as a 'paper manufacturer' in 1861 and ran a paper-mill in Deddington (Oxfordshire) but had to close it in 1870 as the business was unprofitable. He was forty-eight when he took over the Bulford Mill the next year and employed the workforce in his own right. [18]

Papermaking processes and its demise at Bulford

To complete the picture of papermaking in the village, consideration must be given to the processes involved. Rags were sorted depending on quality of paper being produced and put into shallow depressions where they were beaten by trip hammers driven by the waterwheel, the 'maching' of the opening verse. The wet, pulped rags, or stuff as it was known, were soaked in the stuff chest and then pumped into a head box where the papermaker, or vatman, worked. Lime was sometimes added to the heated stuff to help break the cloth down into fibres and this may well have been done at Bulford as a spot near Upper Manor Farm/Hooper's Farm, is still called the 'limekilns'. The papermaker had a wire sieve of the size of the paper that he was making which he dipped into the stuff; he gently nursed the fibres as the water drained out and then left the paper to dry in a sieve or mould. When it had drained the paper was tipped out and piled up with sheets of felt between each piece and then pressed. The felts were removed and the paper was pressed again between zinc sheets to give it a good surface. The man who pressed the paper between the felt and zinc was called a paper layer and this is the description of the job done by Thomas Truckle in the 1871 census. The paper was then left to dry in a loft, suspended from ropes covered with cow hair to prevent staining. Finally it was taken down and sorted, graded and packed with imperfect sheets being recycled. Ellen Godwin was described as a 'paper stripper' in 1861 and she must have been involved with these later stages of production. The nondescript 'employed at the mill' were probably involved in the menial jobs but more especially the sorting and preparation of the rags for different types of paper. The 1789 advertisement quoted earlier stated that the constant supply of water was 'of a quality for making the best papers', but in 1848 the paper from Bulford was described as 'coarser kinds of paper'. Later Anthony Southby made 'blottings, filtering and small hands' the middle one of which was made from muslin rags. In some mills the sorting was done in an upper room above the vats so that rags could be thrown through holes in the floor straight into them, but this was not the case at Bulford as the rag store was situated over the cart shed, which still stands. It is a brick building with a wooden interior which has subsequently been converted into a cottage. It was common practice for a papermaker to work at a head box with an apprentice and, judging by the number of papermakers and their ages at Bulford Mill, it seems likely that there were three of these, at least. A male papermaker earned about twenty-two shillings a week in 1813, whereas women received about seven pence a day piece work. [19]

The millrace can still be seen and the two mill cottages, one on either side of it. Nothing remains of the mill building which the 1773 Andrews and Dury map shows straddling the millrace, its place now taken by part of Mill House. The 1833 map of Sir Edward Poore's lands and the 1841 tithe map of Durrington show the mill and the millrace in detail. The 'Mill House' cottage is substantial with the mill itself over the river being fully part of it, leading into a long narrow building on the opposite bank, incorporating the other cottage (*Plate 28*). Mill House was built at the end of the nineteenth century using a mill cottage as one of its two wings. The central portion joining the wings predates the extension and was part of the original mill complex as the map shows. The two mill cottages were built next to the millrace with all the discomforts and hazards this must have entailed. At least one papermaker's child was drowned in the millrace and one papermaker, William Godwin, suffered from rheumatism and had 'for some years before his death [in November 1850] been a great sufferer'. He was in pain from the mid 1830s at least and had to take medicine to relieve it. It cannot have been a pleasant place to live before the days of modern damp courses and central heating. [20]

Papermaking in the village reached its peak in about 1861 when ten people were employed at the mill; ten years later there were seven, pointing to a contracting business which finally ceased operating between 1872 and 1875. It was the second time around for Joseph Hobday who came to Bulford after winding up his papermaking business at Deddington Papermill (Oxfordshire) in 1870. He appears to have wound up another paper manufacturing business at the same time at Hambridge Mill, Thatcham (Berkshire), dissolving his business partnership with William Stanway. Bulford, no doubt like the other mills, succumbed to technological innovation and ceased as a mill of any sort, whereas Deddington Mill was reconverted to a corn mill. Joseph Hobday made another attempt at running his paper manufacturing business from Clifford Mill at Beckington, near Frome (Somerset) but it is significant that he was not relying totally on paper making. The 1881 census describes him as an 'Engineer and Paper Manufacturer'. Papermaking needed machinery to be operated on a large scale and raw materials had diversified from rags. Bulford Mill along with scores of other mills could no longer keep up with these innovations which, along with the old age and demise of its owner, must have been the death blows to an industry which had existed in the village for over a century. Perhaps a contributory factor may have been Anthony Southby's hankering after past ways blocking modifications and progress. His life experience of self sufficiency in the pioneering society of Upper Canada was not conducive to industrialisation. He was an anachronism when he died in 1883, as was the mill and it was about this time that it was dismantled, probably in 1880. There was certainly nothing remaining in March 1898 when Bulford Manor, including the mill site, was sold for £36,000 to the Secretary of State for War. While the army owned the mill site, a lake was excavated for the cavalry to practise river crossings. The Mill House was sold to General Sir Richard Bryne Haking, C in C of HM Forces in Egypt, as a private residence in 1926 for £500. It has remained a private house ever since then and the papermaking business in the village is now a faint memory with only the converted cart shed and cottage, Mill House and a few surviving sheets of paper left in evidence. [21]

10
Education and Social Mobility

Bulford's first schools

I COME TO THIS chapter with the experience of being deputy headteacher of the new Bulford village school in the late 1970s and early 1980s. The school intake was split between the village community and children of army families who came and went as regiments moved from posting to posting. One of my clear memories of the village children is an occasion when one parent, of a boy who was not progressing well, seemingly unconcerned, remarked, 'You don't need computers to drive tractors'. He was echoing the traditional form of education where children learned what they needed from their elders and betters, alluded to by Allan Young when he said, 'The man who is going to thatch a stack should have taken up the sticks to his father as a boy'. This is the simplest form of apprenticeship which is how skills were traditionally passed from father to son. This approach is also illustrated by the farmer of Upper Farm, William Parsons, who sent his eleven year old son William to school (in Amesbury) in 1895. He was described as being, 'Weak in everything except writing. Has never been to school. Instructed at home'. At the other end of the scale we have details of two eighteenth century formal apprenticeships for villagers. William Perce entered into an apprenticeship contract with a butcher in West Lavington (1725), and James Rattew to a cordwainer in Ablington (1721). Apprenticeships continue through the nineteenth century; we have already seen that James Chalk, the shoemaker was accused of 'misconduct towards an apprentice boy' in 1810, and census returns show bricklayer and baker journeymen. [1]

Educating children in a more formal way, that is to say going to school, had long been an aspect of village life. A report written in 1870 stated that 'the present school has been maintained for generations' mentioning a five hundred year lease dating from 24 March 1643. Education of children has always been an important part of the outreach of the church, backed by the landowner. In Bulford's case, in the absence of a strong church structure with neither glebe nor a resident parish priest until the middle of the nineteenth century, the driving force appears to have been the Lord of the Manor. The challenge was taken up by Richard Duke, who in his 1755 will (proved three years later), instructed his trustees,

> 'to apply the sum of 100 l.[£] for the erection of a tiled school-house in the churchyard of Bulford aforesaid, where the old house there stood, with an enlargement into the old garden, so far as should be thought necessary ... and also that his trustees should apply sufficient monies for the purchasing a free land estate in the name of the person who should be then entitled to his said estate, of the value of 8 l.[£] a year, in North Wilts, which he directed to be for ever applied to the uses following; viz. 7 l.[£] 10s. to be yearly paid to a proper schoolmaster, who was to live in the said school-house, for the teaching and instructing six poor boys and six poor girls (the children of labourers within the said parish of Bulford, who could not afford to pay for their schooling,) to write, read and cast accounts; and the remaining 10s. to be yearly dispersed of to find them in books necessary for the purposes aforesaid. And his will and desire was, that the person or persons who should be in possession of his said estate in Bulford aforesaid, should have for ever thereafter unlimited power of electing the said schoolmaster, and also the six poor boys and six poor girls who were to be instructed by him, and to charge and displace either the said schoolmaster or children at his and their wills and pleasures.

Richard Duke was looking to put the school on a sound footing, run by a 'proper schoolmaster', to teach the twelve poor children whose parents could not afford to pay the school pence to send their children, in addition to those children whose parents could pay.

A tiled school-house was erected in conformity to Richard Duke's will, saving the wall and fence, which would have been an encroachment on

30 Richard Duke's School. The back of the building was the school built in accordance with Richard Duke's will with the house for the school mistress incorporated into the building. When James Hann converted it into the farmhouse of Manor Farm, he extended the building upwards. (Photographed by author in 2011)

the churchyard. The school-house is now [1833] occupied, rent-free, by a schoolmistress, who receives 8 l.[£] a year, by quarterly payments, from Thomas Robbins, the tenant of a farm-house, and about 800 acres of land in the parish of Bulford, formerly belonging to Lady Pollen, and now the property of Miss Southby, who appoints the schoolmistress, and places the children in school.

Both Lady Charity Ann Pollen and then her sister Mary Southby followed Richard Duke's instructions to appoint a teacher to give free instruction to six poor boys and girls, but unfortunately, 'It was considered that a schoolmaster could not be obtained to give the instruction required by the will for 8 l.[£] a year', namely 'to write, read and cast accounts'. In his stead a schoolmistress was employed to educate the children to a lesser standard. 'Miss Southby requires the schoolmistress to instruct six boys and six girls in reading, and also to teach the girls to work. In 1818 an attendance of twelve was reported but by 1833 this had risen to sixteen, which shows that the free children had been joined by four whose parents could pay, and considered it worthwhile to pay, for their attendance.

Prudence Sawyer recalled that, 'There was not much schooling in those days, only the better off could afford to send their children to school, so the school was very small.' ²

Although the Manor was the driving force behind the school, its links with the church were close and in fact the school used the church which was next to the school. This is hardly surprising as the Manor held the patronage of both the church and the school. At times this could be a cause of tension. In their meeting in August 1829, the vestry resolved 'that the school children may be permitted to sit on the outside of the Railing in front of the Communion Table and no longer in the inside as heretofore and it is ordered that a copy of this resolution be respectfully transmitted by the Chairman [Thomas Webb Dyke] to Lady Pollen and Miss Southby'. The request was ignored because at the next vestry meeting a year later, it was reported that, 'The children of Lady Pollens School [are] continuing to sit within the rails of the Communion Table, which Lady Pollen has been by a vestry requested to have removed to another and more proper place.' Lady Pollen appears to have been an awkward customer, aware of her dignity and rights as has already been seen in her other dealings with the church which she regarded as her property, and in her determination to safeguard the Southby name in her will. There was probably no agreement about this issue until the change of ownership of the Manor. The school continued under the next Lord of the Manor, Anthony Southby, who in 1850 allowed the deeds to be purchased from him. The day school still went to the church to attend minor festivals in 1864 but it seems that the invasion complained of under Lady Pollen was a thing of the past. Dr Southby continued to patronise the school and regarded it as his responsibility and in a report of that year it was stated that, 'The School being supported by Dr Southby, he declines all interference' and would not let any grants offered by the Diocese be accessed, no doubt fearing a loss of control. In 1858 it was stated that '15 to 20 children, mixed, [were] taught by a mistress in a low room, in a cottage, near churchyard; the room is occasionally employed "for culinary and other domestic purposes;" … The room is probably large enough for the needs of the parish … '. It had a £20 endowment and it was attached to a house and garden for the mistress. ³

Impact of schooling

THE 1851 CENSUS gives us the first detailed information about schooling in the village. The village school is shown on the 1851 census map, situated next to the church (*Figure 2, no.6*). The school was added to the cottage given to the schoolmistress. The cottage was extended upwards in the beginning of the twentieth century when James Hann converted it into Manor Farm, also known as Church Farm. The two back rooms were part of the first school built in about 1760. The walls are thick with the remains of a bread oven in one. By the 1851 census, however, this village school was not the only school in the village; the Independent chapel had set up its own free school 'with an attendance of 20 to 30 children (in a schoolroom adjoining the Independent chapel), taught by a mistress'. The village therefore boasted two schools and two schoolmistresses with the chapel school being the larger of the two. The village school was run by thirty year old Annabel Douse from Everleigh, younger sister of Mary who married the village thatcher William Batchelor. Four years later the burial register records the death of forty-two year old Martha Rolfe, who is decribed as a 'schoolmistress', presumably of the same school. The chapel school was run by Elizabeth Swatton, aged forty-four. Elizabeth was from one of the old village families of agricultural labourers and husband John was also an agricultural labourer. Both were chapel members, Elizabeth joining in 1829, and John later (first mentioned in 1840). The 1851 census shows her running the Independent school attached to the chapel, which she continued to do until at least 1869. [4]

In 1864 the Rev. Millner reported to his bishop that children enter school at three years old and leave at ten at the latest, with some leaving at eight for farm labour. This last statement reminds us that child labour was very much part of the economic equation for family life and the management of farms. It was acknowledged by Rev. Millner when he reported that he did not say Morning and Evening Prayer due to 'men women and children being all employed in farm labour from sunrise to sunset'. How does the census information three years earlier support his statement? In that year there were 135 children up to and including fourteen year olds, and just under a half of these, sixty-four, were described as scholars (and sixty-one, ten years later). The two schools, if fully attended, catered for a maximum of fifty children implying that either ten or so children attended school outside the village, or that the number of children 'registered' was always greater than the number attending as there were always some children helping in the fields or at home. Analysis of the census figures shows that boys attended mainly between the ages of four and seven, whereas the girls from three to twelve. At either end of the range there were three two year old scholars and two fourteen year old girls (perhaps acting as pupil teachers). Nearly a third of two year old children in the village attended school, rising to half of the three year olds and then rising rapidly until all the six year olds were 'scholars'. From this high point proportions started declining until about half were attending at twelve, and, as we have already noted, only two girls at fourteen. Set against these statistics are the number of children who were in employment other than helping out with the family, especially at harvest time. The youngest was a seven year old boy and altogether there were twenty-one children in work up to the age of fourteen, with all but two of the boys being either ploughboys or shepherd boys (the remainder being a bricklayer's labourer and an agricultural labourer). There were only two girls, both in domestic service in the village but three others, aged fourteen, had found positions elsewhere in the area. By and large, the Rev. Millner's assessment was correct. There were only two children in the village aged between six and twelve who were neither working nor described as 'scholars'.[5]

There were those in the parish for whom the village schools were not sufficient and looked to educate their children elsewhere. They were primarily the tenant farmers and landholders. John Robbins of Upper Farm sent his son Frederick to Rose's Grammar School in Amesbury, as did the papermaker William Godwin who sent his son, William. This view is best expressed in an 1811 tuition bond to care for the needs of George and James Chalk on the death of their father James who was a Bulford yeoman and one of the signatories for licensing the Bulford Mill as a place of Independent worship. The bond drawn up between Thomas Croome of Lower Farm and Mary Hicks of Amesbury who was to act as 'guardian and curator [and to] well and truly educate them the said George Chalk and James Chalk the said minors to their Quality Degree and Estate' – no village school for them. These were almost certainly the children of the sad Mr Chalk whose suicide was recounted in Chapter 1, explaining why he had not made provision for his children's education. The 'farmer friend' could well have been Thomas Croome who might have been induced to act as guardian through a sense of guilt, but knowing his compassion to the poor in his will, this was

Education and Social Mobility

31 *Politeness. Flowers that never fade*, by Lucy Leman Rede, published in 1811. A much loved book, carefully repaired by stitching. It originally belonged to Fanny Long of Salisbury. It was subsequently used by the children of Elizabeth and Francis Stephen Long at Watergate Farm. (Wiltshire and Swindon Archives)

probably not the case. Education cost money and when Matthew Devenish was on his deathbed, the education of his eight children aged between one and eleven years old was at the forefront of his mind. Nine days before he died he added a codicil to his will stipulating that, 'All expenditure for education and maint^{nce} of each child' was to be met from the personal property he bequeathed to his wife Elizabeth. An interesting case of a villager being educated in Amesbury is the case of Wilmot Henry Knight, son of the village schoolmistress, who attended Rose's Grammar School from March 1885 till January 1887. Another villager who attended the same school was Walter Sturges, son of the agricultural labourer William Sturges, reminding us that there are always exceptions to generalities. [6]

A good early education was held in high esteem by those at the top of village society and not labouring in the fields for their living as this doggerel, *The Good Scholar*, shows:

> Harry is the best of boys,
> He does not waste time on toys
> As idle dunces do,
> But has nicely learned to spell,
> And read his books distinct and well,
> And soon he'll write well too.

These lines come from a gem of a little, much loved book entitled *Flowers that never fade* by Lucy Leman Rede belonging to Fanny Long of Salisbury in 1801. It is a little book of verses with beautiful colour illustrations which was handed down in the Long family at Watergate Farm. It was a well loved little book with childish graffiti and torn pages, but these have carefully been stitched up to ensure the integrity of the book (*see Plate 31*). The poems reflect the gentry's attitude to child upbringing with titles like *Come when you are called*, *Going to bed*, *Impatience of illness*, *Politeness* and *The idle boy*. It promotes 'Good humour' which is 'the greatest charm that children can possess' and warns against *The Greedy child* who 'is so selfish that she thinks she cannot have too much'. There is a strong moral tone throughout the verses which aim to put the child in their right place and to accept the responsibilities of their class. In a poem about *The Match Woman*, the child is exhorted to,

> Think then, and be grateful, that Heaven has blessed
> You with parents so good, and by whom you're caressed
> And pray for those poor little things.

Reading the book reminds one of Hilaire Belloc's *Cautionary Tales* with, for example, a tone of 'serves you right' to the boy who ran out to greet his father's carriage and was run over and killed. The sense of responsibility and the valuing of education underpinning this book are clearly reflected in the importance that the local gentry placed in promoting the education of the village children in Bulford's two schools. [7]

Governesses were a feature of the wealthier households with young children. Gertrude Lacy from Laverstock held this position in the Long household when Annie was twelve and Lizzie was eight years old. Their London nephew aged five was also living with them as a 'scholar' no doubt taking advantage of the education that she offered. When the vicar Cecil North Arnold moved into the new Vicarage with his family of four aged between nine and one, he employed Winifred Crompton from Chiswick as a governess, and at the same time (1901) Ada White was governess for James Hooper's three children. All these governesses were aged twenty-five, no doubt having just completed their own advanced education. When children of the top echelons of village society needed to progress their education beyond the home environment, they went away for their schooling. The basic education provision for the village children, however, carried on with little change until the beginning of the 1870s. The Independent free school situated at the chapel still continued under Elizabeth Swatton, but the village school saw staff changes. The mistress in 1865 was a Miss Cull who was born in 1839 at Fawley, Southampton. She had come with her nine year old stepsister but their stay was short as two years later the new schoolmistress was Miss Ann Godwin, a villager born in 1849 to Henry and Charlotte Godwin, both papermakers at the mill. There is a record in 1859 of David Sturges, married to Elizabeth (née Pearce), who at his son Herbert's baptism in 1856 is described as a 'schoolmaster'. When however his daughter Ellen was baptised three years later the description had turned to 'labourer'. He was probably involved in the wider educational input of the chapel which will be looked at later on.[8]

All was not well, however, with the Independent chapel free school's support structure causing it to be closed in the autumn of 1869. A document in 1870 putting the case for a new village school could state that, 'There is no other in [the] Parish and no prospect of the late attempt to support a Dissenting School being revived, owing to the death of its principal promoter and supporters'. The 'principal promoter' was the chapel founder Henry Blatch's daughter Elizabeth Butler who died in 1870. Her death left a great hole in the chapel's finances, including its school. The school accounts at the time of her death show that she provided over a half of its quarterly expenditure of £9 10s 0d. Other principal supporters could well have been Elizabeth's brother and sister Henry and Sarah Blatch, with whom she lived in Durrington. Sarah had died in 1852 but Henry, who was unmarried, died the same year as Elizabeth, 1870. The document putting the case for a new village school went on to say that the pupils were absorbed by the village school as the 'families of the labouring population ... all now send to the Parish Day School, since the Dissenting Day School was finally closed last Autumn'. The 1876 visitation return for the bishop, filled in by the Rev. Jacob Mountain, says that there were sixty-four children on the village school's books, with an average attendance of forty-five. This high absence rate is probably explained by children working in the fields. What is more, there was little change to the school make up with the boys stopping attendance from eight years old, but more usually ten, and the girls staying on longer, till between twelve and fifteen. The 1870 report referring to the state of the chapel school quoted above was the result of the 1870 Education Act which had to, consider whether any and what public school accommodation is required for the district, and in so doing they shall take into consideration every school, whether actually situated in the school district or not, which in their opinion will be suitable for the children of the district. [9]

The act was to transform schooling across the country, but before turning to its impact on the village we ought to try and assess how well the old schools met the needs of villagers. This is impossible to do fully but there are one or two indications. The papermaker John Sawyer's copybook from the old school survives. It is beautifully written and mathematical calculations are set out precisely and clearly. The following was transcribed in well formed copperplate:

> Demand how many Barley Corns will reach Bristol to London it being accounted 9 9 miles

$$\begin{array}{r} 1760 \\ \hline 5940 \\ 693 \\ 99 \\ \hline 174240 \\ 36 \\ \hline 1045440 \\ 522720 \\ \hline 6272640 \\ 3 \\ \hline 18817920 \end{array}$$

Barley corns of ans'r 1 8 8 1 7 9 2 0

What though were the general levels of literacy? One indication was the ability of villagers to sign their names on the marriage registers. In the decade 1841 to 1851 there were twenty-seven marriages celebrated at the parish church with only seven of those entering into wedlock coming from outside the village. The entrepreneurial class could all sign their names: a bricklayer, a collar maker, a shopkeeper, and the daughters of a bricklayer, shopkeeper, carpenter, papermaker, inn keeper and a tanner.

32 *School Copybook belonging to John Sawyer, the future papermaker.*
(Courtesy of Ann Sawyer)

The professional class, a surgeon and a minister's daughter, were literate but they were not village educated. Those unable to sign their names included a groom and the daughters of the parish clerk, a tinker and a shepherd. The biggest group were the twenty agricultural labourers of whom about a third were illiterate by this measure. This level rose with the nineteen daughters of agricultural labourers, two thirds of whom were illiterate. If the picture is true for the whole village about fifty per cent of villagers were illiterate. There was work to be done on the literacy level of the labourers and the chapel's response was to run reading classes as part of the work of its Sunday school in 1844.

The parish responded in a different way; the Rev. Millner reported in 1864 'An Adult Evening School for farm lads and plough boys, between 13 and 21 years, has been held at my private residence from October to January twice a week', when farm work was at its slackest. Whereas the chapel taught both boys and girls, the church taught only boys. Nine years later evening classes were still running twice a week run by the Rev. Mountain and his wife Anna assisted by the mistress of the school. 'Lads a suitable age attend (about 30 in all). The instructions which are given gratuitously and without any Govt Grants seems to be appreciated. The progress made is increasingly good. Discipline is now established.' The needs of villagers were recognised and an effort was being made to meet them. [10]

These educational needs, however, were viewed through utilitarian eyes by the upper echelons of the village. The Rev. Millner and Francis Stephen Long, both of Bulford, along with Dr Mountain of Milston and representatives of other local parishes, for example, pondered in 1861 whether,

> the Education which the Labouring Classes received fitted them for the state of life which it had pleased God to call them, and it was generally thought that the Education had in a measure failed in this respect – that it had not led them to be more industrious in their daily work, nor were they better qualified to discharge the duties of domestic service ... it being even a great truth that "A little learning is a dangerous thing".

Education for its own sake was not deemed to be relevant at all levels of society, except perhaps at the Manor House. The opening statements in this chapter were echoed at the end of the century by a schoolmaster in Amesbury who wrote that, 'It is painful to observe the change wrought in boys consequent upon their withdrawal from school to labour in the fields. They become sluggish and apathetic and manifest little interest in their work'. What is more, the Deanery Meeting reported that 'the crowded state of the cottages where often there was only one bedroom for the whole family, or even if there were two, the limited accommodation was taken up by lodgers or double families' was disadvantageous to the village children. These conditions were seen as detrimental to a good education.[11]

Sunday Schools

THE CHURCH HAD always seen education as part of its mission, hence the questions about its provision in the bishop's questionnaires. It was biblical teaching and a grounding in Christian morality, grooming children to be active members of the church, that inspired these efforts but there is no doubting that there was a wider educational agenda as well. The efforts of both church and chapel in the village were a mixture and so the secular and religious aspects intertwined and overlapped as the 'reading' classes of the chapel Sunday school in 1844 clearly show. On 16 October 1856 when

Pastor John Protheroe and Sarah Godwin wanted to share the celebration of their marriage with their chapel community, they 'gave tea to all members and school, in commemoration' showing just how much the educational effort was an integral part of chapel life. [12]

The first contemporary mention of a Sunday school at the chapel was in 1843, but it had been a feature of its outreach from its earliest years. 'This school was established about the year 1805', before the chapel was opened, which reflects the priority given to the work with children by Dissenters in the village. The parish church's Sunday school is first mentioned in the bishop's returns of 1852. We cannot be as sure that it had been thriving in the earliest years of the century because the lack of a resident clergyman impacted negatively on the church's outreach in the village. 'Agricultural cottagers have a strong bias towards Dissent in one form or another' according to Richard Jefferies and the chapel no doubt capitalised on this undercurrent, so that in 1843 Pastor Protheroe could exclaim that the Sunday school was 'never in a more prosperous condition'. The surviving registers, starting a year after Pastor Protheroe's remark, bear out his satisfaction. There were twenty-one girls and thirty-three boys on the books, organised into six classes, three for each sex, each with its own teacher. The girls were taught by Samuel Sturges, John Swatton, Kezia Godwin, Louise Swatton, Mary Sturges and Eliza Truckle before Mrs Love took over her class. The boys were taught by William Love, Henry Hickman, Charles Godwin, William Swatton, William Sawyer and Thomas Andrews. This dedicated input into the children no doubt helped underpin the dramatic religious revival that we have seen in the chapel's fortunes. [13]

In November 1843 the Sunday school Superintendent, Mr Todman, and the teachers 'thought it necessary to have certain rules and regulations drawn up'. The following extracts show, these regulations placed a heavy obligation on both scholars and teachers, and also how seriously the chapel took its educational mission.

> That the School, to be opened in the morning at 9 o'clock, and in the afternoon at ½ past 1, and closed in the morning at ¼ past 10, and in the afternoon at 3 o'clock, be commenced and concluded with singing and a short prayer ...
>
> That a fine of one penny be inflicted on every Teacher who shall enter the school after 9 in the morning, or half past one in the afternoon, unless

such Teacher assign such a reason as shall satisfy the Superintendent, or his deputy, for doing so ...

That the reward tickets be kept in the possession of the Superintendent and distributed by him or by his deputy.

That no ticket be given to any child who enters the School room after the prayer and singing be concluded.

That any of the Children, belonging to the School, found profaning the Sabbath shall forfeit their tickets for two Sundays succeeding such profanation.

That the children after the school be over shall attend the Chapel unless sufficient reason to the contrary, be assigned.

That the first Teachers Meeting in every November, the Parents of the Scholars be invited to attend, that the objects contemplated by the school be laid before them, and their co-operation, with the Teachers in their work & labour of love, be solicited.

All fines were given to the superintendent to be 'appropriated to the objects of the school'. Teachers all met the fourth Wednesday of the month at seven o'clock, chaired by the Minister, and they were also on a rota to sit with the children during the morning on the Sabbath, and from April 1844 a sermon had to be preached annually 'for the benefit of the school'. Staff had to be committed. David Todman, the Superintendent, was an excise officer living in Amesbury who attended the chapel in 1843 with his wife Mary. Charles Godwin, the papermaker, was appointed to deputise for him, and later that year was upgraded to 'Deputy Superintendent'. Mr Todman's residing 'at a distance' from Bulford led to administrative problems and so it was decided that 'a person be appointed to receive the forfeits, and that John Swatton fill that office'. The 1851 census sees David Todman living in Middlesex and perhaps he had moved from Amesbury during 1843 which necessitated these changes. [14]

Thirty-seven years later in 1880, John Protheroe was still pleased with the health of the Sunday school, reporting that,

It is at present in a very flourishing condition having lately had several additions made to it. When we consider the population of Bulford is small – or less than 400 – it is a matter for gratitude to the Great God that so many as 50 boys and girls attend it. The No of Teachers is 7.

The chapel accounts of c1870 give more insight into how the Sunday school was run. There were, 'Books, tickets, cards, rewards of Bibles and Testaments and Hymn books for good behaviour, given by Mrs Butler', and further, 'Rewards of garments, made by the girls of the Day School', with the Protheroes and Miss Devenish supplying the materials, which were 'distributed, occasionally with books in addition, on Christmas Day'. It was a regime of positive encouragement and there was 'Tea on Christmas Day given to Teachers and Scholars by Mrs Butler'. Expenses for the chapel amounted to six pounds a quarter being paid by the two ladies in equal shares. [15]

The Nonconformists used the schoolroom attached to the chapel and similarly the parish church made use of the next door school building. The parish Sunday school in 1852 was gaining strength as in April it had fifty-three children on its books but this dropped to thirty-four in August, no doubt linked to work peaking to gather in the harvest. After the second afternoon lesson during Lent the scholars had to recite part of the Catechism. It would seem that they were well provided for as its patron, Anthony Southby, had given thirteen Bibles, twenty-five Tests [Testaments?] and twenty-five Prayers as a gift which was no doubt shared between the Sunday school and the day school. We do not have any more attendance figures, other than a reference in 1870 'that ¾ of the families of the labouring population ... are members of the Church of England; of the other families, some send their children to the Church of England Sunday school'. The Sunday school met (in 1873) an hour before the service in the schoolroom next door to the church. Both church and chapel in the village were well placed to deliver an educational input due to the incorporation or close proximity of schoolrooms to the places of worship. The labour demands of a nineteenth-century agricultural community were such that Sunday, or evenings, were the only times when both children and adults were free for schooling which explains why it is sometimes difficult to draw a distinction between secular and religious education. This overlap is clearly documented for the chapel Sunday school which, in 1843, noted that on the Sabbath, there were religious 'Lessons in the morning, and spelling and reading in the afternoon'. Analysis of the children in the two reading classes of the following year shows a class of fourteen boys and girls, aged from two to thirteen (at least), and a second smaller class of five to seven year olds, it looks like these were the better readers. What is clear, however, is that once the children reached working age for employment in the fields or in service, they no longer attended.[16]

The results of the drive to make everyone literate threw up new challenges. If the illiterate could learn to read, what were they going to read? This was a time of workers' agitation and 'free education for all' was one of the demands of the Agricultural Labourers' Union. The establishment perceived that making the workers literate was in danger of feeding this agitation. It is for this reason that there was a movement epitomised by Hannah More who earlier had set up a school in Cheddar in 1789, where at first the reading was of the Scriptures only. She later started writing stories, homilies and poems with a moral purpose, for she believed as John Wesley did, that it was no use to teach people reading, if all there was to read was the 'seditious or pornographic literature of commercialism'. The object of the schools was also to make honest and virtuous citizens which is the theme of her *Shepherd of Salisbury Plain* tract quoted in earlier chapters. The churches had an incentive to play an important role in the promotion of mass literacy, least of all for reasons of self interest. The mission statement of Bulford's Independent Sunday school reads,

> Ignorance is the mother, not of devotion, but of destruction: my people is destroyed by a lack of knowledge. The soul, then, to be without knowledge, is not good.
>
> The value of Christian knowledge is inestimable: it expands the mind and elevates the character. To impart the knowledge to the young and many generations is the grand object contemplated by the Bulford Independent Sunday School.

It was 'Christian knowledge' that the churches wanted. The local Established Church was nervous about the educational effort and successes that the Dissenting churches were reaping, recognising that they themselves had to do better. They needed lay people to come forward as scripture readers, district visitors, and Sunday school teachers but had reservations. For 'if uneducated and untrained men were allowed to preach the word as was at present done among the various Bodies of Dissenters it could not fail of being itself a means of disseminating dissent and must work against the interests and well being of the church either through ignorance or prejudice'. Church interests were paramount. [17]

The Education Act of 1870 and the new Village School

THE WIDER MOVEMENT for universal elementary education culminated in the 1870 Education Act which weakened the hold of the churches over education. It stated that, 'It shall not be required, as a condition of any child being admitted into or continuing in the school, that he shall attend.... any Sunday school, or any place of religious worship' and that the child 'may be withdrawn by his parent' from any religious instruction or religious observance. Equally it recognised the crucial role that the churches were already playing in education, especially in rural communities, and so set up parameters for a partnership. Each Poor Law Union in the country had to set up a school board to oversee the requirements of the Act in their own area without having a detrimental effect on neighbouring areas, and schools had to be subject to a national system of inspection. Bulford parish responded to the new requirements which included standards for buildings, standards which the existing school failed to meet, necessitating a case having to be made for a new school to meet the criteria set out in the act. The case, 'That the school is to be in connection with the Church of England and is to be called "Bulford Parish School"' was submitted in December of that year by the rector, Rev. Jacob Mountain and his two churchwardens. It established, as has been seen, that it would develop the only school in the village which 'is attended by all the Labourers children of the Parish'. The existing school is 'backed entirely by private benevolence' but 'being exclusively agricultural and without men of wealth, this Parish is not able of itself to build a school house and such as the Government requires'. Education was to be offered to all children between five and twelve years old, and pressure was put on for them to attend. At the local Deanery Meeting held 19 April 1876, there was general approbation for the motion that 'all legitimate means (consistent with the liberty of the subject) should be used to ensure their [children's] attendance between the ages of four and ten'. Later, in 1880 it was made compulsory for children to attend up to the age of ten. School pence still had to be paid but the local boards could pay for those who could not afford it. In 1891 schooling was made free for everyone. The proposed new school was for sixty-four children with 'one mistress principal teacher with an assistant'. The level of annual income that the parish expected to raise to support it was,

Annual Subs + donations £30
From School-Pence   £10
Annual Endowment   £ 8 This sum is charged upon the estate of the Patron
                         £48

The proposals for the new school were passed but, first of all, existing and potential accommodation had to be assessed, the result not being reached in July 1873. The existing village school was ruled out as it only had accommodation sufficient for twenty-four children in a room only a height of six and a half feet to the cross-beams and a floor of brick. It was judged to be 'probably large enough for the needs of the parish' in conjunction with the larger 'dissenters school' back in 1859, but clearly not fit for purpose in the new era of education. Another potential building somewhere in the village was assessed, (it could it have been part of Orchard End recently acquired by Anthony Southby, or an outbuilding attached to the old 'Rose and Crown', pulled down when it was rebuilt in 1896) but,

> The dimensions of the building proposed to be purchased (30ft x 21ft x 8½ft) wd give accommodation for 65 children. But a room of this height seems too low, and there is no way of increasing the height, except by sinking the floor. If this were done, the building might be acceptable, otherwise the new S.[school] for 64 as passed wd be necessary.

This option was ruled out and approval given in May 1874 for a new, purpose built school on land given by the Patron. [18]

The new school was to be brick built with no internal plaster thirty feet by sixteen feet, rising to fourteen feet from floor to the apex of the ceiling. The deal floor was on oak sleepers and it was to have wood windows and 'ventilation by an open fire and chimney' and it was 'proposed to have a stove in the centre of room'. The total site was to be 651 square yards surrounded by boundary walls and a 'fence dividing the Boys and Girls playgrounds will be close boarded'; no chance of looking through then. The total estimated cost was £200 which included the 'desks, benches, and other internal fittings'. The Lord of the Manor, residing at the time in Lyndhurst, and the three tenant farmers were to contribute fifty pounds between them towards the costs, the rest of the funding coming from outside the parish, as a 'sum

Education and Social Mobility

33 Farmhouse and new Manse. John Grist's farmhouse, inherited by Jane Castleman (FIG 3, no.23), now two cottages. Beyond is the house used as a parsonage of the parish church (FIG 3, no.24) before becoming the house of the School Mistress in 1875. It is now the Chapel Manse. On the far side is the schoolroom of the first village school. (photographed by author in 2011)

given in 2 nearly equal Grants; the second of which was added because of our difficulties owing to the Poverty of the Parish which has no rich and able men either among its inhabitants, Proprietors or Benefactors'. Building started straight away and the following year the architect reported that it was in 'all respects completed in accordance with the plans'. £15 15s had been raised towards the building through church collections, the Wiltshire Fund contributed £20 and a further £23 10s came from the Diocesan Special Fund but costs had overrun by £21 which was made up by further contributions from the tenant farmers. The village had a new, modern, purpose built school and Rev. Jacob Mountain could report to his bishop that the parish had 'added a brick schoolroom to a very good and mainly new brick house given as a teacher's residence, which had been thoroughly fitted up'. The new school was built by the Sturgesses and the original plans still exist, showing the schoolroom, the playground and the detached 'back offices' (toilets). The school still stands although no longer the village school; a new school replaced it in 1971 on the new estate. The derelict school was bought by the chapel in 1977 with the attached old school house bought two years later.

No 1 Bulford School
Girls Play Ground
APPROVED
Present House for Teacher's Residence
School Room
30'0"
16'0"
Boys' Play Ground
Scale

No 2 Bulford School
Present House
West End Elevation
APPROVED
Present House
North End Elevation
Present House
Proposed School House & Present House Roofs
East End Elevation
Feet
Scale

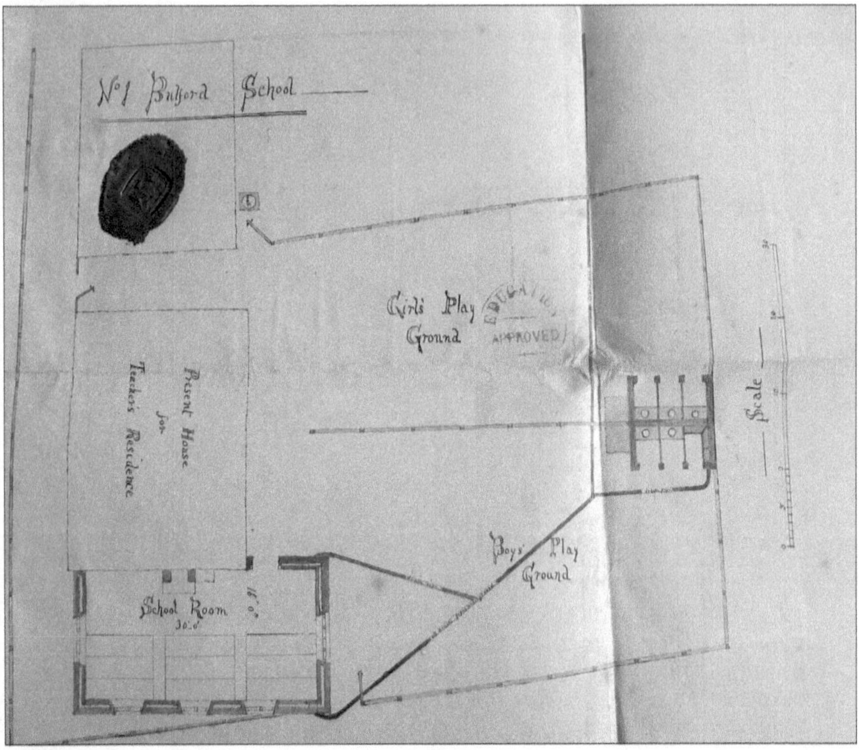

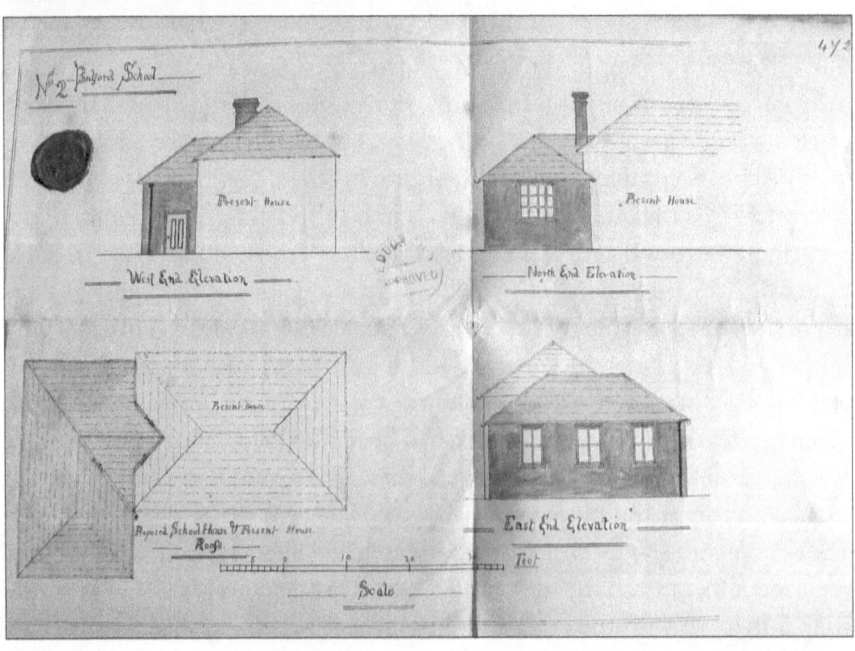

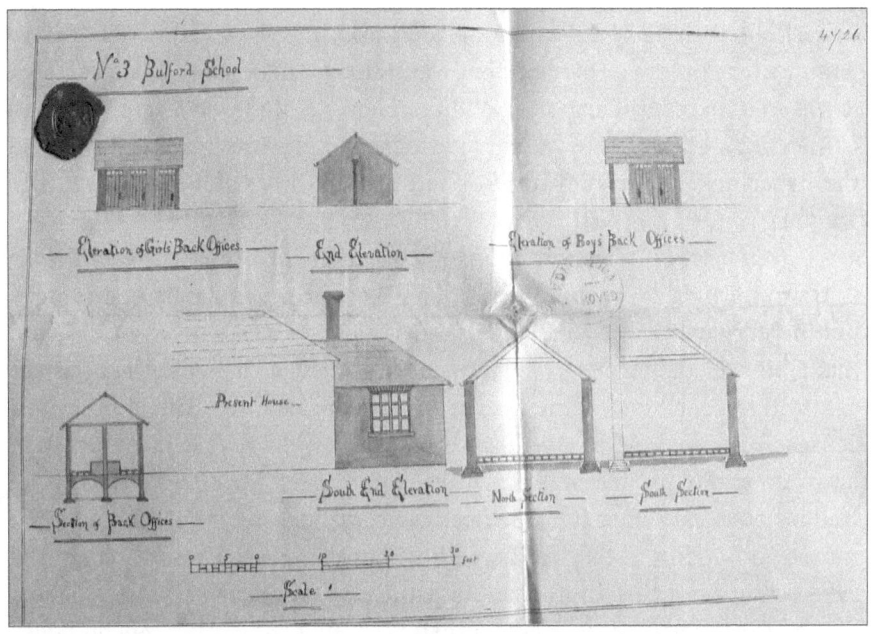

34 School plans. The approved 1872 Plans for the new Bulford Parish School, drawn up by the Sturgesses. The school opened in 1875 and was closed in 1966 with the building of the present school. The building is now the Lawes Hall attached to the Manse. (Wiltshire and Swindon Archives)

The school is now the Godfrey Room and Lawes Hall and the house the new Manse. [19]

On 14 May 1875 the Managers appointed the first mistress of the school, Mary Ann Knight, and she continued in this post into the twentieth century. Her role in village society was important in influencing the outlook of the children in her charge so it is worthwhile looking at her experience of life in more detail. Mary Ann Knight (née Cannings) was a village girl, sister of Elizabeth who married John Sawyer, the papermaker. Her mother Rebecca had married the shepherd William Cannings in February 1831 and Mary Ann was born in 1839. As a young lady, she was employed by Anthony Southby as the cook at the Manor House, along with her younger sister Lucy as a domestic servant. Mary Ann was almost identical in age to Anthony Southby's youngest daughter, Claudia, and a friendship grew up between them. (Mary Ann's family still possess one of Claudia's own paintings that she gave her.) Working in the Southby household with their international outlook must have influenced Mary Ann, which could well explain that when she got married in January 1866, it was to a mercantile captain, William Henry Knight. William, too, had connections with the Bulford papermakers. He was brother-in-law to the papermaker James Hyatt who had married his sister Margaret Alice Knight. [20]

William Henry Knight soon took his new wife on board ship with him to travel the world. At some point Mary Ann crossed a desert in a caravan but in February 1870 their ship 'Cavalier' was in Liverpool where William made his will. Later that year they are recorded in the American census as staying in Michigan – the couple do not appear in the British decennial censuses, always held in April, as this was the time of year that they were away at sea for the tea season. Mary Ann's sister Lucy had married the Bulford born carpenter John Bedford, who worked at Lambeth Palace, and moved to London. Mary Ann was staying with her at Vauxhall when she gave birth to her first child Claudia Annie, no doubt named after Claudia Southby, in August 1871. Claudia then accompanied her parents on board the 'Cavalier' sailing to America via China, but she sadly died of convulsions the following May at Sulawesi Tengah in Indonesia. Mary Ann gave birth to her second daughter Francesca Mabel in March 1873 on board the 'Cavalier'. In August, when landfall was made at San Francisco, after which Francesca was named, her birth and her sister's death were registered at the Consulate. In July 1874, Mary Ann gave birth to a son, Wilmot Henry Pentith, ashore at Netley Cottages, Southampton but was separated from her husband William who had sailed to Australia as master of the 'Bebington', where he arrived that November. He then tragically died in January 1875 of heart disease on board the 'Tararua' steamer, bound for Adelaide in search of cargo to bring back to England. Mary Ann did not know that she was a widow with two young children until the ship arrived back in England three months later in April. The following month, May 1874, she became schoolmistress of the newly opened Bulford parish school under the joint patronage of Anthony Southby and Alfred Seymour, no doubt on the recommendation of Anthony Southby who had learned of her bereavement and knew her well. [21]

Mary Ann Knight moved into the school house with her two young children, a general servant and, in 1881, a boarder from Dorset working as a farm bailiff. Francesca helped her mother in the school, being described as a 'monitor' when she was fifteen year old, and then a 'pupil teacher' when she was eighteen. She was appointed to the staff in December 1888, obtained a P.J. Scholarship in 1892 and attended the Teachers' College in the Close, Salisbury where, after a leave of absence 'to attend the Certificate Examination' in July 1898, she obtained her qualification. She gave her mother much needed help as the average attendance in 1895 was forty-eight, rising to sixty-five in 1906, including children from Milston. In 1886 the Board had already appointed an assistant teacher, Annie Rowden, who had been certified as a teacher in 1868 and was the village postmistress's daughter. Both Mary Ann Knight and her unmarried daughter Francesca were still running the school in 1901, the latter being promoted to 'schoolmistress'. Francesca was also the organist at the parish church. In 1902 she married the son of the landlord of the 'Rose and Crown', George Rumbold, who in 1901 was a carrier lodging in Raglan House with his sister Emma who had married Albert Densley the civil engineer working on the new army camp. Francesca, or 'Esca' as she was called, left teaching. Mary Ann Knight died in 1915 at her son Wilmot's house in Salisbury. Annie Rowden took over as the new headmistress of the school on Mary Ann Knight's retirement at Easter 1902. [22]

Surviving records for the new school begin in May 1897 with the preservation of the school log book, with the exception of one indirect record. This was an entry for April 1882 in Rose's Grammar School log book, in Amesbury, which records that the headteacher's wife 'Mrs Flowers has taken temporary charge of Bulford school during the absence of the mistress from ill health'. Back to Bulford's log book, reading it one is immediately struck by the importance given to attendance figures. Each week's average attendance was recorded along with any reasons for a low attendance, and these figures were regularly checked by the Managers in person of the vicar, and attendance officers. The reason for this assiduous recording and checking is that schools were partly funded on attendance and so this data was economically significant. The funding was encapsulated during the a parliamentary debate in 1871,

> The sum of 6 shillings is granted for each scholar on account of attendance, and 4 shillings each for the three subjects, making 12 shillings for reading, writing, and arithmetic. Thus each scholar can earn 18 shillings apart from extra subjects, and as 14 shillings a-head (or 15 shillings where music is taught) is the maximum payable ... Indeed, it is obvious that if 75 per cent

of the children pass in reading, writing, and arithmetic, the school will earn the maximum grant; and, in fairly good schools, this amount of success has been, and we doubt not will be, attained without difficulty.

This was payment by results; her Majesty's Inspectors came round to assess the quality of the teaching to see whether or not it justified the funding and explains why singing was so assiduously recorded in the log book. A report on the village school in 1899 however concluded that,

> The condition of the school was not altogether satisfactory. The general influence of the teachers is good, but they fail to secure the attention of the scholars or to make them take an active part in oral lessons. The result in Geography are of no value ... Improvement will be expected if the Grant under Article 105 of the Code is to be continued.

It seems a surprise, given Mary Ann's travels, that geography results were judged to be 'of no value'. It was no doubt that her and the inspector's ideas as to what should be taught were poles apart. Funding was threatened but the next report was able to say that, 'The scholars doing a little better'. Another thing to strike the reader of the log book is the influence of the weather on the school. There are frequent references to adverse weather conditions preventing the children's attendance; 'heavy rain', 'much affected by stormy weather', 'heavy fall of snow, only seven children in attendance', and teaching negated by 'a heavy thunderstorm rendering it impossible to carry on the usual work'. It is a reminder that life was still governed by the elements to a degree unrecognisable to most people today. [23]

The school year began on 1 December, in line with the beginning of the Christian year, and was regulated by a combination of religious and agricultural events. There were school holidays for Christmas and Whitsun, but the longest for the whole of August was to help in the fields. It was called the 'Harvest holiday', not the summer holiday. When there was a demand for all available hands, this was the priority which took over from school, even in term time. There are frequent references to low attendance as 'several of the scholars being employed by their parents in the potato fields', or 'the elder boys being employed in the ingathering of the hay'. The demands of agriculture were paramount and the picture painted by Richard Jefferies for boys at this time rings true for Bulford.

Trudging to and fro .... in wind, and wet, and snow, to school, his letters were thrashed into him. In holiday time he went to work - his holidays, in fact, were so arranged as to fall at the time when the lad could be of most use in the field. If an occasion arose when a lad was wanted, his lessons had to wait while he lent a hand.

He also paints a picture of parents eager to get their young children to school so that they can get to work, writing,

Now that good schools are open to every village, so soon as the children are old enough to walk the distance, often considerable, they are sent off every morning. At all events, if it does nothing else, it causes the mothers to give them a daily tidying up, which is in itself an advantage. They travel under the charge of the girl; often two or three such small parties join company, coming from as many cottages. In the warmer months, the lanes and fields they cross form a long playground for them, and picking flowers and searching for birds'-nests pass away the time. In winter they have to face the mire and rain.

Some mothers, though, did not give their children 'a daily tidying up' so that Mrs Knight, 'Warned several scholars that if they were not more cleanly in their persons they would be sent home again'. Attendance at Bulford was always a challenge with some children, especially before 1880 when it was not compulsory. Some names, boys, frequently appear in the log book for, for example, not turning up at the beginning of term. On 7 July 1897 Mrs Knight, 'Sent notice to attendance officer that Macklin and Hargraves have not returned to school and also informed him of other scholars irregular attendance'. Not long afterwards the Managers' scheme for giving praise for regular attendance was adopted and later they, 'Distributed prizes for regular attendance'. [24]

The curriculum and compulsory education

THERE IS A limited amount of information on the curriculum to be gleaned from the log book. The youngest children's learning was focused around a series of object lessons which were mainly topics familiar to their world. One year's curriculum, for example, included lessons on 'The

Cat, The Pig, The Lion, The Hen, The Cow, The Sheep, The Owl, The Wolf, A Fish, Coins, Milk, Currants, Tea, Coal, Iron, Salt, A Table, The Potato, and Water'. It is interesting to note that in 1898 'A Railway Station' was included in the list in preparation for the extension of the railway to Amesbury in 1902, and then subsequently to the village. Judging by the log book of Rose's Grammar School in Amesbury for the same period, we can see that this focusing on their world was standard practice, but Bulford children were taught by someone who had travelled the world by sea, ridden on camels through the Sahara, and led a life regulated by the tea trade. This experience was shared with the children with lessons on topics like ships, the mariner's compass, camel, dates, cocoa, cotton, coral and sponges and sugar cane. She impressed her grandson, telling him stories about her travels, and showing him souvenirs that she had at home with her, including: a collection of Oriental ornaments, tail feathers of birds from 'foreign' parts, a porcupine quill box, hand painted rice paper mats, and a beautiful Japanese pillow. She no doubt shared all this with her young pupils. They must have had a greater knowledge of the world than most children from other villages.[25]

The children were organised according to Standards I through to VI and details of the skills they were required to master were laid down by law. The 1872 standards are shown opposite. Regular examinations were required, mainly by the school itself, moderated by inspectors when they visited, but some were taken externally and an entry in the log book, for example, reads, 'Two scholars attended the examinations at Amesbury School for proficiency certificate'. It would appear that it was an uphill struggle to extend the children to reach the requirements for the higher standards which must have been aspirational for many of the village children. The Rev. Arnold wrote in exasperation, 'I know no other school where it is harder to extract knowledge from the children and only hope it is from shyness on their part, though I fear their intelligence is not fully cultivated. Reading and Grammar are backward, but in other respects the instruction is very fair'. A report, for example, on boys' drawing described it as 'Excellent'.[26]

The education of the older children was a cause of ongoing concern in the latter years of the century. In 1898 the Managers secured an Aid Grant of seven pounds a year to increase expenditure on staffing and to pay an 'organising master' a pound a year to come and give advice to the school. He was a Mr Gates from Salisbury who visited once a term. Two years later

STANDARD I
Reading   One of the narratives next in order after monosyllables in an elementary reading book used in the school.
Writing   Copy in manuscript character a line of print, and write from dictation a few common words.
Arithmetic   Simple addition and subtraction of numbers of not more than four figures, and the multiplication table to multiplication by six.

STANDARD II
Reading   A short paragraph from an elementary reading book.
Writing   A sentence from the same book, slowly read once, and then dictated in single words.
Arithmetic   The multiplication table, and any simple rule as far as short division (inclusive).

STANDARD III
Reading   A short paragraph from a more advanced reading book.
Writing   A sentence slowly dictated once by a few words at a time, from the same book.
Arithmetic   Long division and compound rules (money).

STANDARD IV
Reading   A few lines of poetry or prose, at the choice of the inspector.
Writing   A sentence slowly dictated once, by a few words at a time, from a reading book, such as is used in the first class of the school.
Arithmetic   Compound rules (common weights and measures).

STANDARD V
Reading   A short ordinary paragraph in a newspaper, or other modern narrative.
Writing   Another short ordinary paragraph in a newspaper, or other modern narrative, slowly dictated once by a few words at a time.
Arithmetic   Practice and bills of parcels.

STANDARD VI
Reading   To read with fluency and expression.
Writing   A short theme or letter, or an easy paraphrase.
Arithmetic   Proportion and fractions (vulgar and decimal).

there was still a problem and an Inspector's Report stated that, 'The infant and lower standards are fairly good, but the work of the upper standards is not sound, and class subjects are not well known. I advise the Head Mistress to take only one class subject and to get the younger teachers to help more with the upper standards'. The prevailing culture in the village was probably to view school as a means of occupying the children until the boys were ready to be wage earners in the rural economy. Compulsory schooling delayed this but Jefferies reported that,

> The lads, as they grow older and leave school, can almost always find immediate employment with their father on the same farm, or on one close by. Though they do not now go out to work so soon, yet, on the other hand, when they do commence they receive higher weekly wages. The price paid for boys' labour now is such that it becomes a very important addition to the aggregate income of the cottager.

On the other hand, 'The girls go less and less into the field. If at home, they assist their parents at harvest time when work is done by the acre, and the more a man can cut the better he is off; but their aim is domestic service, and they prefer to be engaged in the towns'. Jefferies writes a lot about village girls going into domestic service arguing that,

> The cottage is a poor preparation even for the humblest middle-class home. Those ladies in towns who have engaged country servants are well aware of the amount of teaching they require before they can go through the simplest duties in a satisfactory manner. But most of these girls have already been out several times before reaching town. What a difficulty, then, the first farmer's wife must have had in drilling the rudiments of civilised life into them! Indeed, the vexations and annoyances connected with servants are no light weight upon the patience of the tenant-farmer. His wife is perpetually preparing servant girls for the service of other people. …. She is a kind of unpaid teacher, for ever shaping the rough material which, so soon as it is worth higher wages than a tenant-farmer can usually pay, is off, and the business has to be begun over again.

Was this a true picture for Bulford? Of fourteen girls in service in 1891, four were employed on farms at Imber, Codford, Alvediston and Broad Chalke and only one out of the fourteen, Emma Knight (b. 1866) came back to live in the village and her career seems to fit this picture. She was servant to a builder/contractor in Newbury before becoming a housemaid to a solicitor in Norfolk, returning to live in Bulford as Mrs Andrews. The farm employees went on to marry a carter, a clocksmith foreman, a police constable and the fourth, Jane Sturgess, married the bailiff of the farm in Alvediston where she was employed. It is difficult to state categorically that Jefferies' opinion was correct for Bulford, but it seems to strike a chord. [27]

The education in the village school continued to be an uphill struggle, a struggle against the culture of an agricultural community which, although at the end of the century was rapidly disintegrating, still held on to its traditional roots with each person knowing their place. They were, in Jefferies' view, 'an old-fashioned farming people [where] if a man once drove pigs to market he should always continue to do so, and all his descendants likewise..... . It is a crime to move out of the original groove; if a man be lowly he must remain lowly, or never be forgiven'. Although it is straying a few years beyond the scope of this book, the report of an inspection on the 10 and 18 December 1907 by George Hodson, Her Majesty's Inspector, paints a picture of this uphill struggle.

> The infants of this school have been nicely taught, though their teacher has been restricted too much in the amount of work attempted. Next year the standard of attainment in Reading and Number should be somewhat higher.
>
> For the rest, there is little to be said of a satisfactory nature. Neither the instruction nor the discipline is as it should be. No appeal is made to the intelligence of the children and the teaching, though vigorous, is unintelligent and ineffective.
>
> In Arithmetic, the books of the two lowest classes are untidy, dirty and abounding in blots and smudges, both inside and out; and there is no evidence of any effort to remedy the state of things. There is but little understanding of some of the simplest processes employed, and figures are merely put down and juggled with according to "rules". This applies, also, to the upper classes, but they though better are by no means satisfactory.
>
> The Reading, throughout, is slovenly, and there has been no systematic attempt to make the children think about what they read. Even among the ablest scholars it is with great difficulty that any indication can be got of any understanding of a passage read, either to them or by themselves, though these passages be selected from books in everyday use and from matter which is not new to them.

> The writing, almost without exception, is bad, while the correction of the exercises in composition is both careless and unintelligent, resulting in a lack of knowledge of some of the most elementary principles of writing in all but one or two of the brighter children.
> The elementary work, therefore is far from satisfactory.

The discipline does not redeem the above state of affairs as,

> The children are uncouth in manner. They have not acquired the habit of obedience, with the consequence that an undue amount of time and energy have to be expended in the repetition and enforcement of orders and directions, the while the work is carried on in an atmosphere of noise and petty disorder which is inexcusable. [28]

Social mobility

FINALLY IN THIS survey of education in the village, it is worth stepping back to look at the bigger picture to see how much it played a part, if at all, in promoting social mobility. The evidence is hard to come by in the short period covered by this book as longitudinal studies of village families over several generations are needed. Opportunities for self advancement were few and far between within the village where, for the majority, employment was restricted to agricultural work with low wages. Richard Jefferies was of the opinion that 'it takes sixty years, two generations, to accumulate a village fortune by saving fifty pounds a year'. Even villagers like Daniel Smith who owned property still worked as agricultural labourers and, as we have just noted, those who changed their station in life were viewed with suspicion. There was, however, some movement within the strands of village society as we have seen with William Kinsman. He worked on Upper Farm as a ploughboy and then became a papermaker for a while before returning to agriculture as a labourer. Education was not seen as a way to advance a person's station in life but rather, as the local Deanery Meeting put it, 'fitted them for the state of life which it had pleased God to call them'. Children of higher stations, like the orphaned minors of yeoman James Chalk, were educated away from the village to the 'Quality Degree and Estate' which befitted them. [29]

Villagers could, on the other hand, gain social respect. One such villager was Samuel Sturges who was employed as a labourer on Watergate

Farm by Francis Stephen Long. He played a prominent part in the life of the chapel for nearly fifty years, being on the appointing committee for new ministers, giving out hymn books on Sunday and teaching in the Sunday school. He was much loved and referred to as 'Dear Samuel Sturges' when he died in 1862. He was literate and wrote with a firm, confident hand and when his son died, Francis Stephen Long acted with him as guardian for his grandchildren. Nevertheless, his station in life remained unchanged. The same could be said of the parish clerks who were also literate agricultural workers, whose services were appreciated by village society. [30]

Social advancement was only really possible by moving from the village and one common route was via service – especially for girls. The case of Mary Cannings is a prime example, as we have seen. She was the daughter of an agricultural labourer who went into service at the Manor and through travel with the household, met her future husband, a ship's captain from Southampton. As Mary Ann Knight she rose to the position of village schoolmistress. She naturally valued education, her daughter qualifying as a teacher, and her son Wilmot trained as a bank clerk, eventually becoming a bank manager in Salisbury; farm labourer rising to bank manager in three generations. [31]

There were occasional examples of villagers who were enterprising, moving from Bulford and developing new careers. Such an example, already noted in Chapter 3, was the labourer William Williams and his wife becoming omnibus entrepreneurs in London, and another was William Sturgess who made the most of the opportunities for self advancement. He was the son of Wlliam Sturgess (d. 1788), a butcher who settled in the village with his wife Sarah (née Newman) where they brought up their three children. His son William was also a butcher at the time of his marriage, aged eighteen, in Winchester. Nothing more is heard of him in the village records until the *Chapel Church Book* records William Sturgess as being 'regularly dismissed at his own request ... to [join] the church in Southampton under Pastor Thos. Atkins' in December 1850. The minute book of the Above Bar Congregational Church in Southampton duly records in February 1851 the admission of 'Mr Sturges from the church of Bulford Wilts'. Within six years he had become a deacon, a position he held until his death in 1863. Before leaving Bulford chapel, he had changed his career to become, as his will written in 1839 described him, 'now at Gosforth, Officer of Excise'. The 1851 census for Southampton shows him as an 'Officer of Inland Revenue

– Superannuated'. The PO Directory for Southampton 1859 lists him as 'William Sturges Gent'. Not a bad rise socially for a numerate butcher's boy from Bulford. [32]

With the collapse in agricultural employment and the closure of the paper-mill in the second half of the century, villagers had to move away to support themselves. This inevitably triggered social mobility with new careers being forged in London, Southampton or elsewhere in the Empire, and this will be looked at in the next chapter. The extent of successes that villagers made of their lives can only be revealed through individual family histories, unknown to the present author. And as to the part that universal education played in all this, it is hard to quantify, but must have been significant. As Richard Jefferies wrote in 1880,

> the rapid progress of education in the villages and outlying districts is the element which is most worthy of thoughtful consideration. On the one hand, it may perhaps cause a powerful demand for corresponding privileges; and on the other, counteract the tendency to unreasonable expectations. In any case, it is a fact that cannot be ignored. [33]

11
'Right About Turn':
The Coming of the Army

Changes to the village in the latter half of the century

THE FIRST DETAILED picture from this portrait of nineteenth-century Bulford is that which begins to emerge with the 1801 Seymour Devenish lease of Watergate Farm and so it seems appropriate to stray into the first year of the twentieth century to round off the picture a hundred years later to ascertain the ways in which the village had changed. Changes in agriculture, improved communications, education and the widening of horizons all left their mark, especially in the second half of the century. The dying years of the century then saw the beginnings of a dramatic change in the village. Within a generation, Bulford was to alter from being a village of limited horizons, to becoming an adjunct to a large, permanent military camp caught up in the eddies of national and international events. It was not the change of ownership, after all this had happened a number of times before, but the presence of the camp itself which affected Bulford most. No longer did the village look exclusively up and down the Avon Valley as it had since the dawn of history, but it did a 'right about turn' and looked towards the camp on the downs, with its back to the river. The whole orientation of the village changed in a few short years. This chapter uses the census returns of June 1851, 1891 and 1901 (along with other sources) as a basis to illustrate the beginnings of this change.[1]

The mid century indigenous village had been geared virtually to one end, that of agricultural production, and then this was overlain with a new role of servicing the army camp emerging in 1901 on the downs behind. The structure of the village had changed little. There were sixty-eight households in that year, a decrease of fifteen since 1851, with the intrusion of the army being limited to the withdrawal of the Manor House from the village (being empty at the time except for the caretaker) to embark on its new career as an Officers' Club, and one of the Pennings cottages (the first residences to come under War Office ownership) on the old Seymour estate. This was situated next to the new hutted camp and was occupied by a corporal of the Army Service Corps. Finally there was Raglan House, the first to be finished of the three Officers' houses built on the edge of the village on Bulford Droveway between 1901 and 1903, inhabited at the time, not by an officer in these early days of the camp, but by a twenty-four year old civil engineer from Birmingham employed on the construction of the new hutted camp.

It was still the 'quaint little village' described by Mary Hamilton in 1900 but there were insidious changes harboured within it. There were for example fifty boarders in the village employed on the construction of the camp. The village population in the 1901 census was 343 and when these 50 are discounted as being alien to the indigenous village, this leaves a population of 293, a reduction of fifteen from 1851 explained mainly by the vacancy of the Manor House, which typically housed upwards of six family members and staff, and Orchard End House which as a boarding house for camp workers, has been excluded from the village statistics. There were other boarders, five agricultural workers, all Bulford born, and a police constable but these have been included in the village. There had always been lodgers and boarders in the village, seventeen for example in 1891, six Bulford born and the rest (except one of unknown place of birth) came from within ten miles. They were all agricultural workers and their wives save for a bricklayer and two widows. [2]

How had the village changed therefore over the second half of the nineteenth century, irrespective of the army's presence? Twenty-four per cent of villagers in 1901 still belonged to the extended families of Sturges/s, Keel, Andrews and Swatton, but this was a reduced proportion from 1851 when it stood at thirty-four per cent. The 1891 census portrays the village on the eve of the arrival of the army and gives a good picture of the degree to which it was already enmeshed in the wider economy. The village had a population of 341 of whom nearly two thirds were Bulford born and bred (as opposed to over three quarters in 1851). Nearly forty per cent were born outside the village and the number is exactly the same as the 132 Bulford born living elsewhere in England and Wales. Half of these (116) lived

'Right about Turn': The Coming of the Army

within a fifteen mile radius of the village and ninety-seven of the inward migrants were likewise from within fifteen miles. The village was still firmly rooted in its locality bounded by a day's walk in all directions. The half of outward migrants who went further afield moved mainly towards London and the South Coast with only four people moving further west (including the three in Wales). This reflects the main communication links of the village, the London Road and the railway to London, and the Avon Valley southwards to the coast. The majority of the twenty-five people moving to the Portsmouth, Southampton and Christchurch region were unskilled labourers, but a different picture emerges in those drawn to the capital. The thirty-three Londoners included three coachmen (and one Bulford girl married to a coachman) and a carter, all drawn by the pull of the London Road, and four working on the railway (three of whom were brothers) and two village girls married to railway workers. William Love was a gardener and he married Elizabeth who ran a grocer's shop in the village – both were teachers at the chapel Sunday school. They had three sons all of whom worked on the railway; John, the eldest, became a shunter, William a ticket collector and James a signalman.

London also drew the gentry throughout the kingdom who resided in the fashionable areas of Belgravia and Camberwell along with merchants who had made their money in trade. All these households needed servants. Twenty-two Bulford girls (nine with the surname of Sturgess) ranging in age from a housemaid of fifteen to a nurse of sixty-nine, with an average age of twenty-six, were in service in 1891. Eight of these were working in London, mainly in Hanover Square or Kensington, along with Alfred Sawyer and Sylvanus Sturgess who were a butler and valet to London merchants. Men going into service was another explanation for marriages from outside the village. The extent of this is hard to tell as the census returns only give a ten yearly snapshot leaving us to find out the stories through family histories, like that of the Sawyers. William Sawyer (born 1878), the youngest son of papermaker John Sawyer, went into service near Bath as a footman where he met his future wife Prudence Howse who was also in service as the cook. She came from Latton, north of Swindon, where her father was a lock keeper on the North Wilts Canal, and her mother collected the tolls. William left service at Bath to work as a carpenter and conducted a courtship with Prudence for eight years by post. When his father died in 1901 and his mother became unwell, William married Prudence at Latton and then moved to Bulford in

1903 to look after her, living in the mill cottage with his new wife, Prudence Sawyer. Her writings have been used extensively throughout this book, living there until she died in 1979, aged one hundred. [3]

A very general picture emerges of the village in the latter years of the nineteenth century of a stable core, drawing about of a third of its population mainly from within walking distance to replace a similar number exported towards the south and east. It was already a village with its traditional insularity rapidly breaking down under assault from the transport revolution and the draw of the conurbations in London and the South Coast. Easier transport was the means for this migration but the underlying causes were changes in agriculture. The fall in employment for agricultural labourers fuelled a 'high rate of migration from villages ... to London, the dominions and the United States'. These expanding centres of population were also attracting those with a trade like the two members of the Sturgess clan, David and Mark, who took their bricklaying skills to Islington and Shoreditch respectively. This picture is incomplete though as it ignores villagers serving abroad in the armed services and those who emigrated to the dominions and the United States. A ten year old boy inspired by the military march past in 1872 would be twenty-nine in 1901. One villager, Charles Adlam, was in the Royal Navy serving aboard *HMS Vernon*, and another, John Truckle, was a ship's fireman at Holyhead in Anglesey. [4]

Comparing the snapshots provided by the 1851 and 1901 census returns, we can also see how employment patterns in the village had changed over half a century. The number of people directly employed on the land dropped from a hundred and fifty to forty-eight, a drop of two thirds, and about half the number in 1801 (when the population stood at 228). Bearing in mind that the army had taken many acres for its use, and the village total population had dropped by a quarter, this is still a dramatic decrease of thirty-two per cent in real terms. The effects of mechanization can clearly be seen with the complete obliteration of ploughboys as a group (there were eighteen in 1851 and none fifty years later). Similarly with women working on the farm (there were thirty-three in 1851, and again none fifty years later). The army mainly took over the downland reducing the number of sheep and so there was less need for shepherds, sixteen reducing to three. Another agricultural change was the increased specialisation of farm work, with new occupations such as 'yardman' and 'farm teamsters' to work the machinery.

'Right about Turn': The Coming of the Army

In 1891 William Blanchard from Berwick St James was an 'engine driver on farm' living in the village, this would have been a portable steam engine for farm work, probably made by Taskers. Farmers increasingly needed a 'farm bailiff' to keep a close eye on the more sophisticated farm work and there were two in 1901 (as opposed to none fifty years earlier). One group of agricultural workers which remained constant was the carters. There was an increase in 'gardeners' from one to five, no doubt capitalising on the opportunities provided by the camp for selling their produce, as a Newton Tony landowner predicted in 1897 when he said that 'The markets will be stimulated, small cultivators of fruit and vegetables and poultry owners will benefit immensely.'[5]

The number of villagers plying a trade remained overall constant, although the make up changed. One trade employing nine people in 1851, papermaking, as we have seen had been totally eclipsed. The village's other major trade, building, employed eight people at the same time. It was the exclusive preserve of two Sturgess families in the village which networked in the wider locality with other branches of the extended family, for example in Ludgershall and Cholderton. 1841 (see Appendix 1f) has William from one family and Thomas and his son Edward from the other working as masons/bricklayers in the village while another contemporary family member, James, was based in Ludgershall. We have records of both Thomas and William working on the church; Thomas was paid £2 5s 4d for tiling the church in 1789, and a further £5 18s 4d for more work on the tiling and mending the church wall, and William £2 5s 2d in 1858 for 'whitewashing and colouring the church'. There were probably other builders at work in the village, not identified in the census, for example William's two elder sons Thomas and David who followed in their father's footsteps. Ten years later, in 1851, these two families provided eight builders between them in the village: William and his sons Thomas, David, Sylvanus and Job, and Edward with his son Silas. This was the peak of the village's population, when as we have seen (in Chapter 2), the pressure on housing was at its greatest. It was also the beginning of the diaspora of Bulford's builders, chasing better building opportunities elsewhere. William's son Sylvanus left the building trade and went into service, moving to London with his wife Lois, who also went into service with him. Of his four brothers, two (Thomas and William junior) remained as builders in the village, but David moved first to Thruxton (1861), before working as a bricklayer in Islington, London

(1881). David's younger brother Job also stayed in the building trade, also moving to Thruxton (1861), Appleshaw (1871) and then to Andover (1881). Edward Sturgess's eldest son, Silas, felt the draw of work on the South Coast, and went to Alverstoke (Gosport) in 1861, then lodged at Portsea with his wife and four children (1871) before settling there as a builder (1881). The younger son, Mark, was attracted by building work in the rapidly expanding London and moved to Shoreditch (1881). When Edward died in 1881, this family of Bulford builders no longer worked in the village, leaving the descendants of William Sturgess as Bulford builders. [6]

The Census returns of 1871 show the building trade in the village at its nadir, with only the aged Edward, William Sturgess junior and his nephew Frank working as bricklayers. Edward was still active, despite his sixty-three years, as we have the estimates that he prepared for Rev. John Protheroe for work at the Chapel and on its cottages in 1874 with a commitment to, 'Find all materials & Complete the work in a workman like manner'. Frank unfortunately did not prosper in the bricklaying trade and worked on the land before dying (as we have seen in Chapter 2) an imbecile at the age of thirty-four in the Amesbury Workhouse. William's sister's illegitimate son, John, worked for a time as a builder, but it was left to William's own children to carry the torch. 1901 sees him and his three sons, Henry Atkins, Ira Sylvanus and Sydney William working as village builders, and it is the same picture ten years later. There was work still in the village at the end of the century for the Sturgesses who were, for example, the bricklayers and masons working for a Southampton firm to build a large service wing on the Manor House in 1892, and they built the new vicarage and the 'Stonehenge Inn' in neighbouring Durrington. The picture presented by this saga of the Sturgesses is that those with get up and go left the village in search of employment, drawn by the South Coast and London, fitting the general pattern of emigration that we have already seen. The difference is that the Sturgesses had a trade, and were not agricultural workers looking for alternative employment. [7]

The building associated with the new camp did not provide work for the Sturgesses but there was a rise of those employed in construction work: 'general labourers', an 'excavator of sewerage works', an 'iron moulder', those 'employed on public works' etc. totalling thirty-four is explained by the construction work on the camp, and as we shall see these were mainly lodgers coming into the village from afar. Other trades and professions supported by the village like dressmakers, laundry women, teachers, shopkeepers and publicans, what can loosely be termed as service industries, remained pretty constant at about ten people. The overall picture is of a village structure of services remaining constant, but there was a dramatic shift taking place from agricultural employment to building and servicing the camp, a development that, as we have seen, provided an opportunity to augment household budgets by taking in lodgers. The old self sufficient community looking in on itself with agriculture as its raison d'être, was rapidly changing to one looking to the camp; a 'right about turn'. The strength of the village's attachment to its locality was already weakening significantly as though its tap root was being yanked from the soil. John Protheroe noted in May 1880 that members of the chapel 'have left the village for more eligible situations' and that, 'This has remarkedly been the case of late.' We can see changes in the life of Bulford village, a reflection of the picture painted by a North Wiltshire journalist who, in the same year, wrote that,

> Had any one gone into a cottage some few years back and inquired about the family, most probably the head of the house could have pointed out all his sons and daughters engaged in or near the parish. Most likely his own father was at work almost within hail. Uncles, cousins, various relations, were all near by. He could tell where everybody was. To-day if a similar inquiry wore made, the answer would often be very different. The old people might be about still, but the younger would be found scattered over the earth. One, perhaps, went to the United States or Canada in the height of the labourers' agitation some years ago, when agents were busy enlisting recruits for the Far West. Since then another has departed for Australia, taking with him his wife. Others have migrated northwards, or to some other point of the compass - they are still in the old country, but the exact whereabouts is not known. The girls are in service a hundred miles away - some married in the manufacturing districts. To the middle-aged, steady, stay-at-home labourer, the place does not seem a bit like it used to. Even the young boys are restless, and talking of going somewhere. This may not be the case with every single individual cottage family, but it is so with a great number. The stolid phalanx of agricultural labour is slowly disintegrating. [8]

35 1872 Review at Beacon Hill. (Wiltshire Heritage Museum)

1872 Autumn Manoeuvres

An old gun barrel was sunk into the ground on Beacon Hill in about 1791 by the Board of Ordnance to mark one end of a base line, whose other end was near Old Sarum, to map the country (later called the Ordance Survey). This had literally put Bulford on the map and in a way was a precursor to the village's military career. The military 'invasion' of Bulford first began in 1872 when large scale Autumn Manoeuvres were held in the area by the army for the first time. These culminated in a review and grand March Past on Thursday 12 September before the Duke of Cambridge and the site for this extravaganza was Bulford Downs with Beacon Hill rising behind. The local paper describes the event which must have made a very great impression on the villagers as well as on a shooting party which noted the 'March Past on Beacon Hill on Sept 12th. Fine Sight.'

> With bands playing and colours flying, battalion after battalion, regiment after regiment, and battery after battery, debouched from the fighting

'Right about Turn': The Coming of the Army

ground to the various downs leading to Amesbury. Some 30,000 men and 20,000 horses are now in fields and parks about Durrington.

... On Thursday the march past took place, and thus was brought to an end the autumn manoeuvres of 1872. It was a grand spectacle, well worth going many miles to witness. The scene of the march past was Beacon Hill, and a better ground for such a purpose could not be found or desired. The widely sweeping slopes of Beacon Hill rose up gently from the downs fronting the west, and afforded the most desirable accommodation for hundreds and thousands of spectators, along with a splendid view of the far reaching plain below. The ground is perfectly adapted to military displays on a grand scale, the plain affording scope for the manoeuvring of 100,000 men, while the splendid facilities offered to the spectators by the soft green slopes of Beacon Hill are unsurpassed.

It must have seemed to the villagers that the whole world had come to Bulford and the open downs behind the village had been transformed by a heaving mass of humanity and horses.

At noon, a royal salute ... announced the arrival of the Prince of Wales who was received by the Duke of Cambridge and a very numerous staff of general officers including foreign and military representatives ... About one o' clock the march past commenced ... the last regiment came to the saluting point at twenty minutes to three o' clock, the passing of the 30,000 men thus occupying one hour and forty minutes.

It cannot have but formed an indelible impression in villagers' minds. Their minds, though, were not the only ones to have been influenced. The military establishment and politicians had seen how eminently suitable the countryside was to military manoeuvres with light, quick drying soils overlying chalk, especially as the army at that time depended exclusively on horses (20,000 during the March Past). Even so, the autumn manoeuvres left the roads in a bad state if the photographs taken in December 1900 of the A303 over Beacon Hill after that year's manoeuvres are anything to go by. The road was not metalled, with a surface of small stones being best that could be expected, and this had been reduced to two very muddy ruts striking out across unfenced downland. And this was the 'Great London Road to Andover'. [9]

Bulford Camp beginnings

THESE WERE THE years that marked the beginning of Great Britain's heavy military involvement in South Africa with the Zulu War in 1879 followed immediately by the First Boer, or Transvaal, War in 1880 to 1881 which created a priority for the Government to find areas for cavalry training and military manoeuvres. Salisbury Plain was favoured for three main reasons; the first of which, its suitability for horses and horse transport has already been mentioned, especially as it was mainly unenclosed. In addition the land was not considered an area of great agricultural value – much only used for sheep walks – and consequently commanded an acceptably low price for acquisition by the Government. And thirdly, it was close to London. There was local opposition to the proposed training grounds from landowners. Sir Edmund Antrobus of Amesbury and G. Knowles of Syrencote House, Figheldean, are both included in this number but there is no record of any opposition coming from Bulford, in fact the opposite seems to be the case as we have seen in Chapter 4. The military thinking culminated in the Military Lands Act which received its royal assent in April 1897 empowering the Secretary for War to begin purchasing the necessary land at Bulford and elsewhere. Although the initial purchases were not completed until March 1898, the local paper reported on 10 July 1897 that,

> The War Office have lost no time in taking advantage of the acquirement by the Government of an extensive tract of land on Salisbury Plain, for the purposes of a military training ground and the past week has witnessed the encampment of the 4th Cavalry Brigade at Bulford. The camp ... is situated on Bulford Down about a mile and a half north-east of the village of Bulford and about twelve miles from Salisbury. Beacon Hill rises close to the eastern side of the camp ... and on the western side is Nine Mile Stream ... .

It was the moment that marked the beginning of the army moving into Bulford and the village school *Log Book* reports that on 6 July there was 'a very low attendance this afternoon, the children having gone with their parents to watch the arrival of the soldiers on the downs'. Serious preparations had begun: the problem of the large population of rabbits whose burrows posed a threat of injury to the galloping horses of cavalry and mounted troops,

'Right about Turn': The Coming of the Army

was addressed with an order that tenant farmers of the land 'should be told they must kill rabbits down this year and fill in the holes' and a warrener was to be employed on the open downlands. A clause in James Hooper's 1897 lease reads, 'I will not keep rabbits on lands comprised in Schedules 2 and 3 so as not to cause damage to troops'. This was at a time when rabbits were deliberately bred for sport as is illustrated by the 1885 lease of Lower Farm which gave joint rights between the landlord and tenant 'to preserve and keep up the breed of and to sport shoot and destroy rabbits and carry away the same'. In 1900 when the army had right of manoeuvre over the whole farm, a clause was added to the 1897 lease that the tenant will not keep any rabbits on the farm and should it be deemed necessary by the landlord, he 'will allow him or his agents or any person authorized by him or them to enter and Kill the Rabbits and dig in the holes'. 1898 was also when approval was given to extend a railway line to Amesbury, and in August of that year another newspaper report talked about the military activity, saying that,

> It is long since the old road from Salisbury to Marlborough ... was the scene of so much traffic since the cavalry camp was formed at Bulford for the brigade consisting of the Scots Greys and the 1st (King's), 3rd and 7th Dragoon Guards. ... Officers and men have both expressed themselves as much pleased with the Bulford camping ground and it is certainly about as healthy, pleasant and convenient a place as a body of troops could desire for pitching their tents.

The village was immediately drawn into logistical support for the tented camp on the downs. There was the immediate need of water which had to be drawn from the Avon and from wells. Several wells were sunk in the area for the cavalry but, in January 1898, only one was finished, that at Bulford, delaying their arrival. It was 206 feet deep with twenty feet of headings and its supply of water was described as 'ample'. A year later saw a very long dry summer and this was a problem due to a bacillus scare. Noisy pumps were placed near the Manor House to supply water to both men and horses in the 'the parched up cavalry camp'. [10]

The Manoeuvres were held in the autumn and were restricted to the period between the harvest and the start of the shooting season. There were two 'armies, one playing the role of invading the country from the South Coast, and the other, Northern Army, being charged with opposing it.

The Southern Army began assembling at Wareham on 15 August, and the Northern Army on Salisbury Plain. 'The Cavalry Division was concentrated at Bulford, under General Luck, for some independent exercise, but on the 29th it was divided into two brigades' and each sent to an opposing army. The idea was for the Northern Army based on Salisbury to oppose the Southern Army, having supposedly landed at Weymouth, heading for London. Bulford was on the fringe of the action but on 6 September, positions for an imaginary army were supposed to be in course of preparation between Beacon Hill and Laverstock and on the next day the Northern Army was told to force a crossing of the Avon between Amesbury and Old Sarum in face of enemy fire. Heale and Lake were the sites chosen for the crossings. It was a foggy day and a cease fire was called at noon. The artillery of both sides, 'finding splendid positions on the high ground bordering the valley, had thundered across it without ceasing from the commencement of the action'. The noise of gunfire would have been heard at Bulford and it is inconceivable that villagers had not walked the short distance to watch the action, although their view would have been hampered by the fog. After the action 'both armies amicably crossed the Avon, and camping together near Beacon Hill, prepared for the grand March Past that was to bring the manoeuvres to a close on the following day'. On the 8 September 53,600 officers and men, 9,456 horses, 242 guns, and 486 wagons marched past C-in-C Field Marshall Viscount Wolseley. 'The day was fine, and the parade was a great success.' It was an eagerly anticipated spectacle by both the local people and visitors. The Under Secretary for War, in answer to a request for viewing provision for M.P.s, explained that, 'There will be a roped enclosure on Beacon Hill, a natural point of vantage for sightseers ... Admittance to the enclosure will be obtained by Members of the House of Commons who intimate to the Quarter-Master General, at the War Office ... their intention of being present'. On the day of the review, eight special trains were laid on to bring spectators to Grateley, and then take them home again. The headteacher of a nearby school at Amesbury bemoaned the low attendance in July stating that he could, 'Never remember to have passed through such a quarter in the whole course of my experience. Principal causes hay-making and the soldiers located on the plain. Doubtless all schools in the vicinity of the camp suffered in like manner'. In October, it got worse for the school and 'an additional week's holiday had to be given in consequence of the Review of Soldiers on the Plain'. [11]

'Right about Turn': The Coming of the Army

The needs of the soldiers were not just physical, and the village vicar, Rev. Cecil North Arnold, was 'appointed to officiate to the troops stationed at Bulford Camp ... during the period of cavalry manoeuvres'. Salisbury Diocese subsequently set up a Welfare of Soldiers Committee which worked closely with the Church of England Chaplain subsequently resident in the camp, Rev. R. Deane Oliver. The two clergymen wrote a joint letter to the editor of the *Andover Advertiser* in July 1898, reporting on the progress of their efforts and seeking financial support for their joint endeavour.

> We are glad to be able to tell your readers that this work is going on splendidly. Major-Gen. Sir G, Luck, K.C.B., Inspector-General of the Cavalry, has given us a capital site in the very centre of the camp. We have three large marquees; on entering the middle one visitors find themselves in a beautiful recreational room 60ft. By 30ft.; tables covered with crimson baize show a goodly stock of magazines, papers and games. Red and blue bunting decorate the walls; large lamps give a perfect light. Writing materials are given free, and a letter box is provided. The daily average posting of letters has been 90, while many more have been written and posted elsewhere; the attendance has risen to upwards of 350 in the day from three regiments. To the left opens the refreshment bar, 50ft. By 25ft. Here Mr Bronti, the well-known soldiers' caterer, from Aldershot holds sway, and provides refreshments of a quality and variety never before seen in the camp. The tables are covered with white oilcloth, and can easily be kept clean; there are seats for 56, standing room for many more.
>
> To the right of the recreation tent stands the "Church", connected by a short covered way. This also measures 60ft. by 30ft. There are seats for 300. It is brightly decorated with turkey red, which shows effectively against the white canvas. The chancel is boarded, and against curtains of turkey green the red cover of the communion table stands in bold relief. Over it hangs a large banner "God is love", while numerous green shield texts with silver lettering give brightness, and teach silent lessons of truth. A Bible reading or informal service is held every night about eight o'clock, and Church services on Sundays at 8 (Holy Communion) and 11.30 a.m., 3 and 7 p.m. The work is a joint one between the Diocesan Welfare of Soldiers Committee and the Church of England Chaplain to the forces resident in the camp. The committee have not yet received sufficient funds, and earnestly appeal for support. The warmest approval of the work has been expressed by

the General Officer commanding, by the staff and regimental officers. The very large attendance of soldiers show how they appreciate our work.

There were also other welfare measures afoot and in May 1901 the Regiment of Yeomanry Cavalry provided an escort for Field-Marshal Earl Roberts from Salisbury to Bulford to open a bazaar in aid of the Soldiers, and there was Miss Perk's Soldiers Home. Misses Louise and Emma Perks from the very early days of the camp had erected a tent to provide refreshments, reading and writing materials and evangelical teaching for the soldiers. They decided to make it permanent and the War Office was quite willing to grant them a site, but the local military authorities wanted it well away from the men. The sisters appealed to Lord Roberts, Comander in Chief of the army who was reported to have said, "Give Miss Perks whatever site she wants!". A new Soldiers' Home was opened in 1903 at a cost of £6,000 – and the building still stands in 2012. [12]

Mary Hamilton, whose descriptions of Bulford in 1900 we have already met, accompanied her husband who was a Captain in the Royal Irish Fusiliers stationed in the camp from May to November. They took lodgings in Milston but she describes life in the tented encampment.

> I watched the beginnings of the camp at Bulford; the first bell-tents going up; then expanding by degrees into the vast panoramic spread of white against the green backdrop of the plain ... Most of the troops at Bulford belonging to Militia, Volunteer or Yeomanry regiments. The infantry were nearly all in scarlet and the Yeomanry in blue, but khaki was being issued on the drafts training for South Africa, and some of the officers and men during that long hot summer were wearing the wide-brimmed Australian hats turned up on one side.
>
> Occasionally I would hear firing on the rifle ranges, or bugles in the camp, but there was no traffic in the air and not a great deal on the roads. I would drive for miles and meet only a few farm carts, or perhaps an Army Service Corps wagon. ...
>
> One day Colonel Sir Denis O'Neill invited me to a tea-party at the camp. A trestle-table was set outside his tent, laden with brown tea-pots, big white Army cups and saucers and plates of bread-and-butter, seed-cake and fruit; a contrast to the dainty porcelain and silver of the rectory. ...
>
> On Sunday mornings I would drive to the camp for church parade

'Right about Turn': The Coming of the Army

36   Church Parade at the tented camp in 1901.
(With permission of the National Army Museum)

and attend divine service from the dog-cart. I would hear the fifes and drums and the brass bands of different regiments assembling for parade. The officers and men would kneel on one knee and come up to their feet for the hymns, and the short sermon preached by the chaplain with his surplice fluttering in the breeze.

[After October 24th the weather] became cold and damp and conditions were severe in the camp. The canvas bell-tents, pleasant enough in summer, were inadequate protection against the hard weather. Early in November some men died of pneumonia and it was decided to break up camp.

Her account alludes to two important developments, the first being the outbreak of the Second Boer War in October 1899 which was to involve those who were encamped at Bulford, like the Scots Greys. Salisbury Plain provided an ideal environment for training troops to fight on the open South African velt and the War Office Salisbury Plain Committee directed in August, 'That all land outside the approved limits of the Avon Valley cultivation zone should be laid down permanently to grass, as soon as possible'. The next month James Hooper of Upper and Lower Farms received a letter informing him that,

The Secretary of State for War had decided that a large area of land forming part of the War Department Property which is now in arable some of which is in your occupation shall be sown to grass not later than 1901, so that it may be in pasture in 1902, and that the Military shall after July 15th in that year, when the Hay will have been stacked, have the right of use without paying compensation. [13]

The Plain also had the advantage of the River Avon, the importance of which we have already seen in the 1898 Autumn Manoeuvres. Then again in the 1900 Autumn Manoeuvres there was action on 14 September with the Yeomanry Cavalry successfully holding the line of the Avon from Netheravon to Durrington. The Salisbury Plain Committee stated that, 'There is no military operation which can be more usefully practised than the crossing of a river in face of opposition' and that the Avon was ideal as there was no railway line running up the valley to get in the way - yet. The Great Western Railway was proposing to extend the Amesbury line up the valley through Netheravon, Enford and Upavon to join the main line at Pewsey, but, as this was to cross four and a half miles of military land, it was strenuously opposed by the War Office as 'the construction of this railway will neutralise, if not entirely destroy, the instructional value, in a military sense, of the River Avon'. This proposed line would have run up the valley on the opposite side of the river to Bulford, crossing near Durrington Walls, and cutting across the water meadows of Watergate Farm to reach Amesbury via Ratfyn. The military preferred the London South Western Railway Company scheme which eventually came to fruition, leaving the river valley intact (see below). It was around this time that the excavation at Bulford Mill was undertaken to create a wide expanse of flowing water to practise river crossings. [14]

The permanent camp and the railway

IT IS DIFFICULT to discern what the villagers thought about all of this decision making on high which directly affected them. We have an inkling from the minutes of the newly formed parish council, which admittedly was heavily weighted by its membership to the interests of the tenant farmers. The minutes of their meeting on 16 February 1898 read,

'Right about Turn': The Coming of the Army

The circular letter to Mr Arnold [the vicar] from the Great Western Railway was read on the subject of the Pewsey and Salisbury Railway and it was decided not to take any action in the matter as it was thought that the Country's interest should be considered in preference to local interests ...

Villagers seem to be acting with a sense of patriotism although, admittedly, they were also eager not to antagonise their new landlord. It was a genuine patriotism as illustrated by the school children having 'a half day holiday in honour of the relief of Mafeking, and the Queen's birthday' in May 1900 after the war had resumed. The second development mentioned by Mary Hamilton was the rifle ranges to practise with the new, improved rifles being issued to the army. Salisbury Plain became crucially important in this respect and by 1900 five ranges had been constructed along the line of the later (1909) Bulford to Tidworth road. Mary Hamilton's account also highlights the need for a permanent encampment. This need had already been recognised and decisions had been taken to build a hutted camp and to provide a rail link, but the one down the valley from Pewsey never materialised. The Staffordshire Volunteer Brigade arrived at Ludgershall for the 1899 Autumn Manoeuvres by train, but as *The Times* reported, 'a long march was necessary before they arrived at Bulford, the distance from Ludgershall to the camp being fully 8 miles. The heat was very trying and the roads dusty'. Other troops marched six miles from Porton. [15]

The train line through Ludgershall and Porton was run by the London South Western Railway Company, and they constructed an extension to Amesbury to help with troop movements. Their Traffic Committee minutes have an entry for 4 December 1901 recording that, 'The War Office want to occupy the quarters at Bulford Camp during the winter months and ask if the new line to Amesbury will be opened at an early date. The line may be used at any time for military purposes'. The station was used on 29 March 1902 to transport troops to South Africa prior to the official opening on 26 April. In the March, Colonel Scott of the Royal Engineers requested an extension to Bulford which was approved and work began in 1904. The line was opened in 1906 for passenger use as far as Bulford Village, with the extension to Sling being a military railway. The line cost £28,809 to construct. The strategic vision of linking the camps on Salisbury Plain, with Aldershot and Portsmouth had finally been achieved. There was an earlier scheme proposed in 1891 by the Midland and South Western Junction Railway to link Ludgershall with Bulford camp, with a spur going on to Amesbury. This would have approached from Cholderton, crossed Tanners Down and swung round to the Camp east of Bulford Pennings. It was opposed by landowners in an enquiry at Andover, along with opposition from the rival London South Western Railway Company. Before the Bulford line was approved, there was a public enquiry held at Amesbury in July 1902. There were two objections, one from Sir Edmund Antrobus 'on the grounds of severance which would be caused to his estate' in Amesbury, and the second from the owner of what remained of the Seymour estate. 'Miss Seymour maintained that sufficient accommodation should be provided and maintained by the Railway Company and objected to the proposal to allow an extra 25 per cent over the London and South Western Rates for the carriage of goods traffic on the light railway' to and from the village. The line would cut her property in two and she wanted guarantees to be able to pass services under the line should she wish to develop her land. The main concern of villagers was the 'bridle path and an occupation farm road' from Bulford to Amesbury via Ratfyn which would be affected by the railway. There was 'a great deal of local traffic over the path'. Mr Melsome of Watergate House, who was also 'the occupier of Ratfyn Farm', expressed concern about the proposed level crossing on Ratfyn Farm. He said in evidence that,

> The path now under discussion was an occupation road and sometimes he crossed it with farm wagons as many as fifty times a day. They could only see a train coming for a distance of about a hundred yards and the road sloped down to the crossing so that it was exceedingly difficult to pull up quickly. In his opinion it was absolutely necessary to have a gatekeeper.

The Rev. Arnold had nothing to add to the discussions and Mr Sylvanus Sturgess supported the application on behalf of the parish of Bulford.[16]

The coming of the army to Bulford was in three stages. First there was the excitement of 1872, and then there was the impact of the tented encampment. The greatest shock to the village though was the erection of the permanent hutted encampment which began in the summer of 1899. Its impact was the greater because in addition to the soldiers and horses, there was the labour force and transport of the 45,000 tons of materials needed for its construction, and we have already seen how a traction engine bringing materials was to damage Bulford bridge in 1902. Accommodation was being built 'for the Army Service Corps, for three brigade divisions of Royal Field Artillery, and for four battalions of infantry'. The work was directed by Colonel Mascall with his staff of Mr. P.B.Roberts (surveyor), Mr. F.W.Osborne (clerk of works), and Mr W.E.Hoskins (assistant clerk of works). The contract was won by Mr. John McMans, of Hammersmith, West London, who employed about twelve hundred men at work on the site. An idea of the scale of the works is provided by a newspaper article in November 1900 headed 'The Bulford hutments, some interesting details'.

> The buildings number 534 (in addition to 109 litter sheds), and consists of officers' and warrant officers' quarters, men's quarters, married quarters, schools, laundries, recreational establishments, canteens, guard rooms, cook houses and baths, stables, workshops, forges, forage barns, gun sheds, wagon sheds, stores, &c. If placed end to end they would make a continuous line of buildings more than six miles long, says the *The Timber Trades Journal*.
>
> The whole of the buildings (except the litter sheds, coal sheds, and latrines, which are built of brickwork in cement), are timber framed, covered on the outside with rough boarding, felt and corrugated galvanised iron, and lined on the inside with rebated and V-jointed match-boarding stained and varnished. The foundations, however, vary, those for the Army Service Corps, and those for the Artillery being composed of cement concrete walls and floors, whilst those for the Infantry buildings are composed of brick piers in cement, on cement concrete bases, the sleeper plates resting on creosoted blocks.
>
> In June last there was not a balk of timber nor a sheet of iron on the site, but since then a town has sprung up, and some of the buildings are now occupied, and within a few weeks' time the whole will have been completed and handed over.
>
> As the work had to be completed within a few months (and this is one of the special features of the contract), the necessity of procuring and getting upon the site in a short time the large quantities of material required became a matter of vital importance. The difficulties of conveyance will readily be appreciated when it is understood that the materials used weigh about 45,000 tons, and the site is an average six miles from the four stations from which the goods were being drawn. For this work many traction

engines and horse trolleys have been used. It would take 125 two-horse teams three months to carry the goods from the rail to the site.

Very large quantities of timber have been used, and the contractor, with a view to securing early deliveries, seems to have distributed his orders as widely as possible – London, Liverpool, Bristol, Gloucester, Southampton, Cardiff, Bournemouth etc., each securing a share.

The following figures will give some idea of the extent of the buildings, and the large quantity of material required:-

Over 3,000 standards of timber have been bought, 536 miles of architrave, fillet and skirting have been used, 600 miles run of matchboarding, 404 miles of flooring (in addition to five acres of concrete flooring, and 15 miles of wrought and chamfered framing). There are about 8,000 windows and over 3,000 doors.

The felt if rolled out in a continuous line, would reach from London to Bristol, and the corrugated iron would cover a field of 47 acres.

There are 40,000 locks, bolts, latches, and stays, about 7,000 hat and coat hooks, and 2,500 iron brackets, while such things as screws and washers are reckoned by the million.

The buildings occupy about 3,000 acres of ground and the contract for this vast work comes close to £250,000.

The cause of the urgency behind its construction was the Second Boer War which began in October 1899 with the sieges of Ladysmith and Mafeking which were not lifted until February and May respectively of 1900. The previous Lord of the Manor James Ledger Hill's twenty-six year old son 2nd Lieutenant William Henry Tucker Hill, serving with the 5th Lancers, was killed in action at Wagon Hill, Ladysmith on 6 January 1900. [17]

Impact on the village

THE SCALE OF the military takeover can also be gauged by population statistics; in 1891 the village had a population of 341 people, but within a decade this had quadrupled to 1,386. The census officer succinctly stated that the 'the increase [was] attributed to the formation of a large military camp'. During the next decade the population nearly trebled again to reach 3,232 inhabitants. The 1901 census reveals the extent to which the village became a service centre for the construction of the hutted camp.

'Right about Turn': The Coming of the Army

The resident population included twelve general labourers, five bricklayers and a builder's labourer, a road labourer, two employed on public works, a housepainter, excavator of sewage works, iron moulder and a civil engineer in Raglan House. This was not enough to construct the camp which had no accommodation for the workers other than tents and the new hutments. Bulford village became a dormitory suburb of the camp, putting up as boarders: sixteen carpenter/joiners, four bricklayers, three plumbers, two house painters, an electrical fitter, a boring machinist, a machine minder, a civil engineer and sixteen general labourers. In addition there was a contract manager, a police constable, a church missionary, a domestic valet and a groom; all found a home in the village. It must have been an economic godsend which percolated all social levels with twenty-nine of the sixty-eight households putting up boarders. Orchard End found a role as a boarding house, the 'Rose and Crown' had two boarders, but the majority were found room in ones and twos with the villagers. Agricultural labourers, shepherds, carters, labourers all found room for lodgers as did the Manse and two widows. The village pub must have had a very different character. The 1901 census shows in the camp itself there were hutments being used to accommodate construction workers, totalling 383 in all, which is less than the 1,200 of the newspaper report but this is explained by the project nearing completion. They consisted of 158 labourers, 141 joiner/carpenters, 52 painters and a grainer, 12 plumbers, 9 bricklayers and a plasterer, 4 floor layers, a blacksmith and a steamroller driver and a stone worker on the roads. The clerk of works came from Andover, with his wife and family, and he was assisted by a builders' and a carpenters' foreman. There were four planning staff (a civil engineer, a draughtsman, a surveyor and his clerk). There were nineteen catering staff including a Chef de Cuisine and a missionary in addition to the military personnel. Fourteen construction workers, including the clerk of works, came from within a fifteen mile radius, with the rest coming from further afield, from all over England, and especially large contingents from Scotland and Ireland. 'Old' Farmer Hann recalled how 'when the hutted camp was being built for the South African War, the navvies would come down to the 'Rose and Crown' at midday and lie outside the brick garage recuperating after their drink. They would also lie in the haystacks behind the pub'. It must have been an invasion of any remaining village quietness by a cacophony of accents. This invasion, though, must have paled into insignificance when, 'One day in the early years of the [twentieth] century, there was a pitched battle between two infantry regiments outside the 'Rose and Crown' with bayonets fixed. Since that occasion bayonets were banned in the village except on exercise'. There were also darker dramas, like that which occurred in October 1898. An evening of drinking ended with the murder of one of the revellers once he had returned home to his hutted accommodation in the camp. [18]

The camp was to all intents and purposes a self contained community with its own policeman and telegraph communications. There were the hutted barracks, officers' quarters, married quarters, a canteen, guard room and pumping station. At the time of the census, 31 March – 1 April, there were 608 soldiers in the camp. In total there were 1,011 men, three wives, a girl and two boys. It was in many ways an 'unnatural' community (using Prudence Sawyer's choice of word quoted below). It was a community, though, which needed feeding and it made an environmental impact. The local economy switched its focus from its markets beyond the parish boundaries, and turned inwards on itself, did a right about turn and supplied the camp. When Allen G. Young moved to Bulford from Hereford in 1903 he saw the fresh opportunities that this offered; very fresh opportunities! He entered into a contract to clear manure from the camp and within a year piled up 4,500 tons of it in three heaps on a field he rented for the purpose. His plan was to auction this precious commodity but his hopes were dashed when all he got for each heap was a pound. He persevered though, became a farmer in the parish, living in Watergate House, and farming about 2,500 acres in Bulford and neighbouring parishes. He still looked to the camp for profit and adjusted farming methods. Explaining these he told a reporter that crops that traditionally 'would be clamped or stacked are, instead, sent off the fields straight to the camp. Oats and straw go straight from the threshing machine to the camp. Potatoes, after they are dug up and graded in the fields, are delivered right away, only seed potatoes are clamped'. He had cut out the middleman and at times of pressure to get crops in, 'if word is sent to the military authorities, soldier volunteers are drafted on the spot'. These changes must have been hard to accept by villagers who had worked their lives in the traditional ways of the nineteenth century. [19]

Throughout its history, Bulford had been a community with one raison d'être, agriculture. All this changed with the coming of the army. Farming was at its height when the army arrived if we take the data from the Ministry of Agriculture's returns in the nineteenth century as an indicator.

'Right about Turn': The Coming of the Army

1886 saw 862 acres devoted to cereal crops, 386 acres for vegetable crops and 701 acres of fodder crops, including sainfoin, grasses and vetches planted as part of a crop rotation. In total this was 1,949 acres (fifty-four per cent of the parish area), and when added to the permanent pasture used for sheep and cattle, this amounted to ninety-five per cent of the area of the parish. 1896 shows this percentage shrinking by one per cent. Once the army was established, the cropped area shrunk in 1906 to twenty per cent but was slightly compensated for by an increase in permanent pasture; the farmed area, however, had shrunk from ninety-five per cent to sixty-nine per cent of parish land. Ten years later it had shrank slightly a further two per cent, but the cropped area had shrunk to a paltry nine per cent (as opposed to fifty-four per cent twenty years earlier). What we see here is the true impact of the army; it had destroyed an agricultural community, its traditional way of life, employment patterns and attitudes – a high price was paid. We have, however wandered beyond the nineteenth century but the changes began with the inception of Bulford Camp in the dying years of the century. Changes in traditional patterns can be seen reflected in two, connected ways. First of all, the number of tenants farming the parish mushroomed from five in 1896, to seven in 1906 and ten in 1916, with the size of half of the holdings being less than fifty acres. Secondly, it is hard to imagine in these circumstances farm workers staying with the same employer for the whole of their working lives, men like John Thorn and Joseph Hedges who had worked on Watergate Farm for fifty-eight and fifty-seven and a half years respectively. They were both awarded two pounds for 'long and faithful service' by the Chippenham Agricultural Society (in 1878 and 1880). [20]

The villagers' world was being turned upside down, farming was rapidly changing, the social structure of the village had been destroyed, and they were on the defensive against the outside world. They may have even thought that The Almighty, in good Old Testament manner, was displeased with the way things were going when on 3 August 1900,

> On Friday afternoon between one and two o'clock one of the most terrific thunderstorms ever experienced on Salisbury Plain expended its full force in the neighbourhood of Bulford Camp, where a large number of Volunteers and Militia Regiments were encamped. The morning broke grey and gloomy with a fresh easterly breeze, and it was apparent that there was a decided climatic change. The sun broke through the clouds about 9 o'clock and the

atmosphere became very sultry. Shortly after mid-day dark clouds gathered in the south-west, and half an hour later low growls of distant thunder betokened a coming storm. At 1.15 rain began to fall heavily, and the storm of thunder and lightning soon burst upon Bulford camp. The storm reached its height by 2.30, at which time the jagged forked lightning played among the clouds just over the tents with wondrous brilliancy. When the storm was at its worst, there was a cry raised that tents in the lines of the 1st Batt, South Wales Borderers, and also in the lines of the 3rd Gloucestershire Regiment had been struck by lightning. Great excitement prevailed, but there was soon a rush to the tents where the men lay injured, and everything possible was done for them. Five or six Welshmen were found lying helpless in the tent which had been struck in the Welsh lines, and in a large tent in the Gloucester lines about a dozen men were more or less injured. When the lightning struck the Welshmen's tent the men were sitting down having just finished dinner. The current seems to have run down the tent pole and after striking the guns standing round the pole, and breaking the stocks into splinters, to have laid the men flat on the ground. .....

In all directions the shock was felt and old soldiers who have spent many years of their life under canvas say they have never experienced such a storm. .....

"It was just at the height of the storm," said Stanley to a newspaper man, "when there was a tremendous cannonade just over our heads, and Batts pointed to a tent in B Company's lines, and exclaimed, "That tent is on fire." I looked, and we could see a small flame at the top. We both made a rush for the tent to see what had happened to the inmates. We hauled back the flap, and there lay all the occupants on the ground. Philip Thomas lay quite still.

The unfortunate Philip Thomas was the only human fatality, but fourteen other men were taken to hospital. There were many stories of narrow escapes, like the man who had the pipe knocked out of his mouth, and the Army Service Corps driver coming from Porton Station to the camp when, 'One of the horses was struck by lightning and killed on the spot, and strange to relate the other horse was not hurt, and the driver escaped with a slight shock. When he found that the horse was quite dead, he left it on the road, and drove into the camp as speedily as possible'. The soldiers in their tents on the downs must have looked down with some envy at the nearby village homes nestling in their secluded hollow and sheltered by trees. The storm did have some effect on village life; a note in the school *Log Book* reports that the timetable was 'not strictly followed this afternoon on account of the gloom caused by the thunderstorm'. [21]

It is impossible to quantify the degree of social intercourse between the soldiers and villagers, particularly the girls. Some were no doubt employed in the camp on domestic chores but would have still lived at home and so this is not revealed by the census. Others may have worked as servants in the Officers' Club in the old Manor House, or in the three newly built houses for officers on the edge of the village next to the new Vicarage. The village schoolmistress had to report that some children were absent 'on errands to the camp' in July 1898 which suggests a constant to and fro between village and camp. Certainly there was contact as is evidenced by the marriage of village girl Fanny Vallis to Richard Long, a trooper of the 2nd Lancers stationed at Bulford, in the parish church in 1899 – the first military wedding associated with the Camp in the village. [22]

The arrival of the army at Bulford had changed the village in ways that nobody would have anticipated. From being a sleepy little village tied up in its own and its neighbours' affairs, unheard of by all but a few, it had been transformed within half a century into a household name, known both nationally and internationally. Thousands passed through it during two world wars and each retained their own memory of Bulford. 'And when the trains to Bulford came, the village was not a bit the same', especially as, in addition to the camp station, there was also one in the village itself for passenger traffic. No longer was a day's walk or cart ride the limit of most villagers' horizons. They were presented with the opportunity of cheap transport which totally disregarded their old lines of communication and they were quick to take advantage of the opportunities offered, shattering still further the old outlook and attitudes. The service was withdrawn in 1952, the old permanent way being ripped up in the sixties, but by this time the old restricted horizons had gone forever. The village and its rural way of life, though, were not totally swamped. Ella Noyes on the eve of the First World War in February 1913 could still write that,

> Amesbury and some of the villages suffer a good deal from the dust and disturbance of passing troops and military traffic, but the autumn rains restore sweetness and peace; and when the season of firing practice, which

prohibits free wandering on the downs in the military areas at certain hours of the day, is over, the shepherds feed their sheep there as usual and all is as it was, except for a few ugly tin buildings, and a hard road in places where formerly only a down track ran.

Bulford, though, dwarfed by the monstrous growth of the army camp on its downs suffered more than most and the last word on this subject must go to the villager, Prudence Sawyer, who lived through many changes in her hundred years:

> Times have changed, and with the changing the pleasant byeways have given place to hard dusty roads. Easy transport has brought a much wider outlook to the people of Bulford. And the coming of the Military has taken away for ever some of the most beautiful scenes around Bulford and put in its place something that is very drab and most unnatural. And with this remark I close my book of memories. [23]

Appendix 1: Family Trees

THE TABLES REPRODUCED on pages 296-301 are derived from the following sources:

1a   This family tree is an amalgam of the Duke family tree found in: Duke, Rev. E.H. 1914-1916 'An account of the Family of Duke of Lake', in *Wiltshire Notes and Queries*. Vol. 8, 1914 - 1916: Devizes, and the Gapper family tree found in: Miller, Audrey Sanders. (ed.) 1968. *The Journals of Mary O'Brien 1828-1838*. Toronto: Macmillan, with additional material from: Rhys-Hughes, Rev. J. 1972. *Notes for a History of Bulford*. unpublished notes: (WSA. 2014/24). References are made to other sources of evidence.

1b   There is no main source for this family tree other than from *Census Returns* and those indicated in the references.

1c   The main sources for this family tree are the *Census Returns* and those indicated in the references. I am very grateful to Ann Sawyer for checking the data and supplying additional information.

1d   Rhys-Hughes, Rev. J. 1972. *Notes for a History of Bulford*, unpublished notes: (WSA. 2014/24). He acknowledges information from a descendant, T. W. Robbins of Wareham. References are made to other sources of evidence.

1e   I am very grateful to Janine Hyatt for sharing this family history with me.

1f   Sturgess, Jack. 1995. *The Sturgesses of Bulford*. Copy of unpublished family history in Wiltshire Heritage Museum, Devizes: (DZSWS MSS.2650). Additional information on mason/bricklayer careers added.

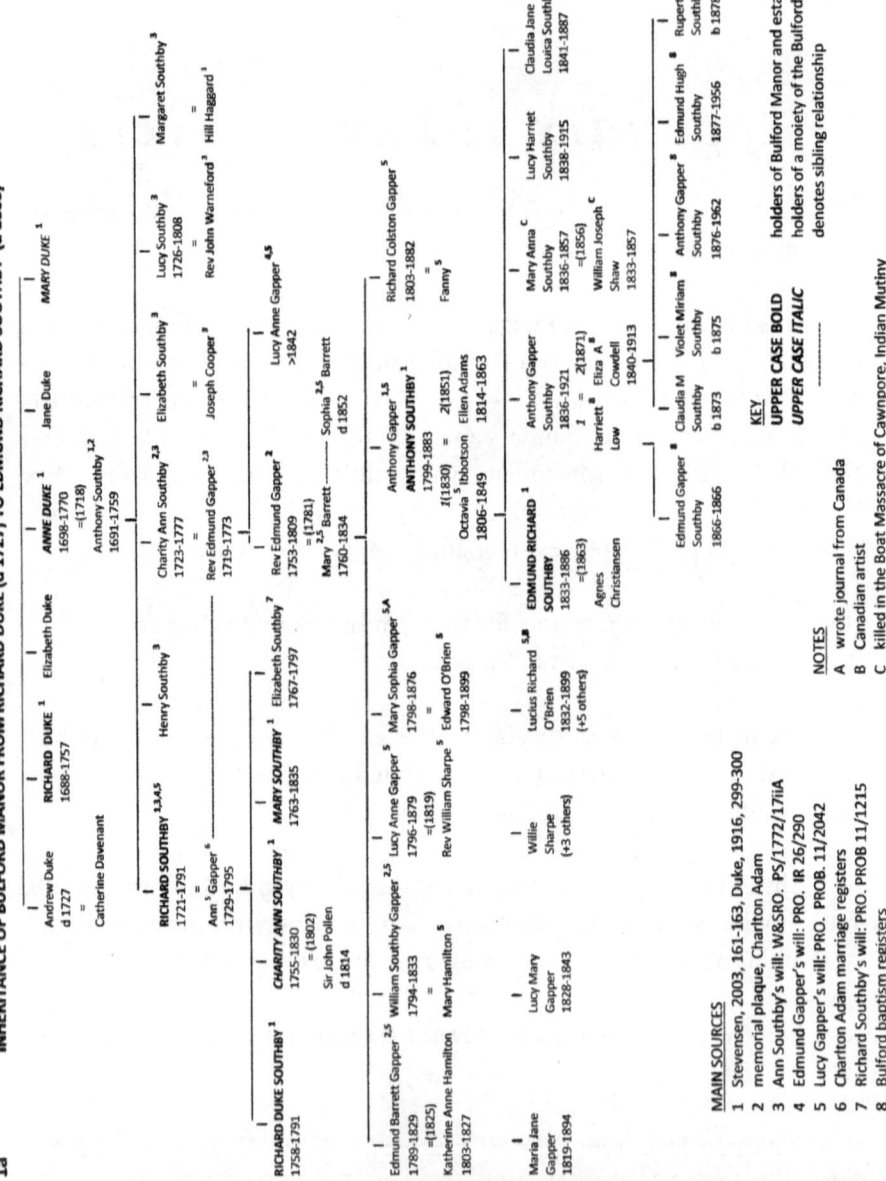

Appendix 1: Family Trees

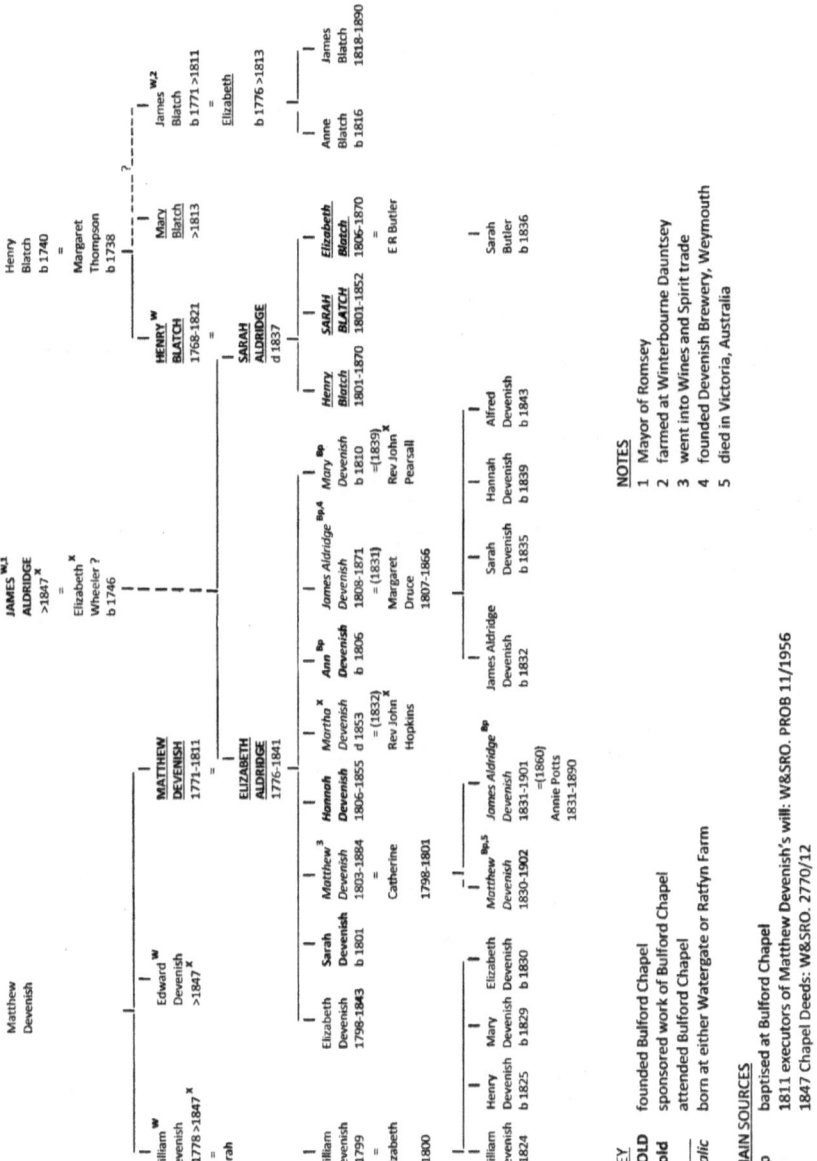

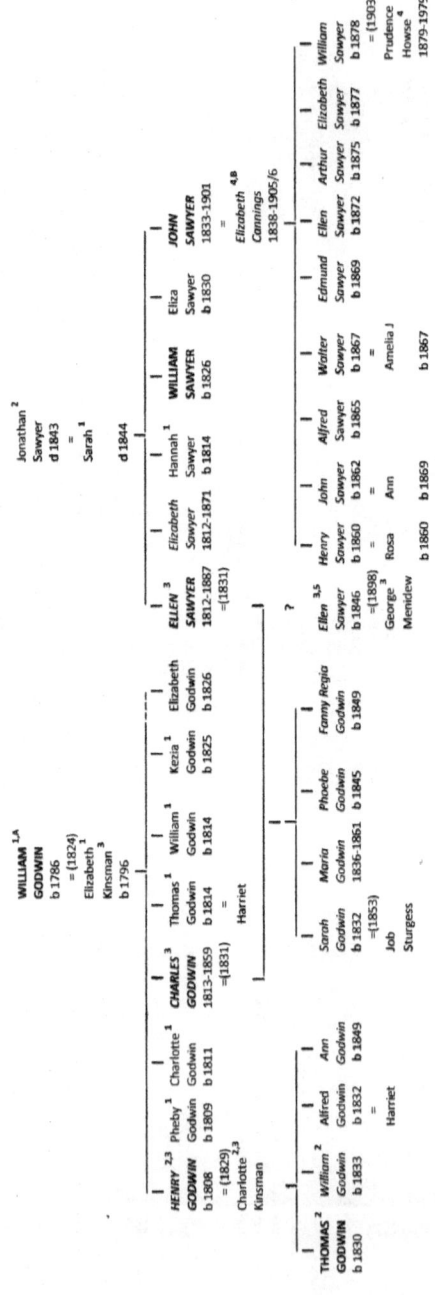

Appendix 1: Family Trees

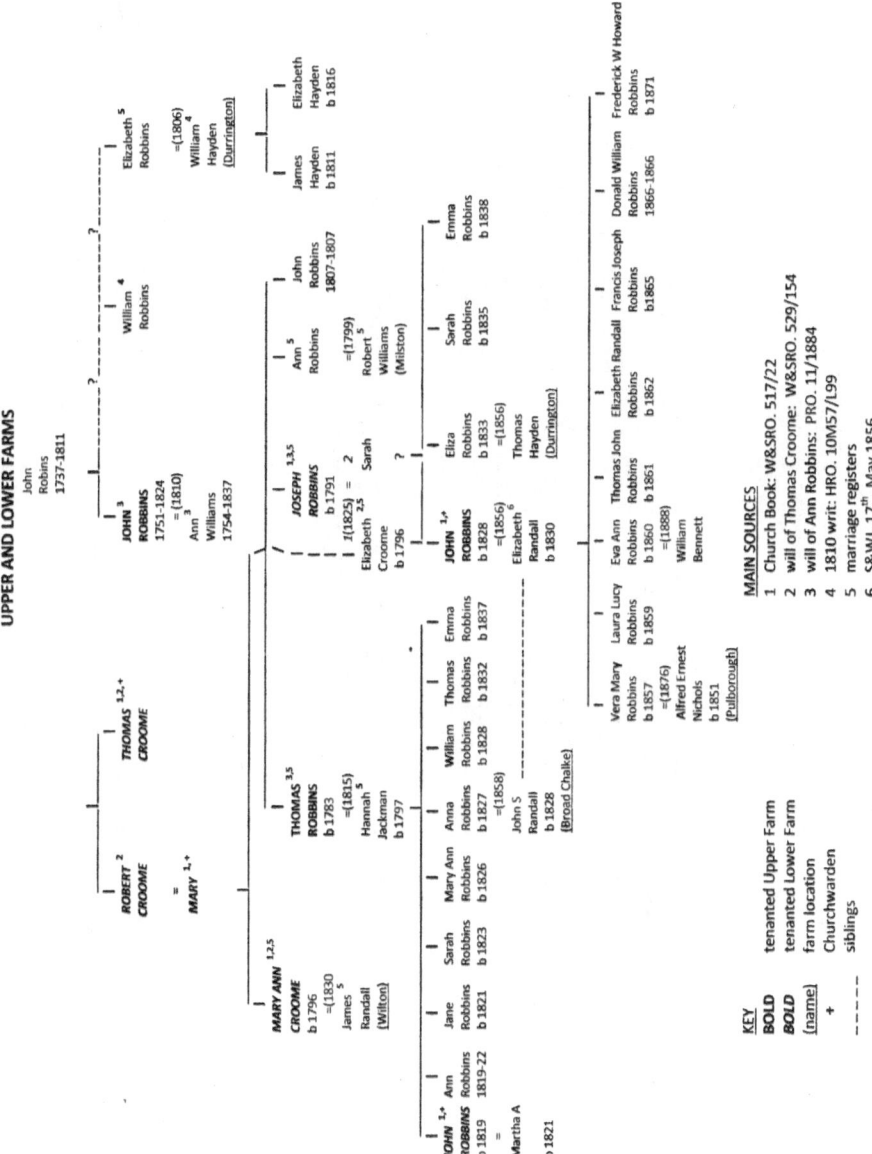

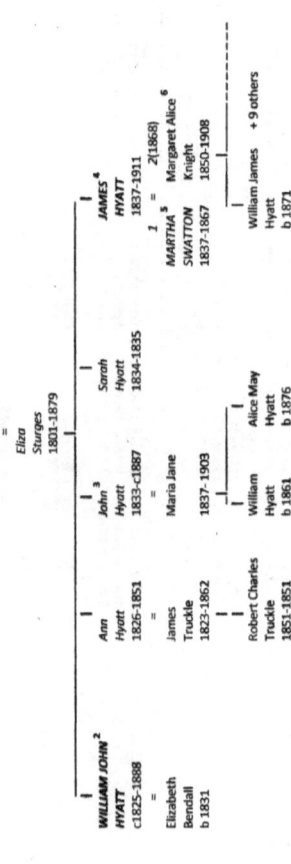

THE HYATT FAMILY: PAPERMAKERS

WILLIAM[1]
HYATT
1802-1855
=
Eliza
Sturges
1801-1879

- **WILLIAM JOHN**[2] HYATT c1825-1888
  = Elizabeth Bendall b 1831
- Ann Hyatt 1826-1851
  = James Truckle 1823-1862
  - Robert Charles Truckle 1851-1851
- *John*[3] Hyatt 1833-c1887
  = Maria Jane 1837-1903
  - William Hyatt b 1861
  - Alice May Hyatt b 1876
- Sarah Hyatt 1834-1835
- **JAMES**[4] HYATT 1837-1911
  1 = ?(1868) *Margaret Alice*[6] Knight 1850-1908
  MARTHA[5] SWATTON 1837-1867
  - William James Hyatt b 1871
  - + 9 others

KEY
UPPER CASE BOLD   Bulford papermaker
UPPER CASE   worked at the Paper Mill
Italic   born in Bulford

NOTES
1. born in Bungay (Suffolk) and married village girl when he moved to Bulford
2. 1851 papermaker; 1861 bricklayer at Nursling (Hants)
3. 1851 agricultural labourer in Bulford; 1861 & 1871 railway porter in Bramshot & Romsey (Hants); 1881 railway signalman, Micheldever (Hants)
4. 1861 papermaker; 1868 coachman/domestic servant Bulford; 1871 living in Hove (Sussex)
5. worked at paper mill and died of TB
6. sister of William Knight, and sister-in-law to Mary Ann Knight (née Cannings), first Mistress of Bulford Village School

This family tree was generously shared with me by Janine Hyatt, a descendant through William James Hyatt (b 1871). It illustrates how the family moved into Bulford as papermakers and then moved away when they were not employed at Bulford Mill, or moved through marriage. Perhaps the business was already struggling for James Hyatt to go into service, and John (on available evidence) not working at the Bulford Paper Mill. Anthony Southby, who knew James through papermaking, took him into service where he met his wife.

1e

Appendix 1: Family Trees

THE 'BUILDER FAMILY' OF STURGESS, IN BULFORD

These must be two branches of the same family, and William was no doubt a mason/bricklayer as well.

William Sturgess = Elizabeth Hayden ? d 1800

THOMAS STURGESS 1765-1846 = Elizabeth

Children of William Sturgess and Elizabeth Hayden:
- Mary Hayden Sturgess b c1781
- Henry Sturgess b c1783
- Arthur Sturgess b c1786
- **WILLIAM STURGESS** b c1788-1868 =(1814) Jane Angel d 1860
- James Sturgess b c1790-1791
- Betty Sturgess b c1794
- Alice Sturgess b c1795
- John Sturgess b c1798

Children of WILLIAM STURGESS and Jane Angel:
- Elizabeth Sturgess b c1815 =(1834) Edward Sarah Powell 1819
- **THOMAS STURGESS** b c1817 =(1841)
- Caroline Sturgess b c1816
- Mary Jane Sturgess b c1827-1845
- Charity Ann Sturgess b c1825-1903 = John Bailey *
- **DAVID**[1] **STURGESS** b c1828
- **SYLVANUS**[2] **STURGESS** b c1831-1926 =(1851) Lois Challocombe 1835-1912 =(1862) Sarah Godwin b1832
- **JOB**[3] **STURGESS** b c1831 =(1853)
- Lucy Sturgess b c1833-1915
- **WILLIAM STURGESS** b c1836-1912 = Elizabeth Jane Atkins ? 1842

Children of THOMAS STURGESS:
- Elizabeth Matilda Sturgess b c1841 =(1876) William Driver
- **FRANK**[6] **THOMAS STURGESS** b c1846 =(1871) Maria Coombes
  - 1 girl

Children of DAVID STURGESS:
- **JOHN STURGESS** b c1854
- Albert[7] Sturgess b c1854

Children of SYLVANUS STURGESS:
- William Charles Sturgess b c1856
- Lilian Gertrude Sturgess b c1858
- Young Sylvanus Sturgess b c1860
- Hugh Tom Sturgess b c1869

Children of WILLIAM STURGESS and Elizabeth Jane Atkins:
- Julia Sturgess b c1858
  - Francis Southy
  - Margaret Melville
  - 2 girls, 1 boy
- Mary Jane Atkins Sturgess b c1861
- Ella Lucy Sturgess b c1863
- **HENRY ATKINS STURGESS** b c1866
  - Claudia Ann Sturgess b c1870
  - William Sturgess b c1874
  - Alice
  - 6 boys, 2 girls
- **IRA SYLVANUS STURGESS** b c1876 = Lois Beatrice Sturgess b c1876 = Fred Spreadbury
- **SYDNEY WILLIAM STURGESS** b c1882 = Eliza
  - 4 boys, 1 girl

Children of THOMAS STURGESS 1765-1846 and Elizabeth:
- Edward Sturgess 1793-1794
- David Sturgess
- **EDWARD STURGESS** 1811-1888
  1 = Charlotte Dominey b1816
  2 = Jane Aisley ? b1832

Children of EDWARD STURGESS:
- **SILAS**[4] **STURGESS** b c1838 = Eleanor
- Edward Sturgess b c1841
- **MARK**[5] **STURGESS** b c1846 = Mary J
- Simon Sturgess
- Jane Sturgess 1851-1851
- Henry White
- Timothy Sturgess
- Ann Sturgess b c1856

NOTES
1. moved to: Thruxton, Islington (London) Appleshaw and Andover (Hants)
2. left bricklaying to go into service with wife Lois in London
3. moved to: Thruxton, Appleshaw, Andover (Hants)
4. moved to: Alverstoke, Portsmouth, Portsea (Hants)
5. moved to Shoreditch (London)
6. ended up a pauper in Amesbury Workhouse
7. joined the Royal Marines

KEY
UPPER CASE BOLD — Mason/bricklayer in Bulford
UPPER CASE BOLD ITALIC — Mason/bricklayer who moved away from Bulford
* — plumber/carpenter

These family trees are taken from: Sturgess, 1995, and with the bricklayer, and other information added. The approximate dates of birth are baptism dates.

1f

Appendix 2
Two Compositions by Prudence Sawyer

Old Bulford Times

Bulford Village so I've heard tell,
Was a nice quiet place in which to dwell.
It boasted of a paper mill,
And acres and acres of land to till,
A Manor, a Church, a Chapel, a Squire,
Three farms and plenty of men for hire.
A School where those who paid, could go,
To learn to read and write and sew,
Those who couldn't afford to pay,
Earned their livings in different ways.
The River Avon flowing past,
Kept the mill wheels turning fast,
Into tanks came tumbling and splashing,
And washed the rags for paper maching,
Then onward flowed through meadow and lea,
Making its course 'way down to the sea.
There were Shepherds, Cowmen, Carters too,
Who found plenty of work to do.
From early rise till set of sun,
A Farmer's work was never done,
Ploughing and sowing, reaping and mowing,
Mangold pulling, or turnip hoeing.

Appendix 2: Two Compositions by Prudence Sawyer

Hedging, and ditching, spreading and pitching,
And a hundred and one jobs in between,
There was animal breeding and poultry feeding,
And many more things that were unforeseen.
The women worked in the fields all day,
Picking up stones or making hay,
Or washing the milk pails, pans, and churns,
And doing the Farmer's wife good turns.
Now I leave the farm behind
To look for work of a different kind.
There were bricklayers masons and carpenters then,
All were most efficient men.
Though buildings did not go up so quick,
And were made of mortar stones and brick,
With wheat, straw and cowhair to bind altogether,
And roofs were thatched to keep out the weather.
The bigger houses were tiled with stone,
Slates were then but little known.
Every cottage had a garden big,
A nice clean sty to keep a pig.
Bacon was their only meat,
A ham no unusual treat.
Baker's bread was unheard of then,
Housewives baked their own,
And butchers meat to many
Was practically unknown.
One little shop, a general store,
Kept the village wants supplied,
But when folks wanted something more,
To the pedlar they applied.
Sunday was a day of rest,
When folks put on their Sunday best,
To Church or Chapel, most of them went,
With that "Day of Rest" they were well content,
And, the only work that was done on Sunday,
Was that that couldn't be left to Monday.
Now this tale started years ago,

> When Bulford was remote and slow,
> When men were content with the village pub,
> Or once a year, when they held their club.
> Some would go to Salisbury Fair,
> But had to walk if they got there,
> As there was neither train or bus,
> Those who couldn't walk, well they didn't fuss.
> And when the trains to Bulford came,
> The village was not a bit the same,
> Changes came as changes do,
> So to "Old Bulford Times" I must bid adieu.

A Nonagenarian remembers . . .

SOME BY-WAYS AND BEAUTY-SPOTS OF BULFORD

THERE HAS BEEN a lot of talk on the Radio and in the papers about the re-opening of by-ways, the beauty-spots of old England. I remember the days when the by-ways of Bulford and other villages were as popular as the highways and airways are today.

Less than a century ago Bulford was just a pretty little village, nestling in the heart of Salisbury Plain, with about 350 inhabitants. Most of these were agricultural workers. There was no means of transport other than by the carrier's van which went to and from Salisbury twice weekly. The village-folk made their own pleasures by joining other villagers for an annual Club Day. These outings were very much looked forward to and thoroughly enjoyed by young and old. This is where the by-ways come in, for, having to walk everywhere, these were short cuts (so to speak). Many walked to Salisbury for the annual Fair; that was a Gala Day for some. But there were others who went in for the purpose of hiring.

There was not much schooling for the children in those days. Only the better-off could afford to send their children to school. The present Church School was built in 1874. Mrs Knight was the first Mistress and kept the post for many years. There were only two small shops - no baker, grocer, or butcher. But there was a bacon-curer and a blacksmith's forge.

Appendix 2: Two Compositions by Prudence Sawyer

The nearest Post Office was at Amesbury; but there was a mail-box in the wall of one of the shops, where the Toll-keeper lived. The postman used to walk from Netheravon to Amesbury every day, a distance of over 6 miles. So punctual was he the villagers called him "The Eleven O'Clock Postman" and many set their clocks by him. He always used the by-ways and must have known every inch of the way. I will take you along the paths he used and, as we go, I will try and picture the countryside as it used to be in those days.

We will start from the bridge which spans the Avon at the foot of Durrington Hill and which marks the parish boundary. The bridge you see today, built in 1913, replaced a pretty little iron bridge; and, while it was being constructed, all wheeled traffic went through the ford part of the river, and a temporary wooden bridge was made for pedestrians and cyclists.

Look around you, as you stand for a while, at the beauty of the surroundings. Over to the right side of the bridge is a narrow path known as "Pecker's Path"; and in the centre of the river is a little island called "Pecker's Island". Just around the bend is the ash-bed where we usually heard the first notes of the cuckoo. This part of the river was indeed a beauty-spot. Over to the left is the waterfall which, whether in Spring, Summer, Autumn, or Winter, provides a picture for an artist to paint. This was the Paper-Mill and employed a few villagers. John Sawyer was the foreman paper-maker. Two cottages adjoined the Mill, one on either side. These were known as Mill House and 2 Mill Cottage". All around this part of Bulford was very picturesque.

A little way up the road stands the Manor House, an early-English mansion, where (it is said) King Charles once entertained. A new wing was added in 1892 by a firm from Southampton; but the Sturgesses of Bulford were the bricklayers and masons. Much of the beauty of the old house was hidden by this new wing.

The Turnpike Road was very narrow. Grass and weeds grew between the wheel-ruts and wild roses formed the hedge on either side. The Church which lies opposite the Manor House dates back to about 1130. For at least two centuries it was called "St John the Evangelist's". It was Mr Arnold who restored its original dedication of "St Leonard". The Church was partly restored in 1870. Some of the old writings (murals) were covered by large wooden frames; but when the Church was restored for a second time these frames were taken away and the original painting of the Ten

Commandments, The Lord's Prayer, and Creed were brought to light – as you see them today.

As we come through the church-yard gate we will turn left. We are now on a bye-path which takes us past the Old Coach Road. As you see, it is a very narrow road. On the left is Church Farm. At one time it was a little school. From here the path leads on to Lime Kiln – why it was called that is further back than I can remember. Here were three cottages for farm-workers. As we go along the path we come to another of Bulford's beauty-spots. Looking down from the high path you can see the river Avon and a little side-stream running alongside, with just a narrow bank to separate the two. The steep bank, now overgrown with trees, was once a picture of wild flowers and an ideal spot for country-lovers. The path leads down into a pretty little dell. Then up a steep incline to the road and to Milston Mill. This was once a flour-mill – but I am out-of-bounds here. The path goes on through Milston, Syrencote, Ablington, Figheldean, and Netheravon, where the postman finished his daily trek, and on to Marlborough.

We will return by the back road, called "Broadway" on account of its width. We pass Upper Farm, and then a long walk brings us into Bulford Village again. It is not so lonely now since rows of houses have sprung up where there was nothing to see but miles of plains. As we come to the Village we see on our left the new Vicarage. This was built with money raised by voluntary subscriptions, for the Vicar, the Rev. Cecil N. Arnold. A tablet was erected inside the porch with this inscription: "TO MY SUCCESSOR. If thou should'st find / A house to thy mind / Built without cost; / Be good to the poor, / Give them of thy store, / Then my labour is not lost." The living then was about £100 yearly.

We go now to the Waterway, which is part of what is called "Nine Mile River". All wheeled traffic came through the water and the bye-path was made for pedestrians alongside, and called Water Street. This is the oldest and most picturesque part of Bulford – a real beauty-spot. The old Vicarage stands on the opposite bank. There was once a little path on that side which the vicar used as a short-cut to the Church.

We come now to the Main Street where the old Toll Gate used to be. Several old houses have been pulled down and others built on better sites. The Manse (now Avondale School) is one of the oldest houses on this road. Bulford's first Post Office was on this road, but when the road was improved it was thought necessary to pull the house down and build a new Post Office

Appendix 2: Two Compositions by Prudence Sawyer

on higher ground. Orchard End was chosen for the new site. An old farm used to stand on the turning and it was called by the children the "Sheen House" (Machine House). Some of the agricultural machinery was housed there. The children were very sorry when the order was given for it to come down, for it was an ideal place to play in on wet days. Only in recent years has there been a road through Orchard End; that used to be a bye-way.

Where the "Rose and Crown" Hotel stands today the villagers held their little fairs, stalls etc. with fairings of all sorts. The hotel was then just a village Pub. The hotel was built in 1894. Next we come to the new school. Just about here, as I said earlier, there used to be a blacksmith's forge. A little further on, on the other side of the road, is Lower Farm. At the end of this road is a little chapel which at one time had an Independent School adjoining. And so we come from one end of the village to the other.

We will leave the village again for another bye-way. We go up a slight incline and follow the path (Upper Path it is called) as far as the approach to Ratfyn. Here the railway, which was made in 1896, cuts across the path. There is a level crossing at this point for pedestrians and farm traffic. This brings us to Ratfyn Farm, down a rather muddy lane, with a few cottages on one side and Ratfyn Farm on the other. I am out-of-bounds here so we will turn back. Taking another path which is known as "Lower Path" we return once more to Bulford. The railway cuts through this path, and Bulford Station can be seen at this point. There are two stiles, one on either side of the railway track, and gates to admit wheeled traffic. A very steep decline starts at this point, coming into a very pretty little lane which we leave on our left with the exception of a few yards which brings us to Watergate House and farm. You can get a very pretty view of the Avon from here. About a quarter of a mile downstream is the "Miracle Stone" with its iron ring set on top. The strange thing about this stone is that the ring is always set against the run of the stream. Some say it belongs to the Stonehenge Stones. As we pass along I will point out to you the old water-wheel. This was turned by water from the little side stream which set the grinding-machinery in motion. Following the little stream we come to the Turnpike and not far away from where we started on our ramble through the by-ways of Bulford.

There is yet another bye-way I should like to embark upon. This is to the top of Beacon Hill, one of the highest spots in Wiltshire, and point out to you all the beauty-spots for miles around, as far as the eye can see. Many visitors to this spot have been curious to know why a cannon should be brought to the top and buried there. This is easily explained. Trig points were marked years ago by burying old cannon barrels. They were not likely to wear for many years.

Times have changed, and with the changing of the pleasant by-ways have given place to hard dusty roads. Easy transport has brought a much wider outlook to the people of Bulford. And the coming of the Military has taken away for ever some of the most beautiful scenes around Bulford and put in its place something that is very drab and most unnatural. And with this remark I close my book of memories.

Appendix Three: Churchwardens

THIS LIST OF Churchwardens has been tabulated from the Parish Records by Rev J. Rhys-Hughes in: Rhys-Hughes, Rev J. 1972. 'Notes for a History of Bulford'. unpublished notes (WSA. 2014/24). I have added the two columns in italics identifying the farms tenanted by the wardens as part of this study.

date	Vicar's Warden	*Farm*	People's Warden	*Farm*
1799	John Robbins	Upper Farm	William Swayne	Watergate Farm
1800	ditto	ditto	Mary Croome	Lower Farm
1801	ditto	ditto	Robert Smith	Orchard End Farm
1802	ditto	ditto	Mary Croome	Lower Farm
1803	ditto	ditto	Thomas Croome	ditto
1804-18	ditto	ditto	Robert Smith	Orchard End Farm
1819-25	Joseph Robbins	Lower Farm	ditto	ditto
1626-27	ditto	ditto	Thomas Robbins	Upper Farm
1828-31	Thomas Webb Dyke	Orchard End Farm	ditto	ditto

There is a gap in the records from 1831 to 1845 (Unless the incumbents in 1831 remained unchanged)

1845-57	ditto	ditto	ditto	ditto
1857	Francis Stephen Long	Watergate Farm	ditto	ditto
1859	ditto	ditto	Henry Pearce	Orchard End Farm
1862	ditto	ditto	John Robbins jnr	Lower Farm
1872	George Melsome snr	Watergate Farm	ditto	ditto
1877	Gilbert Miles	Lower Farm	ditto	ditto
1879	John Robbins	Upper Farm	Edward Weeks	(shopkeeper)
1881	ditto	ditto	George Melsome jnr	Watergate Farm
1894	James Hooper	Upper & Lower Farms	ditto	ditto

The farm names are those used in Chapters 4, 5 and 6. Orchard End Farm is shorthand for the farmer of the seventy-three acre farm sandwiched between the Manor's Upper and Lower Farms, and Watergate Farm on the Seymour estate. The farmhouse for this farm was not necessarily Orhard End House.

Appendix Four: Incumbents

Curates of Parish Church

THIS LIST IS researched by Rev Rhys-Hughes drawing on parish records and appears in his 'Notes for a History of Bulford'. Up to 1870, there was no vicar of Bulford. The patron, who was the Lord of the Manor during the century, was owner of the tithes and advowson (the right to nominate the priest to serve in the Parish Church). Nominated clergy then had to obtain a licence from the Bishop before they could officiate in the Parish. In 1870 Vicars of Bulford were instituted.

1791 to 1801   Francis Gibbs
1802   Samuel Mew

1804	William Greenwood	
1804	Brockley Charles Kennet	
1804	H. Lewis	
1804 to 1806	William Norris	
1806 to 1811	R. W. Hutchins	
1809	Robert Roe	Curate of Odstock[1]
1813 to 1817	Allan Borman Hutchins	Curate of Shipton Bellinger,[2] then Allington[3]
1818	Charles John Coleman	
1818 to 1819	Wilson Becket	Curate of Shipton Bellinger,[4] then Allington[5]
1819 to 1821	George Thomas Rudd	Curate of Shipton Bellinger[6]
1821 to 1826	Fulwar William Fowle	
1826 to 1830	Richard Webb	Curate of Durrington[7]
1830 to 1835	Walter Blunt	Curate of Cholderton[8]
1830	Edward Wilton	Curate of Berwick St James,[9] Winterbourne Stoke[10] and Urchfont[11]
1835 to 1851	James Watts Ellaby	Curate of Milston[12]
1852 to 1861	Thomas Darnton Millner	Incumbent of Bulford,[13] and Chaplain to the Earl of Carlisle
1862 to 1863	Edmund B. Bowman	cover for Thomas Darnton Millner
1863 to 1864	John James Scott	ditto
1864 to 1869	Christopher Salter	ditto

The Curacies where they were licensed have been added as a result of my researches, and the references are as follows:

1 (WSA. D/1/2/30); 2 (HRO. 21M65 E1/1); 3 (WSA. D1/8/1/1); 4 (HRO. 21M65 A2/4); 5 (WSA. D/1/8/1/1); 6 (HRO. 21 M65 A2/4); 7 (WSA. D/1/8/1/2); 8 (WSA. D/1/8/1/3); 9 (WSA. D/1/8/1/2); 10 (WSA. D/1/8/1/2); 11 (WSA. D/1/2/32); 12 (WSA. D/1/8/1/3); 13 (WSA. D1/56/7).

Vicars of Bulford

1870 to 1877	Jacob Jehoshaphat Salter Mountain
1877 to 1879	Robert Liston Johnson
1880 to 1886	John Gray Goodrich
1887 to 1908	Cecil North Arnold

Appendix 4: Incumbents

Pastors at Bulford Independent Church

This list is taken from Rev Peter Beale's list on the back of his leaflet *Bulford Chapel 1806-1986*.

1805 to 1809	Francis William Dury	from Oakham, Rutland
1813 to 1820	Thomas Caffey	
1821 to 1830	James Angear	from Kingsbridge, Devon
1831 to 1840	William Williams	from Wymondley Academy, later became C.E. minister
1840 to 1847	John Protheroe	from Newport Pagnell
1848 to 1852	Thomas Sleigh	from Wavertree
1853 to 1880	John Protheroe	from Newport Pagnell
1880 to 1883	Albion Oram	from Winton, Bournemouth
1883 to 1884	W. Reynolds	"Supplied pulpit"
1884 to 1896	John Pinn	from Lostwithiel, Cornwall
1896 to ?	C. E. Elford	from Fordham, Colchester
1902 to 1913	C. Farr	

Appendix Five
Bulford Papermakers

Early Bulford Papermakers

		evidence
1765	Wingfield Hillman	insured
	Thomas Noyce	insured
1781	Thomas Mould	Mill registered as Nonconformist Meeting House
1784	Mary Mould	insured
1785	William Mould (d1784/5)	settling up of estate
1786	Thomas Mould	Shorter (1959), 245
1786-1790	Isaac Brodribb	leased and insured in 1786, bankrupt and sold in 1790

1791	Lawrence Greatrake	insured 1791, 10 year lease, emigrated to America 1799
1805	Samuel Mould	registration of Nonconformist Meeting House
1810	Joseph Mould	rented Carey Paper Mill in Dorset
1813	William Grivian	Church Baptism Register
1815-1826	John Love	Church Baptism Register
1816-1820	Robert Dymore	Church Baptism Register
1817	H. Noyes	bankrupt
1823	William Hyatt	Church Baptism Register
1830-1833	Henry Godwin	Church Baptism Register
1831	Alfred Godwin	Church Baptism Register

Bulford Papermaker information taken from Census Returns

Additional information on Chapel attendance evidenced from Bulford Chapel Church Book

1841	age	place of birth	attendance
William Godwin	55	Wiltshire*	Chapel
Henry Godwin	30	Bulford	Chapel
William Sawyer	15	Wiltshire*	
John Love	55	Out of County*	
William Hyatt	35	Bungay (Suffolk)	
Charles Godwin	28	Bulford	
1851			
George Adlam	32	Bulford	Chapel
William Hyatt	49	Bungay (Suffolk)	
Henry Godwin	43	Bulford	Chapel
Charles Godwin	38	Bulford	Chapel
1861			
William Kinsman	24	Bulford	Chapel
John Sawyer	28	Bulford	Chapel
Thomas Godwin	31	Durrington	Chapel
John Rowley	22	Kidderminster (Worcs.)	
James Hyatt	23	Bulford	Chapel
Anthony Southby	61	Charlton Adam (Som.)	

Appendix 5: Bulford Papermakers

1871
Joseph Hobday	48	Midhurst (Sussex)	
John Sawyer	38	Bulford	Chapel
Thomas Godwin	41	Durrington	Chapel

\+ not described as a 'papermaker'
* 1841 Census is not specific

Notes

Abbreviations used in the notes and bibliography

BRO	Berkshire Record Office, Reading
DHC	Dorset History Centre, Dorchester
GA	Gloucestershire Archives, Gloucester
HA	Hampshire Archives, Winchester
S&WJ	*Salisbury and Winchester Journal*
TNA	The National Archives, Kew (formerly Public Record Office)
T/Sol.	Treasury Solicitor's Deeds, *penes* Defence Land Agent, Durrington (not publicly available)
WAM	*Wiltshire Archaeological and Natural History Magazine* (also known as *Wiltshire Studies*)
WHM	Wiltshire Heritage Museum, Devizes
WN&Q	*Wiltshire Notes and Queries*
WRS	Wiltshire Record Society
WSA	Wiltshire and Swindon Archives, Chippenham

1 Setting the Scene

1 Opening description from Hamilton, 1911, 121, 123. Although this book was published by Mary Hamilton in 1911, it is based on diaries and so can be relied on to give an accurate picture. The rest of the descriptions are by Prudence Sawyer (see Appendix 2b).

2 An early twentieth century photograph of Water Street showing the thatched houses by the river, unshrouded by trees and high hedges, can be found in Stevensen, 2003,155. Description of the Broadway: Prudence Sawyer (see Appendix 2b). 1851 Census notes and map: WSA. 2916/24. This is a photocopy

of a document owned by the Bourne Valley Historical and Record Society. It is a difficult document to date as it has been interpolated at a later date. Internal evidence for Durrington dates it to the 1851 Census Returns according to John Chandler in his notes with the document. The internal evidence for the later interpolations for Bulford gives these a date of 1861. The evidence for this latter date centres around the note, 'Farm House formerly Mr Pierce's'; he vacated the farm between 1861 and 1867 (see Chapter 6). The Rev. Bowman's name is recorded next to the Church, and he officiated in the village between 1862 and 1863, but most likely did so earlier (see Chapter 8). Any notes/words that I have inserted in quotations are in square brackets. The name Robbins Pennings: WSA. 2770/2, (entry 1877).

3   Population statistics: Census Returns. 1901 analysis of split between village and camp: Stevenson, 2003, 155. Story of Thorns' and Sawyers' bereavements in WSA. 2770/2, (entries 1861). I am grateful to the Rev. Peter Beale for lending me the Chapel Church Book in 1978 prior to its lodging with the WSA.

4   Statistics from analysis of 1841–1851 marriage registers. I am grateful to Jack Sturgess who sent a draft in 1987 of the unpublished work on his family as part of an ongoing correspondence about the Sturgess family. A final copy of this work, now finished, is in the Wiltshire Heritage Museum, Devizes: Sturgess, 1995.

5   Expulsions from Chapel: WSA. 2770/2. The sad tale of James Chalk: *The Examiner*, 29th Jul. 1810, issue 135. This story received national coverage as far as Scotland. Registrations for Dissenter Worship in 1805: WSA. D1/2/29, p.60 (no.626) and p.61 (no.633).

6   Death of Elisa Woods, and the scapegoating of gypsies on the down: *The Times*, 10th Oct. 1878, p.9, issue 2938?; 11th Mar. 1835, p.7, issue 15735, col. B.

7   This paragraph with its conversation with Seth, the old drowner, is taken from Sawyer, 1985, 17, 10. Frank Sawyer was born in the Mill Cottages, Bulford, in 1906 and spent his life on the River Avon, first publishing his experiences in 1952. Managing trees by 'shrouding' in the 1801 lease of Watergate Farm: WSA. 1126/18. Flood damaged to Bulford Bridge in Cowan, 1996, 2 (letter 11).

8   The 1867 sketch by Lucius O'Brien is in the Art Gallery of Ontario, 92/71, p.29. The Watergate Lane location shown in this sketch by Lucius O'Brien is just labelled 'Bulford' with the date. The location of the sketch is my confident interpretation and the spot where it was drawn is marked with a black arrowhead in Figure 2. Recollections of Prudence Sawyer (see Appendix 2b), and Mary Hamilton in Hamilton, 1911, 127.

9   Description of the downland turf in Hudson, 1946, 6 (first published in 1910). Churchwardens paying for polecat and sparrow heads (transcribed from WSA. 517/22) in Rhys-Hughes (1971), 53. Hunting information from the Knoyle House Game Book 1837-1894, WSA. 186/1, and Old Hawking Club Journal 1892-1896. Ravens nesting: Smith, Rev A.G. *Birds of Wiltshire* 1887 (quoted in Hudson, 1946, 87). 1886 advertisement for the sale of Bulford Manor: *The*

Times, 10th Jul. 1886, p.19, issue 31808, col. A. Sale of hounds, and discovery of rhinoceros tooth: *Hampshire Telegraph and Sussex Chronicle*, 19th Oct. 1818, issue 993, and 2nd Oct. 1847, issue 1327. Bevy of quails sprung: *Morning Chronicle*, 1st Sep. 1842, issue 22709. Fish and insect life: Sawyer, 1985, 18. Walking to Salisbury and back: Prudence Sawyer (Appendix 2a). This was equally true the other way round with reports on crowds of people from Salisbury walking to and from Beacon Hill to watch the military review: *S&WJ*, 14th Sep. 1872.

10 Report on cold sharp air: Davis, 1811, 2. Thomas Davis's report was based on a countywide survey undertaken by his father in 1794, which he updated in 1807 for the Board of Agriculture.

11 Plight of soldiers in their tents in November from Hamilton, 1911, 129. Individual cases of ill health are taken from the Chapel Church Book, WSA. 2770/2. Analysis of seasonal illness of the chapel congregation: ibid. At the back of the book, there is a tabulated register of attendance and reasons for absences from the monthly communion services from 1835 to 1840, drawn up by the pastor William Williams.

12 Details of the fictitious shepherd are from *A Shepherd on Salisbury Plain*, More, 1825, 16. Hannah More (1745-1833) was a prominent literary figure, friend to Dr Johnson and David Garrick. She grew up near Bristol and also lived in Somerset. She was also friendly with the Wesleys, William Wilberforce and John Newton and played an important part in the conservative reaction to the French Revolution, turning to religion and philanthropy to counter this. She wrote The Cheap Repository Tracts between 1795 and 1797, of which *A Shepherd on Salisbury Plain* was the most famous. She wrote in 1801, '... as an appetite for reading ... has been increasing among inferior ranks in the country, it was judged expedient, at this critical period, to supply wholesome aliment as might give a new direction to their taste, and also their relish for those corrupt and inflammatory publications [e.g. Rights of Man] which the consequences of the French Revolution have been so fatally pouring in on us.' (quoted in Kelly, T., 1970, *A History of Adult Education in Great Britain*. Liverpool: Liverpool University Press). *A Shepherd on Salisbury Plain* has been used as a source material as it must have been based on a reality, admittedly with a wholesome spin, or else it would have had no credibility for the audience it was aimed at – the disadvantaged poor. Hannah More was prominent in the Sunday School movement which explains the publisher of the edition used here. The story is an account of a Mr Johnson meeting a shepherd somewhere on the Plain, the exact location is not stated. Labourers' ability to afford fuel: Hudson, 1946, 53. Coal prices and scarcity of wood: Davis, 1811, 84-85. Manor's expenditure on coal: BRO. D/ELV E134/2.

13 The letter from Matthew Devenish is transcribed in Chapel Church Book, WSA. 2770/2. The difficulty of growing a specimen of long water meadow grass in May 1810: Davis, 1811, 132 (footnote). 1826 a year of drought: Cobbett, 2001,

280. William Cobbett rode down the Avon Valley, passing through Bulford, in August 1826. Emigration from Durrington in, Tankins, 1975, 60. Low river levels in 1898: *The Times*, 25th Aug. 1898, p.4, issue 35604, col. A.
14 James Chalk's shoe shop: *The Examiner*, 29th Jul. 1810, issue 135. Charles Adlam's shop and payment of church rate: WSA. 517/22 (entry 1829). Location of Jane Rowden's shop/Post Office, and Hannah Candy's shop: T/Sol 2850/50 and 432/51. Hannah's marriage and widowhood from marriage register and Census (1891). Location of Mrs Lake's shop is from personal recollection. Recollections of two small shops and a bacon curer: Prudence Sawyer, (see Appendix 2a). Mary Hamilton's observations in Hamilton, 1911, 123; all other shop details taken from Census Returns, *Kelly's Directory* (1851, 1875, 1880, 1885, 1889, 1895, 1898), and Post Office Directory (1867). Census Map: WSA. 2916/24.
15 Little fairs on site of 'Rose and Crown Hotel' in Prudence Sawyer, (see Appendix 2b). Travelling musician reference found in burial registers. Choral society: Stevenson, 2003, 157. Brass band and the Diamond Jubilee celebrations: *S&WJ* Supplement, 26th Jun. 1897 (in WHM. cuttings file 12, 339). Musical entertainment in the Reading Room: Slocombe, 2012, 60. Bulford Band: WHM. cuttings file 10, 129.

2 Living Conditions

1 Opening quote from, Cobbett, 2001, 282, and quote from 1821 letter in Ian Dyck's introduction, xii. Conclusions of Parliamentary Report of 1867 quoted in Bettey, 1987, 71.
2 The primary source for this and the next paragraph is the Minute Book of the Northern Division of Amesbury Rural Deanery 1856-1874, (Nov. 1863 Meeting of Clergy and Lay Consultees), WSA. D1/21/5/2/1/1, 117-123.
3 The Sturgesses had been builders in the village from at least the seventeenth century: Sturgess, 1995, 4. Three labourers' cottages on Lower Farm: WSA. 2963/10/b, (see Figure 4). Sturgess quotation to build a new cottage for the Chapel, and the extract from the Chapel accounts: WSA. 1418/10. Newspaper report of the explosion given to me by Jack Sturgess, in 1988. Prudence Sawyer's account: Prudence Sawyer, (see Appendix 2a).
4 1883 lease: WSA. 2963/10. 1886 rent account: HA. 93M92/A1.
5 Changes in housing stock deduced by comparing the 1851 Census map and the Army Deeds when the War Office bought the village: WSA. 2916/24; T/Sol Army Deeds (No 26). Housing effect on education quoted from Minute Book of the Northern Division of Amesbury Rural Deanery 1856-1874, WSA. D1/21/5/2/1/1, (meeting Oct. 1861).
6 Manor garden details: BRO. D/ELV E13. The dovecote at Watergate Farm is still extant; pigeon house at Bulford Manor, *S&WJ*, 13th Nov. 1786. Gardens marked on 1861 census map, WSA. 2916/24. Rural Deanery discussion: WSA.

D1/21/5/2/1/1, 117.
7 Description of shepherd's cottage from More, 1825, 38-40. For discussion about this source, see Chapter 1, note 12.
8 Census, *Abstract of the Answers and Returns. Enumeration Abstract* vol.2 (1831). Cobbett, 2001, 286
9 Shepherd's diet, More, 1825, 40. Cider: Davis, 1811, 83. Sir James Caird's Enquiry in, Caird, 1852, 84-85.
10 Prudence Sawyer, (see Appendix 2a)
11 Drink consumption at Manor: BRO. D/ELV E135. Lower Farm brew house: WSA. 2963/10; Watergate Farm brew house and cellar: WSA. 814/16. Matthew Devenish, brewer: WSA. 2770/12. Brewer as occupation for a gentleman: Thompson F. M. L., 1969, 131.
12 Wage statistics taken from Bettey, 1987, 67.
13 Determination of clothiers to enforce laws and Lucy Sturgess's conviction: *S&WJ*, 5th Apr. 1790; her family circumstances taken from, Sturgess, 1995, 6. The details of the poor in Seend: Eden, 1797, 796, 799; the butter in the diet might not be applicable to Bulford because this was subsidised by the dairy farmer at Seend. Bulford was not a dairying area.
14 Cobbett, 2001, 294. The italics are his. The 1830 and 1831 statistics from *Abstract of the Answers and Returns. Ennumeration Abstract*, vol.3 (1831). Salisbury information: Chandler, 1987, 68.
15 Details of John Trowbridge from, Stratford, 1882, 118, and his trade as a carpenter, WSA. 814/17. The probate papers of Thomas Croome include an inventory of farming stock: WSA. 529/154. It is argued in Chapter 4 that this inventory was for Lower Farm/Hindurrington Farm. Watergate Farm inventory: WSA. 814/17. Details of seed drill hire: *The Times*, 11th Mar. 1835, p.7, issue 15735, col. B. 'Sheen House' in Prudence Sawyer, (see Appendix 2b).
16 Frederick Weeks' case: *S&WJ*, 17th Jan. 1852. Two cases of horse theft reported in: *The Times*, 17th Mar. 1829, p .4, issue 13864, col. B, and 11th Mar. 1835, p.7, issue 15735, col. B). Fate of William Reeves: Old Bailey on line t17200115-16, 15th Jan. 1720. Sarum Association for the Prevention of Robberies: *S&WJ*, 26th Apr. 1790. Loveden expenditure at the Manor: BRO. D/ELV E133. Joan Bakehouse's case in Slack, 1975, 20.
17 Will of Lawrence Washington of Garsdon (proved 15 May 1662) in, *WN&Q*. Vol.7, 1911-13, 485. Ann Duke's will: WSA. P5/1772/17iiA. Fictionalised story of shepherd's wife with rheumatism in, More, 1825, 30-31. The eulogy to Sarah Blatch by someone 'who had long enjoyed the friendship of herself and family' in, Anon, 1838, 597-598. Chapel cottages and Sarah Smith's 'diffusive charity': WSA. 2770/5. Ann Smith's headstone is in Bulford Churchyard.
18 This paragraph is based on Stevenson, 2003, 169, with additional information derived from reading the *Poor Law Abstracts*: (1804, 558-59; 1818, 492-23); and *Poor Rate Returns*: (1816-21, 185; 1822-24, 225; 1825-29, 215; 1830-34, 209). Number and cost of loaves distributed, WSA. H/2/110/1.

19 Extracts from the Minute Book, Board of Guardians Amesbury Union 1850-1856 (WSA. H/2/110/5), for example, reveal that maintenance in 1854 was 9s 2d; outdoor relief for the three years was: £56 3s 9d, £36 18s 4d and, £33 8s 1d respectively; and there was no expenditure on lunatics.
20 Tenders sought in local papers, e.g. *S&WJ*. 5th Jun. 1852. Children's routine: WSA. H/2/110/5. Account of marriage and the escape: *S&WJ*, 15th Dec. 1851; *S&WJ*, 15th May 1852.
21 John Weeks's poaching: *S&WJ*, 6th Jan. 1852. The wider picture of poaching is taken from, Thompson F. M. L., 1969, 142-143. Thefts by George Knight and Henry Kinsman: *S&WJ*, Nov. 1825, and 10th Jan. 1852. Concerns about salmon: *S&WJ*, 1st Nov. 1873.
22 Quotation from More, 1825, 17. Absence from chapel: WSA. 2770/2. Account of mushroom picking told to me in 2011 by Ann Sawyer.
23 Cobbett, 2001, 283. The cases of drunkenness in this paragraph are all cited from the local paper: *S&WJ*: 6th Mar. 1852; 10th Feb. 1872; 21st Feb. 1874; 2nd Mar. 1878.
24 Rev Dr Mountain is discussed at length in Chapter 8. His comments about the problem of drinking and his proposed remedies are from the Visitation Query Returns (1873), WSA. D1/56/10. Crossroads Brewery: Stevenson, 2003, 195.
25 Rural Deanery debate in April 1874, and the reporting of the formation of a temperance society on 14th Apr. 1877: WSA. D1/21/5/2/1/1, 254, 256. Rev Dr Mountain's revised scheme quoted from Visitation Query Returns (1876): WSA. D1/56/11. Petition to Parliament: *The Times*, 5th Jun. 1877, p.6, issue 28960. Book by Edmund Southby, future Lord of the Manor: Southby, 1877. Appointment of Churchwarden: WSA. 517/22.
26 For general discussion about the 'Nag's Head', see Stevenson, 2003, 157, 181. Pigeon shoot: *S&WJ*, 18th Oct. 1784. There is no overlap in the documentation of the 'Maidenhead Inn' and the 'Rose and Crown' strongly suggesting that the latter replaced the former. That they occupied the same site is a logical conjecture in the absence of any indication to the contrary. Perhaps the pub just changed its name.
27 The information about Anthony Southby is discussed in Chapter 4 below, and the absences from the village on health reasons have already been discussed in Chapter 1. The suggestion about TB was made to me in 2011 by Martha Hyatt's descendant, Janine Hyatt.
28 Rick fire: *S&WJ*, 28th Feb. 1852. The wider picture of Friendly Societies discussed in, Bettey, 1987, 96; and the local picture in Stevenson, 2003, 157, 181. Breaking up of 'Maidenhead Inn' Friendly Society, and letter about the winding up of the Victoria Society: TNA. FS 4/55, (nos.74, 231).
29 The statistics of the Bulford branch are taken from the annual reports in the *Wiltshire Friendly Society Reports* 1866-8 and 1883-98; and from an 1852 newspaper report: *S&WJ*, 17th Apr. 1852. Bacillus scare: *The Times*, 25th Aug. 1898, p.4, Issue 35604, col. A. The effect of the depression on sheep and corn

farms is quoted from Thompson F. M. L., 1969, 309.
30 Cobbett, 2001, 296-297. Henry Graham's views are taken from his *The Annals of the Yeomanry Cavalry of Wiltshire*, 1886, 63, 70. Unpublished letter to Anthony Southby: O'Brien, 1828-1838, (July 1830).
31 Militia list: WSA. 529/178. Yeomanry Cavalry: Graham, 1886, 65-66, 69.
32 Any local study of the impact of the Swing Riots draws heavily on the work of Jill Chambers and this one is no exception, as evidenced by the detail in this and the next few paragraphs. Separate volumes are published for each County affected by the riots, with those applicable to this study being Wiltshire (1993), and Hampshire (1996). The second volume for Wiltshire was issued as a CD in 2003. References for this paragraph: Chambers, 1993, 25-26, 236- 237, Chambers, 1996, 25, and *S&WJ*, 25th Nov. 1830.
33 Chambers, 1993, 28, 30, 77 with the list of appointments of special constables: GA. D1571/X60; Chambers, 1996, 51-52, 268. For Thomas Jenner's connection with Bulford: TNA. IR 18/10931, WSA. TA Bulford, and WSA. 517/22, (1841 church rate list). Attitude of the radicals to Sir John Pollen: Cobbett, 2001, 394-395.
34 Winter unemployment figures between Lady Day 1832 and 1835: Billinge, 1984, 365-366. Evidence of a thrashing machine at Watergate Farm in 1841 lease: WSA. 814/16, (see also Chapter 5) and the inventory of Watergate Farm: WSA. 814/17. Wiltshire in forefront of the invention and introduction of new machinery and implements: Bettey, 1987, 37. Details of Taskers, although in Chambers, 1996, taken from Endleman in, Hampshire on line.
35 Lavington meeting and its aftermath: Chambers, 1993, 293-294, *Devizes and Wiltshire Gazette*, 9th Dec. 1830, and Chambers, 1996, 25. For extended families: Chambers, 2003. Devenish and Blatch families and the Chapel in, Anon, 1838, 597-598. Batchelor family details from Census Returns.
36 Graham, 1886, 73, Chambers, 1993, 83-84, and Chambers, 1996, 110, 164. Lawrence Greatrake's political views reported in the American Watchman and Delaware Republican, 20th Jun. 1813, vol.5, no. 448. For a fuller discussion see Chapter 9.
37 Piggot's case in, Chambers, 1993, 83-84, 222-223, 243, and Chambers, 2003, 649. Eventually his case was commuted, 'To be imprisoned and kept to hard labour in the House of Correction six years': TNA. HO 6/16. Reconstitution of Everley Troop: Graham, 1886, 93, 233, and TNA. WO 13/4044.
38 Intimidation at Stagg's house and Long's house: *S&WJ*, 29th Nov. 1830, and 29th Jan. 1853. Emigration: *S&WJ*, e.g. 29th May 1852; Cobbett, 2001, 38; and Anon, 1918, article in *Agricultural Gazette*.
39 Durrington emigration in Tankins, 1975, 60. The Errence case is an interpolation in Chapel Church Book, WSA. 2770/2. There was undoubtedly emigration from Bulford as the analysis of the 1851 and 1861 Census Returns makes clear. The case of George Pike is a known example: www.robinsancestry.com/f86.htm; many more await to be uncovered. The comparison with Canadian wages:

Miller, 1968, 36.
40 Details of NALU meetings in Durrington, Figheldean and Netheravon found in Edwina Kingscote-Billinge's PhD thesis: Billinge, 1984, 411-412, 414. The archives of the old NALU could well supply further data on the extent of trade unionism in Bulford which the 1874 case shows was undoubtedly present: *S&WJ*, 14th Mar. 1874. The Trowbridge meeting: *Bristol Mercury and Daily Post*, 27th May 1893, issue 14054. Meanwhile, this book has relied on the work of Bob Scarth for the general picture of trade unionism and the activities of Joseph Arch: Scarth, 1998, 21, 23, 26, 39, 60, 61. Bulford Chapel reference is from the financial return in WSA. 1418/10, (May 1880).
41 Hudson, 1914, 109-110. Sturgess saga: Sturgess, 1995, 9-10

3 Horizons and Communications

1 Shepherd's report in R. Whitlock, 1979, 70. Ralph Whitlock was recounting what his shepherd father recalled from the 1880s.
2 Memories of Old Joe the collier in Hudson, 1946, 54. This book was first published in 1910 and drew on the memories of the old men he met. 'Eleven o'clock postman': Sawyer, Prudence, (see Appendix 2b)
3 Cobbett, 2001, 297. Daniel Defoe quoted in, James, 1987, 190. Armed farmers: Noyes, 1913, 4.
4 Paragraph based on Stevenson, 2003, 153-154, and Andrew and Dury's map. Economic importance of drove-roads: Bettey, 1987, 84. Marlborough Road use by Loveden: BRO. ELV D/ELV E135; and its later use: *S&WJ*, 14th Aug. 1897, and James, 1987, 93. Quarter Sessions summons: WSA. 814/31. Expenditure on roads and militia: *Poor Law Abstract* (1804). The passage from Mary O'Brien's Journal was transcribed as 'Balford', an obvious misreading of 'Bulford' when the context is considered. She was comparing roads in Canada with those she, and those to whom she was writing, knew well in England: O'Brien, 1828-1838, (entry 14th Dec. 1829).
5 Tragedy of Thomas Strange: Rhys-Hughes, 1972, and *S&WJ*, 30th Jul. 1827
6 The main source for this account of Amesbury Turnpike Trust is Chandler, 1979. Details of Folly Bottom Bar taken from the sale notice of the toll houses held at the George Inn Amesbury, 30th. Oct. 1871 : ibid. Richard Sopp: ibid., and marriage registers. The Long's involvement: *S&WJ*, 6th Dec. 1830, and 5th Feb. 1853.
7 As above. Toll accounts: WSA. A3/7/2/1. Details of damage and rebuilding of the bridge taken from the letters of the County Surveyor: Cowan, 1996, 4, 8, 10-11, 59 (letters 11, 23, 62, 76, 59). Note of bridge reopening: *S&WJ*, 5th Dec. 1825. Bidders for Trust property in 1852: *S&WJ*, date? 1852. Shop: Sawyer, Prudence, (see Appendix 2b).
8 Description of old turnpike roads: Sawyer, Prudence, (see Appendix 2b).

Bulford bridge description: Lewis, 1848, 300. Debt and sale of toll house: WSA. A1/205/2. I am indebted to John Chandler for the police report: WCC Sol/Clerk Roads and Bridges Minutes, 1902, no. 80.

9 Hudson's 1910 account of the importance of Salisbury to the villages: Hudson, 1946, 16; and his description of the Salisbury scene on market day, ibid, 17. Carrier services from Bulford taken from various directories, and the verse is from Sawyer, Prudence, (see Appendix 2a). Chough Inn: Chandler, 1987, 146. Ludgershall: Cobbett, 2001, 269-270.

10 Marriage information has been analysed from Census Returns and marriage registers. The need to replace the table of degrees ordered by the church visitation in 1829: WSA. 517/22, (entry 17th Jul. 1829). Sturgess and variations of the name: Sturgess, 1995, 1. I have not been over rigorous in differentiating between the name with one or two 's' in this book as I found examples of the same person's name being spelt different ways.

11 I am grateful to Ann Sawyer for sharing this information about her parents with me when I saw her in 2011. I have also used information from her late brother's writing: Vines, 1984, 18. A photo of their mother at Latton is published in: Small, Doug. 2009. *Wilts and Berks Canal revisited*. Stroud: The History Press. p.60.

12 Pastor Williams's attendance record, recording reason for absences, is the main source for this paragraph: WSA. 2770/2. The Chapel quickly made the village the centre of a wider community, which was the aim of its founders (see Chapter 8).

13 Information mainly from Census Returns. John Bannister of Warminster left 'my friend Francis Stephen Long of Bulford' the residue of his estate in his will: WSA. 14/12/1857.

14 Watergate Farm inventory and Ann Long's recipes: WSA. 563/1. Ann Sawyer's memories of Old Mrs Hill shared with me in 2011. Robbins family based on family tree in: Rhys-Hughes, 1972; and my subsequent research, (see Appendix 1c).

15 Analysis of Census Returns.

16 The probate accounts of Thomas Croome list all the financial debts and liabilities of his estate: WSA. 529/154. Davis, 1811, 145. Reach of Salisbury Corn Market: Chandler, 1987, 105. Sam Sturgess: WSA. G23/1/30. Devizes Corn Exchange: Pugh, 1975, 265.

17 Thomas Croome's probate documents list his sheep purchases and sales for 1820-1821 and are the source of this analysis: WSA. 529/154. Seymour/Devenish lease: WSA. 1126/18.

18 All details in this and the next paragraph, unless otherwise acknowledged, from Sir Edward Loveden Loveden's Bulford inventory for the years 1812-1815 (BRO. D/ELV E133) and his Bulford Housekeeping Book for the same period (BRO. D/ELV E135). Beds advertised by Fidell of Devizes: *S&WJ*, 30th Nov. 1813.

19 Ann Southby's letter: WSA. 367/20.

20 Information about Frances Greensted taken from Watkins, Shoberl and Upcott, 1816. The list of her subscribers was gratefully acknowledged and printed in her book: Greensted, 1796, 60. Her poems include nature poems, elegies, topical poems and 'Burbage, a descriptive poem'. She had contacts in north Wiltshire. Dr Gapper's autopsy on Egyptian mummy: *Gentleman's Magazine* (1824 part 2), 628. Francis Stephen Long's interests in Bank: *Bristol Mercury*, 20th Feb. 1858, issue 3544; *S&WJ*, 17th Feb. 1872 and 14th Feb. 1874. Malignant sheep disorder and the theft of his horse: *The Times*, 9th Sep. 1862, p.8, issue 24344, col. F; and 11th Mar. 1835, p.7, issue 15735, col. B. George Melsome's election support: *S&WJ*, 31st Jan. 1874; and school inspection: Rose's log book WSA. F8/500/6/3/1 (entry 9th Jun. 1890).

21 Francis Stephen Long's investments: WSA. 814/21. Cawnpoor: Parish Church memorial. David Meagher points out in his article (Meagher 2012) that William Shaw was a surgeon with the Bengal Medical Services of the East India Company who just before the massacre, when his wife perished, had been moved to Lucknow where he died a few months later in the siege of that city. Anthony Southby's brother was a magistrate at the time of the Makenzie Rebellion, and his brother-in-law was involved in politics: Berchen, 1977, 140-152. Civil War skirmish: Tibbutt, 1963, 666. Death of William Hill: church memorial plaque. Grace's career: www.lightdragoons.org.uk/history.html, and the Waterloo Medal Book 1815: TNA. MINT 16/112.

22 General background to Anthony Gapper's inheritance: Stevenson, 2003, 162. General background to Gapper family, and family tree: Miller, 1968, ix-xviii, 288; further research on family tree in Appendix 1a. Gapper memorials in Charlton Adam Church.

23 Edmund Gapper's will: TNA. 26/290. Qualifying at Edinburgh University: *Bristol Mercury*, 1st Mar. 1824, p.3. Political situation: Miller, 1968, as in note 22. Edmund's family life: *Gentleman's Magazine* (1825), pt 2, 176; and (1827) pt 2, 697. Journey to Thornhill: Miller, 1968, 3-15, (entries 31st Aug. to 16th Oct. 1828).

24 Details of Lucius O'Brien: English and Bélanger, 1990; also available on line. There are two images that refer directly to Bulford in Lucius O'Brien's 1852-1868 Sketch Book which covers the time of his first visit to England; one is a pencil sketch from 7th Apr. 1869, of a road with trees, a fence and some houses (discussed below in chapter 5). The second looks like a photograph glued to his sketchbook and underneath was written "Bulford Church": Art Gallery of Ontario, 92/71, p.29 and 92/72, p.30. I am grateful to Georgiana Uhlyarik for looking out these images for me in the Gallery's archives. Details of Claudia Southby's prowess in painting was generously supplied to me by Margaret Fay. Anthony Southby's granddaughter, another Claudia, was also an artist. She illustrated the story of St George and the Dragon in a series of delicate line drawings: Matson and Southby, 1893. A source that I have been unable to find is: Broughton and Grant. 1952. *Flower Paintings through Four Centuries*:

Lewis. p.45. This mentions Claudia Southby which is almost certainly Anthony Southby's daughter, considering his botanical passion and expertise.
25 Mary Gapper O'Brien is the major source for this period of her brother's Anthony's life: Miller, 1968, (entries for 18 Oct; 27, 30 Nov 1828 and 17 Jan; 11 May 1829, 18, 26, 32, 49).
26 Miller, 1968, (entries for 12 Feb, 6 May 1829, 39, 48, 292 footnote 11). 'Valuable early record of mammals': Fleming, 1913, 206.
27 One of Mary Gapper O'Brien's letters was addressed to 'Dr Anthony Gapper, College Green Bristol, England' and ends 'God prosper you Anthony. I wish you were amongst us again'. His brother had a house at College Green: Miller, 1968, 122, (entry 6 Jan. 1830). Mayor of Bridgwater: *Bath Chronicle and Weekly Gazette*, 2nd Oct. 1834, p.3. Aunt's death: ibid., 97 (entry for Apr. 1830), 297 footnote. Watson, the 'Father of British topographical botany': Desmond, 1977, 574, 643; and for his acknowledgement of Dr Gapper's contribution: Watson, 1874, 534-535. Dr Southby's vetch observation: Flower, 1863, 118; and Mary's description of him: Miller, 1968, 53 (entry for 15 Jun. 1829).
28 Dr Southby's accompanying Richard Spruce and species named after him: Spruce, 1849, 83, 501; and Desmond, 1977, 574. Return to Brighton in Spruce's List of Botanical Excursions Jun 19 1841 – Apr 30 1863: Linnean Society. Presentation of sample sheets in Essex: *The Essex Naturalist, being the Journal of the Essex Field Club*, 1954 vol. 29, London, 195. Jersey connection: Channel Island Census (1881). Crossing the desert by camel, see Chapter 10.
29 Paper supply: Carter, 2008, 11-12. She notes that the watermark on the paper Mary Gapper O'Brien used has a remarkable resemblance to that produced at the Laverstoke paper mill, Hampshire.
30 Williams Williams's family details from report of marriage: *S&WJ*, 12th Dec. 1825; Census Returns; and baptism register.
31 Anthony Southby's search for a wife: Miller, 1968, 128; O'Brien, 1828-1838, (entry May 1830).
32 Residencies of Colonel Bradshaw and Captain Taylor: *Slater's Royal National and Commercial Directory* (1852-53), and *Mercer and Crocker's Directory* (1872). Living in Lyndhurst: TNA. ED 103/117, 377. This is where his daughter Claudia's picture of ducks in the New Forest was most probably painted: Margaret Fay. The Southbys owned a property in the area which is given as a reason for their cook Mary Ann Cannings meeting and marrying a Southampton man William Knight: ibid. Anthony Southby's attendances of Easter Vestry and Amesbury Rural Deanery meetings: WSA. 517/22; WSA. D1/21/5/2/1/2, (meeting 24th Apr. 1878). Sale of Bulford Manor: *The Hampshire Advertiser*, 28th Aug. 1867, issue 4195. Paying off debt is a family tradition for the Manor being sold on Edmund's death, shared with me in 2011 by Tim Perrot, a family descendant.
33 A detailed account of the coming of the railway line: Grayer, 2011; a more general account: Chandler and Goodhugh, 1979, 40, 64-66. Advertisement: *The Times*, 10th Jul. 1886, p.19, issue 31808, col. A.

34 The career of Jacob Jehoshaphat Mountain is discussed in detail below (Chapter 8), and that of Mary Ann Knight below (Chapter 10).
35 Bulford Manor: Rhys-Hughes, 1972, 41. George Ingles: memorial in the Parish Church.

4 Full Circle of Ownership: Bulford Manor and the Village

Sources for Chapter: WSA. 2963/10 is a file containing a whole series of documents kept by James Hooper. I have given the various documents suffixes a - j for convenience of reference. These documents are:
1880 map of Upper and Lower Farms: WSA. 2963/10/a
1881 advertisement for Lower Farm tenant: WSA. 2963/10/b
1881 Anthony Southby/James Hooper lease of Upper Farm: WSA. 2963/10/c
1885 Edmund Southby/James Hooper lease of Lower Farm, backdated to 1881 WSA. 2963/10/d
1886 Liverpool and London and Globe Insurance Company policy taken out by James Hooper for both Upper and Lower Farms: WSA. 2963/10/e
1893 Sep. James Ledger Hill's side of correspondence with James Hooper about leasing both farms together: WSA. 2963/10/f
1895 James Ledger Hill/James Hooper joint lease for Upper and Lower Farms (backdated to 1893): WSA. 2963/10/g
1897 Secretary of State for War tender document for Upper and Lower Farms, revised in 1900: WSA. 2963/10/h
1899 letter from Rawlence and Squarey, agents for the War Office, changing terms of lease: WSA. 2963/10/i
1907 Liverpool and London and Globe Insurance Company policy taken out by James Hooper for both Upper and Lower Farms: WSA. 2963/10/j.

1 The early history of Bulford needs to be put into the context of Amesbury's history. Two works to address this from a pre-Conquest perspective are: Hinton, 1979, and Pugh, 2003. Specific details for Bulford are best summarised in: Stevenson, 2003, 161-165. In Domesday the Abbess held 12 hides which is equivalent to 720 acres: Morris, 1979, para. 16.1.
2 For the inheritance of Bulford Manor from the Dukes and Southbys to the Gappers, see Appendix 1a.
3 See family tree in Appendix 1a. Mary O'Brien's attitude to sick and needy in Thompson, Samuel, 1968, 141; party at Government House: Miller, 1968, 179. (entry 23rd Mar. 1832). Victorian values of the family: Mulley (1990), 11.
4 Family history of the Dukes of Lake, covering Bulford: Duke, 1914-1916, 296-299. Southby/Gapper marriage: Phillimore and Hayward, 1898, 25. Advertisement for the letting of Bulford Manor: S&WJ, 13th Nov. 1786. Highworth memorial on south wall of the chancel: Hoare, 1825, 45.
5 Bulford Manor accounts for details of transactions: WSA. 367/7. Louisa Pollen's

death and Sir John Pollen's arrangements for Charity Ann Pollen on his death: BRO. D/EL/T111. Mr Fleet's negotiations with the County Surveyor: Cowan, 1996, 2 (letter 10).

6   Quote about ownership of Redenham Mansion is from a faculty granted to Sir John Pollen for a private pew in Thruxton Church: HA. 397/1/8. Description of estate which remained in the Pollen family until it was sold in 1908: Bickley, 1911, 367. Concert in Salisbury: S&WJ, 23rd Aug. 1813. Sir Edward was born Edward Loveden Townsend and subsequently changed his surname to Loveden as stipulated by his great uncle in order for him to inherit the Buscott estate. Anthony Gapper had to change his surname to Southby in the similar circumstances to inherit Bulford Manor and perhaps Charity Ann Pollen (née Southby) got the idea from the Lovedens, although it was a by no means an uncommon practice. The moving in arrangements of Sir Edward Loveden and the purchases from Mr Norton: BRO. D/ELV E133.

7   Sir Edward Loveden's stays were in 1812: 12th Feb. – 4th Mar., 7th – 20th Jul., and 2nd – 23rd Nov.; in 1813: 18th Feb. – 13th Mar., 8th – 26th Jul., and 9th Oct. – 15th Nov.; in 1814: 5th Mar. – 5th Apr., and 12th Oct .– 12th Nov.; and in 1815: 18th Feb. – 27th Mar.: BRO. D/ELV E133. Letter from agent Mr Chapman about Miss Theyer: BRO. D/ELV E134/5. Purchases made from Mr Pickering and Mr Six: BRO. D/ELV E135. Guns: BRO. D/ELV E134/2. Treatment for worms and mange: BRO. D/ELV E133.

8   Pre-nuptial arrangements for Sir John Pollen's estates: BRO. D/EL/T111. Charity Ann Pollen's will: WSA. 2216/62.

9   Souces for family history: (see Appendix 1a); memorials in Charlton Adam Church. John Pollen's executors: BRO. D/EL/T111. Mary Gapper's observations: O'Brien, Mary, 1828-1838, (entry for 14th Dec. 1829).

10 Edmund Gapper's will and Lucy's relationship: TNA. IR 26/290. Spinsters moving in together: O'Brien, Mary, 1828-1838, (entry for 8th Aug. 1830). Charity Ann Pollen's will and codicil: WSA. 2216/62.

11 Whole paragraph based on will of Charity Ann Pollen: WSA. 2216/62. Report of change of name from Gapper to Southby in *Gentleman's Magazine* (1835), pt. 1, 653.

12 Mary Southby's will: TNA. TNAB 11/1846. Lucy Gapper's will: TNA. TNAB 11/2042. Anthony Gapper's letter: O'Brien, Mary, 1828-1838, (entry 2nd Nov. 1834); and his family's concerns for him: ibid, (letter in May 1830, and entry 2nd May 1835). Information on Gapper brothers: (Appendix 1a). Death of Lucy Gapper: *The Standard*, 21st Feb. 1846, p. 8, issue 6719.

13 Anthony Gapper's journey and Aunt Lucy's kindness: Miller, 1968, 66, 97. Church rate: WSA. 517/22, (entry Mar. 1834).

14 Census information. Edmund Southby's marriage announcement in *The Times*, 8th Jun. 1863, issue 24579, col. A. Fellow of Royal Chemical Society from title page, and quote: Southby, 1877, vii.

15 Southby, 1877, title page, vii, 171, 259. Company Listings from the Century's

Progress, 1892, Isle of Man: on-line.

16 Anthony Gapper Southby's 1863 patents: Woodcraft, 1964, (nos. 1899, 2899); and 1877 patent and petition for renewal in *The Times*, 10th Jul.1891, p.13, issue 33373, col. A; *London Gazette*, 24th Mar. 1876, p.2091.

17 Quotes: Southby, 1877, 81, 128; letters patent: *The Times* 1891, p.13, issue 33373, col. A.

18 Southby rent returns: Return of Owners of Land, vol. 2, 1873. Reduced rent expectations: WSA. 2963/10/d. Suicide of William Dymer reported in the *Bristol Mercury and Daily Post*, 15th Apr. 1882, issue 10583.

19 Biographical details from Census Returns: 1841 - 1901; shipping details: *Lloyds Register of Shipping* (1880); involvement in village: Stevenson, 2003, 162. Role of Sturgess family in extending Manor House: Sawyer, Prudence, (see Appendix 2b).

20 Comment on absence through business interests made by Rev Arnold at an enquiry: *Return of Endowed Charities - County of Wiltshire*, vol. 2, Southern Division, 82. Report on pumping engines: *The Times*, 25th Aug. 1898, p.4, issue 35604, col. A. Details of War Office purchase, and the properties excluded from the sale, from Army Deeds: T/Sol 432/51 Wilts no.26. Newspaper report: *S&WJ*, 10th Jul. 1897, quoted in James, 2001, 92. Quote on Water Rights Rents from James Ledger Hill's letter dated 7th Sep. 1893: WSA. 2963/10/f. James Ledger Hill's role in including the village in the sale, at £50 a house, told to me by Ann Sawyer in 2010. Site of coal yard was shown on a map drawn up from memory by Ernie Rich and Dave Taylor who were the village post boys in 1942–1944 and 1944–1947 respectively. New vicarage: see Chapter 8.

21 Details of John Sawyer's career and his photograph were shared with me by Ann Sawyer in 2010. Officers' Club: Rhys-Hughes, 1972.

22 The starting point for a discussion about Hindurrington Farm is Stevenson, 2003, 156, 161, 166-167; and Richard Duke's will: *Return of Endowed Charities - County of Wiltshire*, vol. 2, Southern Division, 81: WSA. 1172/118. Thomas Davis's comments on the siting of farms and the advantages of higher ground: Davis, 1811, 8-10. 1880 map of Upper and Lower Farms: WSA. 2963/10/a; 1838 acreage of Hindurrington and Lower Farms: TNA. IR 29/38/49, 30/38/49 and WSA. TA Bulford. Site of 'old pennings': WSA. 135/37. Various names for the penning found in 1851 Census Map and Chapel Church Book: WSA. 2916/24, and WSA. 2770/2, (entry for 1877).

23 The pre-nineteenth century details of Lower Farm are taken from the English Heritage Listed Buildings Register (ID: 321404); the 1881 details are all from the advertisement for a new tenant: WSA. 2963/10/b.

24 Details of Manor Farm were told to me in 1978 by 'Old' Farmer Hann. The name 'Manor Farm' is a revival of the name for the Manor's farm before it was split into two moieties, and survived into the nineteenth century as an older name for the Seymour/Watergate Farm: WSA. 517/22, (entry 7th Jan. 1841).

25 All details in this paragraph are taken from the 1829 church rate list: WSA.

517/22 and Rhys-Hughes, 1972, 37, tabulation of Churchwardens, (see Appendix 3)

26 Sarum Association for the Prevention of Robberies: *S&WJ*, 26th Apr. 1790. Loveden accounts: BRO. D/ELV E134/1, 134/2 and E133. Thomas Croome's will for family relationships: WSA. 529/154. The will however does not give evidence for Mary Croome whose relationships I have presumed. Mary as tenant of T. W. Dyke: Voters' List (1819). Gamekeeper licence: *S&WJ*, 24th Sep. 1827. Church rate tables for 1829 and 1834: WSA. 517/22.

27 Joseph Robbins's tenancy in 1838: TNA. IR 18/10931. The tenancies of Lower and Upper Farm from *Kelly's Directory* (1855, 1875, 1880). The beginning of James Hooper's tenancy: WSA. 2963/10/c. Churchwardens: Rhys-Hughes, 1972, 37, (see Appendix 3).

28 The Family of Robbins, of Bulford in Rhys-Hughes, 1972 which draws on information provided by a descendant, T. W. Robbins of Wareham. The farming connection is documented on the family tree (see Appendix 1c), with Joseph Robbins's daughter Emma marrying Thomas Hayden a farmer from Durrington in 1856; her cousin Anna, the youngest daughter of Joseph Robbins's elder brother Thomas, married John S. Randall, a farmer from Broad Chalke, and Joseph's granddaughter through his second marriage, Vera May, married Alfred Ernest Nichols who farmed in Pulborough, West Sussex. This has been used as a basis of the family tree in Appendix 1c. The 1824 death of John Robbins: memorial in Churchyard. Letting of Milston cottage: *S&WJ*, 16th Nov. 1812. Robert Smith was People's Warden in 1801, and then again from 1804 till 1825. He was succeeded in this post in 1826 by Thomas Robbins, the new tenant of Upper Farm: Rhys-Hughes, 1972, (see Appendix 3). 1833 record of Thomas Robbins farming 800 acres: *Return of Endowed Charities, County of Wiltshire*, vol.2 Southern Divison: TNA. IR 29/38/49, p.81. Epithets 'the sidesman' and 'churchwarden': ibid. John Robbins's will and probate: WSA. P2/1824/35i. Acreage of Upper Farm: TNA. IR 18/10931. Hursely lease: HA. 58M71/E/B232, Box RB no.11. Employment figures are taken from Census Returns.

29 Upper Farm and Lower Farm rents in 1886: HA. 93M92/A1 and WSA. 2963/10/d.

30 George Parkins: *W.E.Owens & Co Directory* (1878). James Hooper's lease: WSA. 2963/10/c.

31 Biographical information gleaned from Census Returns.

32 1885 lease of Lower Farm: WSA. 2963/10/d, and 1885 Rent of Upper Farm: HA. 93M92/A1. 1886 Insurance Policy: WSA. 2963/10/e. James Ledger Hill's letter: WSA. 2963/10/f. New plantations: WSA. 2963/10/g.

33 Parsons admitted to Rose Grammar School: Volpi, 2011, 31, and WSA. F8/500/6/3/1, (entry 1st Oct. 1895). Description of the Parsons in Hamilton, 1911, 123.

34 War Office lease with maps showing scheduled land in with the lease: WSA. 2963/10/h. Spring Cottage insurance requirement: WSA. 2207/1.

35 Letter from Rawlence & Squarey, Land Agents: WSA. 2963/10/i. 1907 insurance: WSA. 2963/10/j. Scheduling of the farm lands is taken from the amended lease, signed in 1900, and its associated maps: WSA. 2963/10/h.
36 Charity Ann Pollen's will: WSA. 2216/62. 1881 lease: WSA. 2963/10/c. 1885 lease: WSA. 2963/10/d. 1895 lease backdated to 1893: WSA. 2963/10/g. James Ledger Hill offered James Hooper the choice of terms, and payment methods, in a letter dated 16th Sep. 1893: WSA. 2963/10/f. War Office lease of 1897: WSA. 2963/10/h.
37 Leases determinable by two years' notice and extra buildings requiring maintenance in 1881: WSA. 2963/10/c. 1885 split of responsibilities for repairing cottages: WSA. 2963/10/d. Edmund Southby's accounts: HA. 93M92/A1. The Manor's housing stock in 1838 and 1886: TNA. IR 18/10931, and *The Times*, 10th Jul. 1886, p.19; issue 31808; col. A. The Seymour estate cottages: WSA. 212A/27/44/3. Small tithes list: TNA. IR 18/10931. Orchard End as lodgings and guest house: Hamilton, 1911, 121, and Census Return (1901).
38 Toll House: WSA. A/205/2. Jenner's property: Army Deeds T/Sol 432/51, Wilts no.26, and WSA. 517/22, (entry 7th Jan. 1841). Anglo-Saxon Bulford: Hinton, 1979, 24.

5 The Seymour Estate and Leaseholders of Watergate Farm

1 The starting point for the creation of the Seymour Estate is Stevenson, 2003, 161-164. Boundary of the estate is taken from 1820 map of Farm: WSA. 135/37L. Name Manor Farm, e.g.: Voters' List (1838)
2 Biographical details of Henry Seymour in this and the next paragraph in Falk, 1950, 30, 50, 52, 60, 63, 112-115. Landholder attitude to their estates and the financial developments of the eighteenth century: Matthias, 1983, 47-53. 1801 lease: WSA. 1126/18.
3 William Seymour: Stevenson, 2002, 163.
4 Information in this paragraph about Henry Seymour junior from Falk, 1950, 30, 61, 63, 68, 112-113, 115, 127, 156, 159, 162, 173, 177.
5 Henry Danby Seymour inheritance: Stevenson, 2003, 163. Details of business involvement: Beamish, Hillier, and Johnstone, 1976, 33, 38. Biographical information: Falk, 1950, 253-254. Bulford Estate as loan collateral: T/Sol 2850/50, Wilts. No.22, and WSA. 212A/27/44/3. Other Seymour estates at East Knoyle and Stapleford: Sandell, 1975, 67, 94. Swayne lessee and hunting: WSA. 1126/18.
6 Alfred Seymour biographical information: Falk, 1950, 253-254. 1865 election address and property sale cuttings in Game Book: WSA. 186/1. Alfred was following in his father's footsteps as M.P. for Totnes as the Seymour family had extensive lands in South Devon. Jane Seymour inheritance: Army Deeds: T/Sol 2850/50, Wilts. No. 22, and Falk, 1950, 253. 1838 tithe commutation quote:

TNA. IR 18/10931.
7   Seymour/ Devenish 1801 lease: WSA. 1126/18. 1837-1894 hunting statistics: WSA. 186/1. The 1831 Game Act (Ch. 32) regulated the hunting seasons: pheasant 1st Oct. – 1st Feb., partridge 1st Sep. – 1st Feb. All hunts recorded in the Game Book were in September during the partridge season, except one on 9th Oct. 1891, which, being later than usual, fell in the pheasant season as well. Two cock pheasants were bagged by the new Lord of the Manor, James Ledger Hill, and 'Melsome Junior' (Robert Melsome) of Watergate House. There is a portrait of a young Henry Seymour junior posing in his hunting dress, gun in hand and hound asleep at his feet, in Falk, 1950, facing p.112. He is by a well maintained stile with his game sack slung over it. It is a scene which could easily have been located at Bulford, but probably not. The excellent hunting was probably another reason why the Bulford estate was not sold off earlier.
8   The role of the Devenish, Blatch and Aldridge families in the foundation of Bulford Chapel is discussed in full in Chapter 8 below. Death of Matthew Devenish: WSA. 2770/2, (interpolation in list of founder members). Poll Book (1829). 1829 church rate: 517/22. 1841 draft lease: WSA. 814/16.
9   Francis Stephen Long of Amesbury's farm holdings and provision for his sons in his will, attested copy dated 1844: WSA. 814/21/4. Information on Red House Farm from Chandler and Goodhugh, 1979, 28. 1841 draft lease: WSA. 814/16. Horse theft: *The Times*, 11th Mar. 1835, p.7, issue 15735, col. B.
10 The detailed map of 'Bulford Farm' has been dated to c1820: WSA. 135/37 L. 1801 lease improvement stipulations: WSA. 1126/18. Quotes on 'burnbeaking' and sheep husbandry: Davis, 1811, 106, 137-138. The archaic term 'burnbeaked' which was used in the 1801 lease was replaced in the 1841 draft lease by the later term 'burnbaked'. Any downland burnbaked and converted to arable attracted an additional rent of £100 an acre in the 1895 lease of Manor farmland: WSA. 2963/10/g.
11 The information in this paragraph is taken from the 1841 lease. As a draft, it is peppered with abbreviations and contractions which have been faithfully copied in any quotes: WSA. 814/16. 1827 refurbishment plans for the farm house: WSA. 451/58, and Cowan, 1996, 73-74, (letters 601, 607). Description of the Pennings buildings taken from a letter of 19th Mar. 1897: WSA. 212A/27/44/3.
12 Churchwardens: Rhys-Hughes, 1972, 37 (see Appendix 3). Employment details from Census Returns. Seed drill: *The Times* 11th Mar. 1835, p.7, issue 15735, col. B. Thrashing machine: WSA. 814/1, and 1871 inventory and valuation: WSA. 814/17.
13 Biographical details: Census Returns (1841-1901). Churchwardens: Rhys-Hughes, 1972, 37, (see Appendix 3). School closure: WSA. F8/500/44/1/1, (entry 29th Jun. 1899).
14 The information and quotations in this paragraph come from copies of correspondence retained by the War Office leading up to the purchase of the 751 acres in March 1894: (WSA. 212A/27/44/3), and deeds of the sale: T/Sol

2850/50, Wilts. no.22.
15   Army Deeds: T/Sol 2852/50, Wilts. no. 68. George Melsome farming at Ratfyn: TNA. MT 6/1159/9, and at Maddington: *Bristol Mercury and Daily Post*, 9th Dec. 1893, issue 14222. 1943 sale: Stevenson, 2003, 164.
16   Cobbett, 2001, 183-185. Jefferies, 1992, 74, 77, 79, 82.
17   Description of Sir Laurence Washington's house and its extension c.1800: Stevenson, 2003, 168. Andrews and Dury Map (1773). Leases: WSA. 1126/18 and 814/16. 1820 map: WSA. 135/37 L; 1838 tithe map: TNA. IR 30/38/49 and copy in WSA. Bulford TA. For the identification of structures as a cart shed and granary, see discussion of the 1841 lease below. Evidence of wall lines shared with me in 2011 by Dr Goodson-Wicks M.P. The old cottage in need of repair is from 1827 surveyor's report to Henry Seymour's Steward, Mr Fleet, as is the description of work needed in the house: WSA. 451/58, (letter dated 2nd Apr. 1827).
18   'Parlour and chamber over': WSA. 1126/18; service wing: Stevenson, 2003, 168. James Thorn's witness statement: *The Times*, 11th Mar. 1835; p.7, issue 15735, col. B. Quotes from the surveyor's report after the 1827 fire: WSA. 451/58, (letter dated 2nd Apr. 1827).
19   1872 inventory: WSA. 814/17. Water table information was given to me in 2011 by the owner, Dr Goodson-Wicks M.P. 'Fancy key & Lock to Wine Cellar door' costing seven shillings bought for Manor in 1812: BRO D/ELV E133. The 'cellar' of the Manor House was shown to me in 2011 by CSjt Sgt. Povey.
20   English Heritage Listed Buildings Register (ID: 321412) for details of the barn bays. OS Map (1817), first series, sheet 14. 1801 lease and 1841 draft lease: WSA. 1126/18 and 814/16. For details of the barn's condition in 1827: WSA. 451/58, (letter dated 2nd Apr. 1827). The rickyard is identified in the 1820 map: WSA. 135/37L. The leat to the north of the barn is first shown on the OS Map (1887), sheet 14. Ann Sawyer, who was born in 1918, remembers standing on the paddles of the waterwheel in the leat with her friends and making it move like a treadmill, and 'Old' Farmer Hann recalls it in the 1940s. The water wheel is also marked on the 1940 Post Boys' Map: see Chapter 4, note 20. Course of Nine Mile River as it joins the Avon: Andrews and Dury Map (1790). Efficacy of water power: Davis, 1811, 12. 1838 map: WSA. 517/28. OS Map (1887), 1901 edition.
21   Clauses from 1841 draft lease and 1801 lease: WSA. 814/16 and 1126/18. Information about the construction building sequence of the dovecote and stables shared with me in 2011 by Tony Hadfield, owner of 'The Dovecot'.
22   O'Brien, Lucius . 1852-1868 Sketchbook, Art Gallery of Ontario: 92/71, p.29. Details of the 1893 loan and subsequent building work at farm: WSA. 212A/27/44/3.
23   1872 inventory: WSA. 814/17; Census Returns. Michael Stone, coachman: HA. 5M62/17 M368, 471.

6 'Nag's Head' and the Third Estate

1   Links between Chafyn, Staple and Dyke's 73 acre farm in Stevenson, 2003, 164-165.
2   Poore's granting land by copy to member's own family in Stevenson, 2003, 188, and Tankins, 1975, 48. Winchester College sale of leasehold and copyhold: S&WJ, 18th Apr. 1833. Poore's dispute with the Dean and Chapter and the management of their Durrington lands and tenants: Tankins, 1975, 47-48, 51. Edward Poore's Trustees owning 'Nag's Head' in 1841: HA. 11M59/E2/415994. Dyke's Farm: WSA. A1 355/1 and 3. Winchester owning Mill under occupation of John Cooe in 1841: Sandell, 1975, 50.
3   1745 and 1762 leases: WSA. 402/90. 'Nag's Head' seen as part of Bulford in Kelly's Directory (1848). Outline of the history of 'Nag's Head' pub: Stevenson, 2003, 181.
4   Ownership of 73 acre estate: (see note 1 above). Poore family at Syrencote House in Figheldean: Stevenson, 1995, 113. Dykes at Figheldean: Census (1851). Manor debt to Mr Dyke: WSA. 367/17. William Dyke supplying meat: BRO. D/ELV E135. William Dyke's obituary: WHM. cuttings file 1, 71. Thomas Webb Dyke and owning land in Bulford: Poll Book (1819), and Stevenson, 2003, 165; owing church rate in 1824 and 1826, and appointment as Churchwarden 8th Apr. 1831: WSA. 517/22. Potato theft: S&WJ, 28th Nov. 1825. William Bailey tenant of John Cooe: Electoral Register (1833). John and Richard Cooe's property portfolio and William Bailey tenanting the 73 acre farm in Bulford in Sandell, 1975, 27, 69, 89, and TNA. IR 18/10931.
5   Notice of 'George Inn' auction: Devizes and Wiltshire Gazette, 12th Mar. 1833. The notice for auction of the property reads, 'The Property consists of upwards of 400 Acres of Freehold; the remainder being partly Leasehold for 21 years, under the Dean and Chapter of Sarum, re-newable in the usual manner (with power for the Lessee to grant the same as Copyhold for three lives), and partly Copyhold for three lives, held under Winchester College'. The tenure of property of Bulford village not owned by the Manor seems to be in the last throws of reorganisation. The seventy-three acre farm was leasehold but the various properties were almost certainly copyhold. Stevenson thinks that the houses along Water Street were originally copyhold farmhouses. (Stevenson, 2003, 155) The Dukes had consolidated the Manor's holdings but the situation of the Poore /Dyke/Cooe's estate probably lagged behind. Legislation in 1841 and 1851 made it easier for copyhold to be turned into freehold and this may well have helped regularise landholding in the village so that by 1871 there were very few properties not owned by the Manor, mainly those owned by the Chapel. Is it a coincidence that some of the tenant farmers associated with the seventy-three acre farm in Bulford are known over three generations, the Dykes and Hayden/Haydons, then vanish from the village, or is this empirical evidence 'of

the Copyhold for three lives' tenure of the estate? Parish rate list: WSA. 517/22, (entry 7th Jan. 1841). 1838 tithe commutation: TNA.IR 29/38/49 and 30/38/49. Electoral Registers (1832 to 1841): WSA. A1 355/1-9. *Kelly's Directory* (1848); Census Returns. William Bailey at 'Anchor and Hope': *S&WJ*, 24th Sep. 1827. Quarry charity: WSA. 1418/10.

6   1820 sale of lambs to Mr Smith, and sheep with Mrs Croome's mark: WSA. 529/154. Church rate details and elections for Churchwarden: WSA. 517/22. Mary Croome's 1825 bill for 'delapidations': Cowan, 1996, 32, (letter 263). Description of Thomas Croome as a 'corn-dealer': *Hampshire Chronicle*, 20th Dec. 1824. All other sources already acknowledged above.

7   John Williams' 1839 freehold in will: WSA. P2/1839/34. Elizabeth Williams' maiden name: marriage registers. For association of his High Street House with the Williams and James Toomer: WSA. 517/22, (entry 7th Jan. 1841), and Poll Book (1819).

8   Henry Pearce in residence in 1855: *Kelly's Directory* (1855), and marriage registers. Mrs Bailey selling up: HA. 93M92 C2, p.77 no.546. Last mention of Elizabeth Williams: WSA. 517/22, (entry 7th Jan. 1841). Ownership of Orchard End and estate by Charles Edward Rendall: TNA. MAF 11/180.

9   Detailed report of Dyke v Rendall at the Court of Chancery: *The Times*, 28th Jul. 1852, p.6, issue 21179.

10 Biographical information of Pearce's from Census Returns and marriage registers; notice of his marriage to Ellen Adlard: The Morning Chronicle, 28th Apr. 1856, issue 27875. Henry Pearce farmer at Bulford in 1865: *J. G. Harrod and Co's Post and Commercial Directory* (1865). 1871 sale of Orchard End and its farm by Charles Edward Rendall, and details of the subsequent changes in ownership recorded on the deed papers: T/Sol Army Deeds: Wilts no.54.

11 Land exchange: TNA. MAF 11/180. 'Nag's. Head' 1748 lease and plans for new barn: WSA. 402/90. Sale of 'Nag's Head' farming stock: HA 93M92 C2, p.77 (no.546). Cob wall: Stevenson, 2003, 156. Description of Orchard End: Hamilton, 1911, 121.

12 Davis, 1801, 18, 22. Eighteenth century farms and Richard Duke's directive: Stevenson, 2003, 166.

13 John Grist's will: WSA. P2/G/1076. Jane Castleman on parish rate list from 1801-1829, but absent from Nov. 1841: WSA. 517/22. John Gast and 41, 43 High Street: English Heritage Listed Buildings Register (ID: 321403).

7 The Agricultural Heartbeat of Village Life

Sources for Chapter: It is a particular challenge to portray the agricultural life of the village from Bulford specific sources because everyday life leaves little evidence. The approach of this chapter has been to provide an overall picture from wider sources as a frame of reference for any evidence that there is from the village. J.

H. Bettey's *Rural Life in Wessex 1500-1900* (1987) is a modern scholarly general survey which underpins much of this chapter. A contemporary to the early years of the century, Thomas Davis, was steward to the Marquis of Bath; he wrote *A Report on the State of Agriculture in the County of Wilts* 1794 which was revised by his son and published in 1811 by the Board of Agriculture. He says in the introduction (p.xi) that the work is 'the result not only of an actual survey of the county by his late father ... but by an attention to the practice and opinions of the most intelligent farmers in it, during long and extensive intercourse with them'. This work has been drawn on heavily and page references are given. Turning to village sources, there is a series of leases for the various farms which have been referred to a great deal:

1801 (WSA. 1126/18), Henry Seymour/Matthew Devenish for Watergate Farm
1841 (WSA. 814/16), Henry Seymour/Francis Stephen Long for Watergate Farm
1881 (WSA. 2963/10/c), Anthony Southby/James Hooper lease of Upper Farm
1885 (WSA. 2963/10/d), Edmund Southby/James Hooper lease of Lower Farm
1895 (WSA. 2963/10/g), James Ledger Hill/James Hooper joint lease for Upper and Lower Farms
1897 (WSA. 2963/10/h), Secretary of State for War/James Hooper lease Upper and Lower Farms (tender)

There are also two farm inventories and valuations:
1820 (WSA. 529/154), Thomas Croome's probate inventory for Lower Farm
1872 (WSA. 814/17), inventory for Watergate Farm when Francis Stephen Long sold to George Melsome

1. The climatic details in this and the following paragraphs, unless otherwise referenced, from Fagan, 2000, 113, 150. William Cobbett's observations: Cobbett, 2001, 280, 282.
2. Climatic information: Fagan, 2000, 169, 171-172, 178, 196. 'Exceedingly hot day': Cobbett, 2001, 301. Cold temperatures and snowstorm blocking roads in 1881: WSA. F8/500/6/3/1, (entries 10th, 18th and 21st Jan. 1881). Agricultural depression hitting wheat prices, especially in Dorset and Wiltshire: Bettey, 1987, 37, 38.
3. Paragraph based on Davis, 1811, 69, 126. In 1876 there were 344 acres of wheat, 315 acres of barley, 197 acres of oats and 6 acres of rye: TNA. MAF 68/493, sheet 9. 'Making all necessary reparation and amendments whatsoever' from 1801 lease of Watergate Farm: WSA. 1126/18.
4. Quotes about 500 ewes per tenantry acre, timings of sheep coming to and from the water meadows, and summer fields sown with ray grass from Davis, 1811, 68, 77, 127. Hurdles at Watergate Farm in 1872 inventory: WSA. 814/17. John Claridge's *Report of Agriculture of Dorset*, 1793 quoted in Bettey, 1987, 12-13. Although a report for Dorset, it is equally applicable to the chalklands of Wiltshire, especially as there were links between the two farming communities,

e.g. Matthew Devenish was a Dorset man. Sheep still being penned at night on any newly ploughed, or recently sown arable to improve fertility in summer months: Bettey, 1987, 28. Quotes from eighteenth century poet: Thomson, 1865, 160. James Thomson (1700-1748) was a Scottish poet from the Borders who moved to South England. He is famous for writing four long poems, (one for each season) totalling 5,500 lines between 1720 and 1726 (and the words of 'Rule Britannia'). They are fine nature poems describing every aspect of the countryside during the changing seasons. George Peck's Chapel absences: WSA. 2770/2.

5 My conversation with the inhabitants of the Pennings cottages in Bulford Camp in 1979 confirms that they were sheltered from the worst of the weather. Sale of wethers in 1820: WSA. 529/154. William Cobbett's observation: Cobbett, 2001, 277. 1801 lease: WSA. 1126/18. Cost of work on the Hams: WSA. 367/17.

6 Details for Watergate Farm are taken from 1820 map (WSA. 135/37L), the 1838 tithe apportionment: (TNA. IR 29/38/49), and Seymour/Devenish 1801 lease (WSA. 1126/18). Water meadows on Upper Farm, but not on Lower Farm from 1880 map of the farms: WSA. 2963/10/a. Andover Fair frequented by Thomas Croome: WSA. 529/154.

7 Estimate for sheep numbers and flock composition in 1820 and 1838 from WSA. 529/154 and TNA. IR 29/38/49. Details of flocks from leases of 1883 and 1895: WSA. 2963/10/c, and 2963/10/g. Figures for sheep on downs taken from Ministry of Agriculture Returns (1867, 1886, 1896, 1906): TNA. MAF 68/151, 68/1063, 68/1633, 68/2203, sheets 8, 9, 9, 8 respectively.

8 Description of terrain: Davis, 1811, 67. Arable statistics gathered from the 1838 Tithe Apportionment: TNA. IR 29/38/49. The 1867 proportions of arable land: TNA. MAF 68/151, sheet 8. Advertisement for labourer to drive steam threshing machine: S&WJ, 9th Mar. 1878. General decline of water meadows at the end of the century from Bettey, 1987, 29. Water Rights Rent: WSA. 2963/10/f. Advertisement for labourer with knowledge of water meadows: *Western Gazette*, 25th Sep. 1896, p.4. Quote about the state of the irrigation systems: Sawyer, 1987, 18.

9 Details of Watergate Farm taken and quoted from the 1801 and 1841 Seymour leases: WSA. 1126/18 and 814/16. Thomas Davis's description of two year rotation of the 'Hookland' and the crops grown there in Davis, 1811, 59, 70. Ministry of Agriculture Returns (1867, 1876, 1886, 896): TNA. MAF 68/151, 68/493, 68/1063, 68/1633, sheets 8, 9, 9, 9 respectively.

10 General description from Davis, 1811, 58-60, 66. Details for Watergate Farm from 1801 lease (WSA. 1126/18) and those for Lower Farm from 1820 inventory (WSA. 529/154). The provisions of 1895 lease of Upper and Lower Farms: WSA. 2963/10/g. Directory quote: *Post Office Directory* (1867).

11 General description from Davis, 1811, 50, 69-70. Watergate Farm details from 1801 and 1841 Seymour leases: WSA. 1126/18 and 814/16. Lower Farm not being 'burnbeaked' during the Napoleonic Wars: Stevenson, 2003, 167.

12 The details of this paragraph are taken exclusively from the 1872 inventory and valuation of Watergate Farm with the change of leaseholder: WSA. 814/17. Valuation of Upper Farm in a note and letter 16th Sep. 1893: WSA. 2963/10/f.
13 Field names from 1820 map: WSA. 135/37L. Quotations and details of sainfoin agriculture are taken from the contemporary source: Loudon, 1826, 811. Details are taken from the 1872 inventory (WSA. 814/17) and the 1841 lease (WSA. 814/16). Stipulations about sainfoin on Upper and Lower Farms in WSA. 2963/10/g, and the acreage of sainfoin on Upper Farm in Sept. 1893 from WSA. 2963/10/f.
14 Source for this paragraph is from the *Agricultural Gazette*: Anon., 1918, 36. Quote about best farmers getting land clean ploughed before Midsummer from Davis, 1811, 50.
15 Location of reading beds: Geological Survey of England and Wales, Devizes (Marlborough) sheet 266, (Drift) sheet 282. Description of farming the strong red or 'wood sour' land: Davis, 1811, 50, 111-112. Location of field barn is from the 1820 map: WSA. 135/37L. Sainfoin fields: WSA. 814/17.
16 Details drawn from farm inventories for Lower Farm in 1820 and Watergate Farm in 1872: WSA. 529/154 and 814/17. 1835 hiring of seed drill from Amesbury: *The Times*, 11th Mar. 1835, p.7, issue 15735, col.B. Diagram for horse drawn machine to hoe five rows in the Museum of English Rural Life, TR REE/D01/23.
17 Jefferies description: Jefferies, 1992, 49. See inventories (as above), and 1841 lease: WSA. 814/16. Insured machinery with the Liverpool & London & Globe Insurance, policy nos. 112,305, and 8,751,426: WSA. 2963/10/e, and 2963/10/j.
18 Field barns: WSA. 135/37L and 2963/10/h. Details from inventories and 1801 lease as above. Observation of cattle ploughing: *The Northern Echo*, 19th Jun. 1900, issue 9448. Description of the important role of the carter in Jefferies, 1992, 172. Estimate of horses needed to carry corn to market: Davis, 811, 133. Sale of 'Nag's Head' cart horses: HA. 93M92 C2. Statistics of horses from 1876 onwards: TNA. MAF 68/493, 68/1063, 68/1633, 8/2203, sheets 9, 9, 9, 8 respectively. Robert Lake, blacksmith and shopkeeper: see Chapter 1. Location of Smithy: OS Map (1899), sheet LIV, 12. William Toomer blacksmith and farrier: *Pigot's Commercial Directory* (1830). His paying church rate (WSA. 517/22) and the location of property in 1880, owned then by Mrs Toomer (WSA. 2963/10/a).
19 The data on sheep and the quotations unless otherwise acknowledged: Davis, 1811, 141-148. Details of Thomas Croome's transactions: WSA. 529/154.
20 Estimate of the number of sheep: Stevenson, 2003, 167. Allan G. Young's choice of sheep: Anon., 1918, 36.
21 Quotes about milch cows being driven out by "fine sheep" and the effect of the Napoleonic War on the value of dairy produce: Davis, 1811, 136, 154. Watergate Farm details: TNA. IR 18/1093 and WSA. 1126/18, 814/17, 135/37 L. Sixty strong herd and keeping accounts: Anon., 1918, 38. Statistics for cows between 1867 and 1916: TNA. MAF 68/151, 68/493, 68/1063, 68/1633, 68/2203, 68/2773,

sheets 8, 9, 9, 9, 8, 14 respectively; poultry in 1886: TNA. MAF 68/1063, sheet 9. Church restoration: WSA. 517/23.
22 Manor Farm rookery: *Old Hawking Club Journal*, vol.1 1872 – 1892, (entry 28th Apr. 1876). List of necessary implements made from wood: Davis, 1811, 86-87. Henry Seymour's 1801 conditions: WSA. 1126/18. The old drowner's lament: Sawyer, 1987, 20.
23 1767 Manor bailiff's accounts: WSA. 367/17. Lady Pollen's stipulations about timber resources: WSA. 2216/62; and her reluctance to cut back the trees darkening the Church: WSA. 517/22, (entry 6th Jul. 1830). Amazing spirit of tree planting, and want of wood on plain: Davis, 1811, 85, 91. Trees planted at the Manor in 1812: BRO. D/ELV E133; tree planting between 1820 and 1838 and in c1877: Stevenson, 2003, 168; tree planting at the Pennings and at the corner of Milston Road: OS Map (1887), 1901 edition, Wiltshire LIV; copses being created on Bulford Fields: WSA. 2963/10/g. Planting in the 1960s is my recollection. Orchard End orchard and a 'mass of pink blossom': TNA. MAF 11/180, and Hamilton, 1911, 121. Smoking out the 'latent foe': Thomson, 1865, 9.
24 Stewards at the manor in 1824: WSA. 2216/62. The national picture of farm management in Thompson, F. M. L., 1969, 177-178, 183. Richard Cox as bailiff: WSA. 367/17.
25 The role of the agent in drawing up the 1881 lease: WSA. 2963/10/c. Frederick Charles Ellen keeping the Manor rent accounts, and being instructed to sell the Manor: HA. 93M92/A1, and WHM. cuttings file 16, 23. Letter from Elias Squarey (Downton Land Agent) to the War Department and the Trustees of Miss Seymour: WSA. 212A/27/44/3, (24th Feb. 1897). Money for developing Watergate Farm in letter from Ernest Rawlence to War Department: WSA. 212A/27/44/3, (1st Mar. 1879). Firm of Rawlence and Squarey: Bettey, 1987, 37.
26 Parish 'exclusively agricultural': TNA. ED 103/117, p.377. Closing quotation: Sawyer, Prudence (see Appendix 2a).

8 Church and Chapel

1 Tithes in 1838: Sandell, 1975, 27, and TNA. IR 18/10931.
2 Clergy list: Rhys-Hughes, 1972, 36, (see Appendix 4a). Details of clergy taken from Census Returns and Diocesan Records: WSA. D/1/8/1/1 – 3, D/1/2/32, and HA. 21M65 A2/4 and E1/1. Rev. Richard Webb at Milston: Stevenson, 1995, 142. The 1851 Census shows James Watt Ellerby and his family staying in Amesbury with Joseph Olding, a master miller. When Joseph Olding died a few years later, his widow Ellen (née Godwin) then married the Independent Pastor of Bulford, John Protheroe. James Ellaby as 'Incumbent': *Oxford Journal*, 16th Jan. 1847, issue 4890. Vestry attendances: WSA. 517/22. The 1650 Parliamentary Survey: *WAM*, vol.40, 258.

3   Rev. Darnton Millner as incumbent in Visitation Query Return (1864): WSA. D1/56/7, and Clergy list: Rhys-Hughes, 1972, 36, (see Appendix 4a). Stipend: *Post Office Directory* (1855); residence in village: Census (1861), *S&WJ*, 3rd May 1853; appointment of Churchwarden: WSA. 517/22; failure to meet the 275 days' residence prescribed by law: WSA. D1/56/8; admonition from his Bishop: WSA. 814/31. Amesbury Rural Deanery meetings: WSA. D1/21/5/2/1/1. Cover for Rev. Millner's absence noted on Census map (WSA. 2916/24), and in the Visitation Query Return (1867): WSA. D1/56/8. Journeymen pastors: Cobbett, 2001, 308.
4   Visitation Query Returns : Ransome, 1972, 48-49.
5   Cobbett, 2001, 289. Rural Dean's inspection and subsequent actions: WSA. 517/22.
6   Further repairs to Church: WSA. D1/65/7. Minutes of Rural Deanery discussions: WSA. D1/21/5/2/1/2, p.105-107.
7   1783 observation: Ransome, 1972, 48-49; the background to Dissent is taken from Notes on the rise of Nonconformity in Wiltshire in: Rhys-Hughes, 1972, 18. The Chapel Church Book account quoted: WSA. 2770/2. 1805 registration for Dissenting worship: WSA. D1/2/2, 60, (no.626). Mr Rose's income: WSA. 367/17. The site of old chapel marked on army deeds: T/Sol 2852/50. The second registration by Samuel Mould: WSA. D1/2/29, 61, (no.633). It is conceivable that this was the same house as four months earlier and the new registration was necessary through a change of ownership. This is unlikely with the more probable explanation being the growth of the congregation as indicated by the further quote from the Chapel Church Book referenced above.
8   Second registration: WSA. D2/2/28.
9   James Blatch: TNA. TNA 11/1526. Henry Blatch's death and his widow taking on the farm and founding the Durrington Chapel: Anon., 1838, 598. Henry Blatch and the Ratfyn lease: HA. 34M91W/209; Henry's retirement to Durrington and his death: Census Returns and WSA. 1418/10.
10 Devenish family's arrival in Bulford: Anon., 1838, and WSA. 1126/18. Biographical details from census returns and the chapel baptism registers: WHM. nonconformist registers, box 1. The brewing interests of the next generation: DHC D/PRS/F 6. Brewing as an occupation for gentlemen: Thompson, F. M. L., 1969, 131. The Devenish Brewery on Brewer's Key, Weymouth, was in business until it closed in the 1980s.
11 'Two like-minded families' quoted from Anon., 1838, 598. The Devenish's eldest child Elizabeth was born in 1798 which would put the link with the Blatches, through the Aldridge connection, back to at least 1797. The close link endured into the next generation when we find members of both families uniting in 1838 to set up a bond with a Dorchester gentleman: DHC D/PRS/F 6. The 2nd Mar. 1875 letter from Matthew Devenish junior J.P. is transcribed in the Chapel Church Book: WSA. 2770/2.
12 History of the site is taken from the Chapel leases: WSA. 2770/12. William

Andrews was certainly related to the John Andrews who was in occupation of seventy three acres of farmland in the village at the time: WSA. 402/90. Quote about building the first Chapel: WSA. 2770/12.

13. James Aldridge's association with East Wellow: HA. 102M71/T55 and 4M92 PC2. He was Mayor of Romsey in 1813, 1820, 1828 and in 1831 (with Josiah George): Romseynet.org.uk. Hunting incident: S&WJ, 30th Nov. 1813. The evidence of Sir Isaac Pickering's association with Bulford is found in 1812 accounts of Sir Edward Loveden: BRO. D/ELV E135 and D/ELV E133. Regularisation of Chapel Deeds in 1847: WSA. 2770/12. 'Paedo Baptists' are a wing of the Baptist movement practising child baptism.

14. Chapel's opening and early influence: WSA. 2770/2. Need to rebuild Chapel: Anon., 1838, 598. Financing of rebuilt Chapel in Matthew Devenish's 1875 letter (see note 11 above) and the public subscription: WSA. D1/21/5/2/1/2, 107, (entry Apr. 1874).

15. Site of house given by Devenish family and building of Manse: WSA. 2770/2. The 1851 census map marks the Manse built by the Blatches as having been built since the last census. The script of the comment looks to be in the style of the original notation making it before the 1851 Census (WSA. 2916/24), on the other hand the letter 'B' in line with the later interpolation of the Rev Protheroe would perhaps indicate it was built a decade later. On balance I go for the earlier date, especially as the drawing of the two buildings concerned shows no signs of being added at a later date. For further discussion see Chapter 1, note 2. Sale of New Manse and purchase of old school: Beale, 1986, 14, and Rhys-Hughes, 1972, 17. Description of new Manse taken from the 1874 Sturgess quotes for decoration and other works: WSA. 1418/10. Site of prefabricated Manse after the sale of New Manse: T/Sol. Wilts no.56. The Report of the County Union (1876) is transcribed and interpolated in Chapel Church Book: WSA. 2770/2.

16. Chapel Accounts, 1870: WSA. 1418/10. There is no date on this set of accounts but contextual evidence of the consequence of the deaths must date it to this time, or shortly afterwards.

17. Covenant: Beale, 1986, 2. I have correlated the 1848 Chapel attendance list in the Chapel Church Book (WSA. 2770/2) with the Census Returns three years later and marriage registers from 1840 to 1851.

18. John Protheroe's acceptance letter, expressions of Sympathy 30th May, marriages and return to Bulford: Chapel Church Book WSA. 2770/2, Beale, 1986, 7-8 and Rhys-Hughes, 1972, 17. Letter to Mr Mann, 23rd Apr. 1875: WSA. 1418/10.

19. Religious upsurge in Chapel Church Book (WSA. 2770/2), and Beale, 1986, 9-10.

20. Official parish reports and statistics in Visitation Query Returns (1864, 1871): WSA. D1/56/7 and 56/10. Chapel Statistics from Chapel Church Book, WSA. 2770/2. Dissenter background in this and the following paragraph, the role of evening services and the 1870 quote from the vicar of Heddington, Calne, are from Notes on the rise of Nonconformity in Wiltshire in Rhys-Hughes, 1972, 18.

21 John Protheroe's Quarterly Reports to the Wilts & East Somerset Congregational Union, (25th Mar. 1884, and 21st May 1880); the appointment of John Pinn, (24th Jun. 1884), witnessed by John Swatton and William Love; and the Bulford Chapel Visitation Report, (18th Dec. 1906) – all these documents used to source this paragraph are found in WSA. 1418/10. The early career of Canadian born priest, Dr Jacob Mountain: *Crockford's Clerical Directory* (1868); his representation of Milston at the Amesbury Deanery Meetings (Nov. 1860 until Oct. 1862): WSA. D1/21/5/2/1/1.

22 I am greatly indebted to Eve Magee for much of the source material on her distant ancestor Jacob Jehoshaphat Salter Mountain in this and succeeding paragraphs. Biographical details of the two Bishops and Jacob Jehoshaphat Salter Mountain: Marston, 1976, and Millman, 1983. Statistics of his family in Holy Orders from Patterson, 1984, 218. Gapper family connections: O'Brien, 1828-1838, (entries for 12th and 15th Jan. 1829, and 8th Apr. 1830).

23 Mother's 'life of influence', one of first graduates of Bishop's College, bequest for Mission Graduate, and funeral arrangements, are all from the Will of Jacob Jehoshaphat Salter Mountain (25th Jun. 1902), transcribed by Eve Magee from a copy in the East Cornwall Museum, Ontario. His attendance of Cornwall Grammar School, his wife being an archdeacon's daughter: Montreal Herald, 12th Nov. 1910. Ecclesiastical career: *Crockford's Clerical Directory* (1868); known as 'Doctor Mountain': WSA. 517/22, (entry 18th Apr. 1870). A Wreath of Rue, for Lent and the Sacred Lake: MacPhee (on-line). Evening classes: WSA. D1 56/10. Nephew's wife's recollections of him going on 'some tour in out-of-the-world places' in Boa, 2009, 98. The links between Cornwall and Thornhill: O'Brien, 1828-1838, (entry for 18th Dec. 1830).

24 Appointment of Rev. Mountain and later his successor: *The Times*, 14th Dec. 1869, p.3, issue 26620 and 12th Apr. 1878, p11, issue 29227. Residence in 1873: WSA. D1/56/10; he was also diligent in attending Amesbury Rural Deanery meetings: WSA. 1554/1-5. In the latter stages of life he owned property in Canada, USA and Isle of Wight: Will of Jacob Jehoshaphat Salter Mountain (see n.23 above). Sunday School attendance in 1870: TNA. ED 103/117, 377. Drink problem in Visitation Queries Return (1876): WSA. D1/56/11. Making elaborate plans: Boa, 2009, 93.

25 Rev. Charles Amfill covering sabbatical, and the activity of 'so called Evangelists' in Visitation Queries Return (1876): WSA. D1/56/11. Letter about Mountain family: Mountain, 1877. Michael Stone's will: HA 5M62/17, M368, p.471. Last attendance of Rural Deanery meeting: WSA. D1/21/5/2/1/2, (meeting Nov. 1877). Details of the history of Jacob Jehoshaphat Salter Mountain's children and second marriage given to me in 2011 by Eve Magee.

26 Biographical details and appointment as Honorary Canon given to me by Eve Magee. Conditional bequest to nephew, the bells, the windows, the Moses likeness and ambitions for Bishopric: Will of Jacob Jehoshaphat Salter Mountain (see n.23 above). Photographs: Boa, 2009, 98, and another, slightly younger,

generously given to me in 2012 by Ann Boa.
27 Partial restoration under Rev. Johnson: WSA. D1/56/12, and *Kelly's Directory* (1895). No faculty to move pews and the attitude of the patron: WSA. 517/22, (entry 1879), and D1/56/2.
28 Value of Dr Mountain's estate from newspaper cutting in the Canadian Archives, CA. 11/37. Liquidation of Wavertree Chapel debts: WSA. 2770/2, (entry for 16 May 1848). Auction of Manse contents: *S&WJ*, 4th Sep. 1852. Orchard End description: Hamilton, 1911, 121.
29 Jenner owning vicarage site under John Maton's occupation: 1838 tithe map. Corner End: WSA. 517/22. Village bricklayers and builders giving services free told to me by Ann Sawyer, who got it from her mother Prudence Sawyer. Sale of Vicarage: Stevenson, 2003, 170.
30 Parish Council Minutes: WSA. 2005/1, p.1, 12, 33. Closure of old graveyard: WSA. 517/23, (entry 1901, p.33).
31 Letting charges: WSA. 2005/1, p.13. Managers' closure of school: WSA. F8/500/44/1/1, (entries 13th Jan. 1898, 3rd and 16th Oct. 1899). Diamond Jubilee celebrations: *S&WJ* Supplement, 26th Jun. 1897 in WHM. cuttings file 12, 339. The Parish deficit: WSA. 517/23, (entry 1901).
32 Alternate church/chapel attendances and the Chapel Church Book resolution: WSA. D1 56/10, and 2770/2, (entry 27th Jul. 1862). Discussion on the hold of Dissent in the village: WSA. D1/21/5/2/1/2, (entry Apr. 1874, p.107). I am indebted to the Rev. Peter Beale for the quotation about John Mundy's burial in the Chapel Burial Register.
33 Samuel Sturges's tenure of clerk's office: Sturgess, 1995, 10. John Kinsman: Poll Book (1833) and WSA. A1 355/1 and 2. Robert Sturgis: WSA. 517/22, (entry 1839). Robert Hedges' career: Census Returns and WSA. A1 355/3. His relationship with the farmer to whom he was in service is deduced from the farmer's son being called Charles Hedges Horrell, no doubt taking his mother's maiden name as his middle name; his retirement: WSA. 517/23, (entry for 25th Apr. 1889).

9 Bulford Mill and its Papermakers

1 Sawyer, Prudence. (see Appendix 2a).
2 Suitability of Avon for papermaking and sale of Upwey Mill: *S&WJ*, 20th Sep. and 6th Sep. 1790. The water wheel at Watergate Farm is marked on the sketch map of the village and its inhabitants drawn up with information from local postmen in the 1940s (see Chapter 4, note 20). The weir for the wheel is still visible in the leat (2012).
3 The early history of Bulford Paper Mill as evidenced through insurance records: Shorter, 1959, 245. The death of William Mould and the settlement of his estate: *S&WJ*, 7th Nov. 1785. Advertisement for Bulford Mill and dwelling house:

S&WJ, 8th Mar. 1786.
4   Brodribb insured as master papermaker: Shorter, 1959, 245. Noyes' bankruptcy: *The Times*, 24th Mar. 1817, p.2, Issue 10103, col. B. Brodribb's bankruptcy: London Gazette, 24th Jul. 1790, referenced in Shorter, 1959, 245.
5   Leasing property in Bristol: Bristol Record Office 6609/56, 23rd Nov. 1789. Abraham Brodribb as 'clothier': *Boddely's Bath Journal*, 20th Apr. 1771. 1790 letting Bulford Paper Mill and dwelling house: S&WJ, 20th Sep. 1790. Lawrence Greatrake insuring utensils and warehouse: Sun Fire Insurance Policy No. 523473, 26th Oct. 1786. Described as papermaker of Bulford: Archives of Stationers' and Newspaper Makers' Co., London. MS list in notebook of Richard Johnson, Stationer – both referenced in: Shorter, 1959, 245-246.
6   Lawrence Greatrake's Bristol Connection, and death in 1817: *American Watchman and Delaware Republican*, 4th Jun. 1817, vol.9, no.707. Apsley Mill and meeting Thomas Gilpin: Ward, 1998. Voyage to America: Leslie, 1860, 2, 9, 13. Settling in Wilmington and managing Brandywine Paper Mill: Hancock and Wilkinson, 1956, 391, 396.
7   Working for Richardson and Harrison, and being sent to England by Thomas Gilpin: Hancock and Wilkinson, 1956, 397-398. Devoting whole time, thoughts and attention to the promotion of useful and valuable manufactories: *American Watchman and Delaware Republican*, 20th Jun. 1813, vol.5, no.448. Drawings of cylinder papermaking machine when working for John Dickinson, who described him as 'one of his most reliable and trusted employees': Sellers, 1947, 124. Wilkinson was bitter and of the opinion that the Gilpins had bought Lawrence Greatrake in order to copy his invention.
8   Lawrence Greatrake's political views: *American Watchman and Delaware Republican*, 20th Jun. 1813, vol.5, no.448. Thomas Mould registering Paper Mill for Dissenting worship: WSA. D1/2/29, p.61, (no.633).
9   Analysis of Census Returns (1841-1871). John Sawyer joint proprietor with his nephew Thomas Godwin: Post Office Directory (1867).
10 Census Returns for biographical details, and I am grateful to Janine Hyatt for sharing information about her ancestors with me in 2011: (see Appendix 1e). Joseph Mould and the Carey Paper Mill: Shorter, 1959, 245. There was a Hyatt who farmed at Stourhead whose wife was a member of the Huguenot Faugoin family: *WAM* no.73, vol. 25 (1890), p.113, note 1. It is fascinating to think that this could have been the introduction of papermaking into the family, and although William was born in Suffolk, that may well not have been his ancestral home.
11 Isaac Brodribb described as 'master papermaker': Shorter, 1959, 245. John Sawyer's Copy book is still in the possession of Sawyer family, and shown to me in 1978 and 2011 by Prudence and Ann Sawyer (see Plate 32).
12 For the Godwin family's and other papermakers' involvement in the Chapel: WSA. 2770/2 and 2770/5-6. Statement that 'the Greatrakes were Quakers': Wallace, 2005, 226. Thomas Greatrake worked for the Gilpins who were a

Quaker family: Hancock and Wilkinson, 1956, 391. Lawrence Greatrake's daughter Eliza described as 'a Quakeress – not an ordinary Quaker girl, but a strange, unctuous creature, . . . given to awesome silences and sudden ejaculations of a religious character': Coleman, 1947, 286. Benjamin Godwin at Alton: www3.hants.gov.uk/curtis-museum/alton-history/alton-paper-mill.htm. Samuel Godwin as 'millwright' and as 'clothier': Prosser, R. B., 1893, List of Wilts Patentees, *WN&Q*, vol.1, 65. Advantage for clothiers to manage mill: Ramsey, 1965, 18-19; clothier's association with fulling and cloth described as being 'made at the mill': Carus-Wilson, 1959, 143-145.

13 Lucy Sturgess: *S&WJ*, 5th Apr. 1790. Henry Brodribb at Limpley Stoke: Rogers, 1976, 165-166. Advertisement for sale of Bulford Mill where Isaac Brodribb describes himself as 'clothier' from Shepton Mallet: *S&WJ*, 20th Sep. 1790. William Hyatt at Shepton Mallet: Rogers. 1976, 178.

14 Activities of Huguenot émigrés around Andover discussed in Hewitt, 1973, 489-490. Biographical information about John Sawyer given to me in 1978 and 2011 by Prudence and Ann Sawyer respectively, and in: Vine, 1984, 18. Partnership with Thomas Godwin: Post Office Directory (1867).

15 1807 survey of lands owned by St Mary's College, Winchester: HA. 11M59/E2/59594. 1841 Durrington Tithe Commutation: HA. 11M59/E2/415994. The 1838 Tithe Commutation: TNA. IR 29/38/49. Parish rate: WSA. 517/22, (entries 1828, 1834). Thomas Croome's rent payable to the Manor and probate accounts: WSA. 529/154.

16 Mrs Godwin as 'papermaker': *Harrod's Directory* (1865). Ellen Godwin, who was the both wife and the sister of papermakers, was described as a 'paper layer' in the Census (1861).

17 Font cover carved by Anthony Southby: papers in WSA. by Canon Ruddle of Durrington (I have lost the reference). The Arts and Crafts Movement had political associations with the Whigs, whereas Anthony Southby was a Tory. In Upper Canada the High Tory leadership, in which his brother-in-law Edward O'Brien played a prominent part, stood against the radical Makenzie Rebellion in 1837. In the political unrest leading up to it, Anthony Southby (then called Gapper) wanted to sort things out and was tempted in 1829 to stand for a seat in the Canadian Parliament. He was unable to do so as he owned no land: Miller, 1968, 32, (entry 25th Jan. 1829). His insistence that things in the church remained 'as they were a century ago': WSA. 517/22, (entry 1879). Etchings and weathervane: Miller, 1968, 37, 46, 49. Anthony Southby's patent, no.2135: London Gazette, 14th Sep. 1860. The history of Joseph Hobday prior to coming to Bulford is in Wakeman, 1999, 4. In 1855 he was described as a 'papermaker' in a supplementary abstract of title agreement at Bidford: Shakespeare Centre Library and Archives ER4/874; for his details in Bulford: Census Return (1871).

18 The details of the handmade papermaking process in this paragraph are from Stewart, 1969, 38-40. 'Limekilns': Sawyer, Prudence (Appendix 2b). 1789 advertisement: *S&WJ*, 23rd Nov. 1789. Description 'coarser kinds of paper'

in Lewis, 1848, and the mention of 'blottings, filtering and small hands' is in Shorter, 1959, 246. Details of rag store over the cart shed told to me in 1978 by Prudence Sawyer. Earnings of papermakers: Hewitt, 1973, 489-490.

19   The 1833 map has lots marked on it in preparation for an auction at the George Inn, Amesbury, on 24th April: WSA. 402/16. Durrington Tithe map: (WSA. TA Durrington). Information about child drowning told to me by Prudence Sawyer in 1978.

20   The Paper Mill was still operating in 1871: Census Return (1871); it is mentioned a year later: Mercer and Crocker's Directory (1872); but it is not mentioned in 1875: *Kelly's Directory* (1875). Deddington Paper Mill: Wakeman, 1999, 4. The dissolution of his business partnership with William Stanway: *London Gazette*, 16th Aug. 1870. Diversification of raw materials: Stewart, 1969, 86. Sale of the Manor and the subsequent purchase of Mill House: T/Sol 432/51, Wilts no.26 and 222. The excavation of lake for practising river crossings was told to me in 1978 by Prudence Sawyer. Rhys-Hughes states that the Mill was dismantled in 1880. He does not produce any evidence for this statement, but considering his association with Prudence Sawyer, she was probably the source: Rhys-Hughes, 1972, 17.

10 Education and Social Mobility

1   Allan Young's view: Anon., 1918, 38. William Parsons' description in Rose's Gammar School Log Book: WSA. F8/500/6/3/1, (entry 1st Oct. 1895), and in Volpi, 2011, 31. Eighteenth century apprenticeships: Dale, 1961, 117, 126, no.1825, 1957. James Chalk's apprentice: *The Examiner*, 29th Jul. 1810, issue 135.

2   1870 report about 'the present school': TNA. ED 103/117, p.377. Richard Duke's will transcribed in *Return of Endowed Charities, County of Wiltshire*, vol.2 Southern Divison: TNA. IR 29/38/49, p.81. Position under Miss Southby in 1833: ibid. Attendance statistics from *Education of Poor Digest* (1818), and *Education in England Abstract* (1833); both are quoted in Stevenson, 2003, 174. The quote about only the 'better off' affording to send their children to school told to me in 1978 by Prudence Sawyer.

3   Vestry resolutions: WSA. 517/22, (entries 22nd Aug. 1829, 6th Jul. 1830). Purchase of deeds from Anthony Southby: TNA. ED 103/117, p.377. Day school children attending minor festivals and the patron not brooking any interference in the running of his school: WSA. D1/56/7. 1858 quote about the school: *Warburton Census of Wiltshire Schools* (1859), 11, no.242. Endowment and house for mistress: *Post Office Directory* (1859).

4   Situation of the old school (WSA. 2916/24) and the description of it were told to me by 'Old' Farmer Hann in 1978. Independent Chapel Free School in a schoolroom adjoining the Chapel: *Warburton Census of Wiltshire Schools*

(1859), no.242, p.11. Biographical information from Census Returns and Chapel Church Book: WSA. 2770/2.
5   Rev. Millner's report in Returns to Visitation Queries (1864): WSA. D1/56/7.
6   Attendance of Rose's Grammar School: WSA. F8/500/6/3/1, (entries 14th Oct. 1881, 29th Dec. 1884), and Volpi, 2011, 7, 11. Chalk tuition bond: WSA. P1/1811/71. Chalk's suicide: *The Examiner*, 29th Jul. 1810, issue 135. Thomas Croome's will: WSA. 529/154. Licensing of Bulford Mill as a place of Independent worship: WSA. D/2/2/28. Matthew Devenish's will: TNA. TNAB 11/1526.
7   Flowers that never fade, by Lucy Leman Rede: WSA. 563/2.
8   Information in this paragraph from Census Returns, *J. G. Harrod's Directory* (1865) and *Post Office Directory* (1867). Details of David Sturgess: Sturgess, 1995, 3 (in draft).
9   Closure of Dissenting School and transfer of children to Parish School: TNA. ED 103/117, 377. Chapel school accounts, the dating of which has been deduced from the fact that there are two columns of expenditure, one being the amount provided by Miss Butler before her death which occurred in 1870: WSA. 1418/10. Information on Blatch siblings: Census Returns, and Chapel Church Book, WSA. 2770/2. Rev. Mountain's report in Returns to Visitation Queries (1876): WSA. D1/56/11. Final quote from the introduction of The Elementary Education Act (1870).
10 Chapel's reading classes: WSA. 2770/5. Evening classes run by the Rev. Milner in 1864, and the Rev. Mountain in Returns to Visitation Queries: WSA. D1/56/7, and D1/56/10.
11 Amesbury Rural Deanery discussions on the failure of public education and the effects of overcrowding: WSA. D1/21/5/2/1/1, (minute 2nd Oct. 1861). Observation from Amesbury in Rose's Grammar School log book: WSA. F8/500/6/3/1, (entry 12th Sep. 1898).
12 Sunday School lessons in morning with the teaching of reading in the afternoon: WSA. 2770/6. The Protheroes' marriage celebrations: WSA. 2770/2, (entry 16th Oct. 1856).
13 Beginnings of Chapel Sunday School: Beale, 1986, 6, and WSA. 2770/6. Agricultural cottagers' bias towards Dissent in Jefferies, 1992, 126. Richard Jefferies (1848-1887) was born and brought up on a small farm in Coate, near Swindon. He was a journalist who wrote on country matters inspired by his wanderings extensively around the countryside. He was an acute observer of changes in rural society which makes his work a good source for contextualising changes in Bulford at the same time as he was writing. 'Hodge' was a contemporary nickname for an agricultural worker. Chapel Sunday School prospering: WSA. 2770/2, (entry 1843). Sunday School Registers: (WSA. 2770/5).
14 Details of the running of the Sunday School: WSA. 2770/6. The Todmans' membership of the Chapel: WSA. 2770/2.
15 John Protheroe's 1880 report in Chapel quarterly accounts: WSA. 1418/10, (May 1880). Quarterly accounts of c1870 (see note 9 above): ibid.

16 1870 observations about three quarters of families attending the Church: TNA. ED 103/117, 377. All other data from Returns to Visitation Queries (1873): WSA. D1/56/10.
17 Agricultural Labourers' Union demand: Scarth, 1998, 26. Details of Hannah More: Smith, 2002. Sunday School mission statement: WSA. 2770/6. The Established Church's need for scripture readers, district visitors, and Sunday School teachers; and its reservations: WSA. D1/21/5/2/1/1, (entry 15th May 1862).
18 Quotation from Education Act (1870): Introduction, regulation 1. Proposals for Bulford Parish School: TNA. ED 103/117, p.377. Minutes of Amesbury Rural Deanery meeting: WSA. D1/21/5/2/1/2, (meeting 19th Apr. 1876). Dimension of existing parish school: *Warburton Census of Wiltshire Schools* (1859), 11 (no.242); dimensions of another potential building in document dated 4th Jul. 1873: TNA. ED 21/18340.
19 Dimensions of new school, estimates and architect's subsequent letter of Oct. 1895: TNA. ED 21/18340. Balance sheet for new school drawn up by Parish Treasurer, George Melsome: (ibid). Rev. Mountain's report to his Bishop in Returns to Visitation Queries (1876): WSA. D1/56/11. Sturgess's plans for the new school: WSA. 782/18. Subsequent history of the new school: Beale, 1986, 14.
20 Date of Mary Ann Knight's appointment from the staff list on flyleaf of Log Book: WSA. F8/500/44/1/1. The biographical details of Mary Ann Knight and her family have very generously been shared with me in 2011, along with her portrait, by Margaret Fay, her great great granddaughter.
21 Biography: ibid, and United States Federal Census (1870). Joint patronage of school: *Kelly's Directory* (1874).
22 Francesca's teaching career and the appointment of Annie Rowden: Census Returns, and School Log Book WSA. F8/500/44/1/1. Attendance figures in 1895 and 1906: *Kelly's Directory* (1895), and *Return of non-Provided Schools* (1906), p.20. Knight family details and Mary Ann's retirement and death: Margaret Fay, as above.
23 The surviving School Log Book covers the years 1897-1926 and all the entries and reports in this paragraph are from that source except the one from Rose's Grammar School's Log Book about Mrs Flowers replacing Mrs Knight when she was ill: WSA. F8/500/6/3/1, and in Volpi, 2011, 8. Funding encapsulated in Parliamentary debate: *Hansard, HC Debate*, 19th Jul. 1872, vol.212 ch.1454.
24 Quotes from Richard Jefferies: Jefferies, 1992, 23, 184. Quotes from Log Book: WSA. F8/500/44/1/1, (entries 17th Oct. 1900, 17th Jan. 1898).
25 Log Books of Village School: (ibid), and Rose's Grammar School: WSA. F8/500/6/3/1. Details of her story telling and souvenirs are from Margaret Fay. Her father was Mary Ann's grandson.
26 Standards: *Revised Code of Regulations* (1872). Log Book: WSA. F8/500/44/1/1, (entries 30th Nov. and 2nd Dec. 1897).

27 Aid Grant, organising master, and Inspection Report summary: ibid, (entries 2nd Feb. 1898, and 1900). Quotes from Jefferies, 1992, 179, 184.
28 Quote on attitudes of 'old-fashioned farming people': ibid, 30. 1908 Inspection Report: TNA. ED 21/18340.
29 Two generations to accumulate wealth in Jefferies, 2008, 126. Education to fit people 'for the state of life which it had pleased God to call them': WSA. D1/21/5/2/1/1, (entry 2nd Oct. 1861). Chalk's education: WSA. P1/1811/71.
30 Details of Samuel Sturgess: Sturgess, 1995, 7, 10. For Parish Clerks see Chapter 8.
31 Biographical details from Margaret Fay.
32 Career of William Sturgess: Sturgess, 1995, 8.
33 Jefferies, 2009, xvi.

11 'Right about Turn': the Coming of the Army

1 The whole of this section is based almost exclusively on the evaluation of Census Returns (1851-1901).
2 'Quaint little village': Hamilton, 1911, 123.
3 The story of William Sawyer and Prudence Howse was told to me in 2011 by their daughter Ann Sawyer.
4 Easier transport and agricultural changes fuelling migration in Matthias, 1983, 318.
5 1801 population statistics: Enumeration Abstract. Prediction of marketing opportunities provided by the Camp are those expressed by Sir Henry Malet of Wilbury Park, Newton Tony: S&WJ, 13th Feb. 1897, quoted in James, 1987, 17.
6 Information about the Sturgess families of builders is from: Sturgess, 1995, Appendix 1 and 'The Builder Family'. The family trees from this work are used to draw up Appendix 1f, supplemented by information from Census Returns. Payments to Thomas and William by the Church: WSA. 517/22, Rhys-Hughes, 1972, 53, and Sturgess, 1995, 6.
7 Main sources as above. Chapel estimates: WSA. 1418/10. Southampton firm using Sturgesses for the Vicarage was told to me in 2011 by Ann Sawyer. Sturgesses building Stonehenge Inn: Sturgess, 1995, 12.
8 John Protheroe's observation on villagers 'leaving of late': WSA. 1418/10. Quote from North Wiltshire journalist from Jefferies, 1992, 180.
9 Gun base on Beacon Hill, now a trig point: James, 1987, 91. Report quoted on March Past at Beacon Hill: S&WJ, 14th Sep. 1872, and in James, 1987, 13. Hunting party's comment: WSA. 186/1. State of road over Beacon Hill: WSA. F4/800/5/1.
10 I have relied on N. D. G. James's book, heavily in places, for the history of Bulford, especially Chapters: 2 The New Order, 3 Laying the Foundations, and 8 Bulford – The Curtain Rises. It is the sole source for any War Office documents that I have quoted. The need for military training areas and the choice of

Salisbury Plain: James, 1987, 14-15, 17. Encampment of 4th Cavalry Brigade at Bulford, and Salisbury to Marlborough road articles: S&WJ, 10th Jul. and 14 Aug 1897. For details of the purchase of land at Bulford: see Chapters 4 and 5 above. Low afternoon attendance at village school: WSA. F8/500/44/1/1, (entry 6th Jul. 1897). The problem of rabbit holes and the extension of the railway line to Amesbury: Minutes of the Proceedings of the War Office Salisbury Plain Committee, 1897-1902, Jun. 1897, p.13, (minute 6), and p.17, (minute 25), both quoted in: James, 1987, 23. Issue of rabbits addressed in the 1885 and 1897 leases, and its revision in 1900: WSA. 2963/10/g and 2963/10/h. Water problems with the sinking of wells and pumping water from the Avon: *The Times*, 29th Jan. 1898, p.10, issue 35581, and 25th Aug. 1898, p.4, issue 35604; and 15th Jul. 1899, p.15, issue 35882.

11 Timing of manoeuvres: Grayer, 2011, 8. Details of the 1898 Autumn Manoeuvres, and quotes from Graham, 1908, 43-44, 46-50. Viewing enclosure for M.P.s: Hansard, HC Debate, 11th Aug. 1898, vol.64, cc.926-7. Trains laid on for spectators: Grayer, 2011, 13. Details from Log Book of Rose's Grammar School, Amesbury: WSA. F8/500/6/3/1, (entries 29th Jul. and 12th Oct. 1898).

12 Appointment of Rev. North to officiate to the troops, along with clergy from other denominations, but not connected with Bulford: *The Times*, 22nd Jul. 1897, p.7, issue 35262. Letter to newspaper: *Andover Advertiser*, 15th Jul. 1898, and WHM. cuttings file 12, 205. Visit of Field Marshall: Graham, 1908, 160. Miss Perk's Soldiers Home: Grayer, 2011, 77.

13 Life in tented encampment: Hamilton, 1911, 124-125, 129. Extension of the area of permanent grass: *Minutes of the Proceedings of the War Office Salisbury Plain Committee, 1897-1902*, 4th Aug. 1899, p.111, (minute 414), quoted in James, 1987, 22. Quote from letter to James Hooper: WSA. 2963/10/i.

14 The importance of practising river crossing in face of opposition, and opposition of the War Office to building a railway down the Avon Valley: *Minutes of the Proceedings of the War Office Salisbury Plain Committee, 1897-1902*, 1897 p.15, (minute 24), quoted in James, 1987, 25. Proposed route of railway: Grayling, 2011, 9-11. Autumn Manoeuvres 1900 cavalry action: Graham, 1908, 123.

15 Parish Council minutes: WSA. 2005/1, (meeting 16th Feb. 1898). Holiday for the relief of Mafeking and Queen's birthday: WSA. F8/500/44/1/1, (entry 24th May 1900). Construction of rifle ranges and decision to extend railway line to Bulford: James, 1987, 25, 99. Troops marching from Ludgershall: *The Times*, Aug. 1899, quoted in Grayling, 2011, 13.

16 This paragraph is taken from: Grayling, 2011, 16-17, 21, 39, 43. The opposition at the Enquiry and discussion about the bridleway: *Report of Light Railway Company to the Board of Trade*, 15th Jul. 1902, and report in *Salisbury and Wilton Times and South Wilts Gazette*, 18th Jul. 1902. Both in: TNA. MT 6/1159/9.

17 Traction engine damage to bridge: WCC Sol/Clerk Roads and Bridges Minutes 1902 m.80. Details and statistics of camp construction: WHM. cuttings file 3, 120. Death of William Henry Tucker Hill in the siege of Ladysmith: http://

glosters.tripod.com/BoerH.htm.
18 Mushrooming of population and analysis of occupations: Census Returns (1891, 1901). Stories of navvies recuperating after drinking and the pitched battle with bayonets outside the 'Rose and Crown' were told to me in 1978 by 'Old' Farmer Hann. The murder after a drinking bout: *The Times*, 29th Oct. 1898, p.12, issue 35560.
19 Details about Allen G. Young: Anon., 1918, 36-38.
20 Number of tenants farming the land and agricultural statistics: TNA. MAF 68/1063, 68/1633, 68/2203, 68/2773, sheets 9, 9, 8 and 14 respectively. Long service awards: Bristol Mercury and Daily Post, 29th Nov. 1878, issue 9529, and 26th Nov. 1880, issue 10151.
21 Report on the storm: WHM. cuttings file 7, 370; its effect on village school: WSA. F8/500/44/1/1, (entry 27th Jul. 1900).
22 School children absent on errands: WSA. F8/500/44/1/1, (entry 24th May 1900). Fanny Vallis's wedding: marriage registers.
23 The coming of trains changing the village, and the closing quotation: Sawyer, Prudence (Appendices 2a, 2b). Description of vicinity on the eve of the First World War: Noyes, 1913, viii.

Bibliography

Primary Sources

Mary Gapper O'Brien. A series of letters sent home to England from Ontario by Mary O'Brien (née Gapper), which together form a journal, has been drawn upon extensively in this book as a primary source about her brother Anthony. The letters were deposited in the Ontario Archives by her granddaughter, Kathleen O'Brien. Two typed transcripts were made of the journals, the first of which she personally supervised and gave to Audrey Saunders Miller in 1943. The journals contain some three hundred thousand words which Audrey Saunders Miller abridged and edited, publishing it along with an introduction, drawing on Mary O'Brien's family history, told her by her descendants, along with a family tree and notes. I have quoted from this work whenever the material I wanted is contained within it. A second copy transcribed by Helen McClung is now in the Ontario Archives. I have access to this full and unabridged text and have quoted from it where I have used any material that is not in Audrey Saunders Miller's book. The two copies are noted in the bibliography below as: Miller, Audrey Sanders. (ed.) 1968. *The Journals of Mary O'Brien 1828-1838*.

Toronto: Macmillan (from which the information for this paragraph is taken); and O'Brien, Mary. 1828-1838. Journals, (transcribed by McClung, Helen). Ontario Archives: F 592

Prudence Sawyer. I have also made liberal use of unpublished material about Bulford by the late Prudence Sawyer (1879-1979). Included in the papers of Rev. John Rhys-Hughes is an article she wrote entitled "A Nonagenarian remembers . . .' I have also quoted extensively from a poem entitled "Old Bulford Times", a copy of which she gave me when I visited her in 1978. These are both transcribed in Appendix 2. The two works are quoted separately in the Bibliography as: Sawyer, Prudence. (date unknown). Old Bulford Times: Appendix 2a; and Sawyer, Prudence. 1979. 'A Nonagenarian remembers..... Some Byeways and Beauty-spots of Bulford': Appendix 2b. They are referred to in the notes as: Sawyer, Prudence. (Appendix 2a); and, Sawyer, Prudence. (Appendix 2b). I also gained addition oral information on my visit to her which has been acknowledged, as well as from her daughter Ann Sawyer in 2011. Ann Sawyer shares her mother's love of poetry. The book by Ann's brother, the late Frank Sawyer, is another source used. Prudence Sawyer's father-in-law, John Sawyer, was Bulford's last papermaker.

Rev John Rhys-Hughes. He was the vicar of Bulford from 1960, living in the new Vicarage on the corner of Milston Road, and for a time, my neighbour. He was a local historian, following in the footsteps of Canon Ruddle in Durrington. He carried out extensive research, mainly on church records in the Parish and the Diocesan Archives. His paginated notes, are now deposited in the County Archives and have been treated as a written source appearing in the bibliography as: Rhys-Hughes, Rev J. 1972. Notes for a History of Bulford. unpublished notes: [WSA. 2014/24]. They are referred to in the notes as: Rhys-Hughes (1972). His useful list of Churchwardens is in Appendix 3, with additional information on the farms incorporated, culled from my researches.

Treasury Solicitor's Deeds. I was allowed to peruse these deeds at the Durrington Land Agent's Office in 1978 and have used the references that were on the documents. These records are not readily available for general public access and so I have been unable to re-check the references prior to publication.

Secondary Sources

Anon. 1838. 'Obituary: Mrs Sarah Blatch of Ratfyn, near Amesbury, Wilts.' in *The Evangelical Magazine and Missionary Chronicle*: vol.16, London 1838

Anon. 1918. 'Sheep on the Wiltshire Downs. Mr Allan G. Young's Farm at Watergate House, Bulford', in *Agricultural Gazette: 'Farms and Farmers'*, 1918

Beale, Rev Peter. 1986. *Bulford Chapel 1806-1986. 180!.* Bulford: Leaflet quoting extensively from documentary evidence produced by the Chapel to mark the 180th anniversary of its foundation.

Beamish, Derek, Hillier, John and Johnstone, H. F. K. 1976. *Mansions and*

Merchants of Poole and Dorset. Poole Historical Trust

Berchen, F. R. 1977. *The Yonge Street Story 1793-1860. An Account from Letters, Diaries and Newspapers*. Toronto: McGraw-Hill Ryerson

Bettey, J.H. 1987. *Rural Life in Wessex 1500-1900*. Gloucester: Alan Sutton

Bickley, Francis L. 1911. 'Andover Hundred. Fyfield' in Page, William. (ed.) 1911. *A history of Hampshire*. vol.4. London: Oxford University Press. (The Victoria History of the Counties of England)

Billinge, Edwina. 1984. 'Rural Crime and Protest in Wiltshire'. unpublished PhD thesis, University of Kent, Canterbury

Boa, Ann Jarvis. 2009. *Jarvis Pictures and Conversations*. Montreal: published privately

Caird, Sir James. 1852. *Enquiry into English Agriculture 1850-51*. London: Longman, Brown, Green & Longmans

Carter, Kathryn. 2008. 'Neither Here nor There: Mary Gapper O'Brien writes "home" 1828-1838'; in Chambers, Jennifer. *Diversity and Change in Early Canadian Women's Writing*. Cambridge Scholars Publishing

Carus-Wilson, Eleanor M. 1959. 'The Woollen Industry before 1550'. in Crittall, Elizabeth (ed.) *A history of Wiltshire*. Vol. 4. London: Oxford University Press. (The Victoria History of the Counties of England)

Chambers, Jennifer (ed.) 2008. *Change in Early Canadian Women's Writing*. Newcastle upon Tyne

Chambers, Jill. 1993. *Wiltshire Machine Breakers: vol.1: The Riots & Trials*. Letchworth: published privately

Chambers, Jill. 1996. *Hampshire Machine Breakers: The story of the 1830 Riots*. Letchworth: published privately

Chambers, Jill. 2009. *Wiltshire Machine Breakers: vol.2: The Rioters & Appendices*. Letchworth: CD published privately

Chandler, John H. 1979. *The Amesbury Turnpike Trust*. Salisbury: South Wiltshire Industrial Archaeology Society

Chandler, John H. 1987. *Endless Street: a history of Salisbury and its people*. (corrected reprint), Salisbury: Hobnob Press

Chandler, John H. and Goodhugh, Peter S. 1979. *Amesbury: history and description of a South Wiltshire town*. Amesbury: Amesbury Society

Cobbett, William. 2001. *Rural Rides*. London: Penguin edition.

Cowan, Michael. (ed.) 1996. *The letters of John Peniston, Salisbury architect, Catholic, and Yeomanry Officer*. WRS vol.50: Trowbridge

Crowley, D.A. 2003. 'Amesbury' in *A History of Amesbury, Bulford, and Durrington*. Reprint from Crowley, D.A. (ed.) 1995. *A history of Wiltshire*. vol. 15. London: Oxford University Press. (The Victoria History of the Counties of England): Wiltshire County Council and Wiltshire Family History Society

Dale, Christabel. (ed.) 1961. *Wiltshire apprentices and their masters 1710-1760*. WRS vol. 17: Devizes

Davis, Thomas. 1811. *A Report on the State of Agriculture in the County of Wilts*.

Bibliography

London

Desmond, Ray. 1977. *Dictionary of British and Irish Botanists and Horticulturalists*. London: Natural History Museum

Duke, Rev E. H. 1916. 'An account of the Family of Duke of Lake', in *WN&Q*. Vol. 8, 1914 - 1916: Devizes

Edelman, Ian. *Taskers of Andover*. on-line: Hampshire County Council

Eden, Sir Frederic Morton. 1797. *State of the Poor: or, An history of the labouring classes in England, from the conquest to the present period*. London: B. & J. White

Fagan, Brian. 2000. *The Little Ice Age; How climate made history 1300-1850*. New York: Basic Books

Falk, Bernard. 1950. *The Naughty Seymours*. London: Hutchinson

Ferguson, Eugene. (ed.) 1965. *Early Engineering Reminiscences (1815-40) of George Escol Sellers*. Washington DC: Smithsonian Institution

Fleming, James H. 'Mammals', in Faull, J.H. (ed.) 1913. *The Natural History of the Toronto Region*. Ontario, Canada. Toronto: Canadian Institute.

Flower, Thomas Bruges. 1863. 'Flora of Wiltshire' in *WAM* vol 8: Devizes 1863

Gapper, Dr Anthony. 1835. 'Observations on the Quadrupeds found in the District of Upper Canada extending between York and Lake Simcoe, with the view of illustrating their geographical distribution, as well as describing some Species hitherto unnoticed.' in *Zoological Journal*, vol.5, 1832-34: London 1835

Graham, Henry. 1886. *The Annals of the Yeomanry Cavalry of Wiltshire: being a complete history of the Prince of Wales' Own Royal Regiment from the time of its formation in 1794 to October, 1884*. Liverpool

Graham, Henry. 1908. *The Annals of the Yeoman Cavalry of Wiltshire. vol.2: being a complete history of the Prince of Wales' Own Regiment from 1893 to 1908*. Devizes: BiblioLife reproduction

Grayer, Geoffery. 2011. *Rails across the Plain*. Southampton: Noodle Books

Greensted, Frances. 1796. *Fugitive Pieces*. Maidstone

Hamilton, Mary. 1911. *The Silver Road*. London: Allan Wingate

Hancock, Harold B. and Wilkinson, Norman B. 1956. 'The Gilpin Papermaking Machine'. In *Pennsylvania Magazine of History and Biography*. vol.81

Hewitt, E.M. 1973. 'Paper-making' in Page, William. (ed.) 1973. *A history of Hampshire*. vol.5. London: Oxford University Press. (The Victoria History of the Counties of England)

Hinton, D.A. 1979. 'Amesbury and the early history of its Abbey'. in Chandler, John H. (ed.) *The Amesbury Millennium Lectures*. Amesbury: Amesbury Society

Hoare, Sir Richard Colt. 1825. *History of Modern Wiltshire*. vol. 2. London

Hudson, William. 1946. *A Shepherd's Life. Impressions of the South Wiltshire Downs*. London: Methuen

James, N.D.G. 1987. *Plain Soldiering. A history of the armed forces on Salisbury Plain*. Salisbury: Hobnob Press

Jefferies, Richard. 1992. *Hodge and his Masters*. Stroud: Alan Sutton

Leslie, Charles R. (ed.) 1860. *Autobiographical Recollections*. Boston

Lewis, Samuel. 1848. *A Topographical Dictionary of England*. London: Lewis & Co.

Loudon, John Claudius. 1826. *An Encyclopaedia of Agriculture*. London

MacPhee, Dianne. 'A Wreath of Rue, for Lent and the Sacred Lake'. article in *Literature Online*. Logan Collection, Kirkconnell Library, Acadia University, Wolfville, Nova Scotia

Marston, Monica. 1976. 'Mountain, George Jehoshaphat'. in Halpenny, Francess G. and Hamelin, Jean. (eds.) 1976. *Dictionary of Canadian Biography, 1861-1870*, vol. 9: University of Toronto and the Université Laval: and on-line

Matson, Sarah Ann and Southby, Claudia May. (illustrator) 1893. *St George and the Dragon*. London: Fisher Unwin

Matthias, Peter. 1983. *The First Industrial Nation. An Economic History of Britain 1700-1914*. London: Routledge

Meagher, David. 2012. 'The curious life of Anthony Gapper, honoured by the genus Southbya'. in Meagher, David. (ed.) *Australasian Bryological Newsletter*, Number 60, April 2012: University of Tasmania

Miller, Audrey Sanders. (ed.) 1968. *The Journals of Mary O'Brien 1828-1838*. Toronto: Macmillan

Millman, Thomas R. 1983. 'Mountain, Jehosaphat'. in Halpenny, Francess G. and Hamelin, Jean. (eds.). 1983 *Dictionary of Canadian Biography, 1801-1820*, vol. 5: University of Toronto and the Université Laval: and on-line

More, Hannah. 1825. *A Shepherd on Salisbury Plain*. Philadelphia: American Sunday School Union

Morris, John. (ed.) 1979. *Domesday Book, Wiltshire*. Chichester: Phillimore

Mountain, Jacob J. S. 1877. 'The family of Mountain'. in Le Moine, Sir James MacPherson. 1882. *Picturesque Quebec*. Montreal: Dawson Brothers

Mulley, Elizabeth. 1990. *Lucius R O'Brien: A Victorian in North America. American influence on his early work, 1873-1880*. Thesis in Department of Art History, Concordia University, Montreal, Quebec: published on line

Noyes, Ella. 1913. *Salisbury Plain: its stones, cathedral, city, valleys and folk*. London: Dent

O'Brien, Mary. 1828-1838. *Journals*, (transcribed by McClung, Helen). Ontario Archives: F 592

Patterson, William John. 1984. *Joyful is our Praise: Trinity (Bishop Stachan Memorial) Church 1784-1984*. Kingston, Ontario: Brown and Martin

Phillimore, W.P.W. and Hayward, Douglas. (eds.) 1898. *Somerset Parish Registers: Marriages*. vol.1. London

Pugh, R. B. 1975. 'The Borough of Devizes' in Crittall, Elizabeth (ed.) 1975. *A History of Wiltshire*. vol. 10. London: Oxford University Press. (The Victoria History of the Counties of England)

Pugh, R. B. 2003. 'The Abbey, later Priory, of Amesbury' in *A History of Amesbury, Bulford and Durrington*. Reprint from Pugh, R. B. and Crittall, Elizabeth (eds.) 1956. *A History of Wiltshire*. vol.3. London: Oxford University Press. (The Victoria History of the Counties of England): Wiltshire County Council and

Wiltshire Family History Society

Ramsey G. D. 1965. *The Wiltshire Woollen Industry in the sixteenth and seventeenth centuries*. Routledge

Ransome, Mary. (ed.) 1972. *Wiltshire returns to the bishop's visitation queries 1783*. WRS vol.27: Devizes

Rhys-Hughes, Rev J. 1970. 'Notes for a History of Bulford'. unpublished notes: WSA. 2014/24

Rogers K. 1976. *Wiltshire and Somerset Woollen Mills*. Edington: Pasold Research Fund

Sandell, R. E. (ed.) 1975. *Abstracts of Wiltshire tithe apportionments*. WRS vol. 30: Devizes

Sawyer, Frank. (1987). *Keeper of the Stream: The life of a river and its trout fishery*. London: Unwin Hyman

Sawyer, Prudence. c1969. 'Old Bulford Times': transcribed in Appendix 2a

Sawyer, Prudence. c1969. 'A Nonagenarian remembers.... Some Byeways and Beauty-spots of Bulford': transcribed in Appendix 2b

Scarth, Bob. 1998. *We'll all be union men. The story of Joseph Arch and his Union*. Coventry: Industrial Pioneer Publications

Sellers, Charles Coleman. 1947. *Charles Willson Peale*. New York: American Philosophical Society

Shorter, A.C. 1959. 'Papermaking'. in Crittall, Elizabeth. (ed.) *A History of Wiltshire*. vol.4. London: Oxford University Press. (The Victoria History of the Counties of England)

Slack, Paul. (ed.) 1975 *Poverty in early-Stuart Salisbury*. WRS vol.31: Devizes

Slocombe, Ivor. 2012. *Wiltshire Village Reading Rooms*. Wiltshire Building Record: Hobnob Press

Smith, M. K. 2002. *Hannah More: Sunday schools, education and youth work. The encyclopedia of informal education*: http://www.infed.org/thinkers/more.htm

Southby, E. R. 1877. *Brewing: Practically & Scientifically Considered*. London

Spruce, Richard. 1849. 'The Musci and Hepaticae of the Pyrenees.' in *Annals and Magazine of Natural History*, 2nd series, vol.3: London 1849

Stevenson, Janet H. 1995. 'Milston' and 'Figheldean'. In Crowley, D. A. (ed.) 1995. *A history of Wiltshire*. vol.15. London: Oxford University Press. (The Victoria History of the Counties of England):

Stevenson, Janet H. 2003. 'Bulford' and 'Durrington'. in *A History of Amesbury, Bulford and Durrington*. Reprint from Crowley, D. A. (ed.) 1995. *A history of Wiltshire*. vol.15. London: Oxford University Press. (The Victoria History of the Counties of England): Wiltshire County Council and Wiltshire Family History Society

Stewart, Derek. 1969. *Paper* (Modern Industries). Exeter: Wheaton

Stratford, Joseph. 1882. *Wiltshire and Its Worthies*. Brown and Co.

Sturgess, Jack. 1995. 'The Sturgesses of Bulford'. Copy of unpublished family history in Wiltshire Heritage Museum, Devizes: DZSWS MSS.2650

Tankins, Christine M. 'Farming changes in two Wiltshire Villages: Durrington and Shrewton (1760-1860)', unpublished study in History for B.Ed., College of Sarum St Michael: Wiltshire and Swindon History Centre

Thompson, F. M. L. 1969. *English Landed Society in the Nineteenth Century.* London: Routledge, Kegan Paul

Thompson, Samuel. 1968. *Reminiscences of a Canadian Pioneer for the last Fifty Years.* Toronto

Thomson, James. 1865. *The Seasons.* London

Tibbutt, H. G. (ed.) 1963. *The Letter Books 1644-45 of Sir Samuel Luke.* (Historical Manuscripts Commission JP 4). London: HMSO

Vines, Sidney. 1984. *Frank Sawyer: Man of the River.* London: Unwin Hyman

Volpi, Jean. (ed.) 2011. *Amesbury: Rose's Grammar School Log Book, 1872-1899.* Wiltshire Parish Records, No.35: Wiltshire Family History Society

Wakeman, Frances. 1999. 'Deddington Paper-mill', in Cohen, Colin (ed.) 224: *The Newsletter of the Deddington and District History Society*, Oct. 1999, ISSN 1479-5884, issue 1

Wallace, Anthony F. C. 2005. *Rockdale. The Growth of an American Village in the Early Industrial Revolution.* University of Nebraska Press

Ward, A. J. 1998. 'John Dickinson and the Brandywine'. in *Hertfordshire Past* no. 41.

Watkins, John. Shoberl, Frederic. and Upcott, William. (eds.) 1816. *Biographical Dictionary of the living Authors of Great Britain and Ireland.* London: H. Colburn

Watson, Hewett and Cottrell. 1874. *Topographical Botany*: part second. Thames Ditton

Whitlock, R. 1979. 'Just over the horizon: Amesbury, 1700-1979', in Chandler, John (ed.) 1979. *The Amesbury Millennium Lectures.* Amesbury: The Amesbury Society

Woodcroft, Bennett. 1864. *Chronological Index of Patents Applied for and Patents Granted, for the year 1863.* London: Eyre and Spottiswood.

Index

This is primarily an index of personal and place names. Minor places are in Bulford unless otherwise stated. The notes have not been indexed.

A303 56–7
Abbotts Ann 45
   Waterloo ironworks 45
Ablington 192, 227, 296
accounts 169–70
Adam, Ellen 78
Adams, John 184
Adelaide (Australia) 248
Adlam
   Charles 262
   George 302
Adlard
   Charles 11
   Emily 145
advowson 80, 175
Aelfthryth, queen 82
agriculture 23, 147–8, 149–74, 259–60, 280–1
   board of 86
   implements 147
   labourers 237, 256, 257, 260, 262–3, 265
   labourers union 242
   machinery 27–8, 44–5, 124, 126, 162, 163–5, 167, 297
   ministry of 280–1
alders 170–1
Aldershot (Hants) 271, 275
Aldridge
   Elizabeth 119, 187
   James 119, 187–9, 191
   Sarah 119, 187
   family tree 287
alehouse-keeper 100

Alexander, Mary 94
Allahabad (India) 70
Allington 44, 46, 176, 180, 300
almshouses 18, 29
Alton (Hants) 186, 219
Alvediston 254, 255
Alverstoke (Hants) 218, 264
America: *see* United States
Amesbury 15, 28, 31, 34, 44, 48, 54, 55, 57, 61–2, 63, 65, 67, 79, 84, 113, 119, 150, 164, 176, 179, 184, 194, 207, 209–10, 213, 217, 240, 252, 267, 268, 269, 270, 274, 275, 276, 295
   abbey (priory) 46, 82, 112, 175
   Antrobus estate 120
   Countess farm 42–3, 108
   George inn (hotel) 58, 140, 141, 144
   Heaver 28, 126, 164–5
   hundred 31
   New End corner 101
   poor law union 31, 46, 61
   Red House farm 120
   Rose's grammar school 70, 107, 232, 233, 249, 252
   rural dean 18, 180, 181, 182
   rural deanery 16, 19, 21, 35, 79, 178, 179, 188, 198, 203, 238, 243, 256
   schools 227, 233, 238
   turnpike trust 57–60, 112
   West 63
   workhouse 31–2, 52, 61, 264
Amfill, Charles 202
Andover 44, 47, 56, 66, 79, 86, 155, 165,

168, 173, 174, 212, 213, 214, 220, 264, 267, 276, 279
Advertiser 271–2
Westover 213
Andrews
  Caroline 173
  David 61
  Eliza 218
  Emma 265
  George 173
  James 59
  John 139
  Sarah 188
  Thomas 239
  William 188
  family 62, 260
Andrews and Dury's map 55, 132, 225
Angear, James 301
Anglesey 65
animal life 8–9
Antrobus
  Edmund, Sir 48, 210, 268, 276
  Edmund (son) 48
apples 24
Appleshaw (Hants) 264
apprentices 227
Apsley Mill (Herts) 214, 215
Arch, Joseph 50
army 259–84, 298
  service corps 260
Arnold, Cecil North 30, 38, 204, 206, 208, 210, 234, 252, 271, 275, 276, 295, 296, 300
  family 204, 206
Arts and Crafts movement 223
Ashton, Mr 222
asparagus 114
Atkins, Thomas 257
Austen, Jane 83
Australia 25, 45, 47, 49, 77, 265; *see also* Adelaide
Autumn manoeuvres
  (1872) 266–7
  (1898) 269–70, 274
  (1899) 275
  (1900) 274
Avon

river 6, 12, 33, 57, 60, 80, 97, 108, 110, 113, 119, 125, 146, 212, 269, 270, 274, 295, 296
valley 15, 27, 40, 53, 54, 55, 60, 63, 65, 179, 184, 259, 261, 273
Avoncliff 219
Avondale school 190–1, 296

bacon 13, 24–5, 294
Bailey
  Susannah 141–2, 144, 147
  William 99–100, 140, 141
  Mr 192
Bailiff's cottage 173
Bakehouse, Joan 29
bakers, bakery 13, 227
Baltimore (USA) 216
band, brass 208
banking 65, 257
Baptists 184, 216
  Paedo- 189
Barford St Michael (Oxon) 203
barley 151–2, 153, 156–61, 162
barns 132–4, 163, 166
Barrett, Mary 72
Bartlett, Henry Critchett 92
bastardy 4
Bataille, Jeanette 126
Batchelor
  Mariah 31–2
  Robespierre 47, 52
  William, 46, 231
Bath 62, 65, 69, 78, 83, 115, 214, 220, 261
  Marquis of 120, 168, 172
  Royal Crescent 115
bazaar 14, 272
Beacon Hill 14, 57, 79, 95, 113, 117, 124, 126, 161, 162, 166, 172, 209, 266–7, 268, 270, 297–8
Beale, Peter 301
beans 157–8
Bebington (ship) 248
Becket, Wilson 176, 300
Beckington (Som)
  Clifford's Mill 226
Bedford, John 248
Beech Bottom 160

Index

beer 24–5, 34–7, 201–2
bees 22, 33
Belem (Portugal) 72
Belloc, Hilaire 234
bells, church 170
Bemerton 212
Bennet, Rev 190
Berkshire 86: *see also* Buscot Park; Hungerford; Newbury; Thatcham; Wantage
Berry, Rev 190
Berwick St James 180, 263, 300
Bewick, Mr 105
Bible 22
bird scaring 33
birds 8
Birmingham 260
blacksmiths 13, 53, 167, 294, 297
Blanchard, William 126, 263
Blatch
   Elizabeth 186, 192
   Henry 66, 119, 184, 185, 187, 188, 189, 194, 235
   Henry (jun) 186, 235
   James 186
   Sarah 30, 186, 192, 235
   family 29–30, 46, 190–2
   family tree 287
   Mr 66, 106
Blunt
   James 46
   Walter 176, 300
Boer wars 71, 268, 273, 278
Boldre (Hants)
   Newtown farm 101
bonfires 14
Boreham 63
Boscombe 44, 179
botany 74–7
Bourbon family 115
Bourne
   field 138, 146
   road 55, 146
Bournemouth 117, 278
   Winton 301
Bowman, Edward Burkett 178, 300
Brackston, William 47

Bradford on Avon 219, 220
Brading (Isle of Wight) 203, 204
Bradshaw, Col 78
Brandywine (USA) 215
Brasbridge, Joseph 68
brass band 14
   Bourne valley 63, 66
Bratton 45
brewing 35–6, 91–3, 187
Briary cottage 173
bricklayers 71, 227, 232, 236, 260, 262, 263, 264, 278, 291, 295
Bridgefoot cottage 64 96
Bridgwater (Som) 75, 78, 89, 90
   infirmary 75
Brighton (Sussex) 76
Brigmerston 103, 105, 138, 146, 177
Bristol 37, 63, 65, 67, 69, 72, 78, 88, 178, 214, 215, 278
   Clifton 78
   College green 75
   museum 75
Broad Chalke 254
'Broadway' 2, 55, 296
Brodribb
   Abraham 214
   Henry 220
   Isaac 213–14, 216, 218, 220, 301
   family 220
Bronti, Mr 271
brooch 90
Brown and May 45, 165
Browne, Nicholas C 124
Brunswick, Augusta, duchess of 68
Buckinghamshire 28, 148: *see also* Newport Pagnell
builders 95, 263–5, 291
BULFORD (*see also* names of roads, fields and minor places in Bulford)
   bazaar 14, 272
   bridge 5, 6, 36, 55, 59–60, 137, 139, 276, 295
   camp 79, 95–6, 113, 132, 156, 198, 259–84
   downs 95, 266, 268
   droveway 1, 5, 55, 260
   farm 28

fields 1–2, 97, 103, 110
lees 9
mill 137, 139, 142, 154
parish council 274–5
pennings 3, 276
stakes 8
station 60, 297
Bungay (Suffolk) 218, 302
Burges, Silas 188
burial 51
burnbaking (burn-beaking) 121, 158, 159, 162, 166
Burton, William 67
Buscot Park (Oxon) 55, 68, 86
bustards 8
butchers 13, 227, 257
Butler
  E R 186
  Elizabeth 186, 192, 235, 241
  Mrs 106
byways 294–8

Caffey, Thomas 301
Calne 101, 184, 219
Cambridge
  duke of 86, 266–7
  roller 163
Canada 11, 34, 37, 41, 49–50, 51, 56, 64, 71, 72–7, 80, 81, 83, 88, 90, 198–200, 201, 202, 224, 226, 265: *see also* Cornwall; Coteau du Lac; Newfoundland; Nova Scotia; Ontario; Ottawa; Quebec; Simcoe, Lake; Thornhill; Toronto
  academy of arts 74
canals 62, 261
Candy
  Charley 13
  Hannah 13
Canning(s)
  Elizabeth 247
  Lucy 65, 247, 248
  Mary 65
  Mary Ann 77; *see also* Knight
  Rebecca 247
  William 247
Cardiff 278
Carey paper mill (Dorset) 217, 222, 302

Carlisle, earl of: *see* Howard, George William Frederick
Carmarthen 193
carpenters 28, 47, 236, 248
carriers 11, 13, 59, 60–1, 294
carters 21, 23, 50, 53, 59, 166–7, 217, 261, 263
Castleman, Jane 148, 245
Catterick academy 94
cattle 281
Cavalier (ship) 248
cavalry camp 11, 55, 95
Cawnpore massacre 70
Celebrity coach 56
cemetery 95, 96, 207
censuses 62
Chafyn's farm 137
chalk(ing) 163
  soil 161, 163
Chalk
  George 232
  James 4, 11, 185, 227, 256
  James (junior) 232
Channel islands 93
chapel 5, 11, 13, 14, 19, 21, 30, 46, 49, 52, 91, 96, 99, 106, 112, 141, 185–95, 196–8, 209–10, 219, 231, 238–42, 257, 264, 287, 297
  bungalow 191
  church book 184, 194–5
  Cottage(s) 188, 189, 264
  graveyard 188
  manse 178, 190–1, 196, 204–5, 245, 279, 296
  pastors, list of 301
  Sabbath school 194–5, 197
  schoolroom 188
Chapman, Mr 68
Charlton Adam (Som) 72, 78, 84, 87, 302
  abbey 87–8
Cheddar (Som) 242
chemistry 91–3
children 31–2, 33
Chippenham agricultural society 281
Cholderton 43, 44, 63, 66, 113, 117, 126, 176, 263, 276, 300
choral society 14

Index

Christchurch (Dorset, formerly Hants) 234
Christmas 48–9
Church 14, 21, 57, 95, 96, 97, 119, 138, 170, 171, 175–83, 196–211, 228, 238–42, 263, 295
  army 112
  bells 180, 181, 182, 183
  bier 180, 181
  book 100
  choir 206, 208
  dedication 176, 180
  established 83
  farm 99, 231, 296
  field 105
  font cover 223
  lectern 204
  monuments 84–5
  murals 295–6
  organ 206
  path 55
  pews 204, 223
  poor condition 180–1
  repairs 181, 182, 204
  restoration 204, 295–6
  school 228–30
  services 179, 183
  stove 95
  wardens 63, 99, 101, 102, 126, 140, 142, 145, 169, 177, 179, 182, 207
  wardens, list of 298–9
  yard 81, 97, 180, 183
Chute 145
cider 24, 25
civil wars 71
Clarence, duke of 56
clergy 34, 35, 63, 64, 69, 175–83, 198–206
  house 175, 177, 178, 179
clerk, parish 210–11
climate 9–11, 149–51
cloth 219–20
  manufacturers (clothiers) 26, 27, 44, 219–20
  mill 44
clothing 31–2
clover 158, 162
club day 294
coaching 56, 61
coachmen 261
coal 10–11, 94–5
  man 53–4
  yard 96
Cobbett, William 15–16, 23–4, 25, 27, 34, 40, 49, 54, 61, 128, 150, 154, 179, 196
Codford 254
Colchester (Essex)
  Fordham 301
Coleman, Charles John 300
collarmaker 236
Collingbourne 42, 165
constables 60
  special 44, 45, 48
Cooe
  John 138–9, 140, 222
  Richard 140, 141, 144, 145
  Thomas 140, 141, 144, 145
  brothers 175, 222
Cooe's farm 141
cooking 24
Cooper
  Jane 217
  Thomas 217, 222
  William 217
Copley, W 179
cordwainer 227
Cork (Ireland) 214
corn laws 25
Corner end 19, 44, 206
Cornwall 178: *see also* Lostwithiel
Cornwall (Canada) 198, 199, 200, 201, 203
Coteau du Lac 201, 203
cottage tenants 110–12
Cottle, Elizabeth 214
coursing, hare 8–9, 80
cows 175
Cox, Richard 173
cricket 208
Crompton, Winifred 234
Croome
  Ann 142
  Elizabeth 64, 100
  Mary 66, 99, 100, 140, 142–3, 298
  Mary Ann 64, 100
  Robert 28, 100
  Thomas 11, 28, 29, 41, 65, 66, 87, 100,

142, 155, 168, 222, 232, 298
family 64
family tree 289
Mr 67, 99
Mrs 222
Cross road (lane) 13
Crosskills reaper 164-5
Crossroads brewery 35
Cull, Miss 235
curates, perpetual 175-83, 196
   list of 299-300

dairying 160, 169-70, 174
Daventry (Northants) 209
Davis, Thomas 9, 24, 65, 97, 118, 121, 147, 158, 160, 162, 167, 168, 169, 172
death 39
   penalty 48
Deddington (Oxon) 224, 226
Defoe, Daniel 54
Delaware (USA) 215
Densley
   Albert 249
   Emma 249
Derby china warehouse 68
Devenish
   Ann 187, 191
   Catherine 186
   Elizabeth 30, 186, 187, 233, 241
   Hannah 187, 191
   Henry 187
   James Aldridge 25, 119, 187
   Matthew 11, 25, 66, 99, 114, 118, 119, 120, 121, 130, 154, 184-9, 192, 209, 233
   Matthew (jun) 119, 186, 187
   Matthew (III) 187
   Sarah 187, 191
   Seymour 259
   family 46, 190-2
   family tree 287
   Mr 99
Devizes 27, 45, 66, 67, 165, 184, 213, 222
Devon: *see* Kingsbridge; Plymouth; Totnes
Dickinson, John 215
diet 23-5, 31-2
Dimer, William 40

diseases 37-8, 150
disorder 40-9
dissenters 179, 183-98
dogs, hunting 87
Domesday book 212
domestic service 232, 254-5
donkeys 54
Dorchester 11
Dorset 118, 173, 186, 187: *see also* Carey paper mill; Dorchester; Poole; Shaftesbury; Sherborne; Stour Provost; Upwey; Wareham; Weymouth; Wimborne
Douse
   Annabel 231
   Mary 231
dovecote 84, 134-6, 170
downland, downs 53, 54, 159, 162, 168
Downton 71, 194, 212, 219
Dragoons, 15th regiment 71
Draper, Thomas 144
drought 11
Drove, the 96
drovers 55
drowners 151-2, 171
drunkenness 34-7, 80, 195
du Barry, Mme, 114
Duke
   Ann 29, 84
   George 82
   Mary 84
   Richard 82, 83, 84, 97, 148, 171, 173, 228-9
   family 82, 83, 85, 86, 104
   family tree 285, 286
Durham: *see* Hartlepool
Durnford 31, 58, 66
Durrington 2, 10, 30, 31, 35, 39, 41, 44, 49, 50, 58, 63, 64, 65, 101, 106, 112, 137-8, 139, 141, 143, 145, 146, 176, 184, 186, 192, 211, 213, 217, 221, 225, 267, 274, 300, 302, 303
   chapel 186
   East End manor 138
   mill 138-9
   Nag's Head inn: *see* Nag's Head Walls 119, 274

Index

West End manor 137-8
Dury, Francis William 184, 301
Dyke
  Elizabeth 144-5
  Thomas Webb 33, 100, 137, 140, 142, 143, 144-5, 181, 230, 298-9
  William 139-40, 142
  family 139-41, 143, 147
  Mr 67
Dyke's farm 138, 142
Dymer, William 93-4
Dymore, Robert 302

East India Company 215
East Knoyle 66, 113, 114, 116
  Knoyle house 115, 116
East Wellow (Hants) 188
Ecclesiastical Commissioners 206
Eden, Frederick, Sir 26, 27
Edinburgh 72
education 21, 50, 227-56
  act (1870) 243-4
Elford, C E 301
Ellaby, James Watt 176-7, 300
Ellen, Frederick Charles 173-4
emigration 49-52
  committees 49
empire, British 83
employment 23, 26, 50, 217
  child 232
Enford 43, 45, 145, 206, 274
engineering 91, 92
entertainment 14
Errence, James 49
Espair, HMS, 56
Essex: *see* Colchester; Wavertree
Essex Historical Soc 77
Everleigh 43, 46, 231
  yeomanry troop 41-2, 48
Eyres, - 46

fairs 14, 63, 66, 155, 297
farmers 63-6, 69
farming: *see* agriculture
Farnham (Surrey) 15
Farr, C 198, 301
fauna 8-9

Fawley (Hants) 235
fertilisers, artificial 156, 162, 169
fetes 95
Fidell, - 67
Figheldean 27, 31, 44, 50, 51, 63, 139, 156, 206, 296
  Syrencote house 139, 140, 268, 296
fire 38, 42-3
Fisherton gaol 26, 32
fishing 80, 84, 95
Fittleton 57, 206
Fleet, Mr 85-6, 173
floods 6, 59, 86
flora 7-9, 76-7
flowers 7-8
Flowers, Mrs 249
Folkestone, viscount 70
Folly Bottom 55, 57, 59
food 23-5, 31-2
ford 60
Fourdrinier, - 215
Fowle, Fulwar W 176, 300
Foxcott (Hants) 47
foxes 8-9
France 71, 220: *see also* Paris; Pyrenees
  revolutionary 83, 114-15, 185
Freshford (Som) 220
Fricker, Ann 58
friendly societies 38-40
Frome (Som) 226
fruit (trees) 22, 263
fuel 10-11, 22, 24
furniture 22-3, 68, 205
Fyfield (Hants) 86

Gaby, Thomas 44
Gale, Robert 185
gamekeepers 33, 100, 108
  act (1831) 33
Gane, Henry 49
Gapper
  Ann 84
  Anthony: *see* Southby
  Anthony (Rev) 87
  Edmund 72, 88, 89
  Edmund Barrett 72, 88, 89
  Edward (Rev) 88

Gilbert 69
Katherine Anne 72
Lucy 88, 89, 90
Lucy Ann 72
Lucy Mary 73
Mary 72, 88, 198–9
Mary Sophia 72, 73–5, 83
Richard Colston 72, 78, 89
Sophy 88
Susan 88
William Southby 72, 89
family 71, 72, 83, 88, 89, 90
family tree 286
gardeners 96, 261, 263
gardens 22
Gast, John 148
Gates, Mr 252
Gentleman's Magazine 89
gentrification, gentry 63–5, 69, 127–36
geology 162–3
George III, king 168
George IV, king 188
Gibbs, Francis 299
Gilbert, Elizabeth 143
Gilpin
   Annie 200
   Joshua 215
   Thomas 215
glebe 175, 177
Gloucester 278, 282
Gloucestershire: *see* Gloucester; Lechlade
Godfrey Room 191
Godwin
   Alfred 219, 302
   Ann 219, 235
   Benjamin 219
   Charles 239, 240, 302
   Charlotte 235
   Ellen 194, 217, 219, 225
   Henry 143–4, 219, 235, 302
   Kezia 239
   Samuel 219
   Sarah 194, 219, 239
   Thomas 220, 224, 302, 303
   William 37, 63, 219, 225, 232, 302
   William (junior) 232
   family 220

family tree 288
   Mrs 223
Goodrich, John Gray 204, 300
Gosforth (Northumb) 257
governesses 234
Grace, James 71
Graham, Henry 40, 47
Grant, Isabel S, 7
Grateley 176, 270
Greatrake
   Lawrence 47, 214–16, 219, 222, 302
   Lawrence (jun) 216
   Roger 214, 215
Greensted, Frances 69
Greenwood, William 300
Gretna Green (Scotland) 194
Griffin, Rev – 190
Grist: *see also* Gast
   James 148
   John 148, 245
Grivian, William 302
grocer 13
groom 237
guardians 31–2
gun end 162, 298
guns 29, 87
gypsies 4–5

Haking, Sir Richard Bryne 226
Hamilton
   Mary 1, 7–8, 9, 13, 72, 206, 260, 272, 275
   Walter Kerr (bishop of Salisbury) 178
Ham(m)s 157–8, 160
Hampshire 28, 218: *see also* Abbotts Ann; Aldershot; Alton; Alverstoke; Andover; Appleshaw; Boldre; Bournemouth; Christchurch; East Wellow; Fawley; Foxcott; Fyfield; Grateley; Hursley; Kimpton; Lyndhurst; New Forest; Portsea; Portsmouth; Quarley; Redenham; Rendlesham; Romsey; Shipton Bellinger; Southampton; Thruxton; Wallop; Weyhill; Winchester
Hampton Poyle (Oxon) 203
hamsters 75
Handel, George Frederick 86
hanging 48

Index

Hann, James 108, 229, 231, 279
hares 8
Hargraves, – 251
Harrison, George 185
Harrow Way 56-7
harrows 163
Hartlepool (Durham) 95
harvesting 164
Haskett, the 138, 222
Hatch house 124, 125
Hatches, Great 124, 125
Haxton 63
hay 162
Hayden (Haydon)
    Benjamin 139, 145
    James 145
    Robert 145
    family 64, 222
Hayter, Elizabeth 32
Heale 270
health 9-11, 37-40
Hedges
    James 210
    John 61
    Joseph 281
    Orah 210-11
    Robert (two of that name) 210, 211
Hemel Hempstead (Herts) 214
Henry VIII, king 82, 112
Henry, prince of Wales 82
Hereford 280
Hertfordshire: *see* Apsley Mill; Hemel Hempstead; King's Langley; Wymondley Academy
Hickman, Henry 239
Hicks
    Charles 167
    Mary 232
High Street 5, 112, 143, 185
Highal, – (Mrs) 64
highwaymen 55
Highworth 84, 86
Hill
    Dennis 94
    James Ledger 71, 79, 85, 94-6, 105-7, 110, 160, 206, 207, 208, 278
    Mary 94-6
    William Henry Tucker 71, 278
    – (Mrs) 64
Hillman, Wingfield 213, 301
Hindurrington 97
    Farm 28, 96-8, 99, 104, 148
Hitchlands 157-8
Hobday, Joseph 224, 226, 303
Hodson, George 255
Holmes
    Joseph 173
    – 46
Holt, Louise *see* Pollen
Holyhead (Anglesey) 262
Home farm 117
Hooklands 157-8
Hooper
    Henry 104
    James 67, 101, 103-10, 111, 126, 164, 165, 173, 207, 208, 234, 273-4, 299
    William 104
Hooper's Farm 224
Hopkinson, Jane 115
horses 166-7, 180, 182, 267, 268
Hoskins, W E 277
hospital, military 81
housing 15-23
Hove (Sussex) 218
Howard, George William Frederick (7th earl of Carlisle) 177, 300
Howse, Prudence 261; *see also* Sawyer
Hudson, William H. 10, 51
Hudson River 72
Huguenots 220
Hungerford (Berks) 56, 176
hunting and country sports 8-9, 67, 86-7, 116, 118-19, 122, 131
Huron, Lake 75
Hursley (Hants) 102
Hutchins
    Allan Borman 176, 300
    R W 300
Hyatt
    James 218, 302
    Martha 38
    William 218, 220, 302
    William (jun) 218, 302
    family 219

family tree 290

Ibbotson
   Octavia 78, 92
   William 92
illness 10
Imber 104, 218, 254
   Browne Farm 104–5
Imperial Mercantile Finance Co 115
improvement, agricultural 122–4
incomes 25–8
Independent (nonconformist) 189
India 70: *see also* Allahabad; Cawnpore massacre; Kanpur; Lucknow; Satichaura Ghat
   mutiny 70
Indonesia: *see* Sulawesi Tengah
influenza 10
Ingles, George Lycester (Capt.) 81
innkeepers 236
inns 57, 61, 137–43
insects 9
insularity 62–3
insurance 38–40, 108–9, 165
intermarriage 62
investments 70
Ireland 56, 177, 279: *see also* Cork

Jackman, Hannah 102
Jacob, William 43
James I, king 82
Jarman, James 148
Jefferies, Richard 128–9, 164, 166–7, 239, 250–1, 254, 255, 256, 258
Jenkins, Jane 145
Jenner
   Thomas 43–4
   (Mr) 112, 206, 222
   (Mrs) 106
Jennings, Thomas 139, 146
Jersey 77
Johnson, Robert Liston 204, 300
jubilee (Victoria diamond) 14, 95, 208–9
Judd, James 42

Kanpur (India) 70
Keel (Keele)
   Alice 206
   George 60–1
   Hannah M 77
   Jonathan 21
   Mary 21, 111
   Samuel 40
   Sarah 21
   – 46
   family 62, 260
Keinton Mandeville (Som) 72
Kelly's directory 139, 141
Kennet, Brockley Charles 300
Kent: *see* Maidstone; Tunbridge Wells
Kidderminster (Worcs) 302
Kill
   George 11, 13
   family 62
kilns, lime 224
Kimpton (Hants) 86, 176
King, Mrs 222
King's Langley (Herts) 214
Kingsbridge (Devon) 301
Kinsman
   Charlotte 219
   Elizabeth 219
   Henry 33
   John 210
   William 218, 256, 302
Knight
   Claudia Annie 248
   Emma 254–5
   Francesca Mabel 248–9
   George 33, 140
   Mary Ann 74, 80–1, 202, 247–50, 251, 257, 294
   William Henry 248
   Wilmot Henry 233, 248, 249, 257
knitting 33
Knowles, G 268

Lacy, Gertrude 234
Ladysmith (South Africa) 71, 278
Lake
   Robert 13, 167
   – (Mrs) 13
Lake (Wilsford cum Lake) 43, 270
Land Loan and Enfranchisement Co 116,

Index

135, 174
Larkhill 57
Latton 62, 261
Laverstock 140, 234, 270
Lavington 45
   West 66, 139, 227
Lawes Hall 191, 247
Lawrence
   Harry 173
   Thomas 185
Lechlade (Glos) 86
Ledger Hill Close 95
Lewis, H 300
licensing act (1872) 35
lighting, street 207
lime (kiln) 224, 296
Limpley Stoke 220
liquor 67
Lisbon (Portugal) 215
Little Ice Age 149–50
Liverpool 248, 278
   and London and Globe Insurance Co. 105
Lloyds Register 94–5, 115
Local Government Act, 1894 206–7, 211
lodgers 21
London 56, 57, 63, 64, 67, 68, 69, 71, 93, 108, 145, 194, 257, 258, 261, 262, 263, 264, 268, 270; *see also* Middlesex
   and South Western Railway 79
   Belgravia 261
   bishop of 199
   Blackheath 68
   Buckingham Palace 74
   Camberwell 261
   Chiswick 234
   Garlick Hill 92
   Gloucester Road 92
   Great Exhibition 77, 78
   Gresham House 91
   Hammersmith 277
   Hampstead 91
   Hanover Square 261
   Islington 145, 262, 263
   Kensington 261
   Lambeth Palace 248
   Lincoln Inns Fields 99
   Marylebone 77
   Missionary society 197
   Paddington 77
   Queens Crescent 92
   Royal Academy 74
   Shoreditch 262, 264
   Upper Grosvenor Street 115
   Vauxhall 248
   Westminster 109
Long
   Annie 234
   Elizabeth 136, 233
   Elizabeth Sophia 70
   Fanny 233, 283
   Francis Stephen 16, 18, 28, 31, 38, 39, 48, 52, 58, 59, 63–4, 69–70, 118, 119, 120, 122, 131, 136, 155, 165, 177, 179, 233, 238, 257, 299
   Francis Stephen (jun) 119, 122, 124, 126, 130
   Lizzie 234
   Richard 283
   William 120
   family 234
Longbridge Deverill 120
Longleat 9
Long's Pennings 2, 55, 97
Lostwithiel (Cornwall) 301
Louis XV, king 114
Love
   Elizabeth 11, 261
   James 261
   John 261, 302
   Mary 11
   William 11–12, 32, 40, 239, 261
   William (junior) 261
   Mrs 239
Loveden, Edward Loveden (Sir) 29, 55, 67–8, 86–7, 99, 100, 188
Lower Farm 5, 13, 19, 20, 21, 25, 28, 64, 80, 93–4, 97–110, 111, 126, 142, 153–6, 158, 159, 161, 163–5, 166, 173, 222, 232, 269, 273, 289, 297, 298–9
Lower Path 297
Luck, Gen G 270, 271
Lucknow, siege (India) 70
Ludgershall 42, 48, 61, 263, 275, 276

Lyndhurst (Hants) 244
  Bane Cottage 79

machinery
  farm 27-8, 44-5, 124, 126, 162, 163-5, 167, 297
  house 297
  threshing 133-4, 164, 165
Mackenzie rebellion (Canada) 71
Macklin
  Edward 28
  James 40, 251
McMans, John 277
Maddington 101, 104, 126, 127
  Bourton Farm 105
Mafeking (South Africa) 278
Maidenhead Inn 28, 37, 38
Maidstone (Kent) 69
Main Street 13, 167, 296
Man, Isle of 91
management, farm 172-4
mangolds 158, 160, 162
Manor 75, 89, 92, 93, 94-6, 102-3, 110, 140, 172, 175, 180, 188, 223, 226
  Cottage 99, 108
  descent of 82-96
  estate 21, 96-112, 171, 175, 185, 188, 222
  Farm 45, 64, 96-8, 113, 139, 170, 229, 231
  House 11, 14, 21, 22, 25, 28-9, 57, 67, 78-81, 85, 90, 96, 98, 238, 260, 264, 269, 283, 295
    park 106
    summer house 106
markets 65-6
Marlborough 55, 213, 269
  road, old 55, 56, 269
Mascall, Col 277
masons 291, 295
Maton, John 112, 206
mechanisation 27-8, 44-5, 102, 262
medicine 91, 93
  canine 87
Melsome
  Annie 124
  George 59, 70, 112, 124, 126-7, 204, 207, 299

George (jun) 299
Richard 126
Robert 108
Robert Francis 127
William 126
William (jun) 126
Mr 276
Melsome's Pennings 97
Merchant, Mr 207
Methodists 185
Mew, Samuel 299
mice 73
Michigan (USA) 248
Midhurst (Sussex) 224, 303
Middlesex 70, 124, 240: *see also* places listed under London; Staines
Miles, (Joseph) Gilbert 101, 299
milestones 55
Milford (Salisbury) 140
militarisation 108-10
Military Lands Act (1897) 268
militia 41, 56
Mill 99, 138-9, 188, 225, 232, 235, 274; *and see* Paper
  Acre 138, 222
  Cottage(s) 63, 220, 225, 261, 295
  House 186, 212, 220, 225, 226, 295
  race 225
Miller, Isaac 48
Millner, Thomas Darnton 177-8, 201, 231, 237, 238, 300
millwrights 219
Milston 2, 12, 31, 55, 97, 101, 103, 107, 146, 176, 177, 196, 198, 206, 249, 272, 296, 300
  Farm 107
  mill 296
  rectory 205
  Road 1-2, 5, 30, 55, 96, 97, 103, 172, 206
'miracle' stone 297
missionaries 197
  Church Army 112
  societies 197
mobility, social 256-8
Monkton Combe (Som) 96
Montanero, John 14
Moore's Leaze 146

Index

morality 4–5
More, Hannah 242
Morlidge, Anne 64
Morris, William 223
mortality 150
mortgages 114
Moses 203
Mould
  Edmund 218
  Harriet 218
  Joseph 41, 188, 217, 222, 302
  Mary 213, 217, 223, 301
  Samuel 185, 302
  Thomas 185, 213, 216, 217, 301
  Thomas (jun) 217, 301
  William 213, 301
  family 219, 221–2
Mountain
  Annie 200, 202, 237
  Jacob (jun) 198, 203
  Jacob Jehoshaphat S 34–6, 37, 80, 198–204, 235, 237, 238, 243, 245, 300
  Jehoshaphat 198
  family 198–200
Moy, – (Mr) 70
Mundy, John 210
murder 280
mushrooms 34
music 86

Nags Head
  Farm 25, 37, 102, 167, 185, 222
  Inn 2, 36–7, 39, 137–44, 146, 147, 221
Nalder 165
names, Christian 52
Napoleonic wars 25, 55, 72, 83, 121, 159, 162, 169
National Agricultural Labourers' Union 50, 51
natural history 5–9, 72–7
navy 262
Nelson, Paul 35
Netheravon 43–4, 46, 47, 48, 49, 50, 51, 54, 66, 144, 206, 274, 295, 296
New Forest 10, 74
New York 72
New Zealand 25, 50, 51

Newbury (Berks) 254
Newfoundland (Canada) 115
Newman, Sarah 257
Newport Pagnell (Bucks) 193, 301
news 53–4, 70–1
Newton Tony 43, 44, 107, 263
Nine Mile River 1, 5, 55, 57, 95, 103, 108, 113, 133, 146, 154, 160, 172, 268, 296
nonconformity 213, 216; *see also* chapel
Norfolk: *see* Thwaite
Norris, William 300
North Shields 94
Northamptonshire: *see* Daventry
Northumberland: *see* Gosforth; North Shields
Norton, – (Mr) 86
Nova Scotia (Canada) 200
Noyce (Noyes)
  Ella 55, 283–4
  H 213–14, 302
  Thomas 213, 301
nursemaids 65

Oakham (Rutland) 184, 301
Oaksey 126
oats 158, 159, 160, 162, 280
O'Brien
  Claudia 74
  Edward G. 73
  Lucius (Richard) 7, 12, 73–4, 135, 180
  Mary 49–50
  Mary Gapper 73–5, 83
  family 71
Odstock 300
Officers Club 260, 283
Old Coach Road 13, 172, 180, 296
Old Sarum 266, 270
Olding, Joseph 194
Oliver, R Deane 271
omnibuses 77–8
O'Neill, Col Sir Dennis 272
Ontario (Canada) 7, 56, 198–9
  School of Art 74
Oram, Albion 301
Orchard End 100, 105, 111–12, 126, 137, 172, 244, 279, 297
  Farm 102–3, 138, 154, 298–9

House 138, 140, 143–7, 198, 201, 204, 205–6, 260
Orchard Way 13, 28, 146, 172
orchards 175
Ordnance Survey 206
Osborne, F W 277
Ottawa (Canada) 203
outdoor relief 31–3
Over Beacon Hill 163, 166
overseers of poor 207
Overton 120
oxen 166
Oxford
   Queen's College, the 203
Oxfordshire: see Barford St Michael; Deddington; Hampton Poyle; Oxford

Packway 55
Pain, Edward 13
Panthou, Comtesse de 114
paper mill 96, 258, 295
papermakers, papermaking 47, 62, 63, 64, 69, 77, 92, 96, 185–6, 188, 212–26, 235, 236, 237, 240, 263, 288, 290
   list of 301–3
   processes 224–5
Paris (France) 114
parish clerks 257
Parish council 207–8
Park, the 180
Parkins, George 103
parsonage house 196, 245
Parsons
   Arthur 107
   Edwin G. 108
   William 107, 227
   William (junior) 227
   – (Mrs)
   family 107
partridges 8
Pearce
   Edward 96
   Emily 145
   George 145
   Henry 143, 144, 145, 147, 299
   Meliora 145
   Thyra 144

peas(e) 157–8, 160
peat 10
Peck
   George 153
   Rebecca 192
Pecker's Path 295
Peninsula War 71, 168
Penn, John 197
Pennings 12, 97, 117, 120, 124, 127, 135, 153, 172
   Cottages 260
Penticosa (Spain) 76
People's Wardens 99, 100, 101
Perce
   Elizabeth 235
   William 227
Perks
   Emma 272
   Louise 272
Perry and Murch 67
petrol station 96
Pewsey 274, 275
   troop (yeomanry) 48
   vale of 40
pheasants 8
Philadelphia (USA) 215, 216
Philps, Edward G. 173
Pickering
   Sir Isaac 188
   – (Mr) 86–7
pigeons 22, 36
Piggott, Thomas 47–8
pigs 13, 22, 24–5, 160, 170, 175
Pike
   Adam 50
   George 50, 51
Pile, Alice 105
Pin(c)kney
   Rachel Frances 146
   Robert 44
Pinn, John 301
Pitt, William 41
Pitton 107
Pittsburgh (USA) 216
ploughboys 232, 237, 263
ploughing, ploughs 163, 166
Plymouth 56, 194

polecats 8
police 34, 195, 207, 260, 280
Pollen
    Charity Ann (Lady) 44, 100, 102, 110, 171, 172-3, 180, 181, 182, 222, 229-30; *see also* Southby
    John (Sir) 44, 85, 86, 87, 88
    John Walter (Sir) 87
    Louisa (Holt) 85, 86
Poole (Dorset) 115
poor laws 29, 31
poor relief 30-3
Poore
    Edward 138, 139, 140, 225
    Edward Dyke 139
    family 137-41, 221
population 2-4, 18-19, 24, 50, 53, 260-5, 278-9
Portbury (Som) 211
Porton 176, 275, 282
Portsea (Hants), 190, 264
Portsmouth 261, 275
Portugal: *see* Belem; Lisbon
post office 12-13, 28, 54, 61, 296
postmen 54, 295, 296
potatoes 24, 162, 280
poultry 170, 175, 263
Pound of Butter 169
poverty 17, 28-34, 47, 51
prices 25-8
Protheroe
    Edward William 194
    John 10, 37, 189, 190, 192, 193-6, 204, 219, 239, 240, 241, 264, 265, 301
    John Godwin 194
pubs 21, 22, 25, 34-7, 195, 201
Pyrenees 76

quail 9
Quakers 219
Quarley (Hants) 44
quarry 141-2, 192
Quebec (Canada) 198, 201
    bishops of 198-200
Queen Anne's Bounty 206

rabbits 53, 268-9

Radnor, earl of 34
Radstock (Som) 10
Raglan House 249, 260, 279
rags 212, 217, 222, 224
railways 70, 79, 127, 252, 261, 269, 274-6, 283, 297
    Pewsey and Salisbury 208, 274-5
Randall
    Elizabeth 65
    James 65, 100
    John Self 65
Ranger
    Mary Ann 10
    – 46
rape (crop) 160
Ratfyn 184, 186, 187, 274, 276, 297
    Farm 30, 46, 55, 66, 113, 119, 127, 186, 187, 297
Rattew
    James 185, 227
    John 185
ravens 8
Rawlence, Ernest 127, 174
Rawlence and Squarey 174
Rawlings 165
Reading beds 162, 172
reading room 14, 38, 95, 207, 208
reapers 64
recreation ground 14, 208
Rede, Lucy Leman 233
Redenham (Hants) 86
Reeves
    John 45
    Robert 45
    William 28
refrigeration 92
Rendall
    Charles Edward 103, 138, 139, 144-5, 146, 222
    Rachel Frances 146
    Shuttleworth 146
    family 146
Rendlesham (Hants) 44
rent 17
Reynolds, W 301
rheumatism 10, 29
rhinoceros 9, 76

Rhys-Hughes, – (Rev) 99, 176, 299
Richardson and Harrison 215
riots 40–9
roads 5, 7, 53–60, 88
Robbins
  Ann (Annie) 62, 102, 142
  Emma 64
  Frederick 232
  John 2, 41, 65, 79, 100, 101, 102, 107, 111, 142, 173, 232, 298, 299
  John (jun) 39, 299
  Joseph 64, 100, 101, 102, 298
  Martha 101
  Sarah 102
  Thomas 101, 102, 298–9
  William 102
  family 64, 101
  family tree 289
  – (Mr) 69
Robbins Pennings 2, 97
Roberts
  Earl 272
  Ellen 65
  P B 277
Robinson, Brooking and Garland 115
Roe, Robert 300
Rolfe, Martha 231
Romsey (Hants) 187, 188, 189, 190
rookeries 170, 172
Rose
  James 85, 139, 184–5
  family 222
Rose and Crown Inn 5, 14, 34, 36–7, 38, 61, 80, 95, 96, 98, 106, 112, 196, 244, 249, 279, 297
Rowden
  Annie 249
  Jane 12–13
Rowley, John 302
Royal Irish Fusiliers 1
Rudd, George Thomas 176, 300
Rumbold
  Emma 249
  George 249
Rushall 140
Rutland: *see* Oakham
rye 160

Sahara Desert 77
sainfoin 159, 160, 161, 163, 165, 166
Sainsbury, Agnes 32
sale catalogue 79–80, 84
Salisbury (Sarum) 13, 26, 27, 29, 48, 50, 53, 55, 56, 60–1, 65, 67, 69, 71, 79, 107, 139, 184, 187, 207, 212, 233, 252, 257, 269, 272, 275, 294
  Anchor and Hope 141
  Association for Prevention of Robberies (Thefts) 28, 100
  cathedral 86
  Chough Inn 61
  close 139
  dean and chapter 138
  diocese 271
  fair 294
  Grey Friars 212
  Hill 160
  market 29, 99
  Plain 268, 270, 273–5, 281
  Road 146, 185
  St Martin's 140
  Scots Lane chapel 184, 187, 204, 218
  Training college 249
  troop (yeomanry) 41–2
salmon 33
Salter, Christopher 178, 300
San Francisco (USA) 248
Satichaura Ghat (India) 70
Sawyer
  Alfred 261
  Ann 34, 64, 96
  Elizabeth 96
  Emma 3
  Frank 6, 157, 220
  John 62, 96, 216, 217, 218, 220–1, 223, 224, 236, 237, 247, 261, 295, 302, 303
  Prudence (Howse) 1, 7, 13, 14, 19, 24–5, 60, 62, 64, 174, 230, 261–2, 280, 284, 292–8
  Samuel 3
  William 62, 239, 261, 302
  family tree 288
Saxmundham (Suffolk) 70
schools 5, 62, 70, 80–1, 126, 191, 202, 208,

227–56, 270, 294
  chapel 231–2, 235, 297
  church (village) 228–32, 235, 294
  house 173, 178, 191
  log books 249–54, 268, 283
  mistress 200, 202
  'new' 244–56
  recent (1971) 245, 297
  Standards 252–3
  Sunday 237, 238–42, 243, 261
Scotland 279: *see also* Edinburgh; Gretna Green
Scott
  Col 275
  John James 178, 196, 300
  Joseph 181
Sedgemoor (Som) 56
Seend 26, 27
Self, Henry 42–3
servants 65, 102
service industries 264–5
Seth (drowner) 6
Seymour
  Alfred 115–16, 119, 248
  Edward (Sir) 82, 113
  Francis 114
  Henriette F 115
  Henry 66, 71, 114, 116, 118, 121, 122, 124, 154, 170
  Henry (jun) 71, 114–15, 118, 119, 134, 172, 173
  Henry Danby 48, 115–16, 119, 135
  Isabella 117
  Jane Margaret 117, 126, 127
  Thomas 154
  William 115
  family 82, 90, 96, 105, 113–18, 120, 123–4, 127, 135, 174
  Miss 276
Seymour
  estate 95, 110, 113–18, 129, 147, 159, 161, 175, 260, 276
  Farm *see* Watergate Farm
Shaftesbury (Dorset) 86
Shaw
  Agnes Christiana 91
  William 70

'Sheen House' 28, 297
sheep, sheep farming 8, 53, 54, 66, 69, 122, 146–7, 151–6, 160, 167–9, 262, 268, 281, 284
  Merino 156, 168
  Southdown 168–9
Sheep Bridge 5, 19, 55, 56, 97, 98, 146, 166
shepherds 22, 24, 29, 53, 54, 55, 237, 262, 284
  boys 232
Shepton Mallet (Som) 214, 220
Sherborne (Dorset) 108
Shillibeer, George 77
ships 94–5
Shipton Bellinger (Hants) 176, 300
shooting 8–9, 36, 87, 188
shops 11–13, 236, 294
Shrewton 55, 62
sidesman 102
Simcoe, Lake (Canada) 73, 75
Sleigh
  Elizabeth 209
  Samuel 65, 204–5, 209
  Thomas 205, 301
Sling 113, 275
  plantation 163, 172
Smallbones, Jonathan 43, 45
Smith
  Ann 30
  Daniel 256
  Frances 5
  John 41, 58
  Lucy 5
  Robert 142, 298
  Sarah 5
  Sophia 37
  Thomas 146
  – (Mr) 66, 69, 155
  family 64
smithy 167
snakes 75
snow 150
social club 52
soils 162–3
Soldiers' Home 272
Somerset 63, 65, 76, 91: *see also* Bath; Beckington; Bridgwater; Charlton

Adam; Cheddar; Freshford; Frome;
Keinton Mandeville; Monkton Combe;
Portbury; Radstock; Sedgemoor;
Shepton Mallett; Taunton; Wells
Sopp, Richard 57–8
South Africa 268, 272, 273, 275: *see also*
Ladysmith; Mafeking
South Marston 29, 84
Southampton (Hants) 102, 248, 257, 258,
261, 264, 278, 295
Above Bar chapel 257
Southby
Agnes Christiana 91, 92
Ann 69
Anthony 7, 9, 37, 39, 41, 63, 69, 70–1,
72–9, 80, 83–5, 88–91, 93, 96, 101, 103,
105, 110, 111, 138, 146, 154, 173, 175,
198–9, 201, 218, 221, 222–4, 225, 226,
230, 241, 244, 247, 248, 302
Anthony Gapper 77, 79, 91–4
Charity Ann 69, 75, 85–90, 110; *see also*
Pollen, Lady
Claudia 247–8
Edmund 21, 69, 88, 105, 110, 173
Edmund Hugh 79
Edmund Richard 78, 79, 91–2, 96
Elizabeth 85, 88, 92
Ellen 78, 79
Mary 44, 69, 70, 71, 75, 85–90, 172, 173,
181, 198–9, 222, 229–30
Octavia 78, 90, 92
Richard 29, 84, 85, 87
Richard Duke 84, 85
Rupert 79
Violet Miriam 79
family 39, 83, 86, 88–90, 114
family tree 286
– (Miss) 102
Spain 71, 168: *see also* Penticosa
sparrows 8
spinning 26–7
Spode and Co 68, 99
Spratt, James 60
Spreadbury, Charles 51
Spring Cottage 109
Spruce, Richard 76–7
Squarey, E P, 174

Stafford, George 214
Staffordshire 64
Stagg
Charles 43
James 48
Staines (Middlesex) 86
Stanley, – 282
Stanton St Bernard 45
Stanway, William 226
Staple, William 137
Stapleford 116
Steal Pease 138, 141, 146
steam engines, power 45, 126, 165, 167
Steeple Ashton 219
Stephens, H. F. 117, 126
Stevens and Gerrard 67
Still, James 124, 173
Stockton 126
Stone, Michael 136
Stonehenge 56, 297
Inn 35, 37, 60
Stour Provost (Dorset) 204
Strange
Jane 112
Thomas 56
Sture, Fanny 173
Sturgess (Sturges)
Charles 61
David 48–9, 235, 262, 263
Edward 21, 71, 111, 263–4
Eliza 218
Elizabeth 235
Ellen 235
Frank 52, 264
Henry Atkins 264
Herbert 235
Ira Sylvanus 264
Jane 255
Job 263, 264
John 34, 264
Lois 263
Lucy 26, 109
Mark 262–3
Mary 239
Noah 52
Priscilla 26
Robert 211

Index

Samuel 12, 52, 66, 210, 239, 256–7
Sarah 21, 71, 111, 257
Silas 263–4
Sydney William 264
Sylvanus 261, 263, 276
Thomas 77, 263
Walter 233
William 12, 40, 52, 185, 233, 257, 263
William (junior) 257–8, 263–4
– (gardener) 22, 67
family 4, 12, 19, 62, 95, 211, 245, 247, 260, 261, 263, 264
family tree 291
Suffolk: *see* Bungay; Saxmundham; Uphill
Sulawesi Tengah (Indonesia) 248
Sun Fire Insurance Co 213, 214
surgeons, surgery 39, 91, 237
surnames 62
Surrey: *see* Farnham
surveyor, county 85–6
Sussex: *see* Brighton; Hove; Midhurst
Sutton Veny 120
Swaine: *see* Swayne
Swatton
   David 21, 111, 178
   Elizabeth 178, 231, 235
   Fanny 61
   Jemima 33
   John 231, 239, 240
   Louise 239
   Martha 38, 218
   William 11–12, 239
   family 260
   family 32, 62
Swayne, William 69, 116, 118, 121, 298
swedes (Swedish turnips) 150, 154, 158, 160, 162
sweep, chimney 47
Sweet
   Mary Ann 52
   T. 28
Sweetapple, William 43
Swindon 50
Swing, (Captain) riots 25, 28, 40–9, 71
swords 29
Syrencote: *see* Figheldean

tanner 236
Tanners Down 276
Tararua (ship) 248
Tasker
   and Sons 163, 165, 263
   Robert 45
   William 45
Taunton (Som) 63
taxation 105
Taylor, John 79
telegraph 280
temperance 35–6
tenants, cottage 110–12
Thames, River 86
Thatcham (Berks)
   Hambridge Mill 226
thatchers, thatching 46, 164
theft 120, 131
Theyer, – (Miss) 86
Thomas, Philip 282
Thorn
   Betsy 3
   James 131
   John 3, 281
Thorne, Mr 199
Thornhill (Canada) 72, 201
threshing (thrashing) 44
   machines 43–5, 47
Thruxton (Hants) 44, 47, 86, 263, 264
Thwaite (Norfolk) 198
Thynne, Henry 70
Tichbourne, James 115
Tidworth 5–6, 101, 275
   Pennings 2, 19, 97
   South 8
Tilshead 66
Tinham, Jane 209
tinker 237
tithes 46, 80, 82, 175
   small 175
Titt, J.W. 45
Todman, David 239–40
toll
   bar 57, 59
   gates 57–8, 59, 296
   house 54, 57–8, 59, 112, 295
Toomer

James 143, 144
William 167
– (Mrs) 106
Toronto (Canada) 72, 75, 81
Totnes (Devon) 116
traction engines 60
traffic 56–9
transportation (punishment) 47–8
Tredgold, Mary 173
trees 6
trout 9
Trowbridge 51, 94
Trowbridge, John 28
Truckle
  Eliza 239
  Elizabeth 52
  John 262
  Thomas 52, 217, 224
Tuges, R. 67
Tunbridge Wells 150
turf 8
turnips 150, 153–4, 158, 160
turnpike roads 55–60, 295
Twenty Ridges 160

unions, trade 50–1
United States 17, 25, 34, 47, 151, 214–16, 262, 265, 302: *see also* Baltimore; Brandywine; Delaware; Michigan; New York; Philadelphia; Pittsburgh; San Francisco; Wilmington
Upavon 274
Uphill (Suffolk) 70
Upper Farm 2, 12, 21, 65, 80, 95, 97, 98–110, 124, 142, 148, 154, 156, 158, 160, 161, 173, 218, 224, 227, 232, 256, 273, 289, 296, 298–9
Upper Path 297
Upwey (Dorset) 212
Urchfont 300

Vallis, Fanny 283
vegetables 22, 263
Ventum, Alice 10
Vernon, HMS 262
vestry meetings 79, 140, 177, 179, 181, 182–3, 207
vetches 157, 158, 160
  milk 76
vicarage 30, 39, 44, 95, 96, 111, 296
  house 105, 143, 204–6, 234, 283; *see also* Orchard End
  old 112; *see also* Orchard End
Vicar's warden 99, 102
vicars (priests) 198–206
  list of 300
Victoria, queen 208–9
Victorian Society 38
voles 75

wages 45–6, 68
Wales Welshmen 261, 281: *see also* Anglesey; Cardiff; Carmarthen; Holyhead
  Prince of 267
Wallop (Hants) 42, 43, 46
Wantage (Oxon, formerly Berks) 165
War
  Department 98
  Office 95–6, 109, 110, 117, 127, 173, 174, 198, 208, 226, 260–84
  Secretary of State for 108–10, 112
Wareham (Dorset) 270
Warminster 45, 55, 63, 66, 190
Washington, Laurence (Sir) 82, 113, 129, 130
water 6, 11
  meadows 6, 9, 84, 95–6, 124, 125, 149, 151–5, 156–7
  power 133–4, 164
Water Street 1, 5, 55, 148, 296
Watergate
  Farm 5, 7, 16, 22, 25, 28, 39, 45, 48, 58, 59, 64, 69, 70, 71, 90, 97–8, 102, 106, 108, 112, 113, 115, 117, 118–36, 125, 152–7, 160–1, 163–7, 169, 186–7, 212–13, 234, 256–7, 259, 281, 297, 298–9
  House 7, 49, 117, 157, 161, 204, 207, 276, 280, 297
  Lane 5, 7, 112, 135, 172, 185
Waterloo, battle 71
Waters, Alice 206
Waterway 296

Index

Watson, H. C. 76
Watts, Isaac 28
Wavertree (Essex) 204–5, 301
weather 9–11, 250, 281–2
weavers' riots 40–1
Webb
  Mary 176
  Richard 176, 300
weddings 62
Weeks (Weekes)
  Edward 13, 299
  Frederick 28
  James
  John 32
  family 32
Wellington, Duke of 41
Wells (Som) 111
Wesley, John 242
West Lavington 66, 139, 227
Weyhill (Hants) 44
Weymouth (Dorset) 25, 187, 270
  Devenish brewery 187
wheat 151, 156–62
Whitchurch Co. 67
White
  Ada 234
  – (gipsy) 5
Wight, Isle of: see Brading
Wilkins, Henry 48
Williams
  Elizabeth 143, 144, 145
  John 143, 144, 145
  Robert 77–8
  Sarah 77
  William 37, 63, 77–8, 140, 143, 144, 209, 257, 301
  William (jun) 78
  – 36
  – (Mrs) 63
Willoughby, PC 34

willows 170–1
wills 89
Wilmington (USA) 215
Wilsford cum Lake 31
Wilson, James 87
Wilton 44, 91, 100
Wilton, Edward 300
Wilts and Dorset Bank 69
Wiltshire Friendly Society 39–40
Wimborne (Dorset) 217
Winchester 257
  College 137–8, 141, 222
Winterbourne Dauntsey 186
Winterbourne Stoke 66, 206, 300
wireworm 158, 162, 163
women, on farms 128–9, 164
wood (fuel) 10–11
Woodcock, Elizabeth 92
Woodford 31, 63
  Upper 105
  valley 44
woodland, and timber 118, 122, 163, 170–2
Woodrow, Messrs 207
Woods, Elisa 4–5
wool 168
Worcestershire: see Kidderminster
workforce, agricultural, 124, 126
workhouse 31–2, 52, 61–2
World War One 81
Wymondley Academy (Herts) 301

yeomanry cavalry 41–3, 48
Yonge Street (Canada) 72
Yorkshire 64, 177: see also Catterick academy
Young, Allan G. 49, 157, 161–2, 169, 174, 227, 280

zinc 224
Zulu war 268

www.ingramcontent.com/pod-product-compliance
Lightning Source LLC
Chambersburg PA
CBHW030850170426
43193CB00009BA/554